UNIX for VMS Users

Digital Press VAX Users Series

Philip E. Bourne
UNIX for VMS Users

Paul C. Anagnostopoulos
VAX/VMS: Writing Real Programs in DCL

James F. Peters III and Patrick Holmay
The VMS User's Guide

Ronald M. Sawey and Troy T. Stokes
A Beginner's Guide to VAX/VMS Utilities and Applications

UNIX for VMS Users

Philip E. Bourne

Digital Press

To Roma for her love and understanding
To Scott for the inspiration that only a 3 year old can give
To my parents for continuing to convince me that anything is possible

Copyright © 1990 by Digital Equipment Corporation

9 8 7 6 5 4 3 2

Order number EY-C177E-DP

Printed in the United States of America

Trademarks and trademarked products mentioned in this book include: Alliant Computer Systems Inc., Concentrix; Apple Computer Inc., AUX; AT&T, UNIX; Digital Equipment Corporation, DCL, DECnet, DECalc, DECspell, DECUS, the Digital logo, DIGITAL, MicroVAX II, Rainbow, TPU, ULTRIX, VAX, VAXcluster, VAXstation, VMS, VT100; International Business Machines, IBM, AIX; Microsoft Corp., MS-DOS, Xenix; Microsystems Engineering Corp., MASS-11; Silicon Graphics Computer Systems, IRIS; Sun Microsystems Inc., NFS, SUN-OS; The Massachusetts Institute of Technology, X Window System.

Design: Sandra Calef
Production coordination: Nancy Benjamin
Composition: Compset, Inc.

Library of Congress Cataloging-in-Publication Data

Bourne, Philip E.
   UNIX for VMS users / Philip E. Bourne.
     p.   cm.
   Includes bibliographical references.
   ISBN 1-55558-034-3
   1. UNIX (Computer operating system)   I. Title.
QA76.76.063B67   1989   89-36398
005.4'429—dc20   CIP

Contents

Preface

When *hen choosing between two evils, I always like to try the one I've never tried before.*

Mae West

An operating system is like an old friend. You may be in daily contact with him or only see him occasionally. Over the years, a firm bond of friendship develops. You come to realize that he is not perfect, and still you feel comfortable with his idiosyncrasies. In short, you accept him for what he is.

VMS, the operating system currently used by more than 80 percent of Digital Equipment Corporation VAX processors, is an old friend to many of us. Rapid changes in both the hardware and software market-place, however, could threaten this friendship. Innovative hardware architectures using RISC (Reduced Instruction Set Computers) technology, vectorization, pipelining, and multiprocessors are invading the turf traditionally held by VAX/VMS machines, from single-user worksta-tions right up to the large VAXclusters. If you are faced with adopting one or more of these high- or low-end processors, you will likely need to learn a version of the UNIX operating system, for UNIX is the oper-ating system of choice for most processors that use innovative hardware architectures. You may be attracted by the stability that UNIX provides as a development medium in a rapidly changing hardware market. After all, UNIX is the closest we have come to a generic operating system, suited to controlling a variety of hardware from many vendors. Whatever your reason for learning UNIX, if you are already familiar with VMS this may well be the book for you.

The book is intended to help you mold the interactive computing skills that you learned using VMS into the skills necessary for computing in the UNIX framework. It is not meant to be a UNIX user's manual, nor is it designed to teach UNIX from first principles. The book draws upon the experience of observing professionals with varying degrees of VMS expertise grapple with the concrete and philosophical issues of UNIX. This book emphasizes Berkeley UNIX (or BSD, Berkeley Software Distribution) and the C shell, although many of the features discussed are pertinent to any version of UNIX. Thus, this text should also be useful to those "migrating" from VMS to ULTRIX, AT&T System V, System III, Xenix, Version 7, or any other version of UNIX.

Chapter 1 begins with a brief history of UNIX and VMS. The ideas underlying the conception of each operating system differ markedly. To a casual user, these differences result in a UNIX user interface that appears to be quite different from DCL's. Chapter 1 does not discuss any of these differences in detail: the remainder of the book does that. Rather, Chapter 1 explains how these differences came about, and gives some of the reasons for them. At first glance, such a discussion may appear superfluous to the central task of learning a subset of useful UNIX commands. However, an understanding of how UNIX and VMS have evolved lets one begin to see the more subtle differences between the two operating systems, differences exemplified throughout this book. For example, VMS is designed as a series of powerful, self-contained commands which the user issues sequentially. UNIX, on the other hand, is designed to be modular, so that users piece together two or more simple modules to form a single complex command string. Thus, effective use of UNIX requires more than learning a new command syntax: it requires a new mode of thinking. The best way to introduce this new mode of thought is to try to capture what the original UNIX developers were thinking when they laid the foundations of UNIX.

Chapter 1 ends with a brief consideration of the future directions of UNIX and VMS, based on emerging standards. They may ultimately evolve into products that look and "feel" very similar.

Before your hands touch the keyboard, you must grasp a number of ideas that will help prevent later frustration. These ideas are the subject of Chapter 2. First and foremost are the particulars of how the UNIX C shell actually interprets a command, in contrast to the VMS Command Language Interpreter. This discussion introduces the concepts of pipes, filters, and input and output redirection, features that give great power to UNIX and which you need to build the complex command strings mentioned above. Second is the concept of a UNIX disk partition and file system, in contrast to a VMS physical device and directory. These UNIX concepts are particularly important for anyone interested in UNIX system management. UNIX and VMS operating system internals (data structures, input/output subsystems, and system services) are compared in only a cursory fashion.

With the formalities out of the way, you are ready to move to the terminal and begin getting acquainted with your new friend. Chapter 3 introduces the basic commands and files governing every terminal session, and indicates how they differ from those of VMS. You will learn how to tailor the environment to get the most from each UNIX terminal session. Chapter 3 concludes with two topics that VMS users making the transition to UNIX find the most irksome: the recall and seemingly cumbersome editing of command lines, and the use of on-line help and the UNIX document set.

At this point, you should be yearning for some serious interactive computing. Chapter 4 introduces a subset of file management commands that you are likely to need in the first few terminal sessions. So as not to bewilder the beginner, we leave the more complex file management commands for Chapter 9. In Chapter 4, you should begin to comprehend the power of the UNIX environment. Chapter 5 follows with a comparison of the most commonly used UNIX and VMS line and screen editors, in preparation for some meaningful application development. Chapter 5 also introduces two utilities, not available to VMS users, that offer powerful features for pattern-matching and subsequent file modification.

At this stage in the learning cycle, you should be ready to communicate with fellow users and systems staff. Chapter 6 covers the basic features of interactive communications and batch communications via electronic mail. For the reader who must communicate with users on remote computers, Chapter 13 revisits electronic mail as part of a discussion of processor-to-processor communications.

Effective use of any computer system requires an examination of how system resources are being consumed. Chapter 7 describes how to perform such an examination of the UNIX environment.

Chapter 8 introduces the UNIX equivalents of queuing batch and print requests and making tape drive requests. There are no surprises for the VMS user when it comes to printing files in UNIX, but the same cannot be said of magnetic tape and batch processing. The use of magnetic tapes in UNIX is in some ways arcane, but the real surprise is the inability of UNIX to handle batch processing. Chapter 8 explains that this is not a shortcoming but a difference in philosophy. UNIX has no need for batch queues, since you can easily manage multiple tasks interactively.

By the time you get to Chapter 9, you will need more complex file management commands. Chapter 9 builds upon the introductory discussion of file management in Chapter 4 by introducing new commands and options.

Chapter 10 discusses programming using a high-level language in the UNIX environment and provides insight into the programming tools for which UNIX is renowned, some of which are available as layered products under VMS. Chapter 10 discusses tools for debugging, profiling, and maintaining large programs, with examples from the C and FORTRAN languages.

In UNIX, programming is not restricted to a high-level language, inasmuch as you can program the user interface, or shell. Chapter 11 discusses features of shell programming and how it compares to writing VMS command procedures.

Chapter 12 briefly compares the text processing utilities distributed as part of the standard UNIX and VMS operating systems. UNIX has an extensive set of text processing tools that are both powerful and difficult to use. The word processing software available for personal computers and desktop publishing software available for workstations are preferable in most cases. Situations in which UNIX text processing tools might be advantageous are discussed.

Finally, Chapter 13 discusses the use of UNIX in a distributed environment of UNIX or UNIX and VMS processors. It considers connections both by fast dedicated networks and by slower asynchronous modems. The chapter groups network communications on the basis of trusted host access: the UNIX equivalent to a proxy login. Chapter 13 concludes with a brief discussion of the Network File System (NFS), the UNIX equivalent of a Local Area VAXcluster (LAVC).

Appendixes A and B summarize all we have learned by means of cross-reference tables that compare VMS and UNIX commands and editor functions. The tables also provide the section number where you may find a detailed discussion of each command. Appendix C summarizes the various UNIX files introduced throughout the text. Finally, Appendix D provides a chapter-by-chapter list of additional reading for those who need to know more about a specific topic.

The text emphasizes the practical aspects of UNIX throughout. It is loaded with everyday examples of performing tasks, each of which is compared to its closest VMS counterpart. Where no counterpart exists, that fact is noted. If you have some familiarity with the VMS example presented, and compare it to the UNIX example and read the explanation, you should become a competent UNIX user in a short time.

Both operating systems are so rich in their versatility and functionality that producing a concise text meant making some harsh decisions about what should be included and what should be left out. Undoubtedly, some readers will feel that certain topics have been covered in excessive detail and that others have received inadequate treatment. Nevertheless, every effort has been made to draw attention to and describe the similarities and differences between UNIX and VMS that are most important to application users and developers. Any learning process is facilitated by drawing upon previous experience, and learning UNIX should be no exception.

Conventions

Throughout this book these conventions are followed:

Convention	Meaning
form:	The general form of a command.
example:	Particular example of a command defined by form.
$	A command to the VMS Command Language Interpreter. Commands are shown in uppercase.
%	A command to the UNIX C-shell program. Commands are shown in lowercase, unless the shell program specifically requires uppercase.

Convention	Meaning
Italics	Emphasizes important terminology or features.
bold	A UNIX or VMS command or file.
#	What follows to the end of the line is a comment (UNIX only).
!	What follows to the end of the line is a comment (VMS only).
[argument]	Optional argument.
⟨CR⟩	A carriage return in UNIX. Assumed for all commands and shown in this book only when a special meaning is implied.
⟨CR⟩	A carriage return in VMS, also assumed for all commands and shown only when a special meaning is implied.
⟨CTRL⟩	The control key on the terminal.
⟨ESC⟩	The escape key (F11 on many terminals).

Unlike VMS, *UNIX interprets uppercase and lowercase characters differently.*

```
          VMS                                    UNIX
example:  $ ShOw UsErS                           % WHO
   VAX/VMS Interactive Users                     WHO: Command not found
   22-OCT-1987 11:25:34.53
Total number of interactive users = 1           % who
Username   Process Name    PID      Terminal    system tty01 Oct 22 10:39
SYSTEM     SYSTEM          0000001AE TXA0:
```

The **who** command, found as **/bin/who**, provides information on each interactive user, including the login name, the terminal in use, and the time they logged in to the system.

Philip E. Bourne
Howard Hughes Medical Institute
Columbia University
New York, September 1989

Acknowledgments

This book began as a weekend project which, because of my obsessive nature, quickly overtook my daily research work. I am indebted to Wayne Hendrickson for permitting this transgression to occur and for considering it an important enough contribution to authorize support from the Howard Hughes Medical Institute (HHMI).

Thanks also to the folks at Convex Computer Corporation who first introduced me to the world of UNIX, and to Daniel Schainholz who helped write the HHMI *UNIX User's Guide,* the forerunner of this book.

A number of colleagues made significant contributions to the book's content: thanks go to Peter Mossel, Mark Reboul, Peter Shenkin, and Janie Weiss, who reviewed the whole manuscript; and to Sorhab Ismail-Beigi, Reidar Bornholdt, Holt Farley, Tim Lee, and Peter Raith, who reviewed particular chapters.

Thanks to Dorothy Geiger, a new friend in the UNIX world, who reviewed the complete manuscript and made significant contributions.

Thanks to Michael Meyer, who edited the whole manuscript and was kind enough to say that he had made one or two minor changes while covering each page with a mass of red ink, which not only improved the readability but also helped keep the content at a consistent level. Thanks also to Debra Hairston, who made sense enough of the red ink to produce the final copy.

The chapter plates were drawn by Maria Ruotolo. Thanks to her for becoming interested enough in the theme of each chapter to spend time researching the most appropriate artwork to vandalize.

A final word of thanks to my colleagues in the Biochemistry and Molecular Biophysics Department at Columbia University. The problems they encountered in making the transition from VMS to UNIX not only convinced me that this book was necessary but also helped me decide on the content.

This book was composed at the terminal using the MASS-11 word processing software from Microsystems Engineering Corporation (MEC) on both a VAX 11/750 running VMS and a Rainbow 100+ running DOS. All the examples were taken from terminal sessions running on a variety of hardware platforms under various versions of UNIX: a MicroVAX II from Digital Equipment Corporation running ULTRIX, a Convex C1-XP from Convex Computer Corporation running Convex UNIX (both BSD derivatives); an IRIS 3020 from Silicon Graphics Computer Systems running UNIX System V; and a Sun 3/160 from Sun Microsystems running Sunos (a UNIX BSD derivative). Each of these systems was connected to the same Ethernet, and the terminal sessions were reviewed concurrently on a VAXstation 2000 running VMS and VWS screen management software. Using the MicroVAX II running ULTRIX as a DECnet-Internet Gateway and the UNIX **script** command, examples could be pasted directly into the MASS-11 document on the VAX/VMS system from script files copied from the various UNIX hosts.

Chapter Plates

1   *Adapted from "The Thinker" by Auguste Rodin (1840–1917).*

2   *Adapted from "The Creation of Man" by Michelangelo Buonarroti (1475–1519).*

3   *Adapted from "The Lovers" by Picasso (1881–1973).*

4   *Adapted from "Jeune Femme Devant le Lit" by Amedeo Modigliani (1884–1920).*

5   *Adapted from "Three Women at the Spring" by Picasso (1881–1973).*

6   *Adapted from an Egyptian Tomb Painting—18th Dynasty Egyptian Mural.*

7   *Adapted from "Peasant Woman Digging" by Vincent van Gogh (1853–1890).*

8   *Adapted from "The Suitor's Visit" by Gerard ter Borch (1617–1681).*

9   *Adapted from "Portrait of Dr. Gachet" by Vincent van Gogh (1853–1890).*

10 *Adapted from "A Portrait of Sultan Selin II" by Ralis Haydar (1570–1638).*

11 *Adapted from "Gare Saint-Lazare" by Edouard Manet (1832–1883).*

12 *Adapted from "The Rape of the Lock" by Aubrey Beardsley (1872–1898).*

13 *Adapted from "The Last Supper" by Leonardo da Vinci (1475–1564).*

Chapter 1

Introduction

History is philosophy teaching by examples.

Dionysius of Halicarnassus

This book provides an introduction to the UNIX operating system. Most introductory UNIX texts assume no prior knowledge of interactive computing. Here, you must have a working knowledge of the Virtual Memory System (VMS), a Digital Equipment Corporation operating system, for this text is designed to help the reader make a smooth transition from VMS to UNIX. It started as a user's guide within our own organization, which saw an increasing need for VAX/VMS users to compute on processors running the UNIX operating system. Recognizing that mixed operating system environments like ours are becoming more common, I decided to expand the user's guide into the more comprehensive text presented here.

This book is a response to current market conditions, which indicate an increase in UNIX usage. This book does not, however, attempt to convince the VMS user that UNIX is a preferable operating system. I do not regard UNIX as a better operating system than VMS, nor VMS as superior to UNIX. Each has strengths and weaknesses, which I note when relevant to the comparative learning process that the text employs throughout.

The text is intended to do more than describe how to perform a given VMS command or function in UNIX. Certainly such descriptions are useful and may represent all that the occasional UNIX user requires. However, for those who intend to develop complex applications, I have tried to show some of the features that make UNIX a powerful development medium.

Unlike VMS, UNIX is not a single product but rather the evolution of an original idea and design philosophy into a number of different products, each of which has unique features. This book concentrates on only one of these evolutionary pathways, the version of UNIX that comes from the University of California at Berkeley, known as Berkeley Software Distribution (BSD). A discussion of BSD begins in Chapter 2. First, let us look at how each version of UNIX originated, and what the original design philosophies behind them mean to today's VMS user making the transition to UNIX.

Much has been written on the subject of UNIX evolution and the current trends toward standardization (see Appendix D). This section gives only a synopsis and compares UNIX evolution to the corresponding development of VMS.

Ken Thompson first conceived UNIX in 1969 at the American Telephone and Telegraph Company's Research Division at Bell Laboratories in Murray Hill, New Jersey, to run a program on a PDP-7 computer. The program, "Space Travel," originally ran on a General Electric GE645 computer, which used an operating system called Multics. Multics was developed at the Massachusetts Institute of Technology, and was one of the first time-sharing operating systems. The first version of UNIX, which was written in assembly language, incorporated many features of Multics.

The decision to rewrite UNIX in a higher-level language and thus to make it portable between computer systems came in 1972, when Thompson rewrote the UNIX software in a language called B. Dennis Richie, also of Bell Laboratories, extensively modified B in 1973, renaming it C. Whether fortuitous or not, the decision to make UNIX portable is the main reason for the popularity of UNIX today. UNIX provides a stable development medium for a rapidly changing hardware market. Applications can be ported directly to hardware of different types without costly redevelopment.

In 1974, the decision to license the UNIX source code to universities established a second major evolutionary pathway, the Berkeley Software Distribution (BSD). BSD Version 3.0, released in 1979, included many enhancements to the original Bell Laboratories version of UNIX, some of which I discuss in subsequent chapters. Notable were several portable language compilers which expanded the transparent operating system fuctionality on different types of hardware to include transparent program development tools. The development of BSD illustrates one aspect of the original design philosophy of UNIX: the system is modular, that is, it can accommodate additional functionality with relative ease.

At about the time BSD was released, the first version of UNIX appeared on VAX computers. Known as 32V, it represented a 32-bit implementation of the 16-bit Version 7 from Bell Laboratories, which was already running on a number of PDP-11 series computers.

With the relaxation of antitrust laws and its release of a line of micro-computer and minicomputer systems, AT&T found itself in a better position than previously to market UNIX aggressively. In 1983, AT&T released UNIX System V, which contained many BSD features. AT&T is now advancing System V Interface Definition (SVID) as the industry standard for UNIX. Other companies, Digital Equipment Corporation included, are contributing to a nonproprietary standard defined by the Institute of Electrical and Electronic Engineers (IEEE), known as POSIX.

In 1984, Digital Equipment Corporation released ULTRIX, a version of UNIX derived from BSD and System V. ULTRIX gradually became available for the complete line of VAX processors. For the personal computer market, Microsoft Corporation developed Xenix, a 16-bit microcomputer version of UNIX System V. Meanwhile, International Business Machines (IBM) had been quietly supporting several disparate versions of UNIX on different hardware platforms in response to market pressures, but without any apparent overall corporate strategy. The IBM position changed with its introduction of Advanced Interactive Execu-tive (AIX) for the IBM RT in 1986. AIX is the standard for UNIX within IBM and can currently run on a variety of IBM processors including the PS/2 Model 80 personal computer.

The proliferation of UNIX versions does not end here. As mentioned, the decision to write UNIX in a high-level language rather than assembly offers computer manufacturers the opportunity to use a relatively inex-pensive operating system for new hardware. Development costs are low because manufacturers do not have to develop an operating system from scratch, but instead can purchase a license for the UNIX source code and write a C compiler (a good idea anyway, given the popularity of this language) and a small amount of assembly code to handle input and out-put and other hardware-specific functions. Table 1.1 lists some compa-nies that have adopted UNIX as an operating system to support their hardware. Some of these companies have added their own tools and utilities, which have themselves become *de facto* standards. Notable are the Network File System (NFS) and X-windows. NFS, developed by Sun Microsystems Inc., provides transparent file access among a variety of hosts running the UNIX operating system. X-windows, developed by Project Athena, a joint venture involving IBM, Digital Equipment Cor-

Table 1.1 Popular Versions of UNIX

Name	Hardware Supported	Company
Accent	Perq	Perq Systems Corporation
Aegis	Apollo Workstations	Apollo Computer Inc.
AIX	IBM RT, PS/2 Model 80	International Business Machines
AUX	Mac II	Apple Computer Inc.
BBN-UNIX	BBN C/60, C/70	BBN Communications
Coherent	Commodore	Commodore Business Machines
Concentrix	Alliant FX series	Alliant Computer Systems Inc.
Convex UNIX	Convex C1 and C2 series	Convex Computer Corporation
Cromix	Cromemco	Cromemco Inc.
For:Pro	Fortune XP	Fortune Systems Corporation
Gould UNIX	Gould	Gould Inc.
HP-UX	HP workstations	Hewlett-Packard
Hub	VAX, PDP-11	Compion Corporation
IDRIS	IBM PC, DEC Pro, Rainbow, etc.	Whitesmiths Ltd.
Minix	IBM PC	Prentice-Hall
MORE/bsd	VAX	Mt Xinu Inc.
PRIMIX	Prime Computers	Prime Computer Inc.
Regulus	Motorola MC68000	Alcyon Corporation
RTU	Concurrent	Concurrent Computer Corporation
ULTRIX	VAX	Digital Equipment Corporation
UN/System V	Motorola MC68000	Charles River Data Systems
UNISIS	Codata 3300	Contel Codata Systems Corporation
UNIX	Celerity	Celerity Computing
UNIX	Titan	Ardent Computer
UNIX	Elxsi Series	Elxsi Computer Corporation
UNIX	Data General Eclipse	Information Processing Techniques Corporation
UNIX	Silicon Graphics Workstations	Silicon Graphics Computer Systems
SUN-OS	Sun Workstations	Sun Microsystems Inc.
UNIX III/4.2	Motorola 68010	Integrated Solutions Inc.
UNIX Sys3	Plexus	Plexus Computers Inc.
UNIX System V	VAX, PDP-11, IS 3B	AT&T Information Systems
UNIX System V	Motorola 68000	Lisp Machine Inc.
Venix/86	IBM PC, DEC Pro, Rainbow, etc.	Unisource Software Corporation
V7M-11	PDP-11	Digital Equipment Corporation
Xenix	PDP-11 IBM PC	Microsoft Corporation
Xenix System V	IBM PC	Santa Cruz Operation

poration, and MIT, provides a standard windowing interface for UNIX hosts.

With so many implementations of UNIX available, one might expect the user interface to differ significantly from one implementation to another. Fortunately, this is not the case, even without a formal interface definition. Only three interfaces, called *command language interpreters* in VMS and *shells* in UNIX, have become popular. They are:

the Bourne shell (**sh**)	First available shell, included in all versions of UNIX
the C shell (**csh**)	Standard for BSD
the Korn shell (**ksh**)	Standard for System V

This book primarily discusses the C shell, the shell developed for BSD.

Table 1.2 shows the comparable milestones in UNIX and VMS evolution. Unlike UNIX, VMS has followed a single evolutionary pathway as a result of its proprietary nature. The VMS pathway is closely related to the development of VAX hardware, the only hardware on which VMS functions. VMS has undergone a major upgrade approximately every two years and minor updates about three times a year. The minor releases generally fix bugs and provide software necessary to support new hardware. Major releases extend the range of VAX processors that VMS supports. For example, full support of VAX clustering became available with VMS Version 4.0.

The evolution of UNIX and VMS has not been completely independent. New versions of VMS contain enhancements first appearing in the various releases of UNIX, and vice versa. This situation will likely continue, and both products will continue to converge towards a common standard.

Operating system emulators are available for those who require computer environments possessing the functionality of both operating systems yet who do not wish to invest in two separate processors. Native VMS can host what appears to be a UNIX environment and vice versa. In some instances, it is possible to emulate specific tools and utilities rather than the complete operating system. Some software products with such capabilities are mentioned in subsequent chapters.

The nonproprietary and modular nature of UNIX suggests that the versions available today incorporate ideas from many different program-

Table 1.2 VMS and UNIX Genealogy

Date[1]	VMS	UNIX[2]
1969		First development for PDP-7
1970		Named UNIX
1971		First version operational at Bell Labs on PDP-11/20, written in B
1973		Rewritten in C
1974		University licenses issued
1975		UNIX V6 Bell Labs
1978	1.0, 1.1, 1.2	UNIX V7 Bell Labs, first portable version
1979	1.3, 1.4, 1.5, 1.6	BSD 3.0; 32V Homdel, first VAX version
1980	2.0, 2.1	BSD 4.0
1981	2.2, 2.3, 2.4, 2.5	BSD 4.1
1982	3.0, 3.1, 3.2	AT&T System III
1983	3.3, 3.4, 3.5	BSD 4.2; AT&T System V; Bell Labs. V8
1984	3.6, 3.7, 4.0	AT&T System V Release 2; Microsoft Xenix; ULTRIX 1.0
1985	4.1, 4.2, 4.3	
1986	4.4, 4.5	BSD 4.3; AT&T System V Release 3; Bell Labs V9
1987	4.6, 4.7	
1988	5.0, 5.1	

1. UNIX dates are approximate.
2. Only the major milestones in UNIX evolution are listed.

mers added over a long period of time. Although this situation has resulted in an extensive set of tools and utilities for application development, it has not produced a completely coherent design strategy. Some VMS users, familiar with more stringent product management, may therefore find certain UNIX characteristics irksome. Here are a few examples:

- UNIX documentation is not as comprehensive nor as well organized as VMS documentation.

- Command names sometimes bear no resemblance to function. Contributors to UNIX often devised names for their own convenience rather than for a large community of users. Other commands owe their names to historical significance rather than function.

- Contributors who added commands that have now become part of the standard UNIX distributions often used syntax that suited their

own needs but did not always follow a logical pattern relative to
other commands.

- Some commands and utilities are complex to use, having been written for programmers by programmers.

- System security is insufficient.

- Redundant code has not been retired. For example, UNIX still supports some hardware that is no longer in use.

1.2   *The Future*

UNIX developers are working toward solutions to the shortcomings described above as the operating system gains popularity in commerce, industry, and the traditional government marketplace. As UNIX moves toward a standard interface definition, the search for solutions will certainly accelerate. What the standard interface definition will be, if indeed there is to be one, remains to be seen. Such a definition will certainly come through common use rather than by fiat. That is, software manufacturers will likely adopt a definition because it meets all the needs of the marketplace, not because some organization has declared it a standard.

If current trends continue, UNIX will appropriate an ever larger share of the VAX processor market, particularly at the low end, and will rival VMS as the operating system of choice. As Figure 1.1 shows, at the end of 1987 UNIX in its various forms was the operating system for 10% of the VAX 11/7xx series of computers, 5% of the VAX 8xxx series, and 12% of the MicroVAX series. It is estimated that within five years, 50% of all VAX processors purchased, with the majority at the low end, will be running the UNIX operating system.

Indeed, several events have taken place in the last year that will surely speed up the evolution of a UNIX product that will appeal to a wider user community. The three most significant of these events appear to be the collaboration between Sun Microsystems Inc. and AT&T to provide RISC (Reduced Instruction Set Computer) based hardware running a version of UNIX based on SVID; IBM's commitment to UNIX with AIX; and the collaboration known as the Open Software Foundation (OSF) to provide a version of UNIX based on AIX and POSIX and that will support applications identically on many hardware platforms. Much has already been written about these events, and I refer the reader to the journals listed in Appendix D for the ongoing discussion.

Figure 1.1a   UNIX on the VAX 11/7xx Series

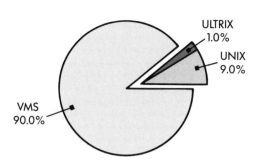

ULTRIX
1.0%

UNIX
9.0%

VMS
90.0%

Figure 1.1b   UNIX on the MicroVAX

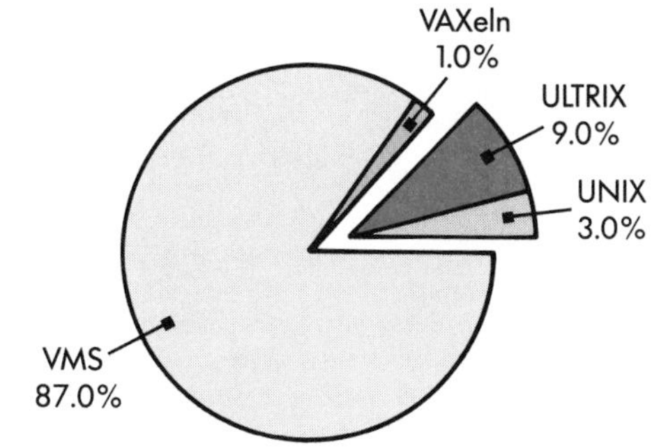

VAXeln
1.0%

ULTRIX
9.0%

UNIX
3.0%

VMS
87.0%

Figure 1.1c   UNIX on the VAX 8xxx Series

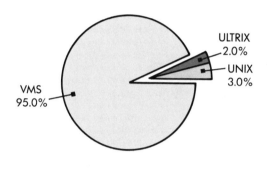

ULTRIX
2.0%

UNIX
3.0%

VMS
95.0%

Figure 1.1d   Planned UNIX Usage on All VAX Computers

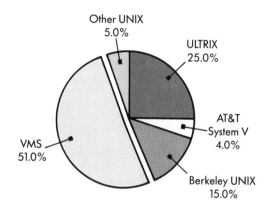

Other UNIX
5.0%

ULTRIX
25.0%

AT&T
System V
4.0%

VMS
51.0%

Berkeley UNIX
15.0%

This is not to say that the future of VMS is in doubt. Too much useful software has been written specifically to take advantage of the VMS operating system for the operating system to become redundant. New generations of improved VAX computers will certainly run some version of VMS.

Computer users can continue to expect faster, smaller processors that run a variety of operating systems and communicate transparently at high speeds. Users no longer have to choose between VMS or UNIX, but have both, with the application dictating the choice of operating system.

Chapter 2

Fundamentals

The golden rule is that there are no golden rules.

George Bernard Shaw

It is recommended that the reader study this chapter before beginning a UNIX terminal session. For it is here that the fundamental features of the UNIX operating system are introduced and compared to those of VMS. Since this book is for the new UNIX user rather than the UNIX system administrator or system programmer, differences in the internal structure of the two operating systems are mentioned only briefly. Section 2.1 provides the new UNIX user with an understanding of the basic functions of the UNIX kernel, the various UNIX utilities and tools, and the user interface, and how these compare with the structure of VMS.

Section 2.1.1 introduces the subject of process creation, which requires more detailed consideration. Users may run UNIX commands simultaneously as separate processes created by the shell. Understanding the interrelationships among these processes is prerequisite to understanding how to use commands effectively. You may synchronize processes so that the output of one is used as input to the next, a procedure known as *piping* (Section 2.1.2). You may also easily *redirect* input and output between files and processes (Section 2.1.3).

Section 2.2 introduces the format of commands. Since many commands involve the manipulation of files, this section also discusses file and directory naming. Section 2.2.1 discusses what happens if you use an incorrect command syntax.

Section 2.3 introduces the concept of a UNIX file system and compares it to a VMS physical device. This section also introduces the different types of UNIX files.

Section 2.4 introduces the concept of *metacharacters,* which perform a special function in command interpretation by the C shell. Section 2.5 discusses the use of wildcards in naming files and directories, indicating the strong similarity to the VMS wildcard syntax.

2.1 System Internals

The internal architecture of most multiuser, multitasking, virtual memory, interactive operating systems are similar; VMS and UNIX are no exceptions. Schematically, an operating system looks like a hierarchical

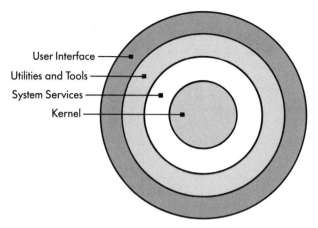

Figure 2.1 Operating System Topology

arrangement of layers or skins not unlike an onion (Figure 2.1). The system grows outward from a central core, or kernel. The functions of any given layer presuppose the functions of layers closer to the core. In both VMS and UNIX, the kernel directly controls the hardware. For example, the kernel handles memory management, scheduling the use of the CPU, and input and output to various devices. The innermost layers surrounding the kernel comprise a set of system service routines which interact directly with the kernel. Assembly code makes direct calls to system service routines: high-level languages can also make calls to these routines to achieve the greatest possible efficiency. Usually, the software resident in the tools and utilities layer, the next outer layer of the hierarchy that includes high-level language compilers, makes the complexity of calling system service routines transparent to the user.

The major difference between VMS and UNIX in the tools and utilities layer[1] has to do with what is included as part of the standard operating system. Both UNIX and VMX provide many tools and utilities, but UNIX provides more of them as part of the standard operating system. VMS requires a separate software license to run some tools and utilities that are standard features of UNIX. Table 2.1 lists some of the major

---

1. Throughout this book, tools and utilities are distinguished from commands on the basis of their complexity. For example, electronic mail, invoked with the UNIX command **mail,** is regarded as a utility, as a number of subcommands may be issued in response to the **mail** prompt. Tools ease the task of application development. The UNIX debugger **dbx** is an example of a tool.

**Table 2.1   Standard UNIX Tools and Utilities and Their
VMS Equivalents**

	VMS	UNIX
Editors		
	EDT	ed
	TECO	ex
	TPU	vi
Communications		
	MAIL	mail
	REPLY	write
	PHONE	talk
	DECnet*	ftp
		telnet
		r commands
Compilers		
	FORTRAN*	f77
	C*	cc
Text Processing		
	RUNOFF	troff
		nroff
		awk
		lex
		sed
	SORT	sort
	MERGE	merge
Program Development Tools		
	LINK	link
	DEBUG	adb/dbx
	LIBRARIAN	ar/ranlib
	DEC MMS*	make
		yacc
	DEC CMS*	scs
Miscellaneous		
	DECalc*	bc/dc
	DECspell*	spell

*Available as optional products from Digital Equipment
Corporation.

tools and utilities available in both VMS and UNIX, emphasizing those
included as part of a standard distribution. The most commonly used
UNIX tools and utilities will be introduced in following chapters.

Both operating systems offer several editors capable of line- or screen-
oriented editing. Both systems offer interactive communications and

electronic mail as well as extensive networking capabilities for file transfer, remote command execution, and remote login. These utilities are standard features of UNIX but require a DECnet license to function in VMS. Many versions of UNIX include compilers, notably C and FORTRAN-77, as part of the standard distribution. Compilers all require separate licenses to run on a VMS system. Code written for UNIX compilers that make calls to UNIX-specific routines will, of course, compile and run on any type of hardware that supports UNIX. Code written with calls to VMS-specific routines such as the run-time library, is restricted to VAX hardware.

Various text-formatting tools are standard features of both systems. UNIX possesses tools for text (string) manipulation not found on VMS, including a lexical analyzer useful for developing a command interpreter or compiler. Program productivity tools are also standard for many versions of UNIX.

At the outermost layer (the surface of the onion) is the user interface: the command language interpreter, or *shell* in UNIX parlance, which surrounds all components of the operating system. The UNIX shell, like the Digital Command Language (DCL) interpreter, is simply a program that parses commands and passes control to other programs that make up the operating system. The UNIX shells introduced in Section 1.1 differ in the functions they perform and the command syntax they accept, but all pass control to the same UNIX programs for processing except for commands processed by the shell itself.

Many of the features introduced in this book are independent of the shell in use. Features specific to the C shell will be noted.

2.1.1 Processes

When you begin either a UNIX or VMS terminal session, the operating system establishes a unique process. This process, which has dynamic access to memory and CPU resources, receives a unique identifier, or process identifier, from the operating system. Whether hardware resources are available to a particular process at any time is determined by its *priority*. The kernel adjusts the priority dynamically every few seconds to control the sharing of resources. The part of the kernel responsible for scheduling determines the priority by means of a complex algorithm. The algorithm uses predefined variables assigned by the system, or in some cases by the system administrator, to determine the priority. Chapter 7 discusses the UNIX commands available for examining and changing the characteristics of a user's processes.

The mechanism the two operating systems use to handle multitasking, that is, concurrent processes initiated by a single user, differ significantly and therefore require further explanation. When a user begins a terminal session, the operating system starts a single *parent process*. It is possible, however, to start multiple processes. If a new process is started by the existing process, this is termed *spawning* in VMS and *forking* in UNIX. The new process, which has its own unique process identifier, is called a subprocess in VMS and a *child process* in UNIX. Forking occurs often in UNIX. Note that submitting a batch job or commencing another terminal session does not involve spawning or forking, as these are not child but parent processes.

When UNIX creates a child process and VMS creates a subprocess, the events that take place are quite different. When VMS creates a subprocess, the parent remains dormant (hibernates) until the user logs off from the subprocess, whereupon control returns to the parent. Alternatively, the VMS **ATTACH** command gives control back to the parent process, at which time the subprocess becomes dormant. The point is that only one process is active at any given time. The exception is the VMS **RUN/ PROCESS = image_name** command, which runs a user-defined executable image as a subprocess while commands are being issued to the parent. In UNIX, however, you may run many parent and child processes simultaneously. A child process that forks another process becomes the parent of the new child, so a process can be both a parent and a child. Child processes are not restricted to user-defined executable images but can involve any valid UNIX operation. UNIX processes either running or stopped but not receiving input directly from the terminal are said to be in *background*.

When you begin a UNIX terminal session, the kernel provides a copy of the shell (the command language interpreter program) in which to work. When you issue a command to the shell, the shell forks a child process, which takes on many of the characteristics of the parent, for the command to run in unless the shell itself processes the command. Compare VMS, where all commands are executed by the parent process. Once it creates the child process, the parent process remains dormant until the child process completes its tasks. The child process then dies, and control returns to the parent. At any time, the parent or the child can fork other processes, which in turn can fork other processes and so on. Hence, a number of parent and child processes may be running simultaneously.

We will discuss the implications of multiprocesses for multitasking in Section 8.3. The following example, although it does not illustrate UNIX multitasking, shows the UNIX analogy to the VMS **SPAWN** command (unique to the C shell) and introduces the UNIX commands **cat**, **fg**, and **f77**.[2]

<table>
<tr><td></td><td>VMS</td><td>UNIX</td></tr>
<tr><td>example:</td><td>$ FORTRAN MYFILE.FOR
⟨CTRL⟩-Y</td><td>% f77 myfile.f
⟨CTRL⟩-Z
stopped</td></tr>
<tr><td></td><td>$ SPAWN
%DCL-S-SPAWNED, process PROCESS_1 spawned
%DCL-S-ATTACHED, terminal now attached
              to process PROCESS_1</td><td></td></tr>
<tr><td></td><td>$ TYPE MYFILE.FOR
. . . . .
$ ATTACH PROCESS
DCL-S-RETURNED, control returned to process PROCESS</td><td>% cat myfile.f
. . . . .</td></tr>
<tr><td></td><td>$ CONTINUE</td><td>% fg
f77 myfile.f</td></tr>
</table>

In this example, partway through a FORTRAN compilation and link (**f77**), which is itself a child process of the parent C shell process, the user suddenly is not sure that the correct source file is being compiled. If the user issues an interrupt (⟨CTRL⟩-C) and then discovers that the correct file was being compiled, the compilation time already used would be wasted. Instead, the child process responsible for the compilation is stopped by typing ⟨CTRL⟩-Z and control passes back to the parent C shell process. The C shell then creates another child process for the **cat** (catenate and print) command to run in. The **cat** command lists the contents of the source file at the terminal, the child process responsible for **cat** dies when the listing is completed (or terminated with ⟨CTRL⟩-C), and control passes back to the parent. When the user determines that the file is the correct one, the command **fg** (foreground) input to the parent process returns control to the child process responsible for the compilation. The command responsible for the compilation is displayed and the compilation continues.

---

2. Throughout this book, ... indicates that text has been omitted for brevity.

The above illustrates the use of ⟨CTRL⟩-C to terminate a child process but not the parent. In the above example, terminating the parent would terminate the terminal session.

All the parent and child processes in the above example use the default input and output device, namely the terminal. Input and output streams in UNIX are called standard input (**stdin**) and standard output (**stdout**). Standard error (**stderr**), not illustrated in the above example, also uses the terminal as its default output device. Redirecting input, output, and error streams away from the terminal in VMS requires the assignment of the logical names **SYS$INPUT**, **SYS$OUTPUT**, and **SYS$ERROR** to a file or alternative device, respectively. The UNIX C shell has an elegant mechanism for redirecting input, output, and error streams when running a number of tasks simultaneously (see Section 2.1.3). In the next section, we discuss a special case of redirection where the output of one command becomes input to the next.

2.1.2   *Pipes*

The creation of a *pipe* is a particular type of multiprocess activity synchronized by the kernel, in which the output of one command becomes input to the next command without creating any intermediate file. UNIX may synchronize two or more processes in what is termed a *pipeline*.

	VMS	UNIX
form:		% command1 | command2 | \
		command3
example:	$ SHOW USERS/OUTPUT = A.TMP	% who | sort | lpr
	$ SORT/KEY = POSITION:40,SIZE:6) -	
	A.TMP SYS$PRINT	

A vertical bar separates the UNIX commands forming the pipeline. In the above example, the kernel starts three child processes simultaneously. However, **sort** (Section 9.4.6; compare the VMS command **SORT**) must wait for input from the processing of the **who** command (Section 7.1.2; compare the VMS command **SHOW USERS**). Likewise, **lpr** (Section 8.1.1; compare the VMS command **PRINT**) must await output from the **sort** command. When all output from the **who** command passes to **sort**, the child process responsible for running the **who** command dies. By default, **sort** uses the first field (delimited by a blank) as the *sort key*. The first field output by the **who** command is the username, hence, **sort** sorts records alphabetically by username. The **lpr** command then accepts as input the output from the **sort** command and the child process responsible for **sort** dies. After printing the output of **sort** on the default printer, the child process responsible for **lpr** dies and control passes back to the parent shell process. The result of the pipeline is a printed listing of all users on the system in alphabetical order.

A comparable sequence of events in VMS requires the creation of an intermediate file. The VMS example above creates a printed listing sorted by terminal device name. The output of the **SHOW USERS** command is saved in a file **A.TMP.** The contents of the file are then sorted on the device key which is six characters long and begins in column 40, and the output passes to the default line printer.

Piping offers the opportunity to perform complex functions by creating a pipeline from a number of simple commands. Examples of piping commands appear throughout this book to emphasize the versatility they give to UNIX. The effective use of piping does not always come easily to VMS users, who are accustomed to the sequential processing of single commands and the occasional redirection of the output of one command to a file for subsequent processing by another command. *Always consider how you can capture a sequence of commands in a single pipeline.*

2.1.3   *Input, Output, and Error Redirection*

Just as the VMS logical names **SYS$INPUT**, **SYS$OUTPUT**, and **SYS$ERROR** point to the terminal by default, so do the UNIX equivalents **stdin**, **stdout**, and **stderr**. However, UNIX uses a simplified method of redirecting input, output, and error messages from or to a file. UNIX does not require the equivalent of an **ASSIGN** statement preceding the command to perform redirection; rather, UNIX includes a redirection metacharacter as part of the command line. In this simple example, **myprog < input.dat > a.lis** causes the executable program **myprog** to read input (<) from the file **input.dat** and send output (>) to **a.lis**.

	VMS	UNIX
example:	$ ASSIGN/USER SYS$OUTPUT A.LIS	
	$ ASSIGN/USER INPUT.DAT FOR005	
	$ RUN MYPROG	% myprog < input.dat > a.lis

Table 2.2   Special Characters Used in Input, Output, and Error Redirection

Character	Meaning
>	Redirect standard output
>!	Redirect standard output, disregarding **noclobber***
>>	Redirect and append standard output
>>!	Redirect and append standard output, suppressing error and opening a new file if output file does not exist*
>&	Redirect standard output and standard error*
>&!	Redirect standard output and standard error, disregarding **noclobber***
>>&	Redirect and append standard output and standard error*
>>&!	Redirect and append standard output and standard error, suppressing error and opening a new file if output file does not exist*
<	Redirect standard input
<<**xxx**	Read input up to a line identical with **xxx***
|	Redirect standard output to another command
| **tee**	Direct standard output to another command and a file*
|&	Redirect standard output and standard error to another command*

*Unique to the C shell.

Note the following:

- UNIX redirection affects only the command line in which the command appears (compare the VMS command **ASSIGN/USER_ MODE**).
- Error messages are not redirected and appear at the terminal.
- If the file **a.lis** already exists, VMS creates a new version of the file with a higher version number. By default, UNIX overwrites any existing file **a.lis**. Overwriting a file through redirection is aptly named *clobbering*. C shell users may prevent clobbering with the shell command **set noclobber**, which warns the user that the proposed output file already exists and prevents the command from executing.
- See Section 3.2.2 and Chapter 11 for more on shell commands.

Table 2.2 summarizes the characters you can use for issuing redirection commands. Let us look at some further examples of their use.

```
                    VMS                              UNIX
example:   $ ASSIGN/USER A.OUT SYS$OUTPUT    % f77 myprog.f >& output
           $ ASSIGN/USER A.ERR SYS$ERROR
example:                                      % f77 myprog1.f >>& output
example:   $ TYPE RUN_PROG.COM               % cat run_prog
           $ RUN MYPROG.EXE                   myprog << end
           1 1 1 1 10                         1 1 1 1 10
                                              end
```

The command **f77 myprog.f >& output** redirects both standard output
and standard error to the file output. If noclobber is not set, the command overwrites any previous version of the file **output**. The command
f77 myprog1.f >>& output has the same effect, except that it appends
standard output and standard error to the file output. If the file output
does not already exist, the command creates it.

The command **cat run_prog** displays a *shell script,* used here to associate data with the compiled program **myprog**. Chapter 11 discusses shell
scripts and how they compare to VMS DCL command procedures. Here
we focus on the use of the redirection to associate data with standard
input to the program **myprog**. A VMS DCL command procedure reads
any records following the **RUN** command and not preceded by a dollar
sign as standard input. In a UNIX shell script, standard input is the
terminal unless redirected. Here <<**end** tells UNIX to read all records
from the script file and not standard input until it finds a record that
begins with "end."

2.2   *Command Structure and File Naming*

VMS is not case-sensitive in its interpretation of a command; that is, it
does not distinguish between commands given in uppercase and commands given in lowercase. In UNIX, on the other hand, commands must
be given in lowercase; the shell will not understand commands in uppercase. Make sure that the caps lock key is not depressed when beginning
a UNIX terminal session.

Filenames are also case-sensitive. That is, UNIX interprets **myfile.dat**
differently from **MYFILE.DAT**. Although the case sensitivity of UNIX
always causes problems to a VMS user during the first few UNIX terminal sessions, it is only a temporary setback. One advantage of case
sensitivity in file naming is that you can use a larger variety of files with
short names. Good news for unimaginative users who are poor typists!

Another advantage of case sensitivity is that it allows the use of upper-case filenames to represent a particular class of files. This advantage offers an alternative to the file type convention used by VMS. For example, directory pointer files to subdirectories exist in UNIX, as they do in VMS. When a subdirectory is created in VMS, the pointer file, which exists in the next highest level of the directory hierarchy, is automatically given a file extension of **.DIR**. UNIX filenames, on the other hand, do not distinguish between directory pointer files and ordinary files. When UNIX displays a default file listing, there is no way of determining which entries are files and which entries are pointers to subdirectories. One way around this situation, which appeals to some VMS users but is not standard UNIX practice, is to name all subdirectories with capital letters or beginning with a capital letter. The following example illustrates this practice with two common UNIX commands: **mkdir** for making subdirectories and **ls** for listing directory contents.

	VMS	UNIX
example:	$ CREATE/DIRECTORY [.TEST]	% mkdir Test
	$ DIRECTORY	% ls
	DIRECTORY DUA1:[HOME]	
	FILE1.DAT;1 FILE2.DAT;1	Test file1.dat file2.dat\
	FILE3.DAT;1 TEST.DIR;1	file3.dat

In a UNIX file listing containing lowercase file entries and an uppercase directory entry, it is immediately obvious which file is the directory file in UNIX even though it has no file extension. Note that uppercase filenames precede lowercase filenames in a UNIX alphabetical listing. It is not advisable to create a subdirectory **TEST.DIR** using the **mkdir** command for reasons that will become apparent in the following section.

Excluding directory pointer files, there is no reason why you cannot adhere to VMS file-naming conventions in UNIX. Since you can legally use a period in UNIX filenames, you can use VMS file extensions to indicate the particular class to which a file belongs. Most VMS users feel comfortable adhering to the VMS file-naming scheme in UNIX. Difficulties arise when the default file extensions used by VMS disagree with UNIX file-naming conventions. For example, object files use the extension **.OBJ** in VMS but **.o** in UNIX. Likewise, FORTRAN source code uses the extension **.FOR** in VMS and **.f** in UNIX. Note that **.o** and **.f** are UNIX conventions to facilitate file recognition and that UNIX commands do not assume file extensions, as do VMS commands. Table 2.3 summarizes commonly used UNIX file extensions.

Table 2.3 UNIX File Extensions

VMS	UNIX	Section	Definition
.OLB	.a	10.5	Library
.BAS	.bas		BASIC source code
.C	.c	10.1	C source code
.FOR	.f	10.1	FORTRAN source code
	.h	10.1	C header files
	.l		**lex** program
.OBJ	.o	10.1	Object code
.PAS	.p		Pascal source code
	.s	10.1	Symbolic assembly code
	.y		**yacc** program
.EXE	a.out	10.1	Executable image
.ADA			ADA source code
.B32			BLISS-32 source code
.CLD			Command description file
.COB			Cobal source code
.COM		11.1	Commands for the language interpreter
.DAT			Data file
.DIS			Distribution list file for **MAIL**
.DIR		2.2	Directory file
.EDT			Startup command file for the EDT editor
.DOC			Documentation
.HLP		3.6	Input source file for **HELP** libraries
.JOU		5.1.5 & 5.2.8	Journal file created by the EDT editor
.LIS			Listing of text
.LOG			Batch job output file
.MAI			**MAIL** message file
.MAR			VAX macro source code
.MEM		12.1	Output file from DSR
.PLI			PL/I source code
.RNO		12.1	Input file for DSR
.SIXEL			Sixel graphic file
.SYS			System image
.TJL			Journal file created by the TPU and ACL editors

Table 2.3 UNIX File Extensions *(continued)*

VMS	UNIX	Section	Definition
.TMP			Temporary file
.TPU			Command file for the TPU editor
.TXT			Text file

	VMS	UNIX
example:	$ FOR MYFILE.FOR	% f77 myfile.f
example:	$ FOR MYFILE	% f77 myfile
	$	**ld:myfile: cannot open**

In UNIX, *command names may not be abbreviated*. In VMS, the portion of the command name that renders it unique is sufficient. UNIX, on the other hand, requires a full specification of the command name. Fortunately, UNIX command names are usually short.[3] Unfortunately, command names are not consistent, nor in some instances do the names have any obvious connection to the functions the commands perform.

Let us now consider the general format of UNIX commands.

	VMS	UNIX
form:	$ COMMAND[/QUALIFIER(S)] [FILENAME(S)]	% command [option(s)] \ [argument(s)]
example:	$ DIRECTORY/SIZE MYFILE.DAT	% ls -s myfile.dat
	Directory DUA1:[HOME]	2 myfile.dat
	MYFILE.DAT;1 3	

	UNIX	
example:	% ls file1 file2	# Check for the existence of two files (no size given)
example:	% ls -s file1 file2	# List the size of two files
example:	% ls -s -a	# List the size of all files
example:	% ls -sa	# List the size of all files
example:	% ls file1 ; ls -s\ file2	# Two sequential file listings
example:	% ls file1 \ file2	# Command continued on next line #
example:	% ls file.{c,o}	# List file.c and file.o (C shell only)

---

3. Further abbreviation or command renaming is possible with the **alias** command (Section 3.2.2).

These examples illustrate the major features of the UNIX command format:

- Options, like VMS qualifiers, modify command functions. UNIX options are usually single letters preceded by a dash. You may combine options and precede them with one dash or give them separately and precede each with a dash. Some options appear as uppercase characters.
- You must use spaces to delimit files in UNIX. A comma is not a valid delimiter when specifying more than one file in a UNIX command line, except when using curly brackets, which are unique to the C shell.
- You can place multiple commands on a single line for sequential processing, provided they are separated by a semicolon. This arrangement is distinct from piping, as the output from one command is not used as input to the next. UNIX interprets the semicolon as a carriage return.
- VMS uses a dash to signify that a command continues on the next line; UNIX uses a backslash. The backslash must be the last character of the line, otherwise the C shell interprets it differently.

2.2.1   Error Reporting

Users familiar with the comprehensive and easily interpreted error reporting features of VMS DCL will likely be disappointed by the features offered by the UNIX shell. This situation is expected to improve (witness the Korn shell) as UNIX gains a wider audience among non-programmers. Until then, users face cryptic error messages, and sometimes no evidence that a command string has failed. UNIX tools and utilities are generally no better at error reporting.

One exception is the simple act of changing the current directory. VMS permits the user to make any directory the current directory, whether it exists or not. Thus, VMS does not report an error until a user issues a command that accesses the non-existent current directory. UNIX, on the other hand, requires that a directory exists before the user can make it the current directory.

2.3   Device, Directory, and File Structures

VMS uniquely defines a file in the following way: **NODE::DEVICE: [DIRECTORY]FILENAME.FILE_EXTENSION:VERSION_NUMBER**, where

NODE	= the name of the host computer on which the file resides
DEVICE	= the physical device on which the file resides
DIRECTORY	= the name of a group of related files to which the file belongs
FILENAME	= the name of the file
FILE_EXTENSION	= a descriptor usually assigned to a class of files
VERSION_NUMBER	= the version number of a file

UNIX uses the following simple scheme to define a file: **host:/directory/ file**, where:

host	= the name of the host computer on which the file resides
directory	= the name of a group of related files to which the file belongs
file	= the name of the file

Both VMS and UNIX have similar rules for naming the components of a complete file specification. For example, UNIX usually abbreviates host names to four to six characters (see Section 13.1.1.1) and file and directory names can have more than 30 characters, avoiding characters that have special meaning.

The differences between UNIX and VMS file specifications are:

- UNIX makes no automatic provision for multiple versions of a file. Therefore, UNIX does not include version numbers as part of the filename. *UNIX saves only the most recent version of a file after any file manipulation.*
- There are no formal file extensions in UNIX. However, as we have already seen, the period can be incorporated into a filename to denote a class of files even though no UNIX commands assume that class of files. In this way, you can use VMS file specifications in a UNIX environment.
- In UNIX, no device specification is ever made.

To understand the implications of this last point, which may sound strange to a VMS user, we must explore the UNIX file structure in some detail.

Like VMS files, UNIX files reside on a physical device. For the purposes of this discussion, we assume that the device is a disk rather than a tape drive (tape drives are considered in Section 8.2). When a user accesses a file, the UNIX operating system determines which physical device the file resides on. The user never explicitly specifies this information. UNIX does this by referencing a file called **/etc/fstab** (file system table), which maps file systems onto physical devices. This may seem confusing. Let us begin with the physical device.

Each disk is divided into *partitions*. Partitions arose due to the inability of 16-bit pointers to address all the space on a large disk. This is not a problem for 32-bit versions of UNIX, and so a large disk can be configured as a single partition. Nevertheless, let us assume the disk has two or more partitions. How the partition is formatted is irrelevant to most users, provided they have a mix of small and large files. A discussion of the partition format, however, may benefit those users who have a predominance of small or large files.

Early versions of UNIX performed all file transfers on 512-byte blocks of data. As the cost of disk storage decreased, the amount of data storage increased, as did file size. For large files, 512-byte addressable blocks do not provide efficient transfer of data between memory and disk. The BSD version of UNIX introduced partitions that allow larger block sizes, facilitating faster block mode transfers. The BSD version allows partitions with different block sizes to exist on the same physical disk. This scheme causes problems when a partition contains predominantly small files. Small files occupy large blocks on disk, so that a large portion of each block is wasted space. BSD solved this problem with the concept of a *fragment,* which is a fraction of a block. Different files can occupy fragments of the same block, reducing disk space wastage. VMS handles the analogous situation by controlling cluster size, which defaults to 3. That is, a VMS file will occupy a minimum of three blocks. Writing to a VMS file with the cluster set to 3 causes the file to expand in three-block increments.

In UNIX, the characteristics of partitions for each type of physical disk drive reside in the file **/etc/disktab** (disk tabulation), which only the system administrator can write to or read. Table 2.4 outlines a sample entry for a Digital RD53 disk drive found on an ULTRIX-based system. The RD53 can be formatted either as a single partition **c** or as three partitions **a**, **b**, and **g**. In all cases the block size is fixed at 4096 bytes, whereas the fragment size for the **c** and **g** partitions is 1024 bytes and 512 bytes for the **a** and **b** partitions. Users whose files do not consist of a mix of large and small should discuss which partitions to use with their system administrator.

Table 2.4   Sample /etc/disktab Entry

```
#
# @(#)disktab     1.12   (ULTRIX)   11/25/85
#
# disktab      from 4.5   4.2 BSD 83/07/30
# Disk geometry and partition layout tables.
# Key:
# ty          type of disk
# ns          #sectors/track
# nt          #tracks/cylinder
# nc          #cylinders/disk
# p[a–h]      partition sizes in sectors
# b[a–h]      partition block sizes in bytes
# f[a–h]      partition fragment sizes in bytes
#
# All partition sizes contain space for bad sector tables unless
# the device drivers fail to support this.
rd53 | RD53 | DEC RD53 Winchester:\
   :ty=winchester:ns#18:nt#8:nc#963:\
   :pa#15884:ba#4096:fa#512:\
   :pb#33440:bb#4096:fb#512:\
   :pc#138672:bc#4096:fc#1024:\
   :pg#89348:bg#4096:fg#1024:
```

A *file system,* a hierarchical arrangement of files and directories, is mounted onto each partition. The file **/etc/fstab** keeps track of which file system to mount in each partition and carries out the mounting operation each time the system is booted. File systems are mounted and dismounted as required (usually by the system administrator), in a manner analogous to mounting and dismounting a VMS physical device. A user can list the mounted file systems and determine the amount of free space with the command **df** (disk free).[4]

example: UNIX
           % df

Filesystem node	total kbytes	kbytes used	kbytes free	percent used	Mounted on
/dev/ra0a	7447	4479	2223	67%	/
/dev/ra0g	42003	23541	14261	62%	/usr

---

4. See Section 7.2.3 for a dicussion of **df**.

Table 2.5 Examples of UNIX Physical Device-Naming Conventions

VMS	UNIX	Description
DUA0:	**/dev/ra0**	Disk drive (block)
	/dev/rra0	Disk drive (character)
LPA0:	**/dev/console**	System console
TTA1:	**/dev/tty01**	Asynchronous terminal
RTA1:	**/dev/ttyp1**	Remote DECnet terminal
LTA01:	**/dev/ttyS1**	Terminal server terminal
LCA0:	**/dev/printer**	Default system printer
MTA0:	**/dev/mt0**	Tape drive (block)
	/dev/rmt0	Tape drive (character)
NL:	**/dev/null**	Wastepaper basket

This example shows two file systems, **/** and **/usr**, mounted in the **a** and **g** partitions of the same RD53 disk specified by **/etc/fstab** in Table 2.4. **ra0a** and **ra0g** indicate the **a** and **g** partitions of the physical device **ra0**. The approximate sizes of the **a** and **g** partitions are 7.5 and 42 megabytes respectively. Note that **/**, known as the *root file system,* is usually mounted in the **a** partition of the **a0** disk. The root file system contains a directory entry for all file systems.

Physical device names vary slightly in different versions of UNIX. Table 2.5 compares ULTRIX physical device names to their VMS counterparts. Note that the physical device names are also the names of files (see Sections 8.1 and 8.2 for the implications of this fact in relation to tape drives). UNIX supports devices as either *block* or *character* (raw), except for disk and tape drives which can be both (see Section 8.1). In simple terms, a character device deals with input and output character by character, whereas a block device buffers characters and deals with them one block at a time. A useful mechanism for discarding output is the *null device*: anything written to it is thrown away. Reading from **/dev/null** will cause an immediate end of file. For example, **cp /dev/null myfile.dat** (compare the VMS command **COPY NL: MYFILE.DAT**) creates an empty file with the name **myfile.dat**. We will see some further uses for **/dev/null** in later chapters.

Each file contained on a VMS physical disk and each UNIX file contained in a file system has a unique identifier, known as a file identifier in VMS and an *inode* in UNIX. Section 2.3.2 describes the UNIX file types and explains briefly how one of these file types uses inodes.

UNIX and VMS directory structures are both hierarchical. Figure 2.2 illustrates the directory structure for a three-disk system, in which one disk contains the operating system and the other two disks contain the user's files. Note the similarity between the directory structures of VMS and UNIX. Both operating systems use particular directories to contain certain types of system files. UNIX directories and related file types are as follows:

/bin	Frequently used system executable files
/dev	Files that address devices (special files)
/etc	Miscellaneous files
/lib	Library files
/tmp	Scratch (temporary) files
/usr/adm	System administrative files
/usr/bin	Less frequently used system executable files
/usr/dict	Dictionary files
/usr/man	Manual page files
/usr/spool	Files spooled to queues
/usr/tmp	Swap and page files

The top level of the VMS directory structure for a physical disk is **[0,0]**. This directory contains all the pointers for the next level of directories. Using the example in Figure 2.2, the directory **DUA0:[SYS0]** has a directory pointer **DUA0:[0,0]SYS0.DIR;1**. To locate the directory **[SYS0]** (or any other directory), the user must know on which device it resides or else search for it. VMS circumvents this problem for system files by defining a common root, as shown in the following example.

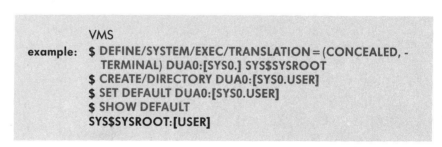

```
                 VMS
example:  $ DEFINE/SYSTEM/EXEC/TRANSLATION = (CONCEALED, -
             TERMINAL) DUA0:[SYS0.] SYS$SYSROOT
          $ CREATE/DIRECTORY DUA0:[SYS0.USER]
          $ SET DEFAULT DUA0:[SYS0.USER]
          $ SHOW DEFAULT
          SYS$SYSROOT:[USER]
```

In the above example, the system directories **[SYS0. . .]** are made equivalent system-wide to the logical name **SYS$SYSROOT** with the **DEFINE**

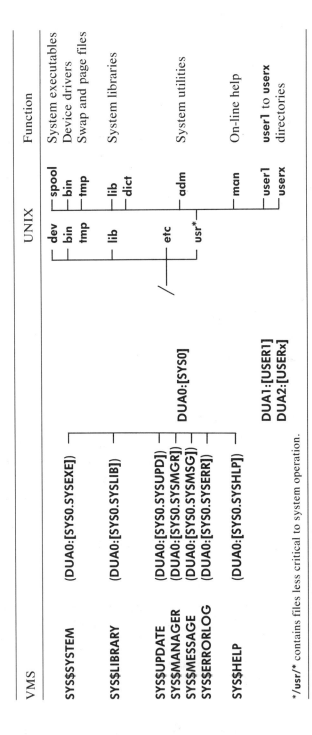

Figure 2.2   VMS and UNIX File Organization

/usr/ contains files less critical to system operation.

command. If you moved the system to a different physical disk, you would change only the definition of the logical name **SYS$SYSROOT:** to redefine the location of all the files it contains, provided all the file references use the logical name rather than the physical device name. In the above example, if a program references a file in **SYS$SYSROOT:[USER]**, you need to make no changes to the program if **SYS$SYSROOT:** is redefined so that it points to a different physical disk. However, if the program references a file using **DUA0:[SYS0.USER]**, then the program must be modified if a change in physical device takes place.

UNIX uses a common root not only for system files but for all files. The UNIX file hierarchy begins with **/** (root directory) for all files on the system irrespective of the physical device. *Each file system, and each subdirectory of the root directory, has a directory pointer in the root directory.*

UNIX
example: % ls -aF /

./	dev/	lost + found/	tp/
../	etc/	mnt/	usr/
bin/	flp/	sys/	vmunix*
boot*	lib/	tmp/	

ls -aF / lists all files in the root directory (refer to Section 2.3.3 for a discussion of hidden files). The **F** (note the use of uppercase) option provides a descriptor at the end of each entry to identify the file type. The slash indicates a directory file. Although **/usr** is a file system (as determined in a preceding example with the **df** command) and the other entries are subdirectories of the root file system, the files contained therein are accessed in the same way. The asterisk indicates that the file is executable: for example, **vmunix** is the executable operating system kernel. The subdirectory **lost + found** resides in the top-level directory of all file systems (the directory **/usr** has one also) and stores files for which the user reference information used by UNIX to associate that file with a particular user has been lost. The system administrator can reassign these files to the owner, if they can be identified. Note also the directory pointers **.** (dot) and **..** (dot dot). These point to the current directory and the preceding level in the directory hierarchy respectively.[5] How these pointers are used is shown in the following section.

---

5. In the root directory only, .. (dot dot) is the same as . (dot), as no higher-level directory exists.

2.3.1　Defining Files to the System

The explicit definition of files in a UNIX system by means of a path from the root irrespective of the physical device is known as *absolute file definition*. Levels down the directory pathway are delimited by a slash (compare to VMS where a period is the delimiter). Any file definition which begins with a slash indicating the root is absolute. Conversely, *relative file definition* defines files not from the root but from the present working directory. Any file definition that does not begin with a slash (/) is a relative definition.

	VMS	UNIX
example:	$ DIR DUA0:[SYS0.SYSEXE[TYPE.EXE	% ls /bin/cat
example:	$ SET DEFAULT DUA0:[SYS0.SYSEXE]	% cd /bin
example:	$ DIR [-]	% ls ..
example:	$ DIR [-.SYSLIB]	% ls ../lib
example:		% ls ~user1

In the first example, **ls /bin/cat** performs a directory lookup using an absolute pathname. Unlike VMS, which may require a device specification, the UNIX file is defined absolutely from the root. The second example, **cd /bin**, introduces the UNIX command **cd** (change directory), which uses an absolute pathname to change to the directory **/bin**. The third and fourth examples illustrate relative pathnames. The command **ls ..** lists the files in the directory above the current directory. The file **..** (dot dot) provides the pointer to the directory above.

The last example, **ls ~user1**, illustrates a feature which is not found in VMS and which, unlike the other examples, is unique to the C shell. A ~ (tilde) followed by the login name of a user points to that user's parent directory. The ~ is an example of filename substitution and is called *globbing*. Wildcards, discussed in Section 2.5, also represent examples of *globbing*. Using the directory constructs from Figure 2.2, **ls ~user1** lists the contents of the directory **/usr/user1**. The tilde without a login name points to the parent directory of the current user, and in this instance is equivalent to the VMS logical name **SYS$LOGIN**.

It should now be evident that using VMS conventions to name directories in UNIX is not useful. For example, if **user1** creates a subdirectory **temp.dir** and then creates a file in that directory called **test**, the absolute pathname to the file **test** is **/usr/user1/temp.dir/test**. The VMS user is more likely to remember the pathname as **/usr/user1/temp/test**.

2.3.2   File Types

There are three types of files in UNIX: *special files, ordinary files,* and *directory files.* UNIX treats all physical devices as if they were special files. Each device on the system has a special file associated with it. These special files reside in the directory **/dev.** As shown in Table 2.5, UNIX treats disks, tape drives, printers, terminals, and pseudo-terminals (used for network connections) as files. Writing to a special file is a matter of course for programs called by the C shell when executing a command; it can also be done explicitly by the user, as later chapters will demonstrate.

Ordinary files contain ASCII characters or binary data. Copying an ordinary file to a special file will output the contents of the ordinary file on the physical device pointed to by the special file. Copying an ordinary file to another existing ordinary file overwrites the target file with the contents of the source file. VMS users accustomed to working with multiple versions of the same file are likely to inadvertently overwrite files in UNIX. Sections 4.9 and 4.10 explain how to avoid losing file contents when copying or renaming files.

An ordinary file consists of a string of bytes arranged in blocks according to the block size defined for the partition. By default, a file is not formatted except for ⟨CTRL⟩-D, an EOF (end-of-file) character. Formatting may be imposed by the user, for example, by writing fixed-length records as output to a FORTRAN program. UNIX still interprets the file as a string of bytes, but the output device correctly interprets carriage returns and line feeds. Formatting is left to a user's program or the UNIX command that is interpreting the file. Thus, all UNIX files have a very simple structure. There is no equivalent to the VMS Record Management Service (RMS), which defines a variety of attributes for files.

We have already discussed directory files. The directory entry contains the file name and *inode number* for each file in the directory. The inode number has an associated entry in an *inode table,* which contains information on the characteristics of a file: for example, the owner, the type of file protection, and the date last modified.

2.3.3   Hidden Files

A subclass of the ordinary file is the *hidden file.* The names of hidden files always begin with a period, and each file has a special function. We will encounter a number of these files in chapters to come. Table 2.6

Table 2.6 Hidden Files

Filename	Section	Function
.cshrc	3.2.2	Define environment to the C shell
.exrc		Define editing environment for **ex** editor
.forward	6.1.4	Define a forwarding address for electronic mail
.history	3.2.1	Save history list
.hushlogin	3.1	Disable some login messages
.login	3.2.1	Define environment at login time, regardless of shell
.logout	3.3	Define environment at logout time
.mailrc	6.1.8	Define environment for the **mail** program
.netrc	13.3.2	Define parameters to **ftp** (file transfer program)
.profile	3.2.2	Define environment to the Bourne shell
.rhosts	13.1.3	Define private remote hosts

summarizes the common hidden files and their functions. Hidden files are so named because using the **ls** command without options will not list them. You must use the command **ls -a** (list all files) to see them. The justification for having hidden files is that if you do not see them you are less likely to damage them!

2.4 *Special Characters*

Characters that the C shell interprets in a special way are known as *metacharacters*. Users should avoid using these characters in filenames, as the results may be unpredictable. Metacharacters will be discussed in subsequent chapters in the context of specific functions. The ˜ (tilde), | (vertical bar), and > (greater than) characters are examples of metacharacters that we have already encountered. Table 2.7 summarizes metacharacters and their functions in the context of the C shell. Table 2.4 lists metacharacters associated with input and output redirection; these do not appear in Table 2.7. The function of a metacharacter may vary depending on whether it is being interpreted by the C shell or by a UNIX utility. Some of the metacharacters listed in Table 2.7 can serve as wildcards for file specifications, discussed in the following section.

Table 2.7 UNIX Special Characters and Their VMS Equivalents

UNIX Character	UNIX Function	VMS Equivalent
&	Perform command in background	
&&	Boolean and*	.AND.
=	Assignment operator	=
= =	Equal to (string)*	.EQS.
!=	Not equal to (string)*	.NES.
=~	Similar to (string)*	
<=	Less than or equal to*	.LE.
>=	Greater than or equal to*	.GE.
‖	Boolean or*	.OR.
;	Command separator	
\	Continuation of command line	
\m	Literal translation of metacharacter **m**	"m
'	Turn off special meaning	/
`	Process immediately	
"	Group characters into a single argument	"
#	Comment follows	!
!	History substitution*	RECALL
%	Signifies a background job*	
-	Indicates input or output to a pipe is that of previous command	
*	Wildcard filename substitution for anything	*
?	Wildcard filename substitution for single character	%
$	Argument substitution follows	'
$#	Argument count	
$$	Process id	F$GETJPI("PID")
$?	Exit status	$STATUS
$<	Read one line from standard input	INQUIRE
@	Perform numerical calculation*	
~	Home directory substitution*	
[]	Selective filename substitution	
.	Current directory	*
{}	Filename expansion delimiters*	

*Unique to the C shell.

Using Wildcards

UNIX wildcards extend those features found with VMS wildcards.

	UNIX	
example:	*	# All files in the current directory and one level below
example:	.	# Files in the current directory
example:	*.*	# All files in the current directory that contain a period in the filename
example:	*.com	# All files in the current directory that end in .com
example:	?.com	# All files in the current directory that end in .com and have one character preceding the period
example:	name[xyz]	# All files in the current directory, namex, namey or namez
example:	name[a-z]	# All files in the current directory, namea through namez
example:	name[a-z4]	# All files in the current directory, namea through namez and name4
example:	name.{o,f}	# All files name.o and name.f in the current directory (C shell only)

There are no absolute rules for the use of wildcards. The output produced when using wildcards is command-dependent. For example, the command **ls** * produces a listing of files for both the current directory and the directory one level down the directory hierarchy. On the other hand, **wc** * (word count) produces output only for the files in the current directory. As you can see, **ls** and **wc** interpret the wildcard differently. The command **ls** . refers to all files pointed to by the . (dot) file, that is, all files in the current directory. The command **wc** ., on the other hand, interprets the . (dot) file literally, providing a word count of the pointer file itself.

VMS users can use wildcards in UNIX in a familiar way. For example, UNIX interprets *.**com** to mean any filename in the current directory ending in **.com**, even though **.com** has no meaning as a file extension. Unlike VMS, which uses the **%** (percentage sign), UNIX uses the **?** (question mark) as a wildcard for single character replacement.

2.6 **Summary**

The software architectures of VMS and UNIX are similar. Nevertheless, the novice UNIX user must grasp several fundamental differences.

First, the novice UNIX user must learn to manage multiple processes, sometimes functioning in a cooperative fashion. In contrast, the VMS user predominantly manages a single process which processes commands sequentially. Chapter 7 introduces the UNIX features for managing multiple processes, although we will encounter many examples before then.

Second, UNIX uses different command syntax. UNIX command names, although short, cannot be abbreviated and do not always bring to mind the command's function. For example, the VMS command **TYPE** is a more logical choice than **cat** for displaying a file at the terminal. Single-letter options modify the functions of UNIX commands in a manner similar to the VMS command qualifiers.

Third, the novice UNIX user must learn new file and directory structures. Although bewildering at first, the elegance of the hierarchical arrangement of files and directories within the UNIX system becomes evident with use. You may address any file or directory irrespective of the physical device, with an absolute pathname from the root or with a relative pathname from the current working directory. Numerous examples of these concepts appear in Chapter 4.

Finally, the novice UNIX user must understand the concept of metacharacters, which have special functions when interpreted by the C shell. We met several metacharacters in this chapter. Chapter 3 introduces the use of metacharacters for the recall and editing of commands lines, known as *history substitution*.

Chapter 3

Getting Started

I was thinking that all these tables [pointing to some logarithms] might be calculated by machinery.

Charles Babbage

You are now ready to begin a terminal session. This chapter explains how to tailor the interactive computing environment to suit your needs and introduces features helpful to the first-time user.

First, we discuss how to set the terminal characteristics to match a host computer environment. This process corresponds to the **SET TERMINAL** command in VMS. Second, we provide instructions on how to customize the UNIX environment. This process corresponds to customizing the user's **LOGIN.COM** file in VMS. Next, we discuss the important features of command line editing and recall, which help you correct incorrect commands. Last, we discuss the UNIX on-line help system and printed documentation.

At first glance, defining a useful environment for interactive computing using UNIX appears complex. Fortunately, the novice user usually has to do very little (or nothing) to establish a usable environment. The system is distributed with default **.login**, **.cshrc**, and other hidden files located in the directory **/usr/skel**. The system administrator may have modified these files to reflect site-specific features. In any case, these files should have been copied to your parent directory when your account was established. If these files are present, then you should already have a usable interactive environment.

Customizing the environment to suit individual needs, on the other hand, requires an understanding of the concepts introduced in Sections 3.1 and 3.2. Many readers may wish to work in the default environment until relatively adept in using UNIX, and then read Sections 3.1 and 3.2 again in preparation for making changes to the interactive environment to better serve their needs.

At the conclusion of this chapter, you should be able to initiate a terminal session, issue commands, and log off: suitable preparation for the manipulation and editing of files, which we discuss in Chapters 4 and 5.

3.1 Terminal Characteristics

UNIX supports a wide range of hardware types. You may connect a terminal to each of these hardware types in a variety of ways; for example, by direct cable, modem, terminal server, or port selector. If your terminal is connected but not displaying a banner message (usually identifying a particular computer) and the log-in prompt from the UNIX host, first check the terminal set-up features. The most common settings for a UNIX system are 9600 baud, 7 data bits, 1 stop bit, even parity (compare 8 data bits, 1 stop bit, no parity for VMS). If your terminal is set up correctly but is still not communicating with the UNIX host, see your system administrator or refer to the additional reading list in Appendix D.

If the wiring of your terminal to the host computer puts Data Terminal Ready (DTR) into operation, turn on the power to initiate a terminal session. If DTR is not in operation, initiate a terminal session by pressing ⟨CR⟩.

Once the log-in prompt appears, UNIX performs a number of operations that determine which characteristics to assign the terminal requesting initialization. These operations illustrate a number of UNIX programs and lookup tables working cooperatively.

When you begin a terminal session, a program named **/etc/init**[1] reads a lookup table residing in a file named **/etc/ttys**. This file contains an argument string for each physical terminal device **/dev/tty** and pseudo-terminal device **/dev/ptty** (used for network connections) available on the system. VMS and UNIX use different descriptors to define terminal devices. For terminals hard-wired to the computer, VMS uses a four-character descriptor followed by a colon: **T** for terminal, **T** or **X** depending on the controller type, a letter of the alphabet to designate the controller, and **0–7** (octal) to designate the device number. Examples of VMS descriptors are **TTA0:** and **TXB7:**. UNIX, on the other hand, uses a five-character descriptor: **tty** for a terminal device, **0–f** (hexadecimal) for the controller ordinal, and **0–f** for the line ordinal. Examples of UNIX descriptors are **tty01** and **ttyff**. You can use the UNIX command **tty**, like the VMS command **SHOW DEVICE/ALLOCATED**, to determine to which device or computer port a terminal is wired.

	VMS			UNIX
example:	$ SHOW DEVICE/ALLOCATED			% tty
	Device	Device	Error	/dev/tty0f
	Name	Status	Count	

---

1. This book uses absolute filenames for programs throughout.

The **/etc/init** program passes the argument string to another program, **/etc/getty**, which looks for the argument string in the lookup table **/etc/gettytab**. If **/etc/getty** does not find the argument, it uses default terminal settings. The settings derived from **/etc/gettytab** include baud rate, parity, and the system banner message (equivalent to **SYS$ANNOUNCE** in VMS). The table **/etc/gettytab** also assigns a function to the ⟨BREAK⟩ key. Usually, pressing ⟨BREAK⟩ changes the baud rate of the host computer port. VMS achieves the same effect more elegantly: the system administrator simply sets the terminal to **AUTO-BAUD**, which automatically matches the speed of the computer port to the speed of the terminal.

When you enter your username at the log-in prompt, **/etc/getty** reads it and passes control to the **/bin/login** program, which prompts you for your password. The **/bin/login** program then checks for your username in the **/etc/passwd** file. If your username is there, it checks for the associated password. If the encrypted password entry in **/etc/passwd** agrees with the password you entered, the program grants you access to the system.

The log-in program updates accounting information and searches the file **/etc/group** to determine to which groups a user belongs. Group names function similar to the VMS User Identification Code (UIC) for the protection of files. All files have group-level protection, which applies to users with the same group name. The difference is that a VMS user always has a single UIC, whereas a UNIX user may belong to multiple groups. Group-level protection is distinct from world-based protection, which applies to all users. Refer to Section 4.2 for more information on file protection. You can determine to which groups you belong with the **groups** command.

                 UNIX
    example: % groups
                 system

The **/bin/login** program invokes **/etc/environ**, a program for setting *environment variables*. Environment variables are similar to system-wide logical name assignments in VMS (see Section 3.2). At this point a copy of the default shell, defined in **/etc/passwd**, is made available to the user. The shell presents a prompt: a dollar sign (**$**) for the Bourne shell, and a percent sign (**%**) for the C shell. The shell is now ready to receive commands.

In VMS, the system administrator can assign an entire range of privileges to each individual user: for example, the ability to change the characteristics of the user's own or other users' processes, or the ability to change the characteristics of physical devices attached to the system. In UNIX, on the other hand, each user has the same limited set of privileges with the exception of the *superuser* (login name **root**). The superuser possesses all privileges, including access to all files on the system irrespective of their assigned protection.

The on-screen messages that appear when a user logs in successfully depend on the host computer, but will likely include features familiar to VMS users, such as the current time and the time when the user last logged in. If the **.hushlogin** file is present in the user's home directory these messages will not appear. Note that **.hushlogin** is an example of a hidden file (see Section 2.3.3). The mere existence of this file suppresses the introductory messages; its contents are irrelevant.

In the following example, the user issues the **touch** command (compare the VMS **CREATE** command, discussed in Section 9.4.7) to create an empty file named **.hushlogin** in the home directory. When the user logs out and logs in again, the system's introductory messages no longer appear.

> VMS
>
> **example:** **CUMBG:: VAX 11/750**
> **Username** SYSTEM
> **Password:**
>   **Last interactive login on Thursday, 15-DEC-1988 10:14**
>   **Last non-interactive login on Tuesday, 13-DEC-1988 19:30**
>   **Welcome to VAX/VMS 4.7**
> **$**
> UNIX
> **Ultrix V2.0-1 (cuhhmd)**
> **login:** root
> **password:**
> **Last login: Thu DEC 15 10:14:00 from tty01**
> **Ultrix V2.0-1 System #3 Wed Oct 26 13:28:16 EDT 1988**
> % touch .hushlogin
> % logout

If your terminal is wired directly to the computer and is unlikely to be changed for long periods of time, the system administrator may unambiguously assign it a terminal type. This terminal descriptor resides in the file **/etc/ttys**, or on some systems **/etc/ttytype**. This descriptor, for example **vt100**, matches an entry in the file **/etc/termcap**, which defines a set of characteristics for the terminal (compare the VMS command **SET TERMINAL/DEVICE_TYPE = VT100**). The file **/etc/termcap** contains information on a large number of terminals from different manufacturers. VMS, in contrast, only carries definitions for Digital Equipment Corporation terminals, although you can define others. The terminal definitions in **/etc/termcap** are usually sufficient. If necessary, you can change a terminal type assignment at any point during a terminal session.

In situations in which different terminals use the same computer port, for example, in the case of modem lines, port selectors, or network connections, you cannot unambiguously define the terminal type. In these situations, UNIX matches a generic terminal definition in **/etc/ttys** or **/etc/ttytypes** (for example, **dialup** or **network**) to a generic definition in **/etc/termcap**. The user may then set the terminal characters, using the commands **tset** and **stty**.

VMS users, presumably already using Digital Equipment Corporation VT-compatible terminals, need do very little to make their terminals respond in a satisfactory manner (see the discussion of the **setenv TERM vt100** command in the following section). For reference, we illustrate some uses of the **tset** and **stty** commands below, even though regrettably, they are two of the more complex commands. To quote the BSD documentation on the **tset** command, "Here is a fancy example to hopelessly confuse anyone who has made it this far." Nevertheless, the documentation for **tset** does contain examples which are helpful in making terminal assignments.

The **tset** command sets the I/O characteristics for a terminal session, and **stty** sets the keyboard characteristics. In the first example, **stty** sets all modes suitable for Digital Equipment Corporation terminal users. In the second example, **stty** explicitly sets characteristics for a terminal (**crt**) rather than for a hardcopy device. The delete key backspaces over the previous character to delete it instead of echoing it and its replacement within string delimiters. Erase character (⟨CTRL⟩-H) functions like the delete key; and delete line is set to ⟨CTRL⟩-U. Note that the user is typing **stty crt erase ⟨DELETE⟩ kill ⟨CTRL⟩-U**, the terminal echoes ^? and ^U for the ⟨DELETE⟩ key and ⟨CTRL⟩-U, respectively. In these two examples, the **stty** command corresponds to the **DEFINE/KEY** command in VMS.

In the third example, **tset -I -Q** suppresses terminal initialization messages (**I**) and the display of keycap definitions (**Q**). In the last example, **tset - -Q -m network:vt100** sets the terminal characteristics to a VT100 when accessing the host UNIX system via a network connection. The minus sign displays the terminal characteristics, once defined, on the terminal screen. The **m** (map) option maps the argument that follows to an entry in **/etc/ttys**, in this case a network device.

Use **stty everything** or **tset** (with no options or arguments) to review the current terminal environment, as illustrated in the following examples:

UNIX

example: % stty everything
new tty, speed 9600 baud
even odd -raw -nl echo -lcase -tandem -tabs -cbreak
crt: (crtbs crterase crtkill ctlecho) -tostop
-tilde -flusho -mdmbuf -litout -nohang
-pendin -decctlq -noflsh

erase	kill	werase	rprnt	flush	lnext	susp	intr	quit	stop	eof
^?	^U	^W	^R	^O	^V	^Z/^Y	^C	\	^S/^Q	^D

VMS   UNIX

example: $ SHOW KEY/ALL   % tset
DEFAULT keypad definitions: Erase is delete
                                       Kill is ctrl-U

tset possesses the functions of both the VMS commands **SET** and **SHOW**. Used without options or arguments, **tset** displays the current terminal characteristics. With options or arguments, **tset** changes the terminal characteristics. This dual functionality is a typical feature of UNIX commands that set variables. Commands that do not set variables and yet require options or arguments behave differently. If you give such commands without options or arguments, UNIX will likely respond with the correct syntax, as shown in the example below. The two commands illustrated here, **cp** (copy) and **mv** (move or rename), are discussed in detail in Sections 4.9 and 4.10 respectively.

UNIX

example: % cp
      usage: cp [-ip] f1 f2;
         or: cp [-irp] f1 ... fn d2
         or: cp -r [-ip] d1 d2
example: % mv
      usage: mv [-if] f1 f2 or mv [-if] f1 ... fn d1 ('fn' is a file or directory)

To a novice UNIX user, the login sequence may seem complex and disconcerting. However, keep in mind that much of the sequence is transparent to the novice user, and is included to illustrate that UNIX has a modular structure enabling a number of programs and lookup tables to function cooperatively.

3.2   *User Environment*

C shell users have two methods for defining the user environment. The first method uses the hidden file **.login** (corresponding to the VMS file **LOGIN.COM**), located in the parent directory. As noted above, **/etc/environ** establishes a set of global characteristics, called environment variables. Users can change the default values of these variables, or add to them, during login by including the appropriate definitions in the **.login** file. Users can also redefine environment variables or add new ones at any time during a terminal session. Environment variables are independent of the shell; that is, they are in effect regardless of what shell is being used.

The second method for defining the user environment applies only to those commands interpreted by the C shell. The hidden file **.cshrc**, located in the parent directory, governs the C shell environment. Entries in the **.cshrc** file define shell variables. When the C shell parses a command line, it either interprets the command (referred to as a *built-in command*) or *forks* a new process, which executes a separate program. By default, the new process receives the characteristics found in both **.login** and **.cshrc**. When the Bourne shell parses the command line it gives new processes the characteristics found in the files **.login** and **.profile**. That is, **.profile** is to the Bourne shell what **.cshrc** is to the C shell. Before discussing how to customize the **.login** and **.cshrc** files, let us deal with the major environment variables and their functions.

The **printenv** command determines which environment variables have been assigned to a terminal session, either by the user or by the system. The following example shows a typical environment for the ULTRIX version of the UNIX operating system. By convention, environment variables appear in upper case.

UNIX

example: **%** printenv
HOME = /usr/users/system   # **Parent directory**
SHELL = /bin/csh   # **C shell as default**
TERM = network   # **Terminal type**
USER = system   # **Login name**
PATH = /usr/ucb:/bin:/usr/users/system-   # **Directories to search**
/bin:/usr/bin:/usr/local:/usr/new:/etc:.   # **for commands**
EDITOR = /usr/ucb/vi   # **Default editor**
MAIL = /usr/spool/mail/system   # **Place to store mail messages**
EXINIT = set ai aw ic sw = 4 redraw -   # **Predefine editing features**
 wm = 4|map g G|map v ~~~~

HOME serves the same function as **SYS$LOGIN** in VMS, defining the user's home, or parent, directory. **SHELL** indicates the shell that is being used to process commands, corresponding to the VMS command language interpreter. **TERM** returns the terminal type, corresponding to the VMS lexical function **F$GETDVI(device_name,DEVTYPE)**. **USER** returns the user login name, corresponding to the VMS lexical function **F$GETJPI(pid,USERNAME)**. **PATH** identifies the directories the system must search to resolve command requests.

When you issue a command, the shell program parses the command line and either processes it directly or passes control to a program in any of the directories specified by **PATH**. Directory paths are separated by a colon. In the example above, note the dot, which specifies the current working directory in the **PATH** list. You should order the **PATH** list so that the directories referenced most frequently appear first in the list.[2] You may add your own directories to the **PATH** list to search for your own specific commands. UNIX users commonly design a directory structure similar to the one used by the operating system: ˜**user/bin** to store executable files, ˜**user/lib** to store libraries, and so on.

EDITOR specifies the default editor, in this case **vi** (see Section 5.2). **MAIL** indicates the location of electronic mail messages, and corresponds to the VMS **SET MAIL_DIRECTORY** command (see Section 6.1.8). **EXINIT** defines the characteristics of the editing environment for the **vi** editor, and corresponds to the definitions contained in the **SYS$LOGIN:EDTINI.EDT** file used to customize the VMS EDT editor (see Section 5.2).

3.2.1 Customizing the .login File

The UNIX command **setenv** defines environment variables in the **.login** file, as shown in the following examples.

	UNIX
form:	% setenv NAME value
example:	% setenv SHELL /bin/sh # make Bourne shell the default
example:	% setenv TERM vt100 # give terminal the characteristics of a VT100

In the first example, **setenv SHELL /bin/sh** sets the **SHELL** environment variable to **/bin/sh**, the Bourne shell program (**/bin/csh** refers to the C shell program). In the second example, **setenv TERM VT100** sets the terminal type to a VT100, recommended for VMS users who have Digital Equipment Corporation VT100, VT200, or VT300 series terminals or compatibles.

Some shell variables have the same names as environment variables, but in lower case. Shell and environment variables with the same names also have the same functions. For example, **HOME** and **home** both define the parent directory. The distinction is only important when the user invokes more than one shell. If **HOME** is defined in the **.login** file as one directory, and the user then invokes the C shell with **home** defined in the file **.cshrc** as a different directory, the latter will be in

---

2. Always place the current working directory last in the **PATH** list to avoid a serious security risk.

Table 3.1   Sample .login File

```
stty dec new cr0
tset -I -Q
umask 027
setenv EDITOR '/usr/ucb/vi'
setenv MAIL /usr/spool/mail/$USER
setenv SHELL /bin/csh
setenv EXINIT 'set ai aw ic sw=4 redraw wm=4 | map g G | map v ~~~~'
set savehist=50
set mail=$MAIL
set prompt = "! - $USER>"
biff y
```

effect. The **set** command defines shell variables. Shell variable definitions can reside in the **.login** file, which is meaningful if you invoke the C shell during login, or in the shell definition file **.cshrc**, discussed in the following section. Table 3.1 illustrates a simple **.login** file for an ULTRIX terminal session, including examples of the **setenv** and **set** commands.

In this example, the **tset** and **stty** commands set the terminal environment (see Section 3.1). The **umask** command sets the default file protection, and corresponds to the VMS command **SET PROTECTION/ DEFAULT**. The three octal digits refer to owner, group, and world access respectively. Unlike VMS, UNIX offers no system-level protection; as noted above, the superuser has access to all files at all times. In this example, a value of 0 indicates read, write, and execute access, 2 indicates read access, and 7 indicates no access. Thus, 027 indicates read-write-execute access for the owner, read access to the group, and no world access. It will be shown that the **umask** notation is the reverse of that used for setting individual file protections. Section 4.2 discusses file protections and **umask** in more detail.

savehist is a C shell variable indicating the number of command lines that you may save for your next terminal session. At the conclusion of each terminal session, the last *n* commands—in this case 50—are saved to the hidden file **.history** located in your parent directory. At the beginning of the next terminal session, the C shell reads the file **.history** into the *history list*. The history list is the name given to those commands that can be recalled with the C shell **history** command (compare the VMS command **RECALL/ALL**). The **history** command is discussed in Section 3.5. VMS does not have a corresponding feature. VMS maintains a history list of the last 20 commands, available only during the current terminal session by issuing the **RECALL** command.

The shell variable **mail** and the environment variable **MAIL** define directories to store incoming and unread mail messages (compare the folder called **MAIL** used by the VMS **MAIL** utility). **mail**=**$MAIL** introduces our first example of *variable substitution*. The dollar sign (**$**) functions as a metacharacter, which when placed before a variable name causes substitution for the value of that variable, in this instance a directory name.

The **prompt** variable defines an alternative prompt to **%** for the C shell (compare the VMS command **SET PROMPT**). The exclamation mark (**!**) is a metacharacter interpreted by the C shell as the beginning of a *history substitution* (see Section 3.4). It indicates the current command number. In this example, the current command number, which precedes the username (based on the substitution of the environment variable **USER**), echoes to the screen. For example, when user **root** issues the first command of a terminal session, the prompt **1 - root**> would appear on the screen. The quotes surrounding the prompt string in the **.login** file delimit the value assigned to the variable **prompt**; without quotes a blank is used as a delimiter. We will meet other examples of the use of the **!** (exclamation) as a metacharacter to invoke a history substitution later in the text.

The last line of the sample **.login** file contains the **biff** command (BSD only), named after the dog of a graduate student at the University of Berkeley. The **biff** command turns notification of incoming mail on and off. Having mail notification turned on (**biff y**) is analogous to having the dog bark whenever mail arrives. The default, **biff n**, corresponds to the VMS command **SET BROADCAST=NOMAIL**; **biff y** corresponds to **SET BROADCAST=MAIL**.

3.2.2   *Customizing the .cshrc File*

The C shell environment definition file **.cshrc** usually consists of two types of commands, **set** and **alias**. As discussed above, the **set** command defines C shell variables. Table 3.2 lists variables that you might use with **set** in the **.cshrc** file. We will discuss the meaning of many of these variables in later chapters. Note, however, the variable **noclobber**. All

Table 3.2 Variables Used with the set Command

Variable	VMS Equivalent	Meaning
argv	P1, P2 etc.	Arguments to the shell
autologout = n		Specifies number of minutes of idle time before an interactive shell terminates*
cdpath = string		Alternative directory tree search
echo	WRITE SYS$OUTPUT	Echoes command lines and arguments
histchars = string		Replaces default of ! for history substitution
history = n	n = 20	Remembers last n commands for recall
home = string	SYS$LOGIN	Sets home directory for C shell command
ignoreeof		Prevents ⟨CTRL⟩-D logouts: require use of logout command
mail = string	SET MAIL __DIRECTORY	Where shell checks for mail
noclobber		Prevents unintentional overwriting during redirection
noglob		Prevents expansion of filenames
nonomatch		Prevents error status if no file match to command is found
notify		Time of notification of job completion
path = string		Sets search path to resolve command calls
prompt = string	SET PROMPT	Sets an alternative prompt to the default C shell prompt of %
savehist = n		Remembers last n commands for recall at beginning of next terminal session
shell = string		Path to the shell program
status	$STATUS	Status as command completion: 1 = error; 0 = no error
time = n		Any command taking longer than n seconds will report CPU and elapsed time
verbose	SET VERIFY	Causes the words of each command to be echoed after history substitution

*Not found in ULTRIX

novice UNIX users should set the variable **noclobber**. Since UNIX maintains only the current version of a file, you must take care to prevent the inadvertent overwriting, or clobbering, of files when redirecting them (see Section 2.1.3). With **noclobber** set, you cannot redirect output to an existing file. If you inadvertently redirect output to an existing file, you will receive an error message.

The command **alias** (compare the VMS construct : = =) redefines command names to make them easier to remember, to abbreviate them, or both. You may abbreviate a command, or a commonly used sequence of commands performing a specific function, to a single user-defined command.

```
         UNIX
form:    % alias name wordlist
example: % alias DIR 'ls -l | more'
example: % alias DIR 'ls -l \!* | more'
form:    % unalias name
example: % alias
         E          emacs
         back       set back = $old; set old = $cwd; cd $back; unset\
                       back; dirs
         cd         set old = $cwd; chdir !*
         cp         cp -i !*
         del        rm -i
         dir        ls -l !* | more
         mv         mv -i !*
         no         /system1/system/scripts/number.scr
         q          /usr/public/queues.scr
         t1500      lpr -P laser
example: % unalias DIR
```

In the first example, **alias DIR 'ls -l | more'**, the name **DIR** is made equal to the **ls -l** command piped to the **more** command. The command **ls**, with the **l** option, produces an extended listing of the file specification. This command corresponds to the VMS command **DIRECTORY/DATE/OWNER/SIZE** (see Section 4.1). The **more** command functions like the VMS command **TYPE/PAGE**, listing the contents of a file one screen at a time (see Sections 4.8 and 9.2). The single quote delimits the string you wish to redefine. You can also use double quotes.

Would the command **DIR *.f** list all FORTRAN source files, one screen at a time? The answer is no. The shell would parse the command line as **ls -l** followed by **more *.f**, that is, list all files in the directory followed by the display of the contents of all files with names that terminate in **.f**. To associate the argument with the first command in the pipe, you must use a history substitution. In the second example, **alias DIR 'ls -l \!* | more'**, the backslash (\, another metacharacter) prevents the immediate parsing of the history substitution when the alias is defined. Instead, the substitution takes place when the alias is invoked. As shown previously,

Table 3.3 Sample .cshrc File

```
set autologout = 30
set prompt = "cuhhmd> "
set cdpath  =  ( $HOME/sys /usr/sys /usr/spool )
set path = (/usr/ucb /bin $HOME/bin /usr/bin /usr/local /usr/new /etc .)
set notify
set history  =  100
set inc  =  /usr/include
alias pwd 'echo $cwd'
alias h history
alias pd pushd
alias pop popd
alias cd 'set old = $cwd: chdir \!*'
alias back 'set back = $old; set old = $cwd; cd $back; unset back; dirs'
```

the exclamation mark invokes a command from the history list and the asterisk (another metacharacter) indicates the last argument to that command. Using the revised definition of **DIR** from the second example, **DIR *.f** now functions correctly: the argument ***.f** is passed to **ls -l**, and the long directory listing of all files ending in **.f** is piped to **more** for display.

In the last example, **alias** without options or arguments illustrates the UNIX convention regarding commands that set variables: If issued without arguments, commands that set variables return the values established with previous use of the command.

The **unalias** command, as the name suggests, undoes the alias command.

Table 3.3 illustrates a typical **.cshrc** file composed of **alias** and **set** commands.

If you make changes to the **.cshrc** file, you must issue the command **source** before the changes take effect for the current shell. The command **source** is built into the C shell (see Section 11.9.4). The command **source .cshrc** corresponds to the VMS command **@SYS$LOGIN:LOGIN.COM**, which the user issues after making changes to the **LOGIN.COM** file to make the changes take effect immediately.

	VMS	UNIX
example:	$ @SYS$LOGIN:LOGIN.COM	% source .cshrc

Note that any child process created will include the characteristics defined in the new **.cshrc** file, for the system executes this file by default each time it forks a new process.

3.2.3   *Setting the Password*

You may change your password at any time using the **passwd** command (compare the VMS command **SET PASSWORD**). Neither the old or the new password echoes to the terminal screen.

	VMS	UNIX
form:	$ SET PASSWORD	% passwd
	Old password:	Old password:
	New password:	New password:
	Verification:	Retype new password:

For security reasons, your password should be at least six characters long. Avoid using metacharacters in naming passwords, as they may provoke an unpredictable response from the UNIX operating system. You may use uppercase and lowercase characters, but remember that the **/bin/login** program is case-sensitive.

3.3   *Logging Out*

You may end a terminal session in one of two ways, depending on whether the C shell variable **ignoreeof** has been set. If **ignoreeof** is set, you must use the **logout** command to log out of the system. If **ignoreeof** is not set, you may use ⟨CTRL⟩-D.

The ⟨CTRL⟩-D command is the EOF (end-of-file) marker, and entering it terminates input from the terminal. Think of the C shell as another program, a program that reads input from the terminal rather than a file. Just as input from a file is terminated with an end of file marker, so is input from the terminal. In either case, the shell program looks in the hidden file **.logout** (compare the VMS file **LOGOUT.COM**) in your parent directory for any user-specific functions to perform before ending the terminal session. It is common practice to place the **clear** command in this file to clear the terminal screen at the end of the session: useful if you don't want anyone to see all the mistakes you've been making! After performing any user-specific functions, the shell searches for the system-wide logout file **/etc/logout** for any further commands to process. Finally, the shell passes control back to **/etc/init**, which initiated the terminal session and now gracefully ends it.

You will not be able to log out if there are any stopped jobs in background. Novice UNIX users often generate stopped jobs in background inadvertently. Novice users who get "stuck" while issuing commands often try ⟨CTRL⟩-Z to get back to the prompt, a common strategy in VMS. In UNIX, ⟨CTRL⟩-Z will return the prompt, returning control to the parent process, while leaving the child process in a stopped background state. The UNIX command **jobs** lists stopped processes in the background. If these are unwanted processes you may enter **logout** or ⟨CTRL⟩-D again, depending on whether **ignoreeof** is set, to remove the stopped processes and end the terminal session.

You do not need to understand the features of background processing at this point. Stopped jobs and background processing, great strengths of the UNIX operating system, are discussed in Section 8.3.

3.4   Control Key Functions

As in VMS, ⟨CTRL⟩ plays a special role in a UNIX terminal session. You may use the **stty** command to modify the functions associated with the control key.

Although ⟨CTRL⟩-Q and ⟨CTRL⟩-S stop and start terminal output on most systems, most users prefer the *hold screen* key found on many terminals. As noted above ⟨CTRL⟩-Z will suspend a child process and return control to the parent process (compare the VMS command ⟨CTRL⟩-Y, followed by **CONTINUE**). The ⟨CTRL⟩-D command will end a terminal session if **ignoreeof** is not set. The ⟨CTRL⟩-L command will refresh the terminal screen (compare the VMS command ⟨CTRL⟩-W). Like the VMS command ⟨CTRL⟩-C, ⟨CTRL⟩-C kills the current child process and returns control to the parent shell process.

3.5   Editing and Recall of Command Lines

We have already touched briefly on the **history** command and the use of history substitution, which are unique to the C shell. We will now discuss them in more detail in reference to the recall of command lines.

VMS Version 4.0 introduced the recall of command lines. Some of the comparable commands in VMS and UNIX are:

	VMS	UNIX	
form:	$ RECALL/ALL	% history	# Provide history list
form:	$ (up arrow)	% !!	# Execute last command
form:	$ RECALL N	% !n	# Execute command number n on the history list
form:	$ RECALL string	% !string	# Execute the last command beginning with # string
form:		% !?string?	# Execute the last command containing string
form:		% !-n	# Execute the nth command ago

There are two important differences between the recall of command lines in VMS and UNIX. First, the command sequence numbers for the VMS **RECALL** command and the UNIX **history** command are different. Command 1 in VMS specifies the last command, whereas command 1 in UNIX specifies the first. Similarly, command **N** in VMS specifies the nth command issued before the current one, whereas in UNIX the **n** command specifies the **n**th command issued since the beginning of the terminal session. Second, when you recall a command in VMS you must press ⟨CR⟩ to execute it, whereas UNIX executes the command immediately, by default.

UNIX can recall only parts of a command line. To explain how this works, we must introduce the concept of *word identifiers*. A word identifier is a piece of a command line delimited by blanks and recognized as a unique entity by the shell. You can break each command line down into a series of word identifiers, which you can then select as part of the current command line. The following examples show the recall of word identifiers from a previous command.

	UNIX			
form:	% command argument1 argument2 argument3			
	0 1 2 3 # word identifier			
example:	% history			
	1 lpr file1 file2 file3			
	..			
example:	% cat !1:1			
	cat file1			
example:	% cat !1:*			
	cat file1 file2 file3			
example:	% cat !1:$			
	cat file3			
example:	% cat !1:2-3			
	cat file2 file3			

Here, the first command on the history list, **lpr** (off-line print; compare the VMS command **PRINT**), has a word identifier of **0**, **file1** has a word identifier of **1**, **file 2** of **2**, and so on. You can introduce metacharacters into the history substitution to manipulate the word identifiers. Each of the above examples associates one or more of the word identifiers with a different command. The first example of word substitution, **cat !1:1**, takes word identifier 1 (**:1**) from the first command in the history list (**!1**) and uses it as an argument to the **cat** command. The second example, **cat !1:***, uses the asterisk to recall word identifiers **1** through **n**, but not **0**. The third example, **cat !1:$**, uses the dollar sign to recall the last word identifier. The fourth example, **cat !1:2-3**, recalls word identifiers **2** and **3**. The last example, **cat !1:2-3 file10**, expands the command line with new arguments.

The recall of command lines, or parts of command lines, in UNIX is versatile, but not as convenient as in VMS, where pressing the up arrow key repeatedly will scroll back through your previous commands. Editing command lines in UNIX is also inconvenient. In VMS, you can position the cursor on the command line using the arrow keys and add or delete text in a manner similar to a full-screen editor. Editing command lines in UNIX is more like using a line editor and performing string substitutions, as shown below.

```
          UNIX
form:     % ^string1^string2^        # Substitute string1 for string2 in previous command
example:  % cat file1
          % ^cat^lpr^
          lpr file1
form:     % !n:s/string1/string2/    # Substitute string1 for string2 in command line n
example:  % history
          . . .
          7 cat file1
          . . .
          % !7:s/cat/lpr/
          lpr file1
form:     % !n:p:s/string1/string2   # Display command substitution but do not execute
          % !!                       # Execute previously displayed command
example:  % !7:p:s/cat/lpr
          lpr file1
          % !!
          lpr file1
```

In the first example, `ˆcatˆlpr` substitutes **string1** for **string2** in the previous command using the caret as a delimiter, and executes the new command. In the second example, **!7:s/cat/lpr/** also performs a substitution (**:s**), but for a specific command; number 7 in the history list. Note that the slash serves as a string delimiter; other characters not found in **string1** or **string2** may also serve as delimiters. In the last example, **!7:p:s/cat/lpr/** previews (**p:**) a command substitution (**:s**) and then executes it with a double exclamation point (**!!**). *Previewing your commands prior to executing them is advisable for all novice UNIX users.* You may use **!!** at any time to immediately execute the previously displayed command again (compare the VMS command up arrow followed by ⟨CR⟩). The novice should not disregard the recall and editing of command lines. You should be comfortable with this feature before moving on to Chapter 4. Spend time at the terminal until fluent in command line recall and editing: time spent now will be time saved later.

3.6 On-Line Help

The major form of UNIX on-line help are the *man pages,* which, as the name suggests, are merely on-line versions of sections of the UNIX documentation set. In reviewing either the machine-readable or written form, VMS users will likely find the UNIX documentation terse, poorly structured, and lacking in examples. Nevertheless, the **man** command, which displays the on-line documentation, will likely appear frequently in a novice user's history list, and it therefore requires detailed discussion.

In VMS, the **HELP** command uses the VMS Librarian Utility to review library entries for each command. Each command in the library is arranged in hierarchical order. At the top is a brief description of the command, followed by a list of qualifiers, parameters, and examples which you may review in any order by using features of the Librarian Utility. The UNIX man page, on the other hand, is a text file which you must read from top to bottom. The general form of the man page is shown below. Not all entries contain each category.

NAME	Lists the name and purpose of a command or subroutine.
SYNOPSIS	Summarizes usage.
DESCRIPTION	Describes usage in more detail.
FILES	Lists the files related to command usage.
SEE ALSO	Points to related information.

Table 3.4 Man Page Locations

/usr/man/manN

N	Contents
1	Shell commands
2	System calls (kernel access points)
3	Subroutine libraries
4	Input/output device driver descriptions
5	Include files and formats
6	Computer games
7	Special files
8	System procedures

Sections 1 and 3 are further subdivided as follows:

1	General purpose commands
1c	Communication related commands
1g	Graphics related commands
1m	System maintenance commands
3	Standard subroutine library
3f	FORTRAN 77 support routines
3r	Internet network library
3m	Mathematical subroutines
3s	Input/output subroutines
3x	Various specialized subroutines

DIAGNOSTICS	Diagnostic messages.
EXAMPLES	Examples on using the command or program.
BUGS	Describes known bugs, or deficiencies, and fixes if available.
RESTRICTIONS	Known limitations.
AUTHORS	Who to blame.

To grasp a particular concept, for example the use of a command option, you may have to read the whole man page several times. Compare the VMS **HELP** system, where you can choose the specific topic of interest and display and redisplay the information easily.

The man pages reside in the directories **/usr/man/man1** through **/usr/man/man8**, according to the classification outlined in Table 3.4. The directory **/usr/man/manl** contains local man page entries, similar to a VMS local help library (for example, **HLP$LIBRARY_1**). UNIX stores the various man pages as unformatted **nroff** files (see Section 12.3), and the **man** command formats and displays them as required. Each man page has an associated section number. For example, the man page for the **cat** command resides in **/usr/man/man1/cat.1**, with a section number of **1**. The **man** command searches all sections for the man page unless you request a specific section. Some man page entries appear in more than one section. In such instances, only one occurrence will be displayed, with preference given to commands over subroutines.

```
            UNIX
form:       %man command
example:    %man cat
            . . .
form:       %man -k keyword
example:    %man -k terminal
ca (see ca(4))                               - terminal multiplexor
clear (see clear(1))                         - clear terminal screen
getty (see getty(8))                         - set terminal mode
gettytab (see gettytab(5))                   - terminal configuration data base
lock (see lock(1))                           - reserve a terminal
pty (see pty(4))                             - pseudo terminal driver
script (see script(1))                       - make typescript of terminal
                                               session
stty (see stty(1))                           - set terminal options
stty, gtty (see stty(3c))                    - set and get terminal state
                                               (defunct)
tabs (see tabs(1))                           - set terminal tabs
term (see term(7))                           - conventional names for terminals
termcap (see termcap(5))                     - terminal capability data base
tgetent, tgetnum, tgetflag, tgetstr, tgoto, tputs (see termcap(3x)) - terminal independent
    operation routines
tset (see tset(1))                           - terminal dependent initialization
tty (see tty(1))                             - get terminal name
tty (see tty(4))                             - general terminal interface
ttynam, isatty (see ttynam(3f))              - find name of a terminal port
ttyname, isatty, ttyslot (see ttyname(3))    - find name of a terminal
ttys (see ttys(5))                           - terminal initialization data
ttytype (see ttytype(5))                     - data base of terminal types by
                                               port
vhangup (see vhangup(2))                     - virtually "hangup" the current
                                               control terminal
form:       %man section command
example:    %man 3c stty
            . . .
```

form:	% man -f command	
example:	% man -f more	
	more, page (see more (1))	**- file perusal filter for CRT viewing**

In the first example above, **man cat** searches the man pages for the specific command **cat**. The **man** command will search all the man directories for a file referring to this command. The man page entry is automatically piped through the **more** command and displayed on the output device. In the second example, **man -k terminal** illustrates a situation where the user knows something about the function of the command, but not the name of the command (compare the VMS command **HELP HINTS**). The user knows that the command relates to the use of a terminal, and therefore displays all terminal-related commands. The user can then select the correct command and display the specific man page. Note that the section number for each command appears in parentheses. In BSD, **man -k** can also be executed as the command **apropos**.

In the third example, **man 3c stty**, a specific section identifier, is used to review the **stty** subroutine; **man 1stty** would display the **stty** command. In the last example, the situation is the reverse of that described above for **man -k**: that is, the user knows the command name but not the function. The **f** option displays the header line, providing a brief synopsis of the command's function. The command **whatis** can substitute for **man -f**.

3.7   *Printed Documentation*

The printed documentation available to a UNIX user depends on the UNIX version and the distributor. Table 3.5 describes the various components of the ULTRIX documentation set, most of which are common to any derivative of the BSD. For a new user, the commands section and Supplementary Volume I provide the most useful reference material.

3.8   *Summary*

Conducting your first terminal session with a new operating system can be a traumatic event. UNIX is no exception. This chapter is intended to minimize that trauma.

Once you have logged in, if the terminal does not respond as expected, issue the command **setenv TERM terminal_type** (Section 3.1), where ter-

Table 3.5 ULTRIX Documentation Set

Section	Contents	On-Line Location
Commands	Commands available to all users	**/usr/man/man1**
System Calls	Routines for making calls to the kernel	**/usr/man/man2**
Subroutines	Subroutines found in various system libraries	**/usr/man/man3**
Special Files	Files relating to device driver and network support	**/usr/man/man4**
File Formats	Describes the format of system files, many of which are discussed in this book	**/usr/man/man5**
Macro Package and Conventions	Miscellaneous information about mail, text formatting, and so on	**/usr/man/man7**
Maintenance	System operation and maintenance	**/usr/man/man8**
Supplementary I	Supplementary information for the user, including system overview, editing, utilities, word processing	
Supplementary II	Supplementary information for the programmer, including languages, debuggers, programming support tools	
Supplementary III	System management support tools	

minal type is one of the terminals described in the file **/etc/termcap** (use the command **more /etc/termcap** to display this file). Users of Digital Equipment Corporation VT series terminals and compatibles should find the appropriate entries, for example VT100, VT200, or VT300. If the terminal still does not respond as expected, consult your system administrator.

Next, use the **cat** or **more** commands to examine any files beginning with a period. Recall that these are hidden files, and that they are important to your terminal session. Particularly important at this point are the files **.login** (Section 3.2.1) for all users (compare the VMS file **LOGIN.COM**), **.profile** for Bourne shell users, and **.cshrc** (Section 3.2.2) for C shell users. If you do not know which shell is your default shell, look at the prompt: **%** is the default C shell prompt, and **$** is the default Bourne shell prompt. Reconcile the commands found in these files with those discussed here.

When the inevitable typing mistakes occur and the arrow keys do not function as they do with VMS, persevere with the UNIX recall and editing of command lines (Section 3.5). Although not as elegant as VMS, they are still useful.

Finally, spend time with the UNIX man pages (Section 3.6); you are sure to use them while experimenting with the material discussed in the following chapters.

Chapter 4

Introductory File Management

Doublethink means the power of holding two contradictory beliefs in one's mind simultaneously, and accepting both of them.

George Orwell

UNIX possesses numerous commands and utilities for the creation, modification, and display of files and directories. Table 4.1, a summary of file management commands, was created from the headers of the man page entries for all sections of the BSD documentation (see Section 3.6). Table 4.1 divides the commands into those that display files and those that manipulate them. Since display commands do not change the contents of files, the novice user may use them in complete safety. Manipulation commands do change the contents of files, and novice users should use them with care.

Like a spoken language, UNIX allows successful communication using only a limited vocabulary. This chapter concentrates on commands and a few options that the novice user will likely need in the first few terminal sessions. Chapter 9 introduces additional commands and options that, although used less frequently, add richness and functionality to the language. In both chapters the focus is commands rather than callable C language routines or utilities. The following chapters deal with important utilities in the context of application development; callable routines are beyond the scope of this book. Table 4.2 summarizes the directory and file commands discussed and indicates where to find them in this book.[1]

After reading this chapter, you should be able to perform the most common tasks involving the management of UNIX files. You should be able to:

- list the files in a directory (Section 4.1)
- determine the current directory (Section 4.3)
- change the current directory (Section 4.4)
- create a directory (Section 4.5)
- delete a directory (Section 4.6)
- locate a file (Section 4.7)

---

1. The commands in Table 4.2 are a subset of the commands found in Appendix A.

- display the contents of a file (Section 4.8)
- copy a file (Section 4.9)
- rename a file (Section 4.10)
- delete a file (Section 4.11)

As you begin displaying and managing files, you will need to learn more about their characteristics. We will begin by learning how to list the characteristics of files in Section 4.1. We will then explain each of these characteristics in Section 4.2. An understanding of file characteristics will be especially useful in Chapter 9, when we discuss commands that change file characteristics. In Sections 4.3 through 4.11, we return to our introduction of interactive file and directory management.

As before, when we give examples of UNIX commands and compare them to their VMS counterparts, we use relative and absolute path-names to emphasize the various ways of defining files in UNIX. The examples come from everyday use, and illustrate piping and input and output redirection. We suggest that you study the examples given here and then experiment with variations of your own.

4.1   *Displaying Directory Contents: ls*

The **ls** command for listing the contents of a directory was introduced in Section 2.2, and it has since been used with different options. The following examples summarize some **ls** options.

	VMS	UNIX
form:	$ DIRECTORY[/QUALIFIER(S)] [FILE-SPEC...]	% ls -[option(s)] [argument(s)]
example:	$ DIR	% ls
	DUA2:[USER1]	myfile.txt program.f tmp
	.LOGIN;1 MYFILE.TXT;1 PROGRAM.FOR;1	
	TMP.DIR;1	
example:	$ DIR	% ls -a
	DUA2:[USER1]	.login myfile.txt program.f tmp
	.LOGIN;1 MYFILE.TXT;1 PROGRAM.FOR;1	
	TMP.DIR;1	
example:	$ DIR [...]	% ls -R
	DUA2:[USER1]	myfile.txt program.f tmp
	.LOGIN;1 MYFILE.TXT;1 PROGRAM.FOR;1	
	TMP.DIR;1	tmp:
	DUA2:[USER1.TMP]	test
	TEST.;1	

Table 4.1 Summary of File Management Commands

UNIX Command	VMS Equivalent	Purpose
Display Commands: Directories		
ls (see ls(1))	**DIRECTORY**	Lists contents of directory
Display Commands: Files		
cat (see cat(1))	**TYPE**	Catenates and prints to a terminal
col (see col(1))		Filters reverse line feeds
colcrt (see colcrt(1))		Filters **nroff** output for CRT previewing
fmt (see fmt(1))	**RUNOFF**	Simple text formatter
fold (see fold(1))	**SET TERMINAL/WIDTH = n/WRAP**	Folds long lines for finite-width output device
fpr (see fpr(1f))	**PRINT**	Prints FORTRAN files
head (see head(1))	**EDIT/READ**	Displays first few lines
more, page (see more(1))	**TYPE/PAGE**	File perusal filter for CRT viewing
od (see od(1))	**DUMP**	Octal, decimal, hex, ASCII dump
pr (see pr(1))	**PRINT/HEAD**	Prints file to **stdout**
print (see print(1))	**PRINT**	Prints to the line printer
sod (see sod(1))	**ANALYZE/OBJECT**	Standard object file-dump utility
tail (see tail(1))	**EDIT/READ**	Displays the last part of a file
Manipulation Commands: Directories		
cd (see cd(1))	**SET DEFAULT**	Changes working directory
chdir (see chdir(2))	**SET DEFAULT**	Changes current working directory—C callable routine
chdir (see chdir(3f))	**SET DEFAULT**	Changes default directory—FORTRAN callable routine
cpall (see cpall(1))	**COPY**	Copies directory
dir (see dir(5))		Format of directories
getdirentries (see getdirentries(2))		Gets directory entries in a file system independent format

Command	VMS	Description
getwd (see getwd (3))	F$DIRECTORY("DEFAULT")	Gets current working directory path name
mkdir (see mkdir(1))	CREATE/DIRECTORY	Makes a directory
pwd (see pwd(1))	SHOW DEFAULT	Working directory name
rmdir (see rmdir(2))	DELETE	Removes a directory file
scandir, alphasort (see scandir(3))		Scans a directory
unlink (see unlink(2))		Removes directory entry—C callable routine
unlink (see unlink(3f))		Removes a directory entry—FORTRAN callable routine

Manipulation Commands: Files

Command	VMS	Description
ar (see ar(1))	LIBRARY	Archive and library maintainer
awk (see awk(1))	EDIT/TPU	Patterns scanning and processing language
basename (see basename(1))	F$PARSE	Strips filename affixes
bcopy, bcmp, bzero, ffs (see bstring(3))	F$FAO	Bit and byte string operations
checknr (see checknr(1))		Checks nroff/troff files
chgrp (see chgrp(1))	SET FILE/OWNER	Changes group
chmod (see chmod(1))	SET PROTECTION	Changes mode—command
chmod (see chmod(2))	SET PROTECTION	Changes mode—C callable routine
chmod (see chmod(3f))	SET PROTECTION	Changes mode—FORTRAN callable routine
cmp (see cmp(1))	DIFFERENCE	Compares two files
comm (see comm(1))	SORT/MERGE	Selects or rejects lines common to two sorted files
compact, uncompact, ccat (see compact(1))	COMPRESS	Compresses and uncompresses files and catenates them
cp (see cp(1))	COPY	Copy
cpr (see cpr(1))	PRINT	Prints C source files
creat (see creat(2))	CREATE	Creates a new file

Table 4.1 Summary of File Management Commands *(continued)*

UNIX Command	VMS Equivalent	Purpose
crypt (see crypt(1))	**ENCRYPT**	Encode/decode command
crypt, setkey, encrypt (see crypt(3))	**ENCRYPT**	Encryption operations—C callable routine
ctags (see ctags(1))		Creates a tags file
dd (see dd(1))	**EXCHANGE**	Converts and copies a file
diff (see diff(1))	**DIFFERENCE**	Differential file and directory comparator
diff3 (see diff3(1))		Three-way differential file comparison
expand, unexpand (see expand(1))		Expands tabs to spaces and vice versa
file (see file(1))	**F$PARSE**	Determines file type
filehdr (see filehdr(5))		File header for standard format object files
find (see find(1))	**DIRECTORY**	Finds files
flock (see flock(2))	**UNLOCK**	Applies or removes an advisory lock on an open file
fsplit (see fsplit(1f))		Splits a multiroutine FORTRAN file into individual files
ftp (see ftp(1c))	**COPY**	File transfer program
grep, egrep, fgrep (see grep(1))	**SEARCH**	Searches a file for a pattern
ident (see ident(1))	**DIRECTORY**	Identifies files
link (see link(2))	**ASSIGN**	Makes a hard link to a file—C callable routine
link (see link(3f))	**ASSIGN**	Makes a link to an existing file—FORTRAN callable routine
ln (see ln(1))	**ASSIGN**	Makes links
lockf (see lockf(3))		Advisory record locking on files
look (see look(1))	**SEARCH**	Finds lines in a sorted list

Command	Keyword	Description
lorder (see lorder(1))	LIBRARY	Finds ordering relation for an object library
merge (see merge(1))	MERGE	Three-way file merge
mknod (see mknod(2))	EDIT/FDL	Makes a special file (character, block, or fifo)
mknod (see mknod(8))	EDIT/FDL	Builds special file
mktemp (see mktemp(3))		Makes a unique file name
mv (see mv(1))	RENAME	Moves or renames files
ncheck (see ncheck(8))		Generates names from i-numbers
nroff (see nroff(1))	RUNOFF	Text formatting
open (see open(2))	OPEN	Opens a file for reading or writing, or creates a new file
qsort (see qsort(3))	SORT	Quick sort—C callable routine
qsort (see qsort(3f))	SORT	Quick sort—FORTRAN callable routine
ranlib (see ranlib(1))	LIBRARY	Converts archives to random libraries
rcp (see rcp(1c))	COPY	Remote file copy
read, readv (see read(2))	READ	Reads input
readlink (see readlink(2))	SHOW LOGICAL	Reads value of a symbolic link
rename (see rename(2))	RENAME	Renames a file—C callable routine
rename (see rename(3f))	RENAME	Renames a file—FORTRAN callable routine
rev (see rev(1))		Reverses lines of a file
rm, rmdir (see rm(1))	DELETE	Removes (unlinks) files or directories
size (see size(1))	DIRECTORY/SIZE	Size of an object file
sort (see sort(1))	SORT	Sorts or merges files
split (see split(1))		Splits a file into pieces
stat, lstat, fstat (see stat(2))	SHOW DEVICE/FILE	Gets file status—C callable routine
stat, lstat, fstat (see stat(3f))		Gets file status—FORTRAN callable routine

Table 4.1 Summary of File Management Commands *(continued)*

UNIX Command	VMS Equivalent	Purpose
strncpy, strlen, index, rindex (see string(3))	F$STRING	Strings operations
strings (see strings(1))	ANALYZE/OBJECT	Finds the printable strings in an object or other binary file
strip (see strip(1))		Removes symbols and relocation bits
sum (see sum(1))	DIRECTORY	Sums and counts blocks in a file
swab (see swab(3))		Swaps bytes
symlink (see symlink(2))	ASSIGN	Makes symbolic link to a file
symorder (see symorder(1))		Rearranges name list
tar (see tar(1))	BACKUP	Tape archiver
tar (see tar(5))	BACKUP	Tape archive, file format
touch (see touch(1))	CREATE	Updates date last modified of a file
tr (see tr(1))	F$STRING	Translates characters
troff (see troff(1))	RUNOFF	Text formatting and typesetting
truncate, ftruncate (see truncate(2))		Truncates a file to a specified length
tsort (see tsort(1))	SORT	Topological sort
umask (see umask(2))	SET PROTECT	Sets file creation mode mask
uniq (see uniq(1))		Reports repeated lines in a file
utime (see utime(3c))		Sets file times
utimes (see utimes(2))		Sets file times
vers (see vers(1))		Sets/displays version numbers
wc (see wc(1))		Word count
what (see what(1))	LINK/MAP	Shows what versions of object modules were used to construct a file
which (see which(1))		Locates a program file including aliases and paths (C shell only)

Table 4.2 Commonly Used File Management Commands

UNIX Command	VMS Equivalent	Location	Purpose
ar	LIBRARY	Section 10.5	Archives files
awk	EDIT/TPU	Section 5.4	Patterns matching utility
cat	TYPE	Section 4.8	Catenates and prints to a terminal
cd	SET DEFAULT	Section 4.4	Changes working directory
chgrp	SET FILE	Section 9.4.2	Changes the group ownership
chmod	SET PROTECTION	Section 9.4.1	Changes protection
cmp	DIFFERENCE	Section 4.5	Compares two files and reports the first difference found
cp	COPY	Section 4.9, 9.3.1	Creates a new copy
diff	DIFFERENCE	Section 9.4.3	Reports all differences between two files
find	DIRECTORY	Section 4.7, 9.4.4	Locates within a directory structure
fsplit		Section 10.2	Splits into functional parts
ftp	COPY	Section 13.3.2	Transfers to/from remote node
grep	SEARCH	Section 9.4.5	Finds a string
head	EDIT/READ	Section 9.2.3	Gives first few lines
lorder	LIBRARY	Section 10.5	Finds ordering relationship
ln	ASSIGN	Section 9.4.10	Creates a symbolic link
ls	DIRECTORY	Section 4.1, 9.1.1	Lists contents of a directory
merge	MERGE	Section 9.4.6	Merges files
mkdir	CREATE/DIR	Section 4.5	Makes a directory
more	TYPE/PAGE	Section 4.8, 9.2.1	File perusal filter for CRT
mv	RENAME	Section 4.10	Moves (or renames)
nroff	RUNOFF	Section 12.1	Text processing
od	DUMP	Section 9.2.2	Octal, decimal, hex, ASCII dump
pr	PRINT/HEAD	Section 9.2.3	Prints file
pwd	SHOW DEFAULT	Section 4.3	Working directory name

Table 4.2 Commonly Used File Management Commands *(continued)*

UNIX Command	VMS Equivalent	Location	Purpose
ranlib*	**LIBRARY**	Section 10.5	Converts archives to random libraries
rcp	**COPY**	Section 13.3.1	Remote file copy
rm	**DELETE**	Section 4.11	Removes or deletes
rmdir	**DELETE**	Section 4.6	Removes a directory file
sort	**SORT**	Section 9.4.6	Sorts by key
tail	**EDIT/READ**	Section 9.2.3	Outputs the last part of a file
tar	**BACKUP**	Section 8.2.1	Tape archive
touch	**CREATE**	Section 9.4.7	Updates file characteristics or creates a null file
tr	**EDIT**	Section 9.4.8	Translates characters
troff	**RUNOFF**	Section 12.2	Text formatting and typesetting
uucp		Section 13.3.3	Remote file copy to neighboring host
uusend		Section 13.3.3	Remote file copy
wc		Section 9.4.9	Counts words

*BSD only.

```
                VMS
example:  $ DIR/PROTECTION/DATE/SIZE/OWNER
          DUA2:[USER1]
          .LOGIN;1        1   10-JAN-1987   08:17   [USER1]  (RWED,RWED,RE,RE)
          MYFILE.TXT;1    2   24-AUG-1988   13:40   [USER1]  (RWED,RWED,RE,RE)
          PROGRAM.FOR;1 1   10-JUL-1988   21:10   [USER1]  (RWED,RWED,RWED,E)
          TMP.DIR;1       1   12-SEP-1988   04:10   [USER1]  (RWE,RWE,RE,RE)

          UNIX
          % ls -l
          total 1
          -rwxr-xr-x       1   user1         1024   24 Aug 13:40    myfile.txt
          -rwxrwx--x       1   user1          512   10 Jul 21:10    program.f
          drwxr-xr-x       2   user1           30   12 Sep 04:10    tmp
```

Each of the four examples above pertain to a directory that contains four files: three ordinary files, **myfile.txt** (text), **program.f** (FORTRAN program), and **.login** (hidden); and a directory file, **tmp**. The subdirectory **tmp** contains one file, **test** (text). The first and simplest example, **ls**, lists the file names in the current directory excluding the hidden file (compare the VMS **DIRECTORY** command). Note that here and in subsequent examples, **ls** does not display the name of the current directory. The second example, **ls -a** (list all), includes the hidden file name in the listing.

The third example, **ls -R**, lists not only the contents of the current directory but also all files in all subdirectories lower in the hierarchical directory tree, which in this example includes the subdirectory **tmp**. This command corresponds to the VMS command **DIRECTORY [. . .]**. The **ls *** command (not shown) lists files in the current directory and all files one level down in the directory hierarchy. Similarly, **ls */*** lists all files in the current directory and all files both one and two levels down in the directory hierarchy. The last example, **ls -l** (long listing), gives additional information on the characteristics of the file including file type, protection, owner, size, and date last modified. See Section 4.2 for a discussion of each of these file characteristics. The options illustrated here may be combined: for example, **ls -al** displays a long listing including the hidden files.

Unless modified by an option, **ls** displays files alphabetically. The following conditions define the sort order for an alphabetical listing:

1. file names beginning with a period
2. numbers

3. uppercase letters

4. lowercase letters

The following example illustrates the order in which **ls** displays files.

> UNIX
>
> **example:** % ls
>
> .123 .Test .test 123 Foo foo

4.2   *File Characteristics*

Let us take a closer look at the **ls -l** command, which produces a long listing of the characteristics of a file. You can add information about the groups to which a file belongs by using the command **ls -lg**, as shown below.

> VMS
>
> **example:** $ DIRECTORY/FULL [-]TESTFILE.
> Directory DUA3:[BOURNE.MASS11]
>
> | | | |
> |---|---|---|
> | TESTFILE.:1 | File ID: | (11044,9,0) |
> | Size: 1/3 | Owner: | [STAFF,DANNY] |
> | Created: 20-FEB-1988 13:15 | Revised: 20-FEB-1988 13:15 (1) | |
> | Expires: <None specified> | Backup: <No backup recorded> | |
> | File organization: | Sequential | |
> | File attributes: | Allocation: 3, Extend: 0, Global buffer count:- 0, No version limit | |
> | Record format: | Variable length, maximum 4 bytes | |
> | Record attributes: | Carriage return carriage control | |
> | Journaling enabled: | None | |
> | File protection: | System:RWED, Owner:RWED, Group:R, - World:R | |
> | Access Cntrl List: | (IDENTIFIER = %X80010003.ACCESS = READ - + WRITE + EXECUTE + DELETE + CONTROL) (IDENTIFIER = $X80010000.ACCESS = READ - + WRITE + EXECUTE) | |
>
> Total of 1 file, 1/3 blocks.
>
> UNIX
>
> % ls -lg ../testfile
> -rwxr--r-- 1 danny   staff   1000 10 Aug   12:20 testfile

In this example, **ls -lg . ./testfile** uses a relative pathname to display the characteristics of **testfile**, which resides one directory level above the current directory. Note that the full listing given by UNIX is more concise than the equivalent listing given by the VMS **DIRECTORY/FULL** command, in part reflecting the simpler file structure of UNIX. First, UNIX does not display record and file attributes; as we saw in Section 2.3, files consist of a string of bytes which, for a given partition, always have the same file characteristics. Second, UNIX does not support an Access Control List (ACL). Third, UNIX does not display the last backup and file creation dates, but only the date the file was last modified.

The first character in a UNIX file description indicates the type of file. File types described by this character include:

d   directory file

b   block-type special file

c   character-type special file

l   symbolic link

s   socket

—   plain file

A plain file contains any ASCII or binary information. A directory file is a pointer to a subdirectory of the current directory. (Compare the VMS file with the extension **.DIR**.) Users usually only manipulate directory files by deleting them to remove a subdirectory. The next nine characters **rwxr--r--** define the file protection (see Section 3.2.1). Each file has three levels of protection: owner, group, and world (all local and remote users), defined by the first, second, and third three-character groups respectively. Unlike VMS, UNIX has no fourth level of protection defining access to the system administrator, who always has full access to UNIX files. Each level of protection permits three types of access: read (**r**), write (**w**), and execute (**x**). Unlike VMS, UNIX does not distinguish between write and delete. A UNIX file which can be written to can also be deleted. In the above example, the owner of **test-file** can read, write, and execute it, and group members and all other users can read it. As in VMS, the protection assigned to a directory file determines the first level of protection for all files in that directory, and takes precedence over the file protection assigned to the individual files. For example, if the directory file has a file protection that precludes writing by the owner, the owner cannot edit any files in that directory even if the individual file protections indicate otherwise.

The second entry in our example, **1**, indicates the number of links the file possesses (see Section 9.4.10 for a discussion of links). As the name suggests, a *link* is a connection between files and directories, or between directories. A file always has at least one link, to the directory file in which it resides. For example, the file specification **/tmp/test1** indicates that the file **test1** has a single link to the directory file **tmp**. Similarly, a directory file always has at least two links, one to all the files in the directory and one to its parent directory file. For example, the directory **tmp** has two links, one to **/** (the root directory) and one to all the files it contains. Creating a further subdirectory to **tmp** would increase the link count of **tmp** by one. Section 9.4.10 discusses making additional links.

The next two entries in our example, **danny** and **staff**, indicate the owner of the file and the group to which the file belongs. You can use groups in a manner similar to the VMS Access Control Entry (ACE) in an Access Control List (ACL). A user may belong to several groups, for example, according to a department or job function. You can assign a file's group permission to give access only to members of the appropriate group. A VMS ACL may comprise multiple ACEs, but only one group can be assigned to a VMS or UNIX file.

If a user belongs to multiple groups and a file can belong to only one group, to which group does a file created by that user belong? The answer can be found in the files **/etc/passwd** and **/etc/group**, introduced in Section 2.3.2. The file **/etc/group** contains a numeric group identifier associated with each group name. The **/etc/passwd** file contains a single group identifier and a unique user identifier for each user regardless of the number of groups to which the user belongs. Therefore, UNIX assigns the group name associated with the user's unique group identifier to a file when the file is created. The file owner can easily change the group ownership of a file with the **chgrp** command (see Section 9.4.2).

The following example shows a record from the **/etc/passwd** file for user **danny**; the fields within the record are separated by colons.

```
                UNIX
example:        % more /etc/passwd
                . . .
                danny:9GeD4S9Hktztl:102:49:Daniel Schainholz,523BB,71846,9284897:/ \
                  system1/danny:/bin/csh
                . . .
example:        % more /etc/group
                . . .
                staff:*:49:danny,fred,george
                . . .
```

The field definitions are as follows:

danny	login name
9GeD4S9Hktztl	encrypted password
102	unique user code
49	group identifier
Daniel Sch. . .	name and demographic information
/system1/danny	parent directory
/bin/csh	default shell

User **danny** has the group identifier **49**, which defines the default group ownership of his files. Referring to the file **/etc/group**, the identifier **49** belongs to the group **staff**. Hence, all files created by user **danny** will by default belong to the group **staff**.

Do not confuse a UNIX group assignment with a VMS User Identification Code (UIC). A UNIX user may belong to many groups, whereas a VMS user belongs only to a single group defined by the UIC. VMS achieves a UNIX-like group file access by assigning an Access Control Entry to a file. An ACE defines an identifier and a level of protection for that identifier. Users possessing that identifier have access to the file in accordance with the identifier's protection. Users who do not possess the identifier have access to the file in accordance with standard VMS file protections. The VMS system administrator assigns identifiers to a user; the owner of the file assigns identifiers to the file.

Returning to the **ls -lg** command, the next entry, **1000**, indicates the size of the file. UNIX file sizes appear in bytes, whereas VMS file sizes appear in blocks containing 512 bytes each. Thus, a VMS file of 3 blocks appears as a file size of 1536 in UNIX.

The next entry, **10 Aug 12:20**, indicates the date and time the file was last modified. The last entry, **testfile**, gives the name of the file.

4.3 Determine the Current Directory: pwd

The command **pwd**, print working directory, determines the current directory (compare the VMS command **SHOW DEFAULT**). The C shell also offers the **dirs** command, which displays a hierarchical list of directories called a *directory stack,* with the present working directory at the top. Section 9.3.2 explains how to build a directory stack and how it facilitates movement between commonly used directories.

	VMS	UNIX
form:	$ SHOW DEFAULT	% pwd
example:	$ SHOW DEFAULT	% pwd
	DUB2:[TEST]	/test

4.4   *Change Directory: cd*

The UNIX command **cd**, change directory, changes the present working directory (compare the VMS command **SET DEFAULT**).

	VMS	UNIX
form:	$ SET DEFAULT device-name[directory]	% cd [directory]
example:	$ SET DEFAULT DUA2:[USER]	% cd /user
example:	$ SET DEFAULT [-.USER]	% cd ../user
example:	$ SET DEFAULT SYS$LOGIN:	% cd

The first two examples above are easy to understand when compared to their VMS counterparts. In the third example, **cd** without a directory argument changes the present working directory to the user's home directory, and therefore provides a simple means of returning to a familiar point in the directory hierarchy.

The C shell extends the use of **cd** through the shell variable **cdpath**. The variable **cdpath** lets you move from the present working directory to a directory defined by **cdpath** without regard to the relative or absolute pathname to that directory. See Section 9.3.2 for a discussion of **cdpath**.

4.5   *Create a Directory: mkdir*

The UNIX command **mkdir**, as the name suggests, creates directories (compare the VMS command **CREATE/DIRECTORY**).

	VMS	UNIX
form:	$ CREATE/DIRECTORY[/QUALIFIER(S)] - directory-spec[, . . .]	% mkdir directory_name
example:	$ CREATE/DIRECTORY [.TEST]	% mkdir test
example:	$ CREATE/DIRECTORY [USER.TMP.TEST]	% mkdir /user/tmp/test

In the first example, **mkdir test** illustrates the creation of a subdirectory, **test**, to the present working directory. In the second example, **mkdir /**

user/tmp/test uses an absolute pathname to create a subdirectory **test**. Note that if the **tmp** directory did not already exist, the subdirectory **test** could not be created. Contrast VMS, where **CREATE/DIRECTORY** creates both the **TMP** subdirectory and the **TEST** subdirectory. In both VMS and UNIX, the creation of a subdirectory requires write access to the parent directory.

4.6   *Delete a Directory: rmdir and rm -r*

UNIX offers two commands for removing a directory, **rmdir** and **rm -r** (compare the VMS command **DELETE**). The latter is one form of the **rm** (remove) command which is used to remove files (see Section 4.9). Like the VMS command **DELETE**, **rmdir** removes a directory only if it contains no files. The directory must be at the lowest level of the directory hierarchy before you can delete it, since only then will it contain no directory files. The command **rm -r**, on the other hand, deletes everything in the directory as well as all files and directories lower in the directory hierarchy, which can be either efficient or devastating. For a novice UNIX user it is more likely to be devastating, so be careful!

	VMS	UNIX
form:	$ DELETE[/QUALIFIER(S)] directory	% rmdir directory
example:	$ DELETE [USER]TMP.DIR;1	% rmdir /usr/user/tmp
form:	$ DELETE/QUALIFIER(S) directory	% rm -r[option(s)] directory
example:	$ DELETE [USER.TMP . . .]*.*;*	% rm -r /usr/user/tmp
	(repeated until all files removed)	
	$ DELETE TMP.DIR;1	

In the first example above, **rmdir /usr/user/tmp** removes the **tmp** directory (that is, the subdirectory of **/usr/user** named **tmp**), provided it contains no files. In the second example, **rm -r /usr/user/tmp** removes the **tmp** directory, all subdirectories of **tmp**, and all files in those directories.

4.7   *Finding Files: find*

The command **find** offers functions in addition to those offered by **ls -R** (see Section 4.1) for locating files in a directory hierarchy. As in VMS, you can use various search criteria to locate files. In UNIX, you can also perform file manipulations on files located with the **find** command. This added functionality requires a complex syntax. The following simple example locates a file; the more complex command syntax for modifying files once they have been found is discussed in Section 9.4.4.

	VMS	UNIX
form:	$ DIRECTORY[/QUALIFIER(S)] file_spec	% find pathname_list criterion action
example:	$ DIR [*. . .]MYFILE.	% find / -name ourfile -print
		/user1/bin/ourfile
		/user3/progs/ourfile

The command **find / -name ourfile -print** searches all files on the system from the root downward for files with the name **ourfile**. The command then prints the path of any file found on the terminal. This example illustrates the elegance of the UNIX file system: you do not need to know the physical device on which a file resides in order to find it. In VMS, you might have to search each disk on the system (issue the command for each device) to find a file.

4.8 Display a File: cat and more

The most frequently used UNIX commands for displaying the contents of a file are **cat** (catenate and print) and **more**, also called **page** (display a file a page at a time). Together these commands provide greater functionality than the VMS **TYPE** command. The less frequently used file display commands appear in Chapter 9: first, **od** (octal dump, Section 9.2.2) dumps files in a variety of formats (compare the VMS **DUMP** command). The **head** command (Section 9.2.3) displays the beginning of a file. The **tail** command (Section 9.2.3) displays the end of a file. Finally, the command **pr** (Section 9.2.3) performs simple formatting for files you wish to print.

	VMS	UNIX
form:	$ TYPE[/QUALIFIER(S)] file-spec[, . . .]	% cat [option(s)] file(s)
example:	$ TYPE MYFILE.DAT	% cat myfile.dat
example:		% cat -n ˜user1/myfile.dat
example:		% cat -s /tmp/myfile.dat
form:	$ TYPE[/QUALIFIER(S)] file-spec[, . . .]	% more [option(s)] file(s)
example:	$ TYPE/PAGE MYFILE.DAT	% more myfile.dat
example:		% more -c file1 file2
example:	$ SET TERMINAL/PAGE = 15	
	$ TYPE/PAGE [--]FILE1.	% more -15 ../ ../file1
example:	$ SET TERMINAL/NOWRAP	
	$ TYPE/PAGE WIDEFILE.	% more -f widefile
example:		% more +10 my_file

The major difference between **more** and **cat** is that **cat** automatically scrolls through a file from beginning to end, whereas **more** pauses between each screen (24 lines by default). The **more** command indicates the percentage of the file already displayed and waits for a response from the user. Striking the ⟨CR⟩ key will scroll the file one line; striking the space bar will scroll the file one screen. If you use the **c** option with **more**, the screen refreshes one line at a time instead of scrolling, facilitating reading while the screen updates. As we shall see in Section 9.2.1, during pauses in file display brought about with the **more** command, you can make alternative responses that provide additional functionality in the display of files.

The **cat** command has useful options, which are shown in the second and third examples above. In the second example, **cat -n ˜user1/myfile.dat** uses an absolute file definition to display the file **myfile.dat** in the parent directory of **user1**. The **n** option displays the file with line numbers. VMS uses an editor to interrogate the file to achieve the same result. The command **cat -s /tmp/myfile**, shown in the third example, removes multiple blank lines from **myfile**.

The **more -15 . . ./. ./file1** command displays **file1**, located two directories above the current directory in the directory hierarchy, with a screen window of 15 lines rather than the default of 24. The **more -f widefile** command truncates long lines rather than wrapping them, which is the default. Finally, **more +10 my_file** begins listing **my_file** at line 10.

4.9   Copy a File: cp

The UNIX command **cp** copies one file to another. If the destination file already exists, **cp** overwrites it with the contents of the file being copied. VMS, in contrast, creates a higher version number of the existing file. UNIX provides two ways to prevent unwanted erasure and replacement of existing files. First, when creating a valuable file, you can set the file protection at no write for all users, including yourself (see **chmod**, Section 9.4.1). Second, you can use the form **cp -i** for all copy operations to request confirmation on the copy when the destination file already exists (compare the VMS **COPY/CONFIRM** command). Novice UNIX users familiar with the multiple version numbers in VMS should use this form for all UNIX copy operations by including an alias in **.cshrc**, as shown below. Note that the use of the shell variable **noclobber** has no effect here: **noclobber** prevents overwriting when redirecting output rather than copying files (for example, **cat file1 > file2**).

	VMS	UNIX
form:	$ COPY[/QUALIFIER(S)] input-file output-file	% cp [option(s)] input_file \ output_file
example:		% alias cp 'cp -i'
	$ COPY/CONFIRM FILE1. FILE2.	% cp file1 file2
	Copy DUA1:[USER]FILE1. to DUA1:[USER] -FILE2.? [N]	Overwrite file2?

4.10   Rename a File: mv

The UNIX command **mv** (move or rename) has the same function as the VMS **RENAME** command.

	VMS	UNIX
form:	$ RENAME[/QUALIFIER(S)] input-file output-file	% mv [option(s)] input_file \ output_file
example:	$ RENAME FILE 1. FILE 2.	% mv file1 file2
example:	$ RENAME/CONFIRM FILE1. FILE2.	% mv -i file1 file2
		remove file2? y
example:		% mv -f file1 file2
example:		% mv - -vn foo

In the same way that **cp -i** invoked interactive mode, **mv -i** prompts the user for permission to proceed with the move operation if a file with the new name already exists. Once again, novice C shell UNIX users should include **alias mv 'mv -i'** in their **.cshrc** file to prevent the inadvertent overwriting of wanted files. You can negate the effect of the **i** option with the command **mv -f** (force), as shown in the third example above. Assuming **file2** already exists and **mv** is made **mv -i** with an alias **mv -f file1 file2** overwrites **file2** without comment.

The last example, **mv - -vn foo**, is particularly valuable to novice users. You can inadvertently create a file that begins with a dash when you intended the dash to precede an option. If this occurs, efforts to address this file with a variety of commands will fail because UNIX interprets the filename as an option. The **mv -** command indicates that the next argument is a filename beginning with a dash. In this example, the command renames the file **-vn** to **foo**, the favorite scratch filename of UNIX diehards.

4.11   *Delete a File: rm*

Section 4.6 discussed using **rm -r** to remove directories and their contents. You can also use **rm** to remove files. As with **cp** (copy file) and
mv (rename file), using the **i** option with **rm** invokes an interactive
form of the command which prompts the user before taking action.
As previously suggested, the novice UNIX user should alias the command to reduce the likelihood of destroying wanted files. Even with
the alias set, you can override confirmation of file deletion with the
f option.

	VMS	UNIX
form:	$ DELETE[/QUALIFIER(S)] file-spec[, . . .]	% rm [option(s)] file(s)
example:	$ DELETE FILE1.;1	% rm file1
example:	$ DELETE/CONFIRM [-]FILE1.;1,FILE2.;1	% rm -i . ./file1 file2
	Delete DUA1:[USER]FILE1.;1? [N]	Delete /usr/file1?
	Delete DUA1:[USER.TMP]FILE2.;1? [N]	Delete /usr/tmp/file2?
example:		% chmod 000 file1
		% rm file1
		**rm: Override protection 0 for **
		file1?

The first two examples of the **rm** command are straightforward. The last
example illustrates the relationship of file and directory protections to
the **rm** command. The **chmod 000 file1** command removes all access to
file1 (see Section 9.4.1), and yet it can still be deleted by the owner and
root. Note, however, that the system asks the user whether to override
the file protection, which indicates that the file has a protection which
renders it undeletable. If the directory containing **file1** is protected
against delete access by the owner then the message "permission
denied" appears. The protection of the directory containing **file1** must
then be changed by the owner with the **chmod** command before deletion
is accomplished.

4.12   *Summary*

A useful way of summarizing the basic commands introduced in this
chapter is to present a scenario of a new UNIX user's first experience
with file management. For the sake of brevity, we omit all but one inten-
tional typographical error and all command abuses!

```
                    UNIX
     example:   % pwd
                /group/george
                % ls
                %
                % ls -a
                . . . .cshrc .login .mailrc
                % more .cshrc

                . . . .
                % find ~sue -name magic.c -print
                /group/sue/progs/magic.c
                /group/sue/new/magic.c
                % ls -lg ~sue/progs/magic.c ~sue/new/magic.c
                -rwxr-----  1   sue     adm     2344    10 Apr 12:20 \
                   /group/sue/progs/magic.c
                -rwxr-----  1   sue     adm     2734    12 Aug 13:11 \
                   /group/sue/new/magic.c
                % groups
                adm payroll
                % mkdir tusk1
                % rmdir tusk1
                % mkdir task1
                % cp ~sue/new/magic.* ~george/task1/.
                % ls task1
                magic.c magic.o
                % rm task1/magic.o
                % mv task1/magic.c task1/magic_wand.c
```

The user George, having logged on for the first time, issues the command **pwd**, which establishes his present working directory and home directory as **/group/george**. The command **ls** turns up a blank for this directory; it finds no files. George is sure that the system administrator said his account would contain some template files that would establish his user environment. He remembers that these are important files and therefore likely to be hidden. The **ls -a** command indeed reveals three hidden files. George then displays one of these files with the command **more .cshrc**, and recognizes many of the features discussed in Chapter 3 for establishing a user environment.

George plans to modify and run a C program, **magic.c**, originally written by Sue. Since he has no idea where Sue keeps the file, George uses **find ~sue -name magic.c -print** to search Sue's directories for the file and to print the path to any file **magic.c** that the system finds. Two versions of the file are found. George uses the long form of the **ls** command, **ls -lg**, to display the dates that the files were last modified. Since **/group/sue/**

new/magic.c was modified most recently and this version of the file is larger, George assumes that this is the file he needs to begin his project. George also notes that only other members of the group **adm** can read the file. By issuing the **groups** command, George discovers that he is a member of the group **adm**, which is also the group assigned to the file. Therefore, he can read the file. Before copying the file, George decides the application should reside in a separate subdirectory. Using **mkdir**, George inadvertently creates subdirectory **tusk1**; he meant to call the directory **task1**. George uses the **rmdir** command to remove the subdirectory and uses **mkdir** again to create **task1**. Note that George could have renamed the directory file with the **mv** command.

George copies the file to the newly created subdirectory using a wild-card; **cp ˜sue/new/magic.* ˜george/task1/..** A directory lookup, **ls task1**, indicates that two files have been copied. The **magic.o** file contains object code, indicated in UNIX filenames by **.o**. Contrast VMS, where **DIRECTORY TASK1.DIR** does not give the contents of the subdirectory but details of the directory pointer file. The UNIX command **ls task1** corresponds to the VMS command **DIRECTORY [.TASK1]**. Since George is planning to make changes to the source code immediately, the object file has no value, and George deletes it with the command **rm task1/magic.o**. Finally, to distinguish his application from Sue's, George issues the command **mv task1/magic.c task1/magic_wand.c** to rename the original C source file.

Chapter 5

Editing

One half of the world cannot understand the pleasures of the other.

Jane Austen

Now that you are familiar with enough file management commands to perform simple tasks, we turn to the next major hurdle in mastering a new operating system: the editor. What alternatives does UNIX offer to the VMS user familiar with EDT, TPU, or EVE? As you may expect, the alternatives are many and varied. The editors **edit**, **ed**, **ex**, and **vi** provide interactive editing; **sed** provides non-interactive editing; and **awk**, a more sophisticated and hence more complex non-interactive editor, provides pattern matching and subsequent file modification useful for extensive file reformatting.

To the new UNIX user, this chapter may appear to cover a bewildering amount of material. The less ambitious reader may feel more comfortable concentrating on a subset of commonly used **ex** and **vi** commands, leaving **sed** and **awk** for later. You need only become familiar with one editor, which you can do only with practice, to move on to subsequent chapters. The user who is ready to develop an application may return to **sed** and **awk** if the use of powerful string-handling utilities seems appropriate.

The editors **edit**, **ed**, and **ex** are *line editors,* whereas **vi** (visual editor) is a *screen editor.* The line editor **ex** (Section 5.1) contains the features of both **edit** and **ed**, plus some of its own. VMS users who are predominantly EDT line mode users need only learn a new syntax when learning **ex**. The same cannot be said of **vi** (Section 5.2), which is designed to work on a variety of terminals and does not depend on a keypad, arrow keys, or VT compatibility. Edits that require a single keystroke in EDT keypad mode may require one or more keystrokes in **vi**, often a combination of the standard keyboard keys and the ⟨CTRL⟩ and ⟨ESC⟩ keys. The implications of using the standard keyboard keys are discussed in Section 5.2.

Appendix B summarizes the commands available to the **ex** and **vi** user and compares them to EDT's line and keypad commands. It is not necessary to document each of these features here. Rather, we will introduce the general principles of **ex** and **vi** and tabulate the common commands in Tables 5.1 through 5.5. The editing required to port a VMS application or write a UNIX application from scratch provides the reader with more than enough opportunity to learn the command syntax outlined in Appendix B.

As in VMS EDT, **ed** and **vi** place the contents of the file you are editing in a *buffer*. When terminating an EDT editing session, the editor writes the contents of the buffer to a file with the same name but with a version number increased by one. By default, **ex** and **vi** write the contents of the buffer back to the same file, overwriting the old version of the file. To prevent overwriting, the novice **ex** or **vi** user should always direct the buffer contents to a file with a new name or copy the original file before editing to preserve the old and the new versions. Both the VMS and the UNIX editors periodically save the contents of the buffer, so that in case of system failure you can recover the majority of your edits from the temporary file.

VMS users reluctant to learn the UNIX editors should ask their system administrator whether EMACS is available. A generic programmable editor found in many UNIX systems, EMACS is to editors what UNIX is to operating systems. It is not too difficult to program EMACS to have the look and feel of EDT.

In the non-interactive editor **sed** (Section 5.3), you do not open a file, move around within it, make changes, see the effects of the changes, and save the changes. Rather, changes to the file are specified externally. You do not see the changes to the file as they are made, only the end result. The changes to be made are specified as part of the **sed** command line or contained in a separate file. The **sed** editor uses the same syntax as **ex** to specify changes to a file. You should use **sed** on large files and when making the same changes to a number of different files.

The **awk** editor (Section 5.4) extends the features of **sed** but maintains the same principles: **awk** scans each line in a file to detect a pattern and performs an action when it finds the pattern. The editors **awk** and **sed** perform different types of actions: **awk** supports complex actions, and users often think of its C-like syntax as more of a programming language than a UNIX utility.

5.1   Line Mode Editing: ex

Like VMS EDT, **ex** functions in line mode. It addresses a line by its line number or a range of lines by a range of line numbers, and then performs some function.

Table 5.1 Summary of ex Commands

ex Command	EDT Equivalent	ex Meaning
a (append)		Appends lines after the current line
c (change)	**CHANGE**	Changes specified lines
d (delete)	**DELETE**	Deletes specified lines
e (edit)		Sets edit buffer to contain a specified file and overwrites original contents
f (filename)		Displays a specified file
g (global)	**ALL**	Applies command to whole file
i (insert)	**INSERT**	Inserts lines before the current line
j (join)		Joins two lines to make one
m (move)	**MOVE**	Moves lines to a new place (cut and paste)
n (number)	(default)	Includes line numbers
p (pointer)	**TYPE**	Displays specified lines
q (quit)	**QUIT**	Leaves editor without saving changes
r (read)	**INCLUDE**	Reads a file into the editing buffer
s (substitute)	**SUBSTITUTE**	Substitutes new character string for old
t (transfer)	**COPY**	Copies lines to a new location
w (write)	**EXIT**	Writes contents of edit buffer to file
W (write)		Appends buffer contents to alternative existing file
=		Shows current numeric value of . or **$**

You can abbreviate the **ex** commands that specify functions to single letters, as shown in Table 5.1, which compares the **ex** commands to their EDT counterparts and finds them quite similar. Nevertheless, note the following features of the **ex** editor:

- The **ex** editor uses the current line as the default (as does EDT).
- The **ex** editor uses one or two characters to specify commands.
- The **ex** editor by default does not display line numbers (compare EDT, which displays line numbers): **ex** uses the command **n** to display line numbers for a specific command, and **set number** and **set nonumber** to toggle line numbering on and off.

- The **w** (write) command writes the whole file back to disk. If **w** is not followed by a filename, it overwrites the original version of the file. Once **w** writes the file, you may quit (**q**) the editor. During a long editing session, you should write the file periodically even though **ex** periodically saves the buffer in case of system failure (see Section 5.1.6). The command sequence **wq** writes the file and then quits the editor, an example of command grouping.

- If you attempt to quit (**q**) without writing the file, **ex** gives you a warning. The command **q!** overrides this warning, quitting the editor and leaving the original file unchanged.

- The period (.) signifies the current line (compare the use of the period in EDT).

- The dollar sign (**$**) signifies the last line of the file (compare the EDT command **END**). This use of a metacharacter to help define a string is called a *regular expression*. Regular expressions are used in each of the utilities described in this chapter.

- Unlike EDT, **ex** automatically resequences the line numbers after each command. EDT resequences only when you save the modified file or issue the **RESEQUENCE** command. For example, if you add a line between lines 1 and 2, EDT refers to the new line as 1.1, but **ex** refers to it as 2 and changes the original line 2 to line 3.

- The **ex** prompt is a colon (:). Compare VMS, which uses an asterisk (*).

5.1.1   *Displaying Lines*

The following examples illustrate the display of lines using the **ex** editor. Note that **ex** uses the command **p** (position pointer and display lines) for this purpose (see Table 5.1). The **p** command is the default: if you enter only the line numbers the editor assumes **p**.

	VMS	UNIX	
form:	* COMMAND [RANGE]	: [range] command	
example:	$ EDIT/EDT MYFILE.DAT	% ex myfile.dat	
	1 This is line 1	"myfile.dat" 59 lines, 1971 characters	
	*	:	
example:	* T 5	: 5 p	# display line 5
example:	* 5:10	: 5,10	# display lines 5 to 10
example:	* T WHOLE	: 1,$	# display whole file
example:	* T .:END	: .,$	# display from current line to end
example:	* T 1:5;10:20	: 1,5	# display lines 1 to 5 and 10 to 20
		: 10,20	

The above examples are straightforward. Note the following **ex** features:

- The **ex** syntax requires that the command follow the target range of lines; EDT places the command before the range of lines.
- When **ex** displays a range of lines, the current line is the last line in the display field (in EDT, it is the first).
- The **ex** editor uses minus and plus to indicate lines before and after the current line respectively, and a period to indicate the current line exactly as in EDT. Thus, **.-5** is five lines before the current line and **.+5** is five lines after the current line.

5.1.2 Inserting, Appending, and Deleting

The following examples illustrate inserting, appending, and deleting lines using **ex**.

	VMS	UNIX	
example:	* INSERT	: i	# insertion occurs
	This is one new line	This is one new line	before the current
	This is two new lines	This is two new lines	line
	⟨CTRL⟩Z	.	
	*	:	
example:		: a	# append occurs
		This is one new line	after the current
		This is two new lines	line
		.	
		:	
example:	* DELETE	: d	# delete current line
example:	* D 1:3	: 1,3 d	# delete lines 1 to 3
example:	* R -1:.+1	: .-1,.+1 c	# delete one line above
	This line replaces 3 old	This line replaces 3 old	current to one line
			below current and
			insert

As you study these examples, note the following:

- The command **a** (append) inserts text after the current line, and **i** (insert) inserts text before the current line.
- Insert mode is terminated by typing a period as the first character of a new line (compare EDT ⟨CTRL⟩-Z), whereupon the **ex** prompt is returned.

- After appending or inserting text, the current line is the last line entered.
- The command **c** (change) changes existing text, that is, a deletion immediately followed by an insertion (compare the EDT command **REPLACE**).

5.1.3 Search and Replace

The following examples illustrate string searching and string substitution.

	VMS	UNIX	
example:	* T "STRING"	: /string/	# display line below containing string
example:	* T -"STRING"	: ?string?	# display line above containing string
example:	* T "STRING1":"STRING2"	: /string1/,/string2/	# display lines between # string1 and string2
example:	* S /STRING1/STRING2/1:5	: 1,5 s /string1/string2/	# substitute string1 for string2 in lines 1 to 5; #first occurrence only
example:	* S /STRING1/STRING2/1:END	: 1,$ s /string1/string2/g	# as above but all occurrences
example:	* S ?/?slash?	: s/\//slash/	# precede with backslash if/ to be taken literally
example:		: s//string2/	# use last defined string1

These examples illustrate the following **ex** features:

- The **ex** editor uses a slash to delimit a string; if the string itself contains a slash, precede the slash with a backslash to tell the editor to read the slash as a character instead of a delimiter (compare EDT, where alternative delimiters may be used).

- If a forward search fails to find the string in the latter part of the file, **ex** will "wrap" the search to the beginning of the file. Compare EDT, where the search terminates at the end of the file. Hence, the line on which the string is found may precede the current line in the file. Similarly, in a backward search the line containing the string may follow the current line in the file. If **ex** does not find the string, it will return a question mark. If the file does not contain the search string, the current line does not change; otherwise the line containing the first occurrence of the search string becomes the current line.
- The **s** command (substitution) replaces only the first occurrence of a string in a line; the **g** (global) command substitutes all occurrences of the string in a line.

5.1.4 Cut and Paste

The command **m** (move) deletes text from one location in the file and places it elsewhere. The command **co** (copy) duplicates text in another location in the file.

	VMS	UNIX	
example:	* MOVE -3:. TO END 4 lines moved	: -3,. m $ last line moved here	# move 4 lines (-3 to current inclusive) to the end of the file
example:	* COPY 10:20 TO 31	: 10,20 co 30	# copy lines 10 to 20 after line 30
example:	* COPY - "string1":"string2" - TO .+1	: /string1/,/string2/ \ co .	# copy lines between the first occurrence of string1 and string2, respectively after the current line

Note the following:

- Remember that **co** is an abbreviation for the copy command, whereas **c** is an abbreviation for the change command.
- The command **co** copies a range following the specified line number; the EDT **COPY** command copies a range preceding the specified line number.

5.1.5 External File Handling

The **ex** command **r** (read) adds all or part of an external file to the file being edited (compare the EDT **INCLUDE** command). The command **w** (write) writes part or all of the file being edited to a new file (compare the EDT **WRITE** command). The command **e** (edit) reads an external file into the file being edited and discards the original contents of the file being edited (compare the EDT commands **DELETE 1:END** followed by **INCLUDE**).

	VMS	UNIX	
example:	* WRITE NEWFILE 1:10	: 1.10 w newfile	# write the first 10 lines of the file being edited to newfile
example:	* INCLUDE MYFILE.DAT	: r myfile.dat	# include myfile.dat after the \ current line
example:	* DELETE 1:END * INCLUDE MYFILE.DAT	: e myfile.dat	# include myfile.dat, deleting \ any original file

5.1.6   *Recovering an Editing Session*

In the event of system failure or inadvertent termination of an editing session—for example, with ⟨CTRL⟩-C—the **ex** editor's **r** option recovers the file being edited (compare the VMS command **EDIT/EDT/RECOVER**). In this example, **ex -r myfile** recovers the editing sesstion inadvertently terminated with ⟨CTRL⟩-C.

	VMS	UNIX
example:	$ EDIT/EDT MYFILE.DAT	% ex myfile
	[changes made here]	[changes made here]
	⟨CTRL⟩-Y	⟨CTRL⟩-C
	$ EDIT/EDT/RECOVER MYFILE.DAT	% ex -r myfile

5.2   *UNIX Screen Editor: vi*

The UNIX editor **vi** (visual) corresponds to EDT when used in keypad mode. Rather than addressing a file by line number, **vi** addresses the file by the position of the screen cursor. Consequently, you can use **vi** only on video terminals and not on hardcopy devices.

EDT functions mostly on VT-series terminals from Digital Equipment Corporation and makes extensive use of the keypad found on all such terminals; **vi** functions on virtually any video terminal. For the VMS user faced with learning **vi** this situation is both good and bad. It is good because its flexibility has led to **vi** being distributed as part of almost every version of UNIX (it was originally part of BSD). On different versions of UNIX and on different types of terminals, **vi** functions identically. It is bad because special keys, which may be terminal-specific, are not assigned to editing functions, making editing more cumbersome. For example, the character **d** deletes the word at the cursor. But what if you wish to insert the character *d* into the file? You must change from passive mode to insert mode by pressing **i**. EDT in keypad mode is always in insert mode because it does not manage editing commands with the standard character set.

Remembering to toggle between passive and insert modes is the major hurdle for the VMS user learning **vi**. All too frequently the novice **vi** user enters insert mode, adds text, and then strikes the arrow key to move the cursor to another location. Rather than moving the cursor, **vi** inserts the character mapping of the arrow key in the file because the user forgot to press the ⟨ESC⟩ key to change to passive mode.

We must note two further points before getting started with **vi**. First, **ex** is to **vi** what EDT in line mode is to EDT in keypad mode; that is, you can invoke many of the **ex** commands from the **vi** editor. Second, **vi** is a complex editor possessing over one hundred commands which you can combine in many ways. We will discuss only a few commands that you are likely to need on a regular basis. Appendix B contains a listing of these commands. Readers requiring a more rigorous discussion of **vi** should refer to the reading list in Appendix D.

5.2.1   *Getting Started*

The command **vi file1 [. . .]** starts a **vi** editing session. For example, **vi file1 file2** starts a **vi** editing session on **file1**. When you save **file1**, **file2** will be opened for editing and so on. If the file you call for does not exist, **vi** will create a new file. New files and short files that do not fill the screen cause **vi** to display a tilde (˜) in column one of every screen line. The tilde is not part of the file and disappears as you add lines. Compare EDT keypad mode **[EOB]**, the end of buffer symbol found at the end of each file. Tilde distinguishes blank lines in a file from no lines.

When you open a file for editing, **vi** defaults to passive mode: you may move the cursor and delete text, but not insert.

5.2.2   Cursor Movement

Table 5.2 introduces a subset of commands that move the cursor. Note the following:

- Movement commands typically require one or two keystrokes.
- Delimiters defining cursor movement in **vi** are similar to those used by EDT in keypad mode: characters, words, lines, and screens all delimit movement.
- In EDT keypad mode, you can precede keystrokes with **[4]**[1] or **[5]** to reverse the direction between forward and backward movement respectively. The **vi** editor uses different commands to define forward and backward movement.
- Both **vi** and EDT keep internal records of line numbers. You can move to a particular line number with the **vi** command **#G**.
- You may combine **vi** movement commands with **vi** action commands (Section 5.2.4).

5.2.3   Action Commands

Action commands change the contents of a file in some way. Table 5.3 summarizes the commonly used **vi** action commands. Note the following:

- Action commands are usually denoted by a single character.
- Commands that permit input must end with ⟨ESC⟩ (**F11** on many terminals) to return the editor to passive mode. It is common for the EDT keypad mode user to forget this.
- In some instances, the single-letter command name when doubled applies to the whole line. For example, **dd** deletes the line at the cursor, then moves the cursor to the beginning of the next line.
- The **vi** editor does not use reverse video to highlight text.

5.2.4   Combining Action and Movement Commands

You may combine movement and action commands to produce a vast number of possible effects. Table 5.4 summarizes a commonly used subset. Note that the movement command follows the action command. Thus, **d** (delete) followed by **w** (move the cursor from its current location

---

1. Keypad characters appear in square brackets throughout this chapter.

Table 5.2 Cursor Movement with vi

vi Command	EDT Equivalent[1]	vi Meaning
arrow keys	arrow keys	Moves the cursor right, left, up, or down
$	[2]	Moves to the end of the line
^	backspace [F12]	Moves to the beginning of the line
H		Moves cursor to top of screen
L		Moves cursor to bottom of screen
M		Moves cursor to middle of screen
⟨CTRL⟩-F	[4][8]	Scrolls file forward one screen
⟨CTRL⟩-B	[5][8]	Scrolls file backward one screen
⟨CTRL⟩-D		Scrolls file forward half screen
⟨CTRL⟩-U		Scrolls file backward half screen
#⟨CTRL⟩-F	[4][8]...	Scrolls file forward # screens
#⟨CTRL⟩-B	[5][8]...	Scrolls file backward # screens
w	[4][1]	Moves forward one word
b	[5][1]	Moves backward one word
#w	[4][1]...	Moves forward # words
#b	[5][1]...	Moves backward # words
e		Moves to last character of current word
fx	[4][PF1][PF3]x	Moves forward to next character x
Fx	[5][PF1][PF3]x	Moves backward to next character x
;	[PF3]	Repeats fx
;	[PF3]	Repeats Fx
)		Moves forward one sentence
(		Moves backward one sentence
/string	[4][PF1][PF3]string	Searches forward for string
?string	[5][PF1][PF3]string	Searches backward for string
#G	[PF1][7]T#	Moves to line number #

1. [4] or [5] are needed only if the direction of movement needs to be reversed.

Table 5.3 Action Commands with vi

vi Command	EDT Equivalent	vi Meaning
i		Inserts text before the cursor
a		Appends text after the cursor
I		Inserts text after the current line
A		Appends text before the current line
o	**[PF1][0]**	Opens blank line after current line
O		Opens blank line before current line
<esc>		Terminates input mode
x	[.]	Deletes character at cursor
X	backspace	Deletes character before cursor
d		Deletes starting at the cursor
dd	**[PF4]**	Deletes current line
c		Deletes starting at the cursor followed by insert
cc	**[PF4]**	Deletes current line and insert
r	[,]	Overwrites single character
R		Overwrites until terminated by <esc>
p	**[PF1][6]**	Pastes deleted or yanked text after cursor
P		Pastes deleted or yanked text before cursor
y	[.]...[6]	Yanks (copies) text into alternative buffer
yy	[.][2][6]	Yanks (copies) current line into alternative buffer

to the end of the current word) deletes all characters from the current cursor location to the end of the word.

5.2.5 *Invoking ex from vi*

The VMS EDT keypad mode user may issue a line mode command by striking the keypad keys **[PF1][7]**. Similarly, when the **vi** user enters a colon in passive mode, a colon prompt appears at the bottom of the screen and the user may enter an **ex** command. Entering **Q** in passive mode has the same effect.

The most important uses of **ex** commands are to write (**w**) the contents of the editing buffer to a disk file and to terminate (**q**) the editing session.

Table 5.4 Common vi Commands Combining Movement and Action

vi Command	EDT Equivalent	vi Meaning
dw	[-]	Deletes from cursor to beginning of next word
d#w		Deletes from cursor # words
d)		Deletes from cursor to beginning of next sentence
d(		Deletes from cursor to beginning of previous sentence
d$	[PF1][2]	Deletes from cursor to end of line
#dd		Deletes # lines
cw	[-]	Deletes word and insert
c#w		Deletes # words and insert
c)		Deletes from cursor to beginning of next sentence and insert
c(		Deletes from cursor to beginning of previous sentence and insert
cc	[PF4]	Deletes current line and insert
c#w		Deletes # words and insert
c$	[PF1][2]	Deletes to end of line and insert

Other common uses of **ex** commands include inserting the contents of another file into the current file and writing all or a part of the current file to a new file. The command **r filename** issued at the colon prompt inserts the contents of filename immediately before the cursor. You can write a section of the current file to a new file. The **ex** command requires line numbers to delimit the text you wish to write. The **ex** command **set number** displays lines in **vi** with line numbers. You may use **n,m w filename** to write lines **n** through **m** to the file **filename**. The **ex** command **set nonumber** turns off line numbering.

Table 5.5 lists these and other useful **ex** commands issued from **vi**. Note the following:

- The command **!command** executes a UNIX shell command. For example **!ls** displays the contents of the current directory. Press a ⟨CR⟩ to redisplay the current file.[2]

---

2. Section 8.3 describes how the C shell user may suspend the editing session, issue UNIX commands, and then return to the editor.

Table 5.5   Common ex Commands Issued from vi

ex Command	EDT Equivalent	**vi** Meaning
r file	**[PF1][7] INCLUDE FILE**	Includes an external file
!		Enters a shell command
n	**EXIT**	Writes edit buffer to disk and opens next file to be edited
n!	**QUIT**	Quits editing without saving changes and opens next file to be edited
set number		Turns on line numbering
set nonumber		Turns off line numbering
set autoindent		Indents text following the cursor
set noai		Turns off indenting
set sw = n		Sets shift width to **n** characters (default = 8)
w	**EXIT**	Writes edit buffer to disk
q!	**QUIT**	Quits editing without saving changes

- The **set shiftwidth = n** command defines temporary right and left margins. The default margin is eight columns.

5.2.6   *Miscellaneous Commands*

Perhaps the most important command in this category is the **u** (undo) command (compare the **[PF1]** or gold key in EDT keypad mode). You may undo only the last command (**u**) or a number of sequential commands affecting a single line (**U**).

Another important command in this category is the period, which repeats the last action command: a convenient shorthand for repeating editing commands.

You may use > (greater than, right shift) and < (less than, left shift) to move lines. Right and left shift move text right or left the number of columns specified by the *shiftwidth parameter* (see the command **set shiftwidth = n** above). Text will not be truncated if an attempt is made to move it beyond the left margin, rather the command is ignored; similarly, text wraps if moved beyond the right margin. The commands >> and << shift single lines right and left respectively.

A powerful feature of **vi** not available in EDT is *filtering,* the ability to pass all or part of a file to a UNIX command such as **sort** (see Section

9.4.6), **spell** (the UNIX spell checker) or **nroff** (see Section 12.2) for text formatting. The following example illustrates the use of a **sort** filter.

```
            UNIX
example:    % vi myfile.list
            jill
            jack
            adam
            ~

            . . . .
            : 1,$ ! sort
            adam
            jack
            jill
            ~

            . . . .
            :wq
            %
```

The colon gets the attention of the **ex** editor, which accepts a range of lines (**1,$**) and passes them to the **sort** command with the construct **!** **sort**. The command **sort** without options uses the first field as the *sort key,* rearranges the text, and redisplays the screen. The command **:wq**, write followed by quit, saves the modified file.

5.2.7   Ending an Editing Session

You may terminate **vi** by issuing the **ex** commands to save the editing changes or quit leaving the file unchanged. The **vi** command **ZZ** issued from passive mode will also terminate the **vi** session, saving any changes that you have made.

5.2.8   Recovering an Editing Session

In Section 5.1.6 we saw how to recover an **ex** editing session in the event of system failure or accidental termination of an editing session with an interrupt. You can recover **vi** editing sessions with the command **vi -r filename**.

5.3   The Stream Editor: sed

sed, which has no VMS equivalent, is useful for editing large files or for making the same changes to a succession of files. In its simplest form,

sed uses line numbers in the same way as **ex** to delimit the text to be edited. The real power of **sed** is its use of *regular expressions* to specify the text to be edited. For example, it is a simple matter in **sed** to edit the last word of each line in a file. **awk**, discussed below, builds on this concept to permit complex string manipulation. Although **awk** is more powerful than **sed**, it is also more complex; some users consider **awk** a high-level language.

We start by introducing **sed** with some simple examples.

```
          UNIX
form:     % sed [-n] [[-e command]. . .] [-f] file
example:  % sed s/this/that/ file1
example:  % sed s/this/that/p file1
example:  % sed -n s/this/that/p file1
example:  % sed -n s/this/that/ file1
```

Each of these examples performs an identical substitution in **file1** but displays the results differently. The command **sed s/this/that/ file1** displays the entire modified file. The command **sed s/this/that/p file1** displays the entire modified file as well as all the lines you have modified (**p**). The command **sed -n s/this/that/p file1** displays only the lines that you have modified (**n**). Finally, **sed -n s/this/that/ file1** (without **p**) displays nothing.

These examples illustrate that the syntax used by **sed** for string substitution is identical to the syntax that **ex** uses. Learning **sed**, therefore, should be straightforward for anyone who has mastered **ex**.

```
          UNIX
example:  % sed 3,4d file1
example:  % sed -e s/this/that/ -e /for/d file1
example:  % sed -e s/this/that/g -e /for/d file1
example:  % cat writefile
          1,2w filea
          /the/w fileb
          s/this/that/w filec
          % sed -n -f writefile file1
```

The command **sed 3,4d file1** deletes lines 3 and 4 from **file1** and displays the modified file. The command **sed -e s/this/that/ -e /for/d file1** illus-

Table 5.6 Operator Characters Used with sed

Character	Meaning	Example
.	Any single character	**d.** Any two-character string beginning with **d**
$	End of line	**d$** Any lowercase **d** which occurs at the end of a line
"	Delimits operator characters to prevent interpretation	**"fred."** fred followed by a period, not **fred** followed by any character
\	Turns off special meaning of a single character	**fred\.** fred followed by a period, not **fred** followed by any character
*	Matches 0 or more characters	**fr*** Matches **fr, fred, frog**; and so on
[ ]	Specifies character classes	**[A-Za-z0-9]** All characters and digits **[^0-9]** All characters except 0 through 9 **[0\-9]** The three characters 0, -, and 9
^	Matches only if string is at the beginning of the line	**^"new line"** Matches the string **new line** only if it is at the beginning of the line

trates the use of the **e** option to specify multiple editing commands: **sed** makes two passes through the file, first changing the first occurrence of "this" to "that" on every line containing "this," then deleting all lines that contain "for." The command **sed -e s/this/that/g -e /for/d file1** performs the same operations except for globally substituting "this" for "that."

The last example illustrates the use of a file containing **sed** commands. The command **sed -n -f writefile file1** modifies **file1** based on the edit commands contained in **writefile** (**f** option); as the command **cat writefile** shows edit commands are given one per line. The result of this command is as follows: **filea** contains lines 1 and 2 of **file1**, **fileb** contains all lines of **file1** that have "the" in them, and **filec** contains all lines of **file1** that originally contained "this" but with "this" changed to "that."

In the examples given so far, **sed** has based line selection on the line number or a character string contained in the line. The **sed** editor can also use operator characters common to a number of UNIX commands that *filter* text to expand these selection criteria, thereby creating a regular expression. Table 5.6 summarizes operator characters. Some simple examples of regular expressions using these operators appear below.

```
             UNIX
example:     % sed -n /^ The/p file1
example:     % sed -n /" "p[a-z]/p file1
example:     % sed s/" . "/" . "/gp file1
```

The command **sed -n/^ The/p file1** displays any line beginning with
"The." The command **sed -n /" "p[a-z]/p file1** displays any line containing a blank followed by a "p" and any other lowercase character of
the roman alphabet. Finally, **sed s/". "/". "/gp file1** substitutes a period
followed by two blanks for any occurrence of a period followed by a
single blank, and displays those lines of **file1** that have changed. Note
that the double quotes insure that **sed** reads the string literally.

These are very simple examples of a complex yet powerful syntax. See
the reading list in Appendix D for more complex examples.

5.4   *Pattern Matching and Processing: awk*

awk extends the features of **sed**. Features of **awk** include:

- field-oriented processing
- predefined variables
- variable assignment
- logical operations
- arithmetic expressions
- scalar variables and arrays
- output redirection and piping

Like **sed**, **awk** does not have a VMS equivalent. To achieve the functionality of **awk**, the VMS user would most likely write a high-level language program or use the string-handling capabilities of DCL.

The C-like syntax of **awk** should pose little difficulty to the user familiar
with the C programming language. Others may feel more comfortable
mastering the basic features of UNIX before turning to **awk**. Note, however, that shell programming, the UNIX equivalent to writing DCL command procedures (see Chapter 11), is also C-like. The hesitant user is
less likely to avoid shell programming than **awk**, for many UNIX applications use shell programming. Non-C programmers should decide
whether to attempt **awk** based on the difficulty they have experienced

thus far and on the extent to which they need to make complex file modifications.

awk searches each record in a file for a pattern and performs some action when it finds that pattern.[3]

UNIX

form: % awk [-Fsep] 'pattern {action} pattern {action} \
  . . .' filename(s)
  % awk [-Fsep] -f pattern-action file filename(s)

To **awk**, each record consists of a number of fields. **awk** uses the **F** option to define a *field separator*. By default, the field separator is any number of blanks between fields. However, you can set the field separator to be any character string. As an example, recall the **/etc/passwd** file introduced in Section 3.1, which contains a record for each UNIX user and uses a colon to separate fields in each record.

Single forward quotes (') delimit the complete pattern-action combination from the file(s) on which to perform the **awk** function. Curly braces surround actions. You may store pattern-matching and action strings that you use repeatedly in **awk** scripts, which are files invoked with the **f** option.

Let us now turn our attention to the available patterns and actions. Table 5.7 outlines the general features of the patterns and subsequent actions available to the **awk** user. At first glance, these strings are somewhat intimidating, so we will start with some simple examples.

UNIX

example: % awk -F: '/smith/ {print $0}' /etc/passwd
example: % awk -F: '$4 ˜ /51/ {print $0}' /etc/passwd
example: % awk -F: '$1 ˜ /ˆh*/ {print $0}' /etc/passwd

The command **awk -F: '/smith/ {print $0}' /etc/passwd** displays any records from the **/etc/passwd** file that contain **smith** in any field. Note that the field delimiter is a colon rather than the default (one or more blanks).

---

3. Recall that a UNIX record is an arbitrary number of bytes terminated by a newline character.

Table 5.7   awk Patterns and Actions

Pattern	Meaning
BEGIN {statement}	Executes statement before pattern matching
END {statement}	Executes statement after pattern matching
/regular expression/	Pattern containing a regular expression
relational expression	Pattern containing relation operator(s)
pattern && pattern	Boolean and
pattern ‖ pattern	Boolen or
(pattern)	Single pattern
!pattern	Boolean not
pattern,pattern	Two patterns

Action	Meaning
if (expression) statement [else statement]	Conditional **if** statement
while (expression) statement	While an expression is true, performs statement
for (expr1:condition:expr2) statement	For each occurrence formulated from expressions 1 and 2 that obey the specified condition, executes the statement
break	Exits immediately from a **for** or **while** loop
continue	Forces next iteration of a **for** or **while** loop
next	Skips to next input record and begin processing from first pattern
exit	If found as part of **BEGIN**, terminates without execution of **END**. If found in main body of script, branches and executes **END**. If found at **END**, causes immediate termination.
variable = expression	Equates a variable to an expression

Table 5.7 awk Patterns and Actions *(continued)*

Pattern	Meaning
print [expression1] > [expression2]	Redirects **expression1** to **expression2**
**print [expression1]	[expression2]**	Pipes **expression1** to **expression2**
for (variable in array) statement	For each array element, executes statement

The search pattern is **smith** and the action is to display (**print**) the whole record. As we shall see in the following section, **$0** is a *predefined variable* that denotes the complete record.

The command **awk -F: '$4 ~ /51/ {print $0}' /etc/passwd** displays the record for any user belonging to group **51**. That is, **awk** displays the record if the fourth field (**$4**) matches (˜) the string **51**.

The command **awk -F: '$1 ~ /^h*/ {print $0} ' /etc/passwd** displays the records of all users whose usernames begins with **h**. The pattern is the expression **$1 ~ /^h*/**. The command searches for the first field (**$1**), which in the file **/etc/passwd** is the username. The tilde matches the username to the regular expression ˆh*, which is any string that starts with **h** at the beginning of a record.

The three examples given above illustrate the most commonly invoked action command: printing. In the following section, we will use this action command to illustrate some predefined variables available to the **awk** user.

5.4.1 Predefined Variables

Table 5.8 shows a subset of predefined **awk** variables. Several appear below, again using the **/etc/passwd** file. For the sake of brevity, the examples show only a sample of the output.

UNIX
example: % awk -F: '{print length}' /etc/passwd
46
63
. . . .

```
example:   % awk -F: '{print NR, NF}' /etc/passwd
           1 7
           2 7
           . . . .
example:   % awk -F: '{print NR, $1}' /etc/passwd
           1 root
           2 sysop
           3 daemon
           . . . .
```

The command **awk -F: '{print length}' /etc/passwd** displays the number
of characters (**length**) in each record. The command **awk -F: '{print NR,
NF}' /etc/passwd** displays the number of the record (**NR**) and the number
of fields (**NF**). Finally, **awk -F: '{print NR, $1}' /etc/passwd** displays the
number of the record followed by the first field (**$1**), which in the **/etc/
passwd** file is the username.

5.4.2   Variable Assignment

Accompanying the predefined variables are variables that the user may
assign. You may assign variables according to context using the form

Table 5.8 Predefined awk Variables

Variable	Function	Example
$0	The entire input record	awk '{print $0}' file
$n	The nth field of the input record	awk '{print $2, $1}' file
length	Length of the current input record	awk '{print length ($0), $0}' file
FILENAME	Name of the current input file	awk '{print FILENAME}' file
NR	Number of the current record; first input record is 1	awk '{print NR, $0}' file
NF	Number of fields in the current record	awk '{print NF}' file
RS	Input record separator (default = new line)	awk '{RS=":"; print NR}' file
OFS	Output field separator (default = blank)	awk '{OFS=":"; print $1 OFS $2}' file
ORS	Output record separator (default = new line)	awk '{ORS=":"; print $0}' file
OFMT	Output format for numbers (default = %.6g)	awk '{OFMT="%.5g"; print $2}' file

variable name = integer or string value. That is, you do not have to declare a variable as a string or integer value as in many high-level languages.

> UNIX
> **example:** x = "3" + "4"
> **example:** x = "some" + "thing"

These two examples illustrate the use of addition (+), first to equate the variable **x** to the integer 7, then to the character string "something."

5.4.3 *Operators*

Table 5.9 gives the operators available to the **awk** user in order of decreasing priority.[4] Operators grouped together have the same priority. The number of operators given in Table 5.9 suggests both the power and the complexity of **awk**. We will use a number of these operators in subsequent sections.

5.4.4 *Scripts*

Many users can meet their needs with single-line **awk** commands. However, to use the extended features of **awk** or to save **awk** commands for subsequent use, you must use an **awk** script. Before looking at how to use operators and variables in **awk**, we consider the rules that govern the **awk** script.

> UNIX
> **example:** % cat awk_test
> BEGIN {nw = 0}
>   {nw + = NF
>   }
> END {print "number of words = ",nw
>   }
> % awk -F: -f awk_test /etc/passwd
> number of words = 1031

The string **BEGIN {nw = 0}** signifies the beginning of an **awk** script. The **BEGIN** statement precedes a statement that sets the variable **nw** (number

---

4. Priority indicates the order in which **awk** executes the operators if used without parentheses.

Table 5.9 awk Operators

Operator	Meaning
+ +a	Increments **a**'s value before using it
a+ +	Increments **a**'s value after using it
--a	Decrements **a**'s value before using it
a--	Decrements **a**'s value after using it
*	Multiply
/	Divide
%	Remainder (modulo)
+	Add
-	Subtract
	No operator between two variables implies catenation; for example, **$1$2** catenates first two fields
>	Greater than
>=	Greater than or equal to
<	Less than
<=	Less than or equal to
= =	Similar to
!=	Not similar to
~	Match, for example, **$1** ~ **/A‖B‖C/** matches if **a, b,** or **c** is in the first field
!~	No match, for example, **$1 !** ~ **/A‖B‖C/**
!	Negate value of expression
&&	Boolean AND
‖	Boolean OR
=	Equal to
+=	**i+ =2** compressed form of i=i+2
− =	**i- =2** compressed form of i=i − 2
*=	**i*=2** compressed form of i=i * 2
/=	**i/=2** compressed form of i=i / 2
%=	**i%=2** compressed form of i=i % 2

of words) to **0**. The string {**nw + = NF**} then increases (**+ =**) the value of **nw**, adding the predefined variable **NF** (number of fields) as **awk** processes each record of the file **/etc/passwd**. After **awk** processes all records, control passes to the **END** statement, and the action command { {**print "number of words= ",nw**} displays the number of fields. You must include the **BEGIN** and **END** commands only if you require some action

Table 5.10   awk Flow Control Statements

Statement	Meaning
for (expr1:condition:expr2) statement	For each occurrence formulated from expressions 1 and 2 that obey the specified condition, executes the statement
for (i element in array) statement	For each element of the array, executes the statement
if (condition) statement1 [else statement2]	Conditional **if** statement
while (condition) statement	While the specified condition holds, executes the statement
break	Exits immediately from a **for** or **while** loop
continue	Forces next iteration of a **for** or **while** loop
exit	If found as part of **BEGIN**, terminates without execution of **END**. If found in main body of script, branches and executes **END**. If found at **END** causes immediate termination.
getline	Forces processing to move to next record
next	Skips to next input record and begin processing from first pattern

before or after record processing, for example, to set a variable or print the value of a variable.

5.4.5   *Flow Control*

Table 5.10 summarizes the **awk** flow control statements. Some of these statements are illustrated below.

```
             UNIX
example:  { for (x=1; x<=NF; x++) print $x }
example:  { for (x in text) {print x, text[x]} }
example:  { i=1
              while (x <= NF) {
              print $x; ++x}
          }
example:  for (x=1; x<=NF; x++) {
                  if ($x == "halt") break
              }
```

```
example:   for (x=1; x<=NF; x++) {
                if ($x == "end") continue
           }
example:   for (x=1; x<=NR; x++) {
                incr += 1
                if (incr > 100) exit
           }
example:   for (x=1; x<=NF; x++) {
                if (NF < 4) getline
           }
example:   for (x=1; x<=NF; x++) {
                if (NF == 1) next
           }
```

The statement { **for (x = 1; x< = NF; x + +) print $x** } will increment **x** from 1 to the number of fields per record and displays each field, one per line. The statement { **for (x in text) {print x, text[x]}** } displays the element number **x** and its value in array **text** (see the following section). The statement { **i = 1 while (x <= NF) {print $x; + +x}** } has the same effect as the first example, printing each field of the record, one per line. The statement **if ($x = = "halt") break** uses **if** (for **while**) to stop processing records when field **x** is equal to the character string **halt**. The statement **if ($x = = "end") continue** stops processing the current record when field **x** is equal to the character string **end**. The statement **if (incr > 100) exit** passes control to the **END** statement of the **awk** script when the value of the variable **incr** is greater than 100. The statement **if (NF < 4) getline** continues processing the next record of the file, from the current point in the **awk** script, if the number of fields is less than 4. The statement **if (NF = =1) next** skips to the next input record if the number of fields in the current record is 1 but begins processing from the beginning of the **awk** script.

5.4.6   *Using Arrays*

In contrast to most high-level languages where array elements are explicitly assigned a data type, for example, integer, real, or character, **awk** assigns array elements implicitly. That is, each **awk** array element assumes a data type according to the assigned value. For example, **record[NR] = $0** assigns the **NR**th element of an array **record** to the current input record: a character string. Note that array elements are enclosed in square brackets.

example: % cat awk_script
{ record[NR] = $0}
END { for i=NR; i>0; i--) print record[i] }
% awk -f awk_script myfile

The statement { **record[NR]** =**$0**} enters each record of the file into the array **record** using the predefined variable **NR** (record number) as the counter. The statement { **for i=NR; i>0; i--) print record[i]** } displays the contents of array **record** from **record[NR]** to **record[1]**; that is, it displays the records of the file **myfile** in reverse order.

5.4.7 *Formatting Output*

The **awk printf** statement, which resembles that found in the C programming language, formats **awk** output.

UNIX

form: printf "format_statement" expression1, . . .
example: { printf "%8.2f" , $i}
example: { printf "%10d\n", $i}
example: { printf "%s" . $i}
example: { printf "%.6g" , $i}

Each example displays the variable **i** in a different format: **"%8.2f"** is a floating point number of eight digits, with two following the decimal point; **"%10d\n"** is a 10-digit decimal number followed by a new line; **"%s"** is an alphanumeric string; and **"%.6g"** makes useful interpretations of numeric values. For example, 11111111 returns $1.11111e+07$, 1001 returns 1001, and 10.1 returns 10.1. A text string returns a value of 0.

5.4.8 *String Operators*

Chapter 11 discusses *shell programming,* the UNIX equivalent of writing VMS command procedures. It will be seen from that discussion that the UNIX C shell does not offer the functionality of the VMS lexical functions when used for string manipulation. That shortcoming is addressed by **awk,** which offers string manipulation features similar to VMS lexical functions (see Table 5.11).

Table 5.11 Commonly Used awk Functions

Function	Meaning
length(string)	Length of **string**
substr(string,position,length)	Substring of **string**, starting at **position**, and **length** characters long
index(string,substring)	Starting position of **substring** in **string**; if not found, returns 0
split(string, array, "separator")	Separates **string** into elements of **array** according to the field separator
int(num)	Truncated integer value of variable **num**
cos(x)	Cosine trigonometric function of variable **x**
sin(x)	Sine trigonometric function of variable **x**
log(x)	Natural logarithm of variable **x**
int(x)	Integer function of variable **x**
sqrt(x)	Square root of variable **x**

The function **length(string)** returns the length of a string. If string is omitted the function **length** returns the length of the current record. The function **substr(string, position, length)** returns a substring of **string** that starts at **position** and is **length** characters long. For example, the statement { **printf "%s\n" , substr($0,1,10)** } below prints the first 10 characters of each record as **awk** processes them. After **awk** processes all records, it displays the total number of characters (**nc**) in the file using **length** to determine the number of characters in each complete record.

```
           UNIX
example:   % cat awk_script
           BEGIN {nc = 0}
               { printf "%s\n" , substr($0,1,10) }
               { nc + = length ($0) }
           END { print "Number of characters =" , nc }
```

The function **index(string, substring)** returns the starting position in **string** that contains **substring**. If **substring** is not found, the function returns a value of 0. The function **split(string, array, "separator")** separates **string** into elements of **array** according to the field separator. If you do not specify a field separator, **awk** uses the predefined variable **FS** (field separator: any number of blanks).

```
            UNIX
example:    % date
            Fri Oct 7 03:07:48 EDT 1988
            % cat awk_script
            { split($4, time, ":")
            print time[1], "hours"
            print time[2], "minutes"
            print time[3], "seconds"
            }
            % date | awk -f awk_script
            03 hours
            07 minutes
            48 seconds
```

For example, the statement **date | awk -f awk_script** pipes the output of the **date** command to **awk** for processing by **awk_script**. The command **split($4, time, ":")** splits the fourth field of the date output, **03:04:48**, into three elements of the array **time** using the colon as a delimiter.

5.4.9   *Mathematical Functions*

Table 5.11 includes the comment mathematical functions available to the **awk** user. The following example shows values returned by some of these functions.

```
            UNIX
example:    % cat foo
            90 90 10 12.7 36
            % cat awk_script
            {
            a = sin($1); b = cos($2); c = log($3); d = int($4); e = \
               sqrt($5);
            print a; print b; print c; print d; print e
            }
            % awk -f awk_script foo
            1
            0
            2.30259
            12
            6
```

Redirecting Output

The following examples illustrate outputting to a file, appending to a file, and piping the results of **awk** to another command.

> UNIX
> **example:** % awk -F: '{print $1 > "myfile.dat"}' /etc/passwd
> **example:** % awk -F: '{file = "myfile.dat"; print $1 >> file}' \
> /etc/passwd
> **example:** % awk -F: '{print $1 | "mail fred"}' /etc/passwd

The statement **awk -F: '{print $1 > "myfile.dat"}' /etc/passwd** writes the first field of the file **/etc/passwd** to **myfile.dat**. The statement **awk -F: '{ {file = "myfile.dat"; print $1 >> file}' /etc/passwd** appends the first field of the file **/etc/passwd** to the variable **file**, defined as **myfile.dat**. Finally, **awk -F: '{print $1 | "mail fred"}' /etc/passwd** mails the first field of each record of the file **/etc/passwd** to the user **fred**.

5.4.11 *Putting It All Together*

The following example illustrates some of the features of **awk** introduced in the previous sections. It is adapted from an example given in *The UNIX Programming Environment* by Kernighan and Pike (see Appendix D). This example checks one or more files for two identical adjacent words, a common typographical error.

> UNIX
> **example:** % cat textfile
> test of awk awk program
> test of same words on two lines
> lines
> % cat awk_script
> FILENAME != prevfile
> { NR = 1
>   prevfile = FILENAME
> }
> NF > 0 {
>   if ($1 == lastword)
>   printf "double %s, file %s, line %d\n", $1, FILENAME, NR
>   for (i = 2; i <= NF; i++)
>   if ($i == $(i-1)
>   printf "double %s, file %s, line %d\n", $1, FILENAME, NR
>   if (NF > 0)
>   lastword = $NF

```
}
% awk -f awk_script textfile
double awk, file textfile, line 1
double lines, file textfile, line 2
```

FILENAME != prevfile
{ NR=1
prevfile = FILENAME
} effectively resets the record counter for each new file where two or
more files are given as arguments to the script. The statement (**if
($i==$(i-1)**)) checks the **ith** field against the **ith-1** field for each non-blank
(**NF>0**) record in the file. If the two words are identical, then the word,
filename, and the line number are printed (**printf "double %s, file %s,
line %d\n" ,i,FILENAME,NR**). The last word of a record is retained as the
variable **lastword** and compared to the first word of the following record
(**if ($1== lastword**)). If they are identical, a message is also printed.
After all records in a file have been processed, **NR** is reset to 1 and the
process is repeated for any additional files specified.

5.5   *Summary*

This chapter describes the various ways a UNIX user may create or
modify the contents of a file. Typical of UNIX are the variety and complexity of the editors and string handlers available. For example, the
editors **edit**, **ed**, and **ex** are available for line editing. **ex** is a superset of
edit and **ed** and the editor discussed. **ex** has similar functionality to EDT
in line mode with the following three exceptions. First, **ex** does not display line numbers, but these may be turned on with the **ex** command **set
number**. Second, **ex** resequences lines after each command, whereas
EDT only resequences line numbers with the **RESEQUENCE** command.
Third, whereas the EDT user places the line or range of lines after the
command, the **ex** user places them before. For example, the **ex** command **9d** deletes line 9 (compare the EDT command **D 9**). Note that the
ex command **d9** deletes 9 lines starting at the cursor, so be careful, and
be aware of the **undo ex** command.

vi (visual) is the closest UNIX editor to EDT in keypad mode. However,
you make changes to a file using the standard keyboard keys and not
the keypad keys. Hence, there are two **vi** modes: passive for moving the
cursor, and active for inserting and making changes to existing text.
Remembering to toggle between passive and active modes is the major

problem encountered by the EDT keypad mode user. Passive and active mode commands may be combined to provide a very extensive command set.

ex and **vi** are interactive editors; you are in a sense part of the file, moving about within it, and making changes. The command **sed** and the utility **awk**, which have no VMS counterparts, are batch editors—all changes are made external to the file. The end result is the same as for the interactive editors, a single updated version of the file. **sed** uses the same syntax as **ex**, and is, therefore, straightforward. **awk**, although very powerful, has an extensive C-like syntax. If you don't need a complex string handler at this time, you should skip **awk**. If **sed** or **awk** commands are used repeatedly, they are stored in a script file for easy recall.

Chapter 6

Communicating with Other Users

*C*an *we talk?*

Joan Rivers

The ability of users to communicate with each other is integral to any interactive operating system. UNIX, like VMS, supports communications between users on the same computer (local host) or between users on different computers (remote hosts) connected via a network. This chapter covers two commands and one utility (that is, two relatively simple and one relatively complex program) whereby users can communicate with each other either on a local computer or on a local and remote computer. This chapter concentrates on communication between users on the local computer only. Chapter 13 discusses communication with remote hosts.

Communication with other users may take place in interactive or batch mode. Interactive communication requires an immediate response from the user receiving the message, who must be logged on to receive it. Batch communications do not require an immediate response from the receiver. The commands **talk** and **write** (Section 6.2) apply to interactive communication (compare the VMS commands **PHONE** and **REPLY**), whereas the **mail** utility (Section 6.1) applies to batch communications (compare the VMS utility **MAIL**). Note that **talk** and **write** are commands and **mail** is a utility. This distinction reflects the relative complexity, and hence versatility, of each program. As indicated above, **write** and **talk** are relatively straightforward: each command performs one simple task. **mail**, on the other hand, has a variety of functions and a more extensive command syntax.

After reading this chapter, you should be familiar with reading, sending, replying to, forwarding, storing, and searching mail as well as communicating interactively with other users. Chapter 13 extends these principles with a discussion of communication with users on remote hosts.

6.1   *Batch Communications: mail*

The UNIX and VMS mail utilities possess similar capabilities. Both use folders to organize stored messages, both permit the user to modify the mail environment, and both permit mailing to lists of users on both local and remote hosts. Most of the differences in the way UNIX and VMS mail function internally are irrelevant to the average user and are therefore not discussed here. Appendix D can refer you to a detailed discussion of the internal operation of the UNIX mailer. This section discusses differences in command syntax important for everyday use.

A UNIX mail message can be any ASCII text. When a user receives a mail message, the system stores it in the file **/usr/spool/mail/user**, known as the *system mailbox*. The command **mail** accesses this file and displays one line of header (address) information for each unread message. The header includes the sender's username, remote computer (if applicable), time the message was sent, and the subject of the message. The **from** command also displays header information but does not permit further access to the system mailbox: it serves as a simple method of listing new mail headers without invoking the **mail** utility. You may wish to place the **from** command in the **.login** hidden file (see Section 3.2.1), where it will automatically display the headers of any new mail messages you have received since your last terminal session.

The system mailbox functions like the VMS **NEWMAIL** folder. A user may read, reply to, forward, delete, or store messages in the system mailbox. Once the user reads a message, mail moves it to the user's own mailbox, by default the file ˜**user/mbox** (the file **mbox** in the home directory of **user**). This file is equivalent to the VMS **MAIL** folder, the default storage bin for messages that have been read. VMS users can gain access to messages contained in the **MAIL** folder only with the **MAIL** utility. The UNIX file ˜**user/mbox**, on the other hand, is an ordinary file which stores mail messages after they have been read. Users can call up this file using the **mail** utility; users can also use any UNIX command that manipulates ordinary files (see Chapters 4 and 9). It is not advisable to edit this file, since changes may render it unreadable by the **mail** utility. However, users may read, search, print, and otherwise manipulate it like any other file. Once messages have been read, they may also be moved to files or folders other than ˜**user/mbox**.

A feature of the UNIX **mail** utility not found in VMS is the **dead.letter** file in the user's home directory. Pressing ⟨CTRL⟩-C twice stores the incomplete draft of a message in the file **dead.letter** instead of sending it. The file **dead.letter** stores the aborted message until the user aborts a second message, at which time the second message overwrites the first.

Users send mail by including either login names or a *mail alias* for a mailing list on the command line.

	VMS	UNIX
form:	$ MAIL[/QUALIFIER(S)] [file-spec] [recipient]	% mail [option(s)] recipient
example:	$ MAIL	% mail user1 user2
	MAIL> SEND	**Subject:** [subject entered \ here]
	To: user1, user2	[message entered here]
	Subject: [subject entered here]	.
	Enter your message below. . . .	**Cc:** [additional recipients \ entered here]
	[message entered here]	%
	⟨CTRL⟩-Z	
	MAIL>	
example:	MAIL> SEND	% mail userslis
	To: @USERS.LIS	

The first example above illustrates how to send mail messages to two individuals, **user1** and **user2**. Note, unlike VMS, the UNIX **mail** command issued without arguments or options does not produce the **mail** prompt unless you have unread mail messages. If you have no unread messages in the system mailbox, **mail** returns the shell prompt without comment. When invoked with user names or an alias for a distribution list on the command line, **mail** responds with a prompt for the subject. You enter the subject, then the message beginning on the following line. Terminate the message with a period as the first character of a line, or with a ⟨CTRL⟩-D (compare the **ex** editor in Section 5.1). You can then carbon copy (**Cc:**) the message to additional users (see the discussion of **askcc** in Section 6.1.8) by entering additional user names. Press ⟨CR⟩ for no users or when done specifying additional users.

The second example illustrates sending a message to a distribution list of names contained in the file **userslis**. In VMS, the distribution list is a file containing a list of mailing addresses, one per line. The UNIX distribution list is a mail alias established in the **.mailrc** hidden file (see Section 6.1.8). Note the similarity between using an alias within **mail** and using an alias within the C shell program. While entering a message in UNIX, you can make changes to the characteristics of the message not possible using the VMS **MAIL** utility. Table 6.1 summarizes the UNIX message modifiers. Changes begin with a tilde as the first character of a new line. For example, ˜**e** can be used to invoke the editor at

Table 6.1   mail: Message Modifiers

UNIX Modifier	VMS Modifier	UNIX Function
˜d		Include the **dead.letter** file
˜e	**/EDIT**	Invoke the editor set by **EDITOR**
˜v	**/EDIT**	Invoke the **vi** editor
˜t user(s)		Add **user(s)** to the list of people receiving the message
˜s new_subject		Change the subject of the message
˜p		Display entire message
˜h		Optionally change all characteristics
˜r filename	**∗INCLUDE FILENAME**	Include a file in the message
˜m message_#		Include message # in the message sent

any point during message input. Correspondingly, changes may be made to the subject of the message (˜s) or the list of users who are to receive the mail message can be enlarged (˜t). The editor used is defined by the mail environment variable **EDITOR** in the **.mailrc** or **/usr/lib/Mail.rc** file (Section 6.1.8). In VMS the editor can be invoked from the **MAIL>** prompt: it cannot be invoked from within the message itself.

6.1.2   Reading Mail

The mail system, by default, notifies you of any new mail messages received since your last terminal session. When you have new mail, **mail** displays the message "You have new mail" when you log on. If you have unread messages received prior to your last terminal session, **mail** displays the message "You have old mail." If both conditions apply, **mail** displays only the new mail message. Notification of incoming mail during a terminal session depends on the command **biff**, discussed in Section 3.2.1. The command **biff y** displays the message header, including sender and subject and the first few lines of the message, when new mail arrives (compare the VMS command **SET BROADCAST=MAIL**). This display interrupts any output from the current process at the current cursor location. The command **biff n** gives no notification (compare the

VMS command **SET BROADCAST=NOMAIL**). You can use the command **from** to review the headers of unread mail messages.

example:

VMS	UNIX
$ MAIL	**% mail**
You have 1 new message	**Mail version 2.18 5/19/83. Type ? for **
	help.
MAIL> DIR	**"/usr/spool/mail/fred": 1 message 1 **
	unread
# From Date Subject	**>U 1 root Wed Apr 27 11:13 9/146 **
	"test"
1 SYSTEM 27-APR-1988 TEST	**&**
MAIL>	

The above example, taken from the ULTRIX **mail** utility, illustrates the effect of invoking **mail** when user fred has messages in the system mailbox **/usr/spool/mail/fred**. The message header **>U 1 root Wed Apr 27 11:13 9/146 "test"** indicates the following:

>	Current message pointer
U	Message status: **U**=unread, **N**=new, *=unsaved, (blank)=read but not saved
1	Message number
root	Sender's user name
Wed Apr 27	Date message was sent
11:13	Time message was sent
9/146	Number of lines/characters in message
"test"	Subject of message

The **&** is the **mail** prompt indicating that the **mail** utility is ready to receive commands (compare the VMS **MAIL>** prompt). Table 6.2 lists the responses you can make to the prompt. The simplest response is ⟨CR⟩, which displays the active message. As discussed above, the active message is indicated by the **>** symbol. The response **n** displays the next message, and **message list** displays one or more messages identified by message number. For example:

1	Message 1
1 7	Messages 1 and 7
1-7	Messages 1 through 7

Table 6.2 Interactive mail Responses

Response	Function
t <message list>	Type messages
n	Go to and type next message
e <message list>	Edit messages
f <message list>	Give header lines of messages
d <message list>	Delete messages
s <message list> file	Append messages to file
u <message list>	Undelete messages
r <message list>	Reply to messages (to sender and recipients)
R <message list>	Reply to messages (to sender only)
pre <message list>	Make messages go back to **/usr/spool/mail**
m <user list>	Mail to specific users
q	Quit, saving unresolved messages in **mbox**
x	Quit, do not remove system mailbox
h	Print out active message headers
!	Shell escape
ch [directory]	Move to directory or home if none given

A <**message list**> consists of integers, ranges of same, or user names separated by spaces. If omitted, <**mail**> uses the last message typed.

A <**user list**> consists of user names or distribution names separated by spaces. Distribution names are defined in **.mailrc** in your home directory.

.-$ The current message through the last
message

Messages are piped through **more** (see Section 4.8), and therefore appear on your terminal one screen at a time, as in VMS **MAIL** message display.

6.1.3   *Replying to Mail*

There are several ways to reply to a message (see Table 6.2). Use **R** to reply only to the originator of the message. Use **r** to reply to the originator and all users who received the original message including the Cc:. By default, **r** or **R** reply to the last message read. If the user wishes to reply to different mail messages, then a message list or individual message number should be included.

6.1.4   *Forwarding Mail*

The UNIX **mail** utility provides no specific command corresponding to the VMS **MAIL** command **FORWARD/EDIT** for forwarding mail to other users. Nevertheless, the procedure for forwarding mail is relatively simple.

	VMS	UNIX
example:	$ MAIL	% mail
	You have 1 new message	Mail version 2.18 5/19/83. Type ? for help.
		" /usr/spool/mail/fred": 1 message 1 unread
		>U 1 root Wed Apr 27 11:13 9/146 "test"
	MAIL> FORWARD/EDIT 1	& m user1
	To: USER1	Subject: forward message
		˜m 1
		.
	⟨CTRL⟩-Z	&
	MAIL>	

The command **m user1** directs **mail** to send a message to **user1**, having entered a new subject (VMS **MAIL** uses the subject of the message being forwarded). ˜**m 1** includes message 1 as part of the text of the current message, which can be further modified.

You can also forward your own mail. This is useful in situations when you have multiple usernames on one computer or usernames on multiple computers, and desire one point of reference for mail. The hidden file **.forward** in each parent directory of each username may contain a common address (see Section 13.1.1 for the format of network addresses) to which all your mail is forwarded. Rather than logging on to each username to check for incoming mail, you need only look under a single username on a single computer (compare VMS **MAIL SET FORWARD**).

6.1.5   *Saving and Deleting Mail*

Once you read a message, **mail**, by default, saves it to the file ˜**user/mbox**, which you can access via the **mail** utility or any command used on ordinary files. You can also print or delete mail messages, append them to a file, or place them in a folder. Each of these options is discussed below.

	VMS	UNIX
example:		% mkdir ~user/mail_folder
		% ex ~user/.mailrc
		:a
		set folder = mail_folder
		.
		:wq!
example:	MAIL> DIR/FOLDER	& folders
	Listing of folders in DUA1:[USER] -	bugs
	MAIL.MAI;1	
	Press CTRL/C to cancel listing	
	BUGS MAIL	
example:	MAIL> MOVE BUGS	& s +bugs
example:		& s 4-6 +bugs
example:	$ MAIL	% mail -f
	MAIL> SET FOLDER MAIL	
example:	$ MAIL	% mail -f ~user/mail_ \
	MAIL> SET FOLDER BUGS	folder/bugs
example:	MAIL> PRINT 10	& s 10 foo
		& !lpr foo; rm foo
example:	MAIL> DELETE 4	& d 4

In the first example, the user establishes a directory, **mail_folder**, in which **mail** stores folders. (You do not need to make a mail folder directory in VMS, as VMS maintains folders as part of the **MAIL.MAI** file.) Then the user appends the command **set folder=mail_folder** to the file **.mailrc** using the **ex** editor (see Section 5.1). The hidden file **.mailrc** customizes the **mail** environment (see Section 6.1.8), and in this instance tells **mail** in which directory to store mail folders. Each folder appears as a separate file. New messages are appended to these files and, like **~user/mbox**, these folder files may be accessed by any UNIX commands used on ordinary files.

The second example, **folders** (compare the VMS **MAIL** command **DIRECTORY/FOLDER**), displays existing folders. The third example, **s +bugs** (compare the VMS MAIL command **MOVE BUGS**), moves the current message to the folder **bugs**. The fourth example, **s 4-6 +bugs**, moves the fourth, fifth, and sixth messages in the message list to the folder **bugs**.

The fifth and sixth examples illustrate how to access old mail files. The shell command **mail -f** (without a file name) accesses the **~user/mbox** file. The command **mail -f ~user/mail_folder/bugs** accesses the folder **bugs**. The seventh example illustrates how to print a message list. First, message 10 is stored in the file **foo** with the command **s 10 foo**. Then, **foo** is sent to the default line printer and once spooled, deleted with the command sequence **!lpr foo; rm foo**. Note that **!** informs the **mail** utility that the command that follows is to be interpreted by the shell rather than by **mail**.[1] By using pipes and input/output redirection, you can initiate complex sequences of commands from within **mail**.

The last example, **d 4**, deletes the fourth message in the message list. Note that until quitting or exiting **mail**, you may recover the last deleted message list with the **undelete** command.

You may also save messages as files, as the following examples illustrate.

	VMS	UNIX
example:	**MAIL> EXTRACT MAILFILE.TXT**	**& s mailfile.txt**
example:	**MAIL> EXTRACT 4 MAILFILE.TXT**	**& s 4 mailfile.txt**
example:		**% mail -f mailfile.txt**

In the first example, **s mailfile.txt** saves the message just read to the file **mailfile.txt** in the current directory. In the second example, **s 4 mailfile.txt** saves message 4 in the message list to the file **mailfile.txt**. In the last example, the command **mail -f mailfile.txt** presents a further example of the UNIX **mail** utility's ability to access ordinary files. Provided that the contents of the file **mailfile.txt** have not been changed, for example, by use of an editor to remove the message header, the **mail** utility treats it as a regular mail message. You cannot do this in VMS MAIL, although you can use messages previously saved to a disk file with the **EXTRACT** command. The VMS **MAIL** utility commands **REPLY/EDIT**, **SEND/EDIT**, and **FORWARD/EDIT** invoke an editor which is used to include the message contained in the disk file, but not until a list of recipients and a subject have been entered.

6.1.6   *Searching Old Mail*

The UNIX **mail** utility offers several mechanisms for searching messages to locate the sender or a keyword in the header that indicates sender, subject, time, or Cc. Once you store messages in ordinary files, you can use the **grep** command (see Section 9.4.5) for searching.

---

1. This use of **!** to escape to the shell is common to a number of utilities.

VMS version 5.0 and later permits you to search mail message headers with the **MAIL** command **DIRECTORY/EDIT**. UNIX **mail** does not have a feature equivalent to the VMS **MAIL** command **DIRECTORY/ SINCE**, which lets you preview the header information of messages received since a specified time.

	VMS	UNIX
example:	$ MAIL	
	MAIL> SET FOLDER MAIL	% mail -f
	MAIL> DIRECTORY	& h
example:		& f user
example:		& f /keyword
example:	MAIL> SEARCH STRING	& !grep string ~user/mbox

In the first example, **h** displays one line of header information for each message stored in **~user/mbox**. Unlike the VMS **MAIL DIRECTORY** command, **h** displays only the first 18 message headers. The command **+h** displays the next 18. Correspondingly, **-h** displays the previous 18. In the second example, **f user** displays messages sent by a specified user. In the third example, **f /keyword** displays headers of messages containing the keyword. In the last example, **!grep string ~user/mbox** issues a shell command from within **mail** (by temporarily escaping to the shell and then returning to **mail**) to search the user mailbox for **string**.

6.1.7 Terminating Mail

Terminating mail represents the most fundamental and annoying difference between the UNIX and VMS mail utilities. In VMS **MAIL**, when a message is deleted, it is moved to a temporary folder called **WASTEBAS-KET**. The command **EXIT** deletes the **WASTEBASKET** folder and terminates **MAIL**. The VMS **MAIL** command **QUIT**, on the other hand, leaves the **WASTEBASKET** folder intact, so that deleted mail messages can be recovered in subsequent mail sessions by moving them from the **WASTE-BASKET** folder. In UNIX, these functions are reversed: **exit** leaves the **mail** environment unchanged so that any deleted mail messages will reappear the next time **mail** is invoked. The command **quit** loses forever mail messages that were deleted.

6.1.8 Customizing the Mail Environment

Just as you can customize the shell to suit individual needs (see Section 3.2.2), so you can customize the mail environment. The system administrator can customize the mail environment for all users by modifying the file **/usr/lib/Mail.rc**. You can further modify your own mail environment with the hidden file **.mailrc**. Details of modifications that you can make to the mail environment appear in the additional reading list shown in Appendix D. The following example represents a typical system and user environment taken from an ULTRIX v2.0 system.

---

example:

VMS

$ COPY SYS$SYSTEM:MAILEDIT.COM -
   MYMAIL.COM
$ EDIT MYMAIL.COM

*s?EDIT?EDIT/TPU?21
* EXIT
$ DEFINE MAIL$EDIT MYMAIL.COM

UNIX

% cat /usr/lib/Mail.rc
**set append dot save ask askcc \
   SHELL = /bin/csh
EDITOR = /usr/ucb/ex metoo hold**

The variables defining the **mail** environment are:

append	Messages are appended to **˜user/mbox** rather than prepended
dot	. (period) alone on a line signifies end of message, and supplements ⟨CTRL⟩-D
save	Saves mail messages in a file or folder
ask	Prompts for subject field
askcc	Prompts for **Cc:** field
SHELL	Shell to use with **!** command
EDITOR	Editor to use while in **mail** (compare the VMS MAIL command **SET EDITOR**)
metoo	Include sender in recipients (compare the VMS MAIL command **SEND/SELF**)
hold	Messages once read do not automatically pass to **˜user/mbox** but are kept in the system mailbox

A typical user-specific modification to this system-wide environment might be as follows.

---

example:

UNIX

% cat ˜user/.mailrc
#   .mailrc - File to tailor mail environment [PEB 4/21/87]
#
set folder = mail_folders   # define directory for folders
set crt = 20   # set number of message lines

```
    set autoprint                          # automatically display next message \
                                             after delete
    set EDITOR = /usr/local/emacs          # define editor for mail
    alias managers george fred             # aliases
    alias cshell jack jill george dragon
    alias gripe root
```

The command **set folder = mail_folders**, as we saw previously, defines the directory to store mail folders. **set crt = 20** sets the number of lines displayed per screen to 20. **set autoprint** automatically displays the next message after a message is deleted. **set EDITOR = /usr/local/emacs** defines an alternative editor while in **mail**. **alias managers george fred** defines a mailing list called **managers**, which currently specifies the two recipients **george** and **fred**.

6.2   *Interactive Communications: talk and write*

This section covers two commands, **talk** and **write**, with which users can communicate with other users logged on to the same or a remote computer. You can use **talk** (compare the VMS **PHONE** command) to conduct an ongoing conversation to the exclusion of any other interactive computing. You can use **write** to exchange messages while performing other interactive tasks. Note the analogy to the VMS **REPLY** command, which is available only to system operators (users with the VMS OPER privilege). You may use **mesg** if you do not wish to be interrupted by **talk** or **write** requests (compare the VMS command **SET NOBROAD-CAST**). The command **mesg n** prevents the receipt of a **talk** or **write** request, **mesg y** (the default) reinstates the ability to receive **talk** and **write** messages, and **mesg** without arguments reports the current state of **mesg**.

	VMS	UNIX
form:	$ PHONE[/QUALIFIER(S)] USER	% talk user [ttyname]
form:	$ REPLY[/QUALIFIER(S)] "MESSAGE"	% write user [ttyname]
		[message]
		⟨CTRL⟩-D
example:	$ PHONE FRED	% talk fred tty17
example:	$ REPLY/USER = FRED "ARE YOU THERE?"	% write fred
		are you there?
		⟨CTRL⟩-D

Notice that both **talk** and **write** accept a **ttyname** argument. You can use this argument to send messages to a specific terminal when the user is logged on at more than one location. In the first example, **talk fred tty17** attempts to establish communication with user **fred** logged on to **tty17**. Fred's terminal will display the following:

Message from TalkDaemon@sender_computer
talk: connection requested by sender_name@sender_computer
talk: respond with: talk sender_name@sender_computer

If Fred responds with **talk sender_name@sender_computer**, then communication is established. Just as with **PHONE**, the screen splits into two segments, so that what the sender types appears in one window and what the receiver types appears in the other. You can refresh the screen with ⟨CTRL⟩-L (compare ⟨CTRL⟩-W in VMS). Communications terminate when either user types ⟨CTRL⟩-C.

In the second example, **write fred**, user **fred** sees the following:

Message from sender_computer!sender_name sender_ttyname
Are you there?

At this point, Fred can respond if he wishes.

6.3   *Summary*

The following scenario, typical of daily mail use, summarizes the material presented in this chapter. User Joyce returns from vacation and checks her electronic mail.

```
            UNIX
example:    % mail
            " /usr/spool/mail/joyce": 10 messages
example:    & h
            >    1 root         Tue May 12 12:11 28/950 "rsh to/from ultrix"
                 2 MAILER-DAEMON Wed May 13 17 16:43 23/615 "Returned mail: Host \
                 unknown"
                 3 poisson      Thu May 21 11:20 16/506 "dcp"
                 4 youkha       Thu May 21 12:55 21/507 "rmf,peters and dly"
                 5 youkha       Tue May 26 14:21 19/451 "brookhaven files"
                 6 youkha       Wed May 27 00:12 33/731 "rcpvms"
                 7 pahler       Wed May 27 22:15 29/864
                 8 murthy       Thu May 28 10:24 17/487 "stream <lf> files"
                 9 horton       Sat May 30 14:38 17/512 "man utility"
                10 cucard!root  Thu Jun 18 18:04 11/282 "Re: test"
example:    & 2
            From joyce May 13 16:43:43 1987
            Received: by cuhhca.UUCP (4.12/4.8)
```

id AA12988; Wed, 13 May 87 16:43:41 edt
Date: Wed, 13 May 87 16:43:41 edt
From: MAILER-DAEMON (Mail Delivery Subsystem)
Subject: Returned mail: Host unknown
To: joyce
Status: RO
----- Transcript of session follows -----
550 reidar@cucard. . . Host unknown: Not a typewriter
----- Unsent message follows -----
Received by cuhhca.UUCP (4.12/4.8)
id AA12986; Wed, 13 may 87 16:43:41 edt
Date: Wed, 13 May 87 16:43:41 edt
From: joyce (Joyce Lastname)
To: reidar@cucard
Subject: test
Hopefully when u poll me u should get this???? Joyce

example: & m reidar@cucard
Subject: Resending message of May 13
~m 2
Interpolating 2
(continue)
⟨CTRL⟩-D
Cc:
example: & d
example: & 1
From root Tue May 12 12:11:28 1987
Received: by cuhhca.UUCP (4.12/4.8)
id AA05129; Tue, 12 May 87 12:11:26 edt
Date: Tue, 12 May 87 12:11:26 edt
From: root (System Administrator)
To: joyce
Subject: rsh to/from ultrix
Status: RO
Dear Joyce:
I fixed the problem. . . .
example: & s +vacation
" /usr1/joyce/mail_folders/vacation" [New file] 28/950
example: & 9
From horton Sat May 30 14:38:57 1987
Received: by cuhhca.UUCP (4.12/4.8)
id AA27943; Sat, 30 May 87 14:38:55 edt
Date: Sat, 30 May 87 14:38:55 edt
From: horton (John Horton)
To: joyce
Subject: man utility
Status: RO
Joyce. help. . . please contact me as soon as you return
example: & !who
horton   tty06   May   2 07:20
murthy   tty07   May   2 07:08
system   tty10   May   2 09:42

```
                    zhaoping    ttyp0    May     2 09:16         (cuhhmd.hhmi.colu)
                    royer       ttyp1    May     2 09:21         (cuhhmd.hhmi.colu)
                    !
example:    &q
            Held 8 messages in /usr/spool/mail/joyce
example:    % write horton
            are you there?
            ⟨CTRL⟩-D
            %
            Message from cuhhca!horton on tty06 at 11:36
            yes. . let us "talk"
            EOF
            %
            Message from Talk_Daemon@cuhhca at 11:37. . .
            talk: connection requested by horton@cuhhca
            talk: respond with: talk horton@cuhhca
            % talk horton
            [Connection established]
            -------------------------------------------
```

Using the command **mail**, Joyce discovers that ten mail messages have
been sent to her system mailbox **/usr/spool/mail/joyce** during her
absence. Using the **h** (header) **mail** utility command, she displays a one-
line summary of each message. Message 2 catches her eye; it is a
response from the **mail** utility (**MAILER_DAEMON**) indicating that it was
unable to deliver a message she sent prior to her departure. She enters
2 at the interactive **mail** prompt **&**, which displays the message. It is in
fact a message she tried to send to **reidar@cucard** (a network address;
see Section 13.1.1). She decides to send this message again, believing
that the network connection is now functioning correctly. The command
m reidar@cucard begins sending the new message by prompting for a
subject, to which user Joyce responds with **˜m 2** to include message 2 in
the text of the new message. Joyce sends the message by pressing ⟨
⟨CTRL⟩-D, then ⟨cr⟩ at the **Cc:** prompt. Joyce then deletes the original
message with the **d** command and reads the first message by typing **1**.
Having read the message, Joyce decides to save it (**s +vacation**) in the
new folder **vacation**, which is a file in the directory **/usr1/joyce/mail_
folders**. She then turns her attention to message 9. Since this message
is a call for immediate help, she decides to use interactive communications. The string **!who** issues a command **who** to the shell (**!**) to determine if user **horton** is logged on and therefore capable of receiving interactive communications. Seeing that he is logged on, she quits **mail** (**q**),
retaining her unread messages in the system mailbox. The command
write horton then opens a dialog with user **horton**. As he is logged on

only once, it is not necessary to include a terminal name in the **write** command. The dialog is terminated with ⟨CTRL⟩-D. User **horton** responds by using the **write** command and requests a **talk** session (whereupon user **horton** would have entered **talk joyce**). Joyce responds with **talk horton**. The screen splits into two segments and a dialog takes place.

Chapter 7

Monitoring and Utilizing System Resources

I can't see who is ahead—it's either Oxford or Cambridge.

John Snagge

This chapter discusses UNIX commands that analyze and affect the use of system resources such as the CPU, physical memory, virtual memory, and disk space. Monitoring system resources is of major concern to the system administrator in maintaining a balanced workload. Users become interested in this subject when, for example, the system responds sluggishly to terminal input, or when they wish to estimate the running time of a particular application. Unfortunately, users can usually do nothing to improve the situation except to alter processes they own, which is often self-defeating.

Applications programmers may consider this position narrow-minded, reflecting only a system administrator's perspective. Indeed, programmers can examine how a particular application consumes resources and often see how to improve the performance of their code. This chapter, however, is not a lesson in programming, and therefore offers no insight into how such improvements might be made. It simply describes the commands that monitor how processes utilize system resources and that affect the system resources devoted to processes.

UNIX users familiar with the VMS commands **MONITOR**, **SHOW**, and **ANALYZE**, with their easily understood output, will likely be disappointed by the commands UNIX offers to analyze system resource utilization due to the original UNIX design constraints. These constraints required that output be displayed as hard copy on slow Teletype devices. The designers of the original operating system could not, of course, avail themselves of the fast screen updating capabilities of today's video terminals. A few vendors of UNIX systems now offer graphical output pleasing to the VMS **MONITOR** user, but such features are not generally available.

Despite differences in convenience, the principles for analyzing resource utilization in both VMS and UNIX are the same. Figure 7.1 illustrates the common UNIX commands for monitoring and changing resource utilization. These commands apply either to single processes (discussed in Section 7.1) or to the sum of all processes (discussed in Section 7.2). Once resource utilization of your system has been analyzed, a community-conscious user (if such a creature exists) can modify his or her

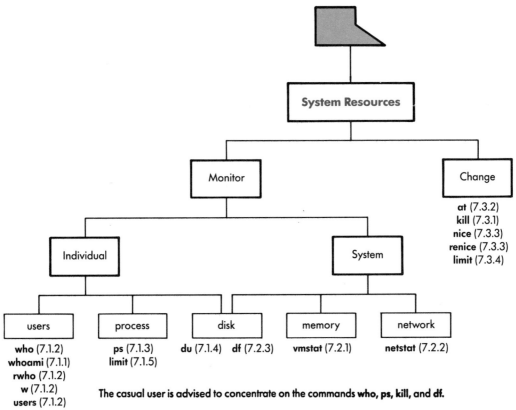

The casual user is advised to concentrate on the commands **who, ps, kill,** and **df.**

Figure 7.1   UNIX Commands for Monitoring and Changing Resource Utilization

processes to reduce their system resource requirements (see Section 7.3).

We will begin by looking at the commands for monitoring system resource utilization as they apply to a single process, a single user, or disk space.

7.1   *Monitoring Users and Their Processes*

Before examining how individual processes are consuming system resources, you should examine how many interactive users are logged into the system as a first indication of the workload. UNIX offers several commands—**users, who, w,** and **rwho**—for displaying a list of interactive users. The BSD version of UNIX even has a command, **whoami** to determine who you yourself are. Once you have determined the number and names of the interactive users on your system, you can list the processes that you and your fellow users are running with the **ps** command. If you need additional information, you can issue **du** to determine the amount of disk space consumed, and if you are a C shell user, the shell command **limit** to get information on the resource limits imposed on user processes.

7.1.1   *Who Am I: whoami*

The **whoami** command (BSD only) is not as ridiculous as it may first appear. It is useful, for example, when you have different usernames on several frequently used UNIX computers. You may invoke **whoami** to determine your current username and hence which computer you are using.[1] You might also use **whoami** when sharing a terminal with other users. If that terminal has been left unattended, you can issue **whoami** to list the name of the user who is currently logged in. You may then locate that user and ask him or her to end the terminal session. In VMS, the corresponding command **SHOW PROCESS** returns the current user's username as well as other useful information; **whoami** returns only the username.

	VMS	UNIX
form:	$ SHOW PROCESS[/QUALIFER(S)] process_name	% whoami
example:	$ SHOW PROCESS	% whoami
	29-JUN-1988 11:20:12.98 RTA3: User: SYSTEM	root
	Pid: 00000219 Proc. name:_RTA3: UIC: -	
	[SYSEM,POSTMASTER]	
	Priority: 4 Default file spec: -	
	SYS$SYSROOT:[SYSMGR]	

BSD is the only version of UNIX that supports **whoami**. System V uses **who am i**, which returns the username, the terminal name, and the time the user logged in.

7.1.2   *Monitoring Interactive Users: users, who, w, and rwho*

The UNIX commands **users**, **who**, and **w** provide information in increasing detail on interactive users using the local computer (compare the VMS command **SHOW USERS**). The command **rwho** provides informa-

---

1. If these computers are from different manufacturers and running different implementations of BSD UNIX, using the **whoami** command indicates that UNIX hides differences in hardware behind a common user interface (Section 1.1).

tion about interactive users using remote computers on the same net-work (see Chapter 13).

	VMS	UNIX
form:	$ SHOW USERS[/OUTPUT] [username]	% users
		% who [file]
		% w [option(s)] [user]
example:	$ SHOW USERS	% users
	VAX/VMS Interactive Users	**beigi hendw jayaram**

```
            VAX/VMS Interactive Users
Total number of interactive users = 3
BEIGI      ALPHA      0000021C   LTA40:
HENDW      HENDW      00000129   RTA1:
JAYARAM    JAYARAM    0000020D   LTA36:
```

UNIX

example:
```
% who
beigi         tty06      Jun 28 12:04
hendw         tty0c      Jun 27 19:15
jayaram       ttyp0      Jun 29 09:42
```

example:
```
% w
 12:09pm    up 14 days,  2:07,  3 users,  load average: 0.78, 0.35, 0.20
User       tty        login@     idle    JCPU    PCPU    what
beigi      tty06      12:04pm    31:02   9       9       rlogin cuhhmd
hendw      tty0c      7:15pm     40:53   7       2       -csh[hendw] (csh)
jayaram    ttyp0      9:42am     2:27    3       1       -csh[jayaram] (csh)
```

example:
```
% who /usr/adm/wtmp | grep fred | tail -4
fred   tty03    Feb 24   11:10
fred   tty03    Feb 24   12:03
fred   tty05    Feb 25   12:10
fred   tty05    Feb 25   15:09
```

The **users** command returns only an alphabetical list of the usernames of interactive users currently logged in. The **who** command, which most closely resembles the VMS **SHOW USERS** command, displays the name of the device to which the user's terminal is connected (for example, **tty06**) and the login time (for example, **Jun 28 12:04**). The command **w** also displays a header line with the time of day (**12:09pm**), how long the computer has been up (**14 days, 2:07**), the number of users (**3**), the system load, and the following information about each user:

idle	how long since the user last typed anything, in minutes
JCPU	the accumulated CPU time of all the user's processes since logging in, in minutes
PCPU	the CPU time used by any currently active processes, in minutes

what   the program being executed by the current process

For example, user **jayaram** logged on at 9:42 a.m., has not touched the terminal connected to **ttyp0** for two hours and 27 minutes, and is running the C shell program. Blanks in the fields **idle**, **JCPU**, and **PCPU** indicate a time of less than one minute.

The three values for system load indicate how busy the system was one, five, and 15 minutes ago. A load of 0.78 indicates that the system was operating at 78% capacity; a load of 2.30 indicates that it would take 2.3 identical systems to process the current load efficiently. Stated another way, a single CPU-intensive application running at a system load of 2.30 will receive 1/2.3, or approximately 44%, of the CPU resources.

The last example, **who /usr/adm/wtmp | grep fred | tail -4**, illustrates the use of **who** to interrogate a system accounting file rather than the default file **/etc/utmp**. The file **/etc/utmp** maintains information on users currently logged onto the system. The file **/usr/adm/wtmp** maintains information on all logins and logouts. Rather than displaying the contents of this file (the default), the example pipes the output to the **grep** command (compare the VMS command **SEARCH** in Section 9.4.5), which searches for records that indicate when user **fred** logged into and out of the system. The example, in turn, pipes this information to the command **tail -4** (see Section 9.2.3), which displays the last four records: namely, the last two times user **fred** logged into and out of the system. This information is useful, for example, if you sent a mail message to user **fred** and wish to know when he is likely to read it. If user **fred** has logged in twice in the last couple of days, then you can assume that user **fred** uses the system frequently and will read the message in the near future. On the other hand, if user **fred** logged in only twice in the last two months, it is less likely that he will read the message in the near future.

The command **rwho** produces a display similar to the **who** command, but for users who are logged in to other computers on the network (see Section 13.1.2).

```
         UNIX
form:    % rwho [option(s)]
example: % rwho
         ari        cunixc:ttype     Jun 29 13:30
         brown      sylvester:ttyp2  Jun 28 10:47   :52
         glenda     zeno:tty17       Jun 29 11:46
         gr         cunixc:tty56     Jun 29 12:50
```

```
heidi        cunixc:tty25      Jun 29 09:04   :06
system       cuhhmd:ttyp3      Jun 29 13:39   :07
zagorski     cuhhmd:ttyp0      Jun 28 12:04   :20
```

The command **rwho** displays the same information as **who**, as well as a name preceding the terminal name and how long since the user last typed anything, in minutes. A blank field here indicates that the user has typed something within the last minute. The name preceding the terminal name is the *hostname* of the remote computer (see Section 13.1). VMS, in contrast, does not offer a convenient way to determine who is logged in to a remote DECnet node. You may use the options **a** and **h** with **rwho**. The option **a** reports on all remote users. Without the **a** option only those users who have touched the terminal in the last hour are reported. The option **h** sorts the output alphabetically by hostname rather than username. On a large network, the system administrator may prevent the computer from broadcasting messages describing who is currently using the system in an effort to prevent the network from becoming overloaded. In this case, **rwho** would not detect a complete list of remote users.

7.1.3   *Monitoring Processes: ps*

The command **ps** (process status) shows the system resources being consumed on a UNIX system at any given time by one or more processes. The VMS analogy to **ps** is a combination of the **SHOW SYSTEM** and **SHOW PROCESS** commands. Although **ps** has many options, the subset described here will meet the needs of the average user.

```
          VMS                                          UNIX
form:     $ SHOW PROCESS[/QUALIFIER(S)] [process]      % ps [option(s)]

          VMS
example:  $ SHOW PROCESS
          29-JUN-1988 15:08:38.91   RTA3:       User: SYSTEM
          Pid: 00000219   Proc. name:_RTA3:   UIC: [SYSTEM.POSTMASTER]
          Priority:    4   Default file spec: SYS$SYSROOT:[SYSMGR.COM]
example:  $ SHOW PROCESS/ALL
          2-JUL-1988 11:03:46.85   RTA2:            User: SYSTEM
          Pid: 00000196   Proc. name:_RTA2:         UIC: [SYSTEM.POSTMASTER]
          Priority:   4   Default file spec: DUA3:[BOURNE.MASS11]
          Devices allocated: RTA2:
          Process Quotas:
            CPU limit:                      Infinite   Direct I/O limit:          18
```

Buffered I/O byte count quota:		99904	Buffered I/O limit:	18
Timer queue entry quota:		20	Open file quota:	59
Paging file quota:		59063	Subprocess quota:	10
Default page fault cluster:		64	AST limit:	22
Enqueue quota:		30	Shared file limit:	0
Max detached processes:		0	Max active jobs:	0

Accounting information:

Buffered I/O count:	147	Peak working set size:	387
Direct I/O count:	55	Peak virtual size:	1159
Page faults:	1285	Mounted volumes:	0
Images activated:	7		
Elapsed CPU time:	0 00:00:09.35	Connect time:	0 00:00:40.75

Process privileges:

GRPNAM	may insert in group logical name table
TMPMBX	may create temporary mailbox
WORLD	may affect other processes in the world
NETMBX	may create network device

Process rights identifiers:
INTERACTIVE
REMOTE

Process Dynamic Memory Area

Current Size (bytes)	25600	Current Total Size (pages)	50
Free Space (bytes)	21648	Space in Use (bytes)	3952
Size of Largest Block	21568	Size of Smallest Block	8
Number of Free Blocks	4	Free Blocks LEQU 32 Bytes	2

Processes in this tree:
_RTA2: (*)

UNIX

example: % ps

PID	TT	STAT	TIME	COMMAND
6682	p1	S	0:01	-csh[system] (csh)
7415	p1	R	0:00	ps

example: % ps -l

F	UID	PID	PPID	CP	PRI	NI	SZ	RSS	WCHAN	STAT	TT	TIME	COMMAND
9808209	103	18228	18227	2	1	7	47	38	14423c	S	p0	0:01	csh[system]
1008009	103	18402	18228	17	108	0	396	140		R	p0	0:00	ps -l

example: % ps -v

PID	TT	STAT	TIME	SL	RE	PAGEIN	SIZE	RSS	LIM	TSIZ	TRS	%CPU	%MEM	COMMAND
28798	p0	R	0:00	0	1	2	416	200	XX	84	40	1.0	0.9	ps
28568	p0	S	0:00	0	99	5	76	84	XX	184	172	0.4	0.4	csh

example: % ps -u

USER	PID	%CPU	%MEM	SZ	RSS	TT	STAT	TIME	COMMAND
system	24778	47.0	2.4	220	166	p0	R	0:00	ps -u
system	24521	0.7	1.1	130	71	p0	S	0:05	-csh (csh)

In the first example, **ps** without options (compare the VMS command
SHOW PROCESS) provides a brief summary of your own processes. In
this example, the user is running only two processes: one child running
the **ps** command, and the C shell parent process that forked the child

process (see Section 2.1.1 for a discussion of parent and child processes). The user initiated each process from the terminal **ttyp1**, a pseudo-terminal used in a network connection (see Section 3.1). The **csh** process has been stopped (**S**) for a short period of time, and **ps** is running (**R**). The **csh** process has consumed one minute of CPU time.

In the second example, **ps -l** (compare the VMS command **SHOW PROCESS/FULL**) provides additional information on the user's processes as follows:

UID	Numerical process identifier (compare the VMS **PID**)
PPID	Numerical process identifier of parent process
CP	Short-term CPU utilization factor
PRI	Process priority (compare VMS priority)
NI	Process scheduling increment
SZ	Virtual memory size of the process in kilobytes (compare VMS peak virtual size)
RSS	Real memory size of the process in kilobytes (compare VMS peak working set size)
WCHAN	Event address for which process is waiting

The average user will likely never need some of the information given by **ps -l**. Therefore, we discuss only the commonly used fields.

PPID displays the identification number of the parent process that forked the process under examination. This information is useful if you need to trace the parent process. In this example, the **PPID** of **18228** for the process running the **ps** command is the **PID** of the parent shell process. The priority (**PRI**) determines the amount of the available CPU resources that the system will devote to the process. Unlike VMS, where base priorities range from one to five, UNIX priorities use zero as the baseline, with positive numbers indicating lower priority and negative numbers higher. Section 7.3 describes how you may lower the priority of a running process or a process about to run a command. **SZ** and **RSS** indicate the relationship between how much physical memory a process may theoretically use and how much it has access to. Processes where **SZ** vastly exceeds **RSS** may be running inefficiently. **RSS** corresponds to the peak working set size of a VMS process, the former expressed in kilobytes and the latter in pages of 512 bytes.

If you need to know more about memory utilization, you should use **ps -v**. As shown in the example, **ps -v** displays additional fields relating to memory utilization:

SL	Sleep time of the process, in seconds
RE	Residency time of the process in main memory, in seconds
PAGEIN	Number of disk I/Os resulting from reference to pages not in main memory for a process
SIZE	Same as **SZ** above, that is, virtual memory size of the process in kilobytes
LIM	Soft limit on memory available to process, in kilobytes. The message **xx** means no limit; the process could theoretically use all the available address space
TSIZ	Size of whole program image, in kilobytes
TRS	Size of memory-resident part of program, in kilobytes

The last example, **ps -u**, provides perhaps the most useful display for the average user, for it sorts the percentage of the total CPU (**%CPU**) resources and memory (**%MEM**) consumed by the user's processes in descending order according to CPU utilization. The processes using the most CPU time appear first.

The examples of **ps** given thus far display features of your own processes. You may also display the characteristics of other types of processes (compare the VMS commands **SHOW SYSTEM**, **SHOW PROCESS/IDENTIFICATION**, and **MONITOR PROCESS**). Other UNIX processes fall into two classes: user (both your own and others') and processes not attached to a terminal and owned by **root**. The latter processes, called *daemons*, usually start when the system is booted and are part of the operating system. You may display these two classes of process with the **a** and **x** options respectively.

example:

UNIX

% ps -aux | head

USER	PID	%CPU	%MEM	SZ	RSS	TT	STAT	TIME	COMMAND
fred	24790	31.0	2.6	240	178	p0	R	0:00	ps -aux
george	24881	22.0	1.8	131	119	p3	R	0:12	/usr/george/myprog
fred	24791	4.0	0.3	36	14	p0	S	0:00	head
root	24520	2.3	1.1	85	74	p0	S	0:19	dlogin
fred	24521	0.5	1.1	130	72	p0	S	0:07	-csh (csh)
root	3624	0.2	1.8	131	119	?	S	324:23	/etc/rwhod
root	3611	0.1	0.2	5	3	?	S	65:36	/etc/update
root	3614	0.0	0.3	31	11	?	I	15:54	/etc/cron
root	1	0.0	3.6	270	251	?	I	3:08	init
root	3580	0.0	1.1	99	74	co	S	0:55	swapin

The command **ps -aux | head** pipes the output of the **ps** command to **head** (see Section 9.2.3), which displays the first 10 lines of the output, in this case the 10 processes consuming the largest percentage of CPU resources. Unlike **ps -u**, this command includes processes owned by other users (option **a**) and processes not attached to a terminal or the system console (option **x**). Since the processes owned by the operating system are not associated with a terminal, the **TT** field displays a question mark. Examples of such daemons include **/etc/rwhod**, a program which acts as both a collector and broadcaster of network information. Current users are broadcast over the network, while information on remote users is collected for use by the local **rwho** command; **/etc/ update**, which periodically updates the file system pointer file (see Section 2.3) to assure file integrity in the event of a system crash; **/etc/cron**, which executes commands at preset intervals, such as a time stamp used for accounting purposes (compare the VMS process **OPCOM**); **init**, which initiates a terminal session (see Section 3.2) and **swapin** (compare the VMS process **SWAPPER**), which controls the swapping of data from physical memory to a secondary cache.

7.1.4   *Monitoring Disk Usage: du*

The command **du** (disk utilization) provides information on how much disk space the system's users are utilizing (compare the VMS command **DIRECTORY/SIZE/TOTAL**). You can use **du** to examine your own files or any user's files that are world-readable.

	VMS	UNIX
form:	$ DIR/SIZE file-spec[, . . .]	% du [option(s)] directory
example:	$ DIR/SIZE/TOTAL DUA1:[FRED. . .]*.*;*	% du ˜fred
	Directory DUA1:[FRED]	512 /usr/fred
	Total of 10 files 1000 blocks	256 /usr/fred/scratch
	Directory DUA1:[FRED.SCRATCH]	
	Total of 1 file 500 blocks	
	Grand total of 2 directories, 11 files, 1500 blocks	
example:		% du -s ˜fred
		768 /usr/fred
example:		% du -a
		[not shown]

The command **du** reports the total size of all files in each directory in kilobytes, starting with the directory specified or the current directory if no directory is specified, and moving down the directory tree. In the first example, **du ˜fred** without options reports the disk usage of all directories belonging to user **fred**. In the second example, **du -s ˜fred** (summary) gives only the total size of all files owned by user **fred**. In the last example, **du -a** lists the size of all files in the directory hierarchy, starting at the present working directory (not shown).

7.1.5   *Monitoring Process Resource Limits: limit*

The command **limit**, which is a built-in feature of the C shell program (see Section 11.9), lists the system resources available to a given user process. As we shall see in Section 7.3.4, you may also use **limit** to decrease (but not increase) the value assigned to a particular resource.

	VMS	UNIX	
form:		% limit resource value	
example:	$ SHOW PROCESS/FULL	% limit	
	[not shown]	cputime	unlimited
		filesize	unlimited
		datasize	2097151 kbytes
		stacksize	512 kbytes
		coredumpsize	32768 kbytes
		memoryuse	unlimited

The values displayed by **limit** which are important to the average user are:

cputime	The maximum amount of CPU time assigned to any one process, usually unlimited
filesize	The maximum size, in kilobytes, of any one file, usually unlimited (that is, it could be the size of the whole file system)
coredumpsize	The maximum size, in kilobytes, of the core dump file (see Section 7.3.4)
memoryuse	The amount of physical memory that one process can consume, usually unlimited; that is, all the physical memory not being used by the operating system is theoretically available to a user's process

7.2   *Monitoring the System*

Section 7.1 considers how individual processes consume system resources. This section discusses three commands that review how the sum total of all user processes or all user files affects the available system resources: **vmstat** reviews virtual memory usage and provides other useful statistics, **netstat** analyzes network usage, and **df** reviews the amount of free disk space on each file system.

7.2.1   *Virtual Memory Utilization: vmstat*

You can use **vmstat** (compare the VMS command **SHOW MEMORY**) either statically or dynamically. In static mode, without a counter or interval option, **vmstat** reports average utilization of certain system resources since boot time. In dynamic mode, **vmstat** reports the current values at intervals until it is terminated or it reaches the count option (the number of times the **vmstat** program is run). An interval of five seconds is useful.

```
UNIX
form:      % vmstat [interval] [count]
example:   % vmstat
           procs    memory        page      po  fr  de  sr  faults          cpu
           r b w  avm   fre    re at pi                      in   sy   cs vs  us  sy  id
           0 0 0  8412  15584   0  1  2    0   0   0   0    42  108  27  0  45  10  45
example:   % vmstat 5 10
           procs    memory        page                      faults          cpu
           r b w  avm   fre    re at pi po fr de sr          in   sy   cs vs  us  sy  id
           0 0 0  3048  18408   0  1  2  0  0  0  0         42  107  27  0  45  10  44
           0 0 0  4844  18352   0  0  0  0  0  0  0         42  147  16  0   3  16  81
           0 0 0  4432  18328   0  0  0  0  0  0  0         46   87   5  0   2   6  92
           0 0 0  3088  18324   0  0  0  0  0  0  0         39   52  12  0   3   5  92
           0 0 0  3088  18324   0  0  0  0  0  0  0         68  112  22  0   4  21  76
           0 0 0  2856  18324   0  0  0  0  0  0  0         92  191  40  0  11  18  71
           0 0 0  2856  18324   0  0  0  0  0  0  0         53   86  19  0   1   3  96
           0 0 0  4584  18324   0  0  0  0  0  0  0         62  177  24  0   2  19  79
           0 0 0  4172  18324   0  0  0  0  0  0  0         51   91  19  0   1   5  94
           0 0 0  2828  18324   0  0  0  0  0  0  0         36   42  10  0   1   4  95
```

In the first example, **vmstat** without arguments reports average statistics since boot time. The most important fields are:

procs   Process statistics: running (**r**), awaiting resources (**b**), and swapped (**w**)

memory   Memory utilization: virtual pages of 1024 bytes in use (**avm**) or free (**fre**)

page   Paging activity: reclaims (**re**), pages in (**pi**), pages out (**po**), and anticipated short-term memory shortfall, that is, how much paging is likely to occur (**de**)

faults   Faulting: device interrupts per second (**in**), system calls per second (**sy**), indicating the demand being placed on the kernel, averaged over the last five seconds. The fields **cs** and **vs** show features found only on a vector processor and represent a vendor-specific enhancement to UNIX. These fields are not discussed further.

cpu CPU utilization: user (**us**), system (**sy**), and idle (**id**) in seconds

The second example, **vmstat 5 10**, reports statistics every five seconds for 10 counts.

7.2.2   *Network Utilization: netstat*

The command **netstat** is used principally by the system administrator. Therefore, this section discusses **netstat** only briefly for the benefit of those users for whom network utilization may be an issue. If you are unfamiliar with the nomenclature introduced here, you may wish to return to this section after reading Chapter 13, "Processor-to-Processor Communications."

Like **vmstat**, **netstat** operates in both a static and a dynamic mode, as illustrated in the following examples.

UNIX

form: % netstat [options] [interval] [system] [core]
example: % netstat -i

Name	Mtu	Network	Address	Ipkts	Ierrs	Opkts	Oerrs	Collis	Queue
ex0	1500	128.59	cuhhca.hhmi.	30602	0	11632	0	3	0
lo0	1536	loop	localhost	73135	0	73135	0	0	0

example: % netstat -i 5

input		(lo0)			input		(Total)		output	
packets	errs	packets	errs	colls	packets	errs	packets	errs	colls
73294	0	73294	0	0	103977	0	84951	0	3
0	0	0	0	0	30	0	15	0	0
64	0	64	0	0	81	0	72	0	0
18	0	18	0	0	22	0	19	0	0

example: % netstat

Active Internet connections

Proto	Recv-Q	Send-Q	Local Address	Foreign Address	(state)
tcp	0	0	cuhhca.hhmi.colu.1028	cuhhca.hhmi.colu.batch	TIME_WAIT
tcp	0	0	cuhhca.hhmi.colu.4988	cuhhca.hhmi.colu.batch	TIME_WAIT
tcp	0	78	cuhhca.hhmi.colu.login	cuhhmd.hhmi.colu.1022	ESTABLISHED

Active UNIX domain sockets

Address	Type	Recv-Q	Send-Q	Vnode	Conn	Refs	Nextref	Addr
9c08a0c	stream	0	0	1bf32d0	0	0	0	/etc/cronsock
9c12a0c	stream	0	0	1bf4560	0	0	0	/dev/printer

The command **netstat -i** provides information on each available interface. In the example above, **ex0** is the Ethernet interface and **lo0** is a loopback circuit used in testing. **Mtu** expresses the maximum size of a packet. **Network** gives the Internet address, and **Address** gives the Internet hostname. The remaining fields describe network activity since the computer was last booted: input packets (**Ipkts**), output packets (**Opkts**), input errors (**Ierrs**), output errors (**Oerrs**), and collisions (**Collis**). The number of collisions provides a clue as to how heavily the network is being utilized: two host computers must attempt to send data at exactly the same time to produce a collision. This situation is known as *network contention*. Given the high speed of transmission, network utilization must be heavy before **netstat** registers a significant number of collisions. The command **netstat -i 5** updates this information every five seconds. The first entry provides the statistics accumulated since the computer was booted, and the following entries provide statistics at five-second time intervals.

The command **netstat** without options provides information on the status of each Internet connection. **Recv-Q** and **Send-Q** indicate the number of packets waiting to be received and sent, respectively, to a particular host.

7.2.3   *File System Utilization: df*

The command **df** (disk free) determines the amount of free disk space on all mounted file systems, including the file system containing a user's files (compare the VMS command **SHOW DEVICE/FULL**). **df /dir** reports disk space utilization for the file system **/dir** only. If **df** reports that the file system is full, you will be unable to create a new file or save the editing session of an existing file. In VMS, if you wish to save the editing session of an important file to a disk device that is full, you must either ask the system administrator to make space available or move to another terminal and delete some of your files from the disk that is full. In UNIX, you can stop the current process, fork a new copy of the shell, delete unwanted files, return to the editing session, and save the file. That is, you can rectify the situation without changing terminals or contacting the system administrator.

VMS

form: $ SHOW DEVICES [device-name[:]]
example: $ SHOW DEV/FULL DUA2:
Disk DUA2:, device type RA81, is on-line, mounted, file-oriented device, shareable, available to cluster, error logging is enabled.

Error count	0	Operations completed	321135
Owner process	" "	Owner UIC	[SYSEM,POSTMASTER]

Owner process ID	00000000	Dev Prot	S:RWED,O:RWED,G:RWED,W:RWED
Reference count	19	Default buffer size	512
Total blocks	891072	Sectors per track	51
Total cylinders	1248	Tracks per cylinder	14
Volume label	"USR$DISK1"	Relative volume number	0
Cluster size	1	Transaction count	18
Free blocks	12597	Maximum files allowed	222768
Extend quantity	5	Mount count	1
Mount status	System	Cache name	"_DUA0:XQPCACHE"
Extent cache size	64	Maximum blocks in extent cache	1259
File ID cache size	64	Blocks currently in extent cache	1065
Quota cache size	0	Maximum buffers in FCP cache	273

Volume status: subject to mount verification, file high-water marking, write-through caching enabled.

UNIX

form: % df [option(s)] [filesystem]
example: % df

Filesystem node	total kbytes	kbytes used	kbytes free	percent used	Mounted on
/dev/ra0a	7415	6354	320	95%	/
/dev/ra0g	41847	33635	4028	89%	/usr

The command **df** without options or arguments reports on all mounted file systems, in this example, two. The fields provide information on two file systems, **/** and **/usr**, mounted in the **a** and **g** partitions of the physical device **ra0**. The fields are self-explanatory. The UNIX command **df** reports only file system utilization, whereas the VMS command **SHOW DEVICE/FULL** also reports the physical characteristics of the device. Section 2.3 describes how to determine the physical characteristics of a file system.

The command **df -i** (not shown) reports the file system block and fragment size.

7.3   *Modifying Processes*

UNIX provides five commonly used commands to modify user processes: **kill**, to terminate a process completely; **at**, to start a process at a later time; **nice**, to lower the priority of a process to be executed; **renice**, to lower the priority of a process already running; and **limit**, to reduce the resource limits of a process. Only the system administrator can increase the priority of a process or kill other users' processes.

Some VMS users can modify features of their own processes other than the priority using the **SET PROCESS** command. The ability to make these modifications depends on the privileges assigned by the VMS system administrator. UNIX does not provide the same flexibility, since the system administrator cannot assign a subset of privileges to individual users.

7.3.1 Delete a Process: kill

The command **kill** (compare the VMS command **STOP/IDENTIFI-CATION**) deletes processes. It is a built-in feature of the C shell, but is a separate command in the Bourne shell. To use **kill**, you must specify a process identification number, which you can determine with the **ps** command. The effect of **kill** may vary in different shells. The feature of **kill** described here relates to all shells.

	VMS	UNIX
form:	$ STOP/ID = pid	% kill -[option(s)] processid
example:	$ STOP/ID = AA2019	% kill -9 2019

In this example, **kill -9 2019** deletes the process with the process iden-tification number **2019**. The man page for **kill** indicates that the **9** option is a "sure kill" and will therefore remove a process under all circum-stances. Most users will not need to use more than this version of the **kill** command.

7.3.2 Delaying Execution: at

The command **at** instructs the shell to begin processing command(s) at a later time. The commands may reside in a UNIX file known as a *shell script,* which corresponds to a VMS command procedure, or commands may be entered at the terminal. In either instance, you do not need to be logged in when the system executes the commands. You must redi-rect output from the command(s) to a file or else you will lose it. You may specify various formats for the time of execution, as shown in the following examples.

	VMS	UNIX
form:	$ SUBMIT/AFTER = time file	% at time [day] [file]
	$ RUN PROCESS/DELAY = delta-time file	
example:	$ SUBMIT/AFTER = 23:00 TEST.COM	% at 2300
		test > test.out
		⟨CTRL⟩-D
example:	$ SUBMIT/AFTER = 24-JAN-1988:08:00 TEST.COM	% at 8am jan 24
		test > test.out
		⟨CTRL⟩-D
example:		% at 1530 fr

example:

test > test.out
⟨CTRL⟩-D
% at 1530 fr week
test > test.out
⟨CTRL⟩-D

The command **at 2300** processes the commands contained in the file test, starting at 2300 hours (11 p.m.) on the day the **at** command was issued. If the command was issued at 11:30 p.m., then the system will execute the commands at 11:00 p.m. the following day.

You must type the script file name, and any redirection, on the following line(s). The system will not execute a shell script if entered on the same line as the **at** command. Rather than the name of a shell script file, you may enter any sequence of commands on the following lines. In either instance input to the **at** command is terminated by entering ⟨CTRL⟩-D.

The command **at 8am jan 24** begins processing at 8:00 a.m. on January 24 of the current year if issued before January 24 or of the next year if issued after. The command **at 1530 fr** begins processing on Friday at 3:30 p.m. The command **at 1530 fr week** begins processing at 3:30 p.m. a week from the coming Friday. In all of these examples, the output is directed to the file **test.out**. Error messages will be lost (but could have been saved with a >**&** redirection).

The daemon **cron** will start the **at** program at intervals. The program **cron** looks in the file **/usr/lib/crontab** to determine how often to process **at** requests. A typical interval is 15 mintues, and so a job scheduled to start at 15:31 may not actually start until 15:45.

One basic difference between VMS and UNIX that affects **at** is that UNIX can "remember" the directory from which a command was issued. For example, a VMS user submitting a command file to a batch queue must include commands to set the default directory if commands address files not found in the parent directory. UNIX assumes that the default directory is the one from which the command was issued and not the parent directory.

7.3.3   *Lowering the Priority: nice and renice*

The command **nice** lowers the priority of a command, or a file containing a group of commands (a shell script) prior to execution. The C shell includes **nice**, but it is a separate program for Bourne shell users. Recall that the higher the number associated with the priority, the lower the priority.

	VMS	UNIX
form:	$ SET PROCESS/PRIORITY = n	% nice + [number] command \ [arguments]
example:	$ SET PROCESS/PRIORITY = 1	% nice + 10
example:	$ SET PROCESS/PRIORITY = 1	% nice + 10 f77 myprog.f

The command **nice + 10** adds 10 to the priority of the current shell, that is, it reduces its priority. Similarly, **nice + 10 f77 myprog.f** adds 10 to the priority of the FORTRAN compilation of the source file **myprog.f**.

The command **renice** reduces the priority of processes that are already running. The operating system reduces priority automatically, but you can do so manually. You can reduce a single process, all of a user's processes, or all processes owned by members of the same group. Once you reduce them, you cannot raise the priority of these processes. Only the system administrator can increase the priority of any process running on the system.

	VMS	UNIX
form:	$ SET PROCESS/PRIORITY = 1/ID = nn	% renice priority -[p pid] \ -[g group] -[u user]
example:	$ SET PROCESS/PRIORITY = 1/ID = B34	% renice 10 -p 71823
example:		% renice 10 -g admin
example:		% renice 10 -u fred

The command **renice 10 -p 71823** decreases by 10 the priority of the running process with the identification number **71823**. The command **renice 10 -g admin** lowers the priority of all processes owned by members of the group **admin**, provided the command is issued either by a member of the group **admin** or by the user **root**. Finally, **renice 10 -u fred** lowers the priority of all processes owned by user **fred**, provided **fred** (or **root**) makes the request.

7.3.4   *Lowering System Resource Utilization: limit Revisited*

You have already used **limit** to display the system resources available to a process. You may also use **limit** to reduce them.

	VMS	UNIX
form:	$ SET PROCESS[/qualifier(s)] - process name	% limit resource value
example:		% limit coredumpsize 0

The command **limit coredumpsize 0** prevents the creation of a core dump file in the advent of program failure. Users who do not intend to analyze a memory dump might do well to set this value to 0, thereby preventing large unwanted files from occupying disk space.

7.4   *Summary*

The following scenario uses some of the commands introduced in this chapter. Fred wishes to compile and then run a large C program.

UNIX

example: % w

```
6:24pm    up 8 days,    6:07,    6 users,    load average: 5.23, 5.18, 5.42
```

User	tty	login@	idle	JCPU	PCPU	what
joyce	tty14	4:09pm		4	4	rlogin cuhhmd
jack	tty15	4:09pm		16	4	rlogin cuhhmd
jill	tty27	5:46pm	12	1:12	1	more tmp.F014229
root	ttyp5	2:31pm		12:07	23	-csh[sharp] (csh)
mary	ttyp6	3:14pm	1:11	38	15	-csh[royer] (csh)
fred	ttyp7	5:05pm		1	1	w

```
% cc -o myprog.exe myprog.c >& myprog.out &
[1]    16335
% ps -aux | head
```

USER	PID	%CPU	%MEM	SZ	RSS	TT	STAT	TIME	COMMAND
fred	14516	39.8	11.0	536	244	p7	R	0:01	cc myprog.c >& myprog.out &
joyce	4857	24.8	16.0	236	224	14	R	47:52	f77 /usr/joyce/list.f
jack	14064	19.8	10.3	104	44	15	R	0:00	/usr/public/xplor
jill	14093	16.8	20.2	28	16	27	R	61:39	/usr/public/fft
fred	14517	0.6	0.2	56	28	p7	S	0:00	head
root	81	0.4	0.5	160	100	?	I	45:17	/etc/routed
root	14468	0.4	0.3	104	44	p0	I	0:12	rlogind 803b6202.1022
root	87	0.3	0.4	128	80	?	S	19:31	/etc/rwhod
fred	14065	0.2	0.4	260	64	p7	S	0:00	-csh[system] (csh)

```
% df /usr
```

Filesystem node	total kbytes	kbytes used	kbytes free	percent used	Mounted on
/dev/ra0g	41847	35060	2603	93%	/usr

```
% at 2300
myprog.exe > output
(CTRL)-D
```

Fred first issues the command **w** to determine the number of users and the load on the system. The system is being heavily utilized, having sustained a workload of greater than 5 over the past 15 minutes (that is, five similar computers are necessary to process the workload efficiently). Fred decides to compile and link his program now and, provided no errors occur, run the application later in the evening when the system load will likely be less. The command **cc -o myprog.exe myoprog.c >& myprog.out &** performs the compilation in the background and directs terminal output and error messages to the file **myprog.out** and the executable image to **myprog.exe**. See Section 8.3 for a discussion of background processing. For now it is sufficient to understand that multiple processes may be running simultaneously. Hence, while the system performs the compilation, Fred determines the percentage of system resources utilized by the compilation with the command **ps -aux | head**, which forks a new process and displays the 10 processes currently consuming the most CPU time. Seeing that he is utilizing 39.8% of the available CPU resources, Fred waits for the compilation to finish. Then Fred issues the command **df /usr**, which shows 2.6 megabytes of disk space available on the file system on which he wants to run his application. The disk space is sufficient for the output of **myprog.c**, assuming that the amount of free disk space is not going to change significantly between now and the time that **myprog.c** writes output to the file system. The command **at 2300** will start the application at 11:00 p.m. this evening, regardless of whether or not Fred is logged in. The command **myprog.exe > output** will run the program, directing output to the file **output**; no error messages will be saved. Fred terminates input to the **at** command with ⟨CTRL⟩-D. Fred then goes home, having performed his good deed for the day.

Chapter 8

Devices, Queues, and Background Processing

ho's on first?

Bud Abbott and Lou Costello

This chapter covers the use of printers, magnetic tape drives,[1] and the UNIX equivalent to batch processing. At first glance, these topics may appear unrelated. What they have in common, however, is that each is an example of *multitasking,* the ability to perform two or more tasks simultaneously. VMS users perform most multitasking activities through the use of queues and device allocation. One VMS user queues a job to a printer and performs some other interactive task without having to wait until the job is finished printing. Another VMS user reserves a magnetic tape drive for later use while performing an interactive task. A third VMS user submits a CPU-intensive task to a batch queue and while that is processing edits a file.

This chapter discusses the extent to which UNIX accommodates multitasking features similar to those implemented in VMS, and then goes on to describe features of multitasking unique to UNIX. In UNIX, the printing of files (see Section 8.1) corresponds to VMS: both systems queue files and print them in the order received. The availability of printers to handle UNIX print requests is, of course, site-dependent. Section 8.1 also shows you how to determine the printers available on a UNIX system and how you can use them.

Section 8.2 describes the commands available for reading and writing magnetic tapes. As with printers, the availability of magnetic tape drives and their characteristics are site-dependent. This section also shows you how to determine the magnetic tape drives available on a system and how you can use them for reading and writing files. Section 8.2 concludes with a discussion of methods for exchanging files between UNIX and VMS.

Section 8.2 reveals the shortcomings of UNIX in handling tape drive requests. To be sure, UNIX offers the equivalents of the VMS **BACKUP** and **COPY** commands for reading and writing magnetic tapes. However, it seems that the designers of the early versions of UNIX assumed that individual users would not need to read and write their own magnetic tapes, and that only the system administrator or system operator would

---

1. Throughout this chapter, magnetic tape means any sequential tape medium, for example, ½-inch tape reels and ¼-inch tape cartridges.

have access to tape drives. The result of this assumption is that *anyone can access any mounted magnetic tape in UNIX*. VMS, in contrast, allocates a given tape drive to a single user process.

Section 8.3 introduces the concept of UNIX *background* and *foreground* processing, which shows multitasking at its best. Unlike VMS, which frequently utilizes batch queues, UNIX implementations rarely support batch processing.[2] UNIX achieves multitasking through the use of concurrent foreground and background processing. UNIX users do not submit tasks to a queue, the characteristics of which (for example, process priority or CPU limit) may differ from a user's interactive process. Instead, UNIX users run tasks as separate, detached background processes with the same characteristics as the foreground process. The only difference between foreground and background processes is that only foreground processes may receive input from the keyboard. However, you can easily interchange foreground and background processes, so that you can easily make any process receive input from the keyboard. This powerful feature of UNIX is unfamiliar to VMS users, who can handle only one interactive process in the foreground. We shall explore this UNIX alternative to batch processing as used by the C shell in some detail.

8.1   Using Print Queues

Most versions of UNIX support a *print spooler* for queuing print jobs to one or more printers. The print spooler software may differ from one version of UNIX to another. However, the average user who needs access only to the commands that use the spooler need not be perturbed: the commands that queue files for printing are identical in all versions of UNIX. You need to examine the print spooler software only if you must determine the available printers and their characteristics. In the case of a BSD print spooler, you can determine the printers available by examining the file **/etc/printcap**, a typical example of which appears below.

UNIX

example: % cat /etc/printcap
Printer Definition File 4.2 BSD
lp =   decwriter III

---

2. If, by definition, spooling is regarded as batch processing, then printing and transmitting files via **UUCP** (see Section 13.1) are also.

```
#              lp1 =        talaris t1500 laser printer
# definitions:
#              mx#0         unlimited file size
#              pl#66        page length (lines)
#              pw#80        page width (characters)
#              br#          baud rate
#              lp           device name for output
#              if           accounting text filter /usr/tbin/if
#              of           output filter /usr/tbin/of
#              sd           spool directory
#              lf           error logging filename
#              af           accounting file
#              fc           clear flag bits
#              xc           clear local bits mode
#              fs           like fc but set bits
#              xs           like xc but set bits
lp|local line printer:\
            :af=/usr/adm/lpd-acct:if=/usr/lib/lpf:mx#0:\
            :lp=/dev/tty0f:sd=/usr/spool/lpd:lf=/usr/adm/lpd-errs:\
            :rf=/usr/lib/flpf:br#1200:fs#06320:\
            :sb=default Printer:
lp1|laser|laser printer:\
            :af=/usr/adm/laser:ms#0:pl#66:pw#80\
            :lp=/dev/tty12:sd=/usr/spool/laser:lf=/usr/spool/laser/\
            error:br#4800:fc=0:xc=0:fs=06320:xs=00460:


VMS
example:  $ SHOW QUEUE/DEVICE/FULL
          Terminal queue TTA4, on TTA4, mounted form PORTRAIT/BASE_PRIORITY=4
          /CHAR=(0) /DEFAULT=(FLAG=ONE,FORM=PORTRAIT) /NOENABLE_-
            GENERIC
          /LIBRARY=LN03 Lowercase /OWNER=[SYSEM,POSTMASTER]
          /PROTECTION=(S:E,O:D,G:R,W:W) /SEPARATE=(RESET=(RESET))
```

Note the similar formats of **/etc/printcap** and **/etc/termcap** (see Section 3.1). If you need information on the variables used to define the characteristics of each queue, display the on-line man page entry for **printcap**, consult your system administrator, or simply attempt to print a file on each of the available printers. To do the latter, you must know the name(s) your system uses to address each queue. The BSD version of UNIX provides this information in the **/etc/printcap** file.[3]

---

3. Other versions of UNIX, for example, some implementations of System V, support a version of the BSD print spooler and therefore use an **/etc/printcap** file.

The sample **/etc/printcap** file above begins with a number of comment lines, identified as usual by # occurring as the first non-blank character of a record. Definitions of two printers follow. The backslash (\) at the end of a line indicates that the definition continues on the following line. Colons (:) separate the fields within each definition. The first field in each printer definition gives the printer's names; vertical bars (|) separate each name. In the above example, the first printer is addressed as either **lp** or "**local line printer**," and the second printer is either **lp1**, **laser**, or "**laser printer**." If the printer name is a phrase rather than a single word, you must surround the phrase with double quotes in all commands so that the shell can distinguish the queue name from the names of the files being printed. If the command line does not address a specific printer, the system defaults to **lp** (the same as **lp0**; compare the VMS logical name **SYS$PRINT**). You may modify the definition of the default printer with the environment variable **PRINTER**. The two sample printer definitions described in the **/etc/printcap** file will be used in examples of the print commands described below.

Printing files in UNIX differs from VMS in two major ways. First, by default, VMS print queues sequence jobs on the basis of size, irrespective of the order received.[4] UNIX, on the other hand, queues print jobs in the order received. Second, unlike VMS, BSD UNIX does not support a *generic queue*, which places jobs in a single queue supporting more than one printer, and then prints jobs on the first available printer. UNIX print queuing is explicit: there is a separate queue for each printer.

8.1.1   *Submitting Print Jobs: lpr*

The commands **lpr** (offline print, available in all versions of UNIX) and **print** (print to the line printer, available in BSD only) queue any files with a protection that renders them readable by the user for printing (compare the VMS command **PRINT**).[5] The command **print** is a one-line shell script (see Chapter 11) containing the command **lpr -p**, also written as **pr file | lpr**. Both **print** and **lpr -p** invoke the **pr** command to format a

---

4. The VMS system administrator may use the command **INITIALIZE/QUEUE/ SCHEDULE=NOSIZE** to override the default condition, thus printing jobs in the order received.

5. The term "line printer" is a historical quirk; today it means any kind of printer, including character and laser printers.

file prior to printing. One function of **pr**, discussed in Section 9.2.3, places a header at the top of each page (compare the VMS command **PRINT/HEADER**).

The following examples illustrate the major options of the **lpr** command. The following discussion omits site-dependent features, such as addressing different fonts on printers that support multiple fonts.

	VMS	UNIX
form:	$ PRINT[/QUALIFIER(S)] file-spec[, . . .]	% lpr [option(s)] file(s)
example:	$ PRINT FILE1.,FILE2.	% lpr file1 file2
example:	$ PRINT/COPIES = 3/QUEUE = LASER FILEA.	% lpr -Plaser -#3 filea
example:	$ PRINT/DELETE FILEB.	% lpr -r fileb
example:	$ PRINT/NOFLAG/QUEUE = LASER FILEC.	% lpr -hPlaser filec
example:	$ PRINT/HEADER FILED.	% lpr -p filed # or print \ filed
example:	$ DEFINE SYS$PRINT TTA4: $ PRINT FILEZ.	% setenv PRINTER laser % lpr filez
example:		% lpr -s filee
example:		% lpr -f filef

The command **lpr file1 file2** queues two files to the default printer, and **lpr -Plaser -#3 filea** queues three copies (**#3** option) of **filea** to the printer named **laser** (**Plaser** option) defined in the **/etc/printcap** file. The command **lpr -r fileb** prints **fileb** on the default printer and then deletes it (**r** option). **lpr -hPlaser filec** queues **filec** to the printer named **laser** and prints it without the banner page (**h** option). **lpr -p filed** (or **print filed**) prints a header at the top of each page, and **setenv PRINTER laser** establishes an environment variable that redefines the default system printer **lp**. All print requests that do not use the **P** option are sent to the laser printer rather than **lp**.

The six examples of **lpr** discussed thus far are similar to variations of the VMS **PRINT** command; the following two are peculiar to UNIX. You can use **lpr -s filee** to print large files. This command does not queue **filee** in the spool directory (defined as **/usr/spool/lpd** in the **/etc/printcap** file for the default printer), since the spool directory could reside on a file system with insufficient free disk space to accommodate it. Rather, **lpr -s filee** prints the file directly from the user's directory. If you use **lpr -s** to print a particular version of a file, and then later unthinkingly make changes to that file, **lpr -s** prints the latest version of the file available at the time the file begins printing. In other words, the printed file would incorporate any changes made to the file between the time you added the print job to the queue and the time the file actually prints. If the file had been spooled, that is, copied to the spool directory, the version printed would be the version that existed when you issued the print command.

The command **lpr -f filef** prints **filef** using any FORTRAN carriage control characters present in column 1. Without the **f** option, UNIX ignores these control characters and prints them like any other characters.

8.1.2 Examining Print Queues: lpq

The **lpq** (line printer queue) command lists the contents of a print queue; that is, it displays a list of jobs that are printing or waiting to print (compare the VMS command **SHOW QUEUE**). Like **lpr**, **lpq** assumes the default queue unless you specify an alternative.

	VMS	UNIX
form:	$ SHOW QUEUE[/QUALIFIER(S)] queue-name	% lpq [option(s)] [-Pprinter] [job #] [user]
example:	$ SHOW QUEUE LASER	% lpq -Plaser

VMS:
Terminal queue laser, on tta4

Jobname	Username	Entry	Blocks	Status
-------	-------	------	------	------
LOGIN.COM	SYSTEM	70	3	Printing
RESET.DAT	SYSTEM	71	3	Pending

UNIX:

Rank	Owner	Job	Files	Total Size
active	root	70	.login	913 bytes
2nd	root	71	/tmp/reset	22 bytes

example: % lpq fred
example: % lpq 71

The command **lpq -Plaser** displays information about the queue **laser**. By default, VMS displays information only about those jobs owned by the user making the request.[6] UNIX, on the other hand, displays all jobs. As with the VMS **PRINT** command, each UNIX **lpr** command constitutes a single job irrespective of the number of files specified on the command line. The command **lpq** displays jobs in the order to be printed (rank). For each job, **lpq** displays the owner, the job number, the file(s) to be printed, and the size of the job in bytes.

The command **lpq fred** displays information only on those jobs owned by user **fred** in the default print queue; **lpq 71** displays information about job **71** in the default print queue.

---

6. Most VMS users invoke the **SHOW QUEUE/ALL** command to display all queued jobs.

8.1.3   *Removing Queued Print Jobs: lprm*

The command **lprm** (line printer remove) deletes one or more of your jobs from the print queue; you cannot remove other users' print jobs (compare the VMS commands **DELETE/ENTRY** and **STOP/ABORT**). The syntax for specifying an alternative print queue is consistent with that of the **lpr** and **lpq** commands. The job being deleted may be printing or pending.

	VMS	UNIX
form:	$ DELETE/ENTRY = entry-number queue-name	% lprm [-Pprinter] [job #] \ [user]
example:	$ DELETE/ENTRY = 71 LASER	% lprm -Plaser 71 dfA071cuhhca dequeued cfA071cuhhca dequeued
example:		% lprm - dfA072cuhhca dequeued cfA072cuhhca dequeued

The command **lprm -Plaser 71** removes job **71** from the laser print queue. Unlike the VMS **DELETE/ENTRY** command, **lprm** informs you of dequeued jobs. The command **lprm -**, which has no VMS equivalent, removes from the default printer queue all jobs owned by the user making the request. UNIX offers no mechanism to requeue a job; you must first delete the job from one queue and then submit it to another.

8.2   *Using Tape Drives*

It is common practice to use tape drives to make personal archives of important files or to import and export data. UNIX provides several commands for reading and writing magnetic tapes: **tar** (tape archiver) is the most frequently used for creating personal archives and for importing and exporting files between UNIX systems, since all UNIX systems support it. The command **dd** (convert and copy a file) reads and writes files in non-standard formats. The command **mt**, although not specifically used to read or write magnetic tape data, positions a magnetic tape, writes an EOF (end-of-file) mark on a magnetic tape, or places a magnetic tape off-line. Finally, the system administrator uses the **dump** and **restore** commands (not discussed here) to archive and retrieve whole file systems. Note that **restore** is valid only for magnetic tapes written with the **dump** command; it will not read a magnetic tape written with **tar**. Like the VMS **BACKUP** command, **tar** and **dd** can also perform disk-to-disk copying.

UNIX handles tape drive requests clumsily. In VMS, you can determine the availability of a tape drive, allocate the drive, and mount the magnetic tape for reading or writing; most versions of UNIX do not support these features. Without the ability to allocate a tape drive, UNIX has no mechanism to prevent a user from inadvertently (or purposefully) reading from or writing to another user's tape while it is on the tape drive and on-line! Not surprisingly, some versions of UNIX have been enhanced to permit the allocation of a tape drive to a specific user.

To determine which tape drives are available on a UNIX system, a principle introduced in Section 2.3 is brought into play. You use a special device file to address devices. That is, tape drives are accessed as if they were files. The address of each tape drive resides as a file entry in the directory **/dev**. A single tape drive may have multiple entries, each entry defining a different way to use the device: for example, to read or write at different densities (compare the VMS command **BACKUP/DENSITY**) or to specify whether or not to rewind the tape after each read or write (compare the VMS command **BACKUP/REWIND**). Different versions of UNIX use different names for these device files, but most names include the string **mt**.

	UNIX
example:	% ls -l /dev/*mt*

crw-rw-rw-	1	root	36,		12 May	2	15:26	/dev/nrmt0h
crw-rw-rw-	1	root	36,		4 May	2	15:26	/dev/nrmt0l
crw-rw-rw-	1	root	36,		8 Jun	22	17:13	/dev/rmt0h
crw-rw-rw-	1	root	36,		0 May	2	15:26	/dev/rmt0l

This example, from the ULTRIX version of UNIX, defines two devices, **mt0l** and **mt0h**. **/dev/rmt0h** is a raw character device (**rmt**): it processes input and output as a stream of characters. **/dev/nrmt0h** buffers character input and output (**nrmt**). Since raw character devices are commonly used in the reading and writing of UNIX tapes, we use them for the examples in this book. See Section 2.2 for more information about raw character devices and their relation to disk devices. You can also check the on-line man pages for each system.

Your system may have several device files, but there is no guarantee that each of these files represents a device available to users. You should therefore check with your system administrator for information on available tape drives, the device files with which to access them, and the default. To illustrate how to use different tape drives or different features of the same tape drive at the command level, we will use the two character device files **/dev/rmt0h** and **/dev/rmt0l** from the example shown above.

Each version of UNIX defines one of the available tape device files as the default; in ULTRIX it is **/dev/rmt0h**. In the C shell, you can define your own tape drive default with the **TAPE** environment variable, in the same way that you can define a specific printer as the default with the **PRINTER** environment variable. For example, the command **setenv TAPE /dev/rmt0l** changes the default tape drive to **rmt0l**.

8.2.1   *Archiving Files: tar*

The UNIX **tar** command (compare the VMS **BACKUP** command) reads and writes personal archive tapes and imports and exports files from one UNIX processor to another. Note the following contrasts and similarities:

1. Unlike VMS **BACKUP/VERIFY**, **tar** does not support file verification, which checks the files on the magnetic tape against the files on the disk.

2. **tar** does not support writing to multiple magnetic tapes. In VMS, **BACKUP** requests additional magnetic tapes be mounted as necessary; the **tar** user, on the other hand, can archive only those files that fit on a single magnetic tape.[7] If the target tape lacks the capacity to accommodate all the files you want to transfer, you must complete the copy operation by listing the contents of the first tape, mounting a second tape, and issuing a new **tar** command specifying the files that remain to be copied.

3. In VMS, **BACKUP** writes a directory hierarchy to a **BACKUP SAVE-SET** either on disk or magnetic tape, which you may then treat as a single file using VMS file manipulation commands. The command **tar** also copies directory hierarchies to magnetic tape and disk for treatment as a single file.

4. You can append files to an existing **tar** magnetic tape as a separate **tar** file. You can use the **mt** command to skip **tar** files. In VMS,

---

7. A single **tar** tape can accommodate approximately 100 megabytes of data at 6250 bits per inch (bpi) and 30 megabytes at 1600 bpi.

BACKUP appends files as a separate save-set, with a separate header including the save-set name and the date it was written. The VMS user then selects the save-set using the appropriate save-set name.

5. Both VMS **BACKUP** and **tar** are recursive when saving or extracting files if the appropriate file specification is given. That is, if the file specification for **tar** includes a directory, the contents of that directory and any subdirectories will also be included in the save or extract operation. In the simplest form, with no file specification, **tar** will save all files from the current directory and any subdirectories in a save operation or extract all files on the tape in an extract operation.

6. Both VMS **BACKUP** and UNIX **tar** support absolute and relative pathnames for naming files. If you write files to tape using absolute pathnames, the files must be copied from tape back to their original directories. If you use a relative pathname to save files, the files will be copied from tape to directories relative to the present working directory. As in the case of any command that writes files, you must have write access to the directory which is to contain the restored files.

7. If you restore a file to a directory on disk that already contains a file of the same name, **tar** will overwrite the original file. The behavior of the VMS **BACKUP** command depends on the qualifiers you use. By default, if the file on the magnetic tape and the existing file on disk are identical, **BACKUP** will notify you that the file already exists and will not restore the file from magnetic tape.

UNIX users and system administrators who need to save whole file systems should use the command **dump** for saving files to magnetic tape and the command **restore** for restoring them to disk. The system administrator (user **root**) using the **dump** command can update the file **/etc/dumpdates**, which keeps a record of when a file system was last saved, either completely or in part. The header of a **dump** magnetic tape contains a listing of the files on the tape, including the directory hierarchy of the file system. The **restore** command is used, first to select files or directories to be restored, and then to extract the selected files from magnetic tape.

8.2.1.1   *Writing Files to Tape*

The following examples illustrate writing files to the beginning of a tape and appending files to a **tar** tape.

	VMS	UNIX
form:	$ BACKUP[/QUALIFIER(S)] file-spec[, . . .] - tape_device:saveset	% tar [option(s)] file(s)
example:	$ ALLOCATE MUA0: MYTAPE $ MOUNT/FOREIGN MYTAPE $ BACKUP/REWIND/LOG/RECORD - DUA1:[FRED. . .]*.*;* MUA0:ARCHIVE.BCK	% tar -cv ˜fred
example:	$ BACKUP/REWIND/LIST = NL: - MUA0:ARCHIVE.BCK $ BACKUP/NOREWIND/RECORD/ - SINCE = BACKUP - /LOG DUA1:[FRED. . .]*.*;* - MUA0:ARCHIVE1.BCK	% tar -ruv ˜fred
example:	$ MOUNT/FOREIGN/DENSITY = 6250 MTA0: $ BACKUP/REWIND/DENSITY = 6250 - FILE1.,FILE2. MTA0:EXPORT.BCK	% tar -cf /dev/rmt0h file1 file2

In the first example, **tar -cv ˜fred** copies all the files of user **fred** to the beginning of the tape using the **c** option. The **v** option (verbose) informs the user as each file is copied. The files are written to tape using the default tape device.[8]

The second example, **tar -ruv ˜fred**, illustrates the later incremental save of **fred**'s files. This command appends the new files following any existing files on tape (**r** option); copies only files created or modified since the tape was originally written, that is, different from the files already on tape (**u** option); and once again informs the user as it copies files (**v** option). Note the analogy to the VMS command **BACKUP**, which creates a new save-set after you position the tape at the end of the first save-set by listing the contents of the first save-set to the null device. Positioning the tape should not be necessary if the **/NOREWIND** qualifier (the default) is used with **BACKUP**. However, because of problems with early versions of **BACKUP**, some users feel more comfortable positioning the tape first. VMS then selects files for copying to magnetic tape by looking for the backup recording date in the header record of each disk file.

The last example illustrates the use of an alternative tape device. The command **tar -cf /dev/rmt0h file1 file2** writes two files, assumed to be in the present working directory, to the beginning of a tape (**c** option). Rather than using the default tape device file specification, this com-

---

8. Unlike most other UNIX commands, **tar** does not require a minus sign preceding options. However, for consistency it is included here.

mand uses an alternative, defined by the **f /dev/rmt0h** option (that is, **f** followed by a tape device filename). This command could, for example, write to a tape drive that supports the reading and writing of tapes at a density of 6250 bpi, rather than 1600 bpi as indicated by the default tape device file specification.

8.2.1.2   *Listing Tape Contents*

The **t** option lists the contents of **tar** tapes.

	VMS	UNIX
example:	$ BACKUP/REWIND/LIST MUA0:SAVE.BCK	% tar -t
		/usr/file1
		doc/book.txt
		./myprog.f
		. ./oneup.c
example:	$ MOUNT/FOREIGN/DENSITY = 6250 MTA0:	
	$ BACKUP/LIST = SYS$PRINT MTA0:EXPORT.BCK	% tar -tf /dev/rmt0l | lpr

In the first example, **tar -t** displays the files on the magnetic tape at the terminal. The listing shows file specifications for four different types of files: **/usr/file1** is an absolute file specification, **doc/book.txt** is a relative file specification, **./myprog.f** indicates a file from the present working directory, and **. ./oneup.c** is a file in a directory one above the present working directory. The implications of these different types of file specifications will become clear in the next section, which discusses restoring files from tape. In the second example, **tar -tf /dev/rmt0l | lpr** pipes the output of the **tar** display command to the default printer. The tape is mounted on device **/dev/rmt0l**.

8.2.1.3   *Extracting Files from Tape*

The **x** option of **tar** restores (extracts) files from tape.

	VMS	UNIX
example:	$ BACKUP/REWIND/LOG MUA0:SAVE.BCK *	% tar -xv
		x /usr/file1
		x ./doc/book.txt
		x ./myprog.f
		x . ./oneup.c
example:	$ BACKUP/REWIND/SELECT = MYPROG.FOR -	
	MUA0:SAVE.BCK *	% tar -xm ./myprog.f

In the first example, **tar -xv** without file arguments extracts (**x** option) the contents of the whole tape, reporting on each file as it is restored (**v** option). The file definition **/usr/file1** is absolute; **file1** is written specifically to **/usr**, overwriting any existing file with the same name. Only user **root** could issue this command, for usually **/usr** may not be written to by all users. The response **./doc/book.txt** indicates that the file **book.txt** is being restored to a subdirectory **doc** of the present working directory. This present working directory can be different from the one from which the file was originally saved. The response **. ./oneup.c** indicates that the file **oneup.c** is being restored to a directory one level higher than the present working directory. When restoring files with relative filenames, you should be in the correct working directory before you issue a **tar** restore command.

This example illustrates the flexibility of **tar**, which can use both absolute and relative pathnames. The use of absolute pathnames, however, is not recommended, particularly if you are going to export files to another UNIX computer. You may not have write access to the directory into which you wish to restore the files (assuming it exists), and even if you do, you may overwrite important files already in the directory.

In the second example, **tar -xm ./myprog.f** extracts the single file **myprog.f**. The **m** option updates the file's modification date to the time the file was extracted. The default condition, like the VMS command **BACKUP**, maintains the modification date that existed at the time the file was originally saved.

8.2.1.4   *Disk-to-Disk Copying*

You can use **tar** for disk-to-disk copying. It is particularly useful if you wish to maintain directory hierarchies during the copy operation.

	VMS	UNIX
example:	$ BACKUP [FRED. . .]*.*;* FRED.BCK - /SAVE_SET	% tar -cvf /tmp/tar_save /usr/ \ fred
example:	VMS	
	$ BACKUP [FRED. . .]*.*;* [JOHN. . .]*.*;*	
	UNIX	
	% cd /usr/fred ; tar -cf - . | (cd /usr/john ; -tar -xf -)	

The command **tar -cvf /tmp/tar_save /usr/fred** saves all files from **/usr/fred** down the directory hierarchy to the **tar** file **/tmp/tar_save**. You can restore files later from this **tar** file or list them with the command **tar -tf /tmp/tar_save**. Note that here the **f** option indicates a **tar** file on disk. In the previous examples, the **f** option points to a device special file, synonymous with a magnetic tape drive with a predefined set of characteristics.

The command construct **cd /usr/fred ; tar -cf - . | (cd /usr/john ; tar -xf -)** is more complex. First it changes the directory **/usr/fred**. Then, rather than writing the files read by **tar** to magnetic tape, it pipes them to another command sequence (-), which first changes the directory to **/usr/john** and then extracts the files using the input from the previous command in the pipe. File **/usr/fred/filea** thus becomes **/usr/john/filea**, **/usr/fred/doc/fileb** becomes **/usr/john/doc/fileb**, and so on. An alternative method of copying directory hierarchies, the **cp -r** command, is discussed in Section 9.3.1.

8.2.2   *Special Tape Formatting: dd*

The command **tar** writes files to magnetic tape in a specific format, useful if you wish to read the magnetic tape on another UNIX processor, because all UNIX processors support **tar**. If a non-UNIX processor will read the tape, you can use **dd** to write the magnetic tape in a more generic format. Conversely, you can use **dd** to read magnetic tapes written on a non-UNIX processor. Section 8.2.4, which deals with the exchange of files on magnetic tape between UNIX and VAX/VMS computers, discusses **dd** in detail. Three general examples are given here. Note that the format of the **dd** command is different from anything you have encountered before.

```
          UNIX
form:     % dd [option(s) = value(s)]
example:  % dd if = myfile.dat of = /dev/rmt0h ibs = 3120 cbs = 80 conv = block
          40 + 5 records in
          10 + 1 records out
example:  % dd if = /dev/rmt0h of = ˜fred/ibm.dat ibs = 800 cbs = 80 conv = ascii,lcase
          40 + 5 records in
          27 + 1 records out
example:  % dd if = /dev/rmt0l of = /tmp/catfile ibs = 3120 cbs = 80 conv = ascii,lcase \
              files = 3
          1340 + 385 records in
          4276 + 911 records out
```

The first example illustrates writing a file to magnetic tape with **dd**, and the latter two examples illustrate reading files from magnetic tape. The command **dd if=myfile.dat of=/dev/rmt0h ibs=3120 cbs=80 conv=block** writes the file **myfile.dat** to magnetic tape; **if** defines the input file, **of=/dev/rmt0h** defines the output file, which is the device file for the magnetic tape drive. Unlike **tar**, **dd** does not assume a default for input or output. **ibs** defines the block size, and **cbs** defines the record size.

The second example, **dd if=/dev/rmt0h of=˜fred/ibm.dat ibs=800 cbs=80 conv=ascii,lcase**, resembles the one given in the man page for **dd**. The string **conv=ascii,lcase** converts EBCDIC to ASCII and maps uppercase characters to lowercase.

Normally, you use **dd** to read or write a single file, but you can also append multiple input files on magnetic tape to a single output file, as shown in the third example. The command **dd if=/dev/rmt0l of=/tmp/ catfile ibs=3120 cbs=80 conv=ascii,lcase files=3** reads the first three files from magnetic tape and combines them into a single output file, **/tmp/catfile**. As we shall see in the following section, the user can skip any number of files before reading files.

8.2.3   *Tape Manipulation: mt*

The command **mt** positions a magnetic tape, writes EOF (end-of-file) marks on the tape, or rewinds a tape and places the tape drive off-line. It is often used in conjunction with **dd** to position the magnetic tape while extracting files.

	UNIX
form:	% mt [-f tapename] command [count]
example:	% mt -f /dev/rmt0l rewind
example:	% mt fsf 4
example:	% mt offline

In the first example, **mt -f /dev/rmt0l rewind** completely rewinds the magnetic tape on the tape drive specified by the special device file **/dev/ rmt0l** and leaves it on-line. In the second example, **mt fsf 4** moves the magnetic tape on the default tape drive forward four files from the current position. These four files could be four **tar** files, each containing one or more files. You should issue the command in the final example, **mt offline**, the moment you have finished with the magnetic tape. Once rewound and placed off-line, the tape is inaccessible to other users unless physically loaded and placed on-line again. Other useful **mt** command options are:

eof [count]	Write **count** end-of file marks at the current position
fsr [count]	Move forward **count** records from the current position
bsr [count]	Move back **count** records from the current position
bsf [count]	Move back **count** files (as defined by EOF marks) from the current position

Each of these commands assumes that you know the current position of the magnetic tape relative to the files, and the records it contains.

8.2.4   *VMS-to-UNIX Tape Exchange*

To determine the most straightforward method of exchanging files written on magnetic tape between computers using VMS and computers using UNIX, you should consult the system administrator of each computer. The version of UNIX that the computer uses and any locally written software will likely affect the choice of a method. In any event, it is unlikely that you can read a VMS **BACKUP** tape on a UNIX computer or that you can read a UNIX **tar** tape on a VMS computer, as the magnetic tape formats used by **tar** and **BACKUP** are not easily translated. Nevertheless, the exchange of files written on magnetic tape is possible; this section describes two common methods.

The first method uses the command **ltf** (labelled tape facility), unique to the ULTRIX version of UNIX, for reading magnetic tapes written with the VMS **COPY** command and for writing magnetic tapes readable by **COPY**. The second method uses the **dd** command, available in all versions of UNIX, to read or write files with a fixed record length and block size. Use of **dd** assumes that the VAX/VMS computer can read files with fixed block and fixed record lengths from, or write them to, a magnetic tape with no tape label. VMS does not provide a utility to accomplish this task.[9] However, you can write a simple high-level language program as detailed below.

---

9. The layered software DECShell can read **tar** tapes on a VAX/VMS system.

```
                UNIX to VMS
form:           % ltf [option(s)] file(s)
example:        % ltf -cfB /dev/rmt0h 800 file1 file2 file3
                $ MOUNT/DENSITY = 6250/BLOCKSIZE = 800 MTA0: ULTRIX
                $ COPY MTA0:*.* *.*

                VMS to UNIX
example:        $ INITIALIZE MUA0: VAXVMS
                $ MOUNT/BLOCKSIZE = 800 MUA0: VAXVMS
                $ COPY FILE1.DAT, FILE2.DAT MUA0:*.*
                % ltf -xvBL 800 VAXVMS
                x file1.dat
                x file2.dat
```

The first example illustrates ULTRIX-to-VMS file exchange. The command **ltf -cfB /dev/rmt0l 800 file1 file2 file3** writes three files to the device specified by the special device file **/dev/rmt0l**. The command sets the tape block size to 800 (**B 800** option) and writes the files at the beginning of the tape (**c** option). Note the similarity to the **tar** syntax. The user then moves the tape to the VAX/VMS computer and mounts it as a Files-11 device (the standard VMS device structure) with a volume label of **ULTRIX** (the default written by **ltf**) and a block size of **800**. The VMS **COPY** command copies the files from the tape.

The second example, **ltf -xvBL 800 VAXVMS**, illustrates VMS-to-ULTRIX file exchange. A tape is written using the VMS **COPY** command. The tape is initialized with the volume label **VAXVMS** and mounted with the block size of 800 bytes. With the files copied to tape, the tape is moved to the ULTRIX computer and the files extracted (**x** option). The default tape device file specification is used and a non-default tape label is specified (**L VAXVMS** option). The command **ltf** reports on each file as it is copied (**v** option).

The second method uses **dd** to read files written on a VAX/VMS computer, or to write files to be read by a VAX/VMS computer. Both applications use a fixed-block length, a fixed-record length, and no tape label.

```
                UNIX
example:        % dd if = /dev/rmt0h of = foo ibs = 800 cbs = 80 \
                    conv = unblock
                40 + 5 records in
                27 + 1 records out
example:        % dd if = /dev/rmt0h of = foo1 ibs = 800 cbs = 80 \
```

The command **dd if=/dev/rmt0h of=foo ibs=800 cbs=80 conv= unblock** copies the first file on tape to the file **foo**. The conversion **conv=unblock** converts fixed to variable length records. Without this conversion, UNIX will set the record length to the block size, which is dependent on the disk partition (Section 2.3) and may well be 512 bytes. If the tape is not rewound, you can repeat the command for additional files. As the command **dd if=/dev/rmt0h of=foo1 ibs=800 cbs=80 conv=unblock files=3** in the second example illustrates, you can use the **files** option to concatenate input files to form a single output file. In this example, the command concatenates three files on tape to form a single output file, **foo1**. Finally, **dd if=foo1 of=/dev/rmt0h ibs=800 cbs=80 conv=block** writes the file **foo1** to the tape drive defined by **/dev/rmt0h**, with fixed length records of 80 bytes (that is, as a card image) and 10 records per block. You could read the file **foo1** from tape with a simple program like the one shown below, written in VAX FORTRAN:

example:

```
VMS
$ TYPE TAPEREAD.FOR
C Template program to read fixed block and record magnetic tapes
C Assumes: BLOCKSIZE = 800 bytes ; RECORDSIZE = 80 bytes ; No Label
C
C
        CHARACTER LINES(10) * 80
C Open Input Tape File
        OPEN(UNIT=1, NAME='TAPE', RECORDSIZE=800, BLOCKSIZE=800)
C Open Output Disk File
        OPEN(UNIT=2, NAME='FOO1.DAT', CARRIAGECONTROL='LIST')
C Read a block of data from tape
5       READ(1,10,END=1000) (LINES(JJ),JJ=1,10)
10      FORMAT (⟨10⟩A80)
C Write a block of data to disk
        WRITE(2,10) (LINES(JJ),JJ=1,10)
C Go back for next tape block
        GO TO 5
C File completely read so exit
1000    CLOSE (UNIT=1)
        CLOSE (UNIT=2)
```

```
            END
$ ALLOCATE MUA0: TAPE
$ MOUNT/BLOCKSIZE = 800 TAPE
$ RUN TAPEREAD
```

8.3   *Background Processing*

The C shell (csh) and the Korn shell (ksh), but not the Bourne shell (sh), support *background processing*. A background process is a separate task, called a *job,* that may either be running or stopped. A user may have one *foreground job* and several *background jobs* running simultaneously, constituting a multitasking environment. A UNIX background job has all the features of a foreground job, with one exception: only the foreground job can receive input from the terminal. This fact is not a restriction, as we shall see, since foreground and background jobs are easily interchangeable.

The analogy to background processing in VMS is the spawning of a subprocess (see Section 2.1.1), which is less powerful. VMS makes up for its deficiencies through the use of batch queues, which are not standard in UNIX.

Background jobs in UNIX differ from jobs submitted to VMS batch queues in two ways. First, UNIX background jobs can make the same demands on system resources as any of a user's interactive processes. They are not restricted by the same limitations imposed on a VMS batch queue, such as lower priority, or a CPU time limit, although some implementations of the C shell reduce the priority of a background process that has been running for a predefined period of time (see the command **nice** in Section 7.3.3). Second, VMS batch jobs continue processing when you logout. What happens to UNIX background jobs when you log out depends on whether the background job is running or stopped. If you attempt to log out with stopped background jobs, the system responds with the message, "There are stopped jobs." You may attend to these background jobs or issue the **logout** command again (or ⟨CTRL⟩-D, depending on **ignoreeof**), which terminates all stopped background jobs. Background jobs that are running when you log out continue processing.[10] If you log back in, the background job started in

---

10. This is true of BSD and the C shell, but may differ for other versions of UNIX.

the previous terminal session no longer functions as a child process of the current parent shell; that is, it is not a background job of the current terminal session and cannot be manipulated or examined like other background jobs. However, you can treat it like any other process you own and can examine or modify it using the commands outlined in Chapter 7. Thus, you can issue the command **ps -aux | grep user** to display the characteristics of the process (see Section 9.4.5 for a discussion of **grep**).

8.3.1 Moving Command Execution to Background

To execute a command in the background, end the command with an ampersand (**&**). You can also stop a command which is running in foreground by pressing ⟨CTRL⟩-Z. In both cases, you receive a new copy of the shell with a unique process number for foreground processing. Note that jobs stopped with ⟨CTRL⟩-Z remain inactive until you either restart them in the foreground or start them in the background (see Section 8.3.3).

The following examples, used again in subsequent sections, illustrate the use of background processing to perform interactive tasks in parallel. Compare VMS, which performs tasks sequentially, or in parallel using one or more batch jobs to complement a single interactive process.

```
         UNIX
form:    % command &
example: % find / -name myfile -print > find.out &
         [1] 15781
form:    % command
         ⟨CTRL⟩-Z
example: % grep "hello again" /usr/file1 > grep.out
         ⟨CTRL⟩-Z
         Stopped
         % ps
           PID   TT   STAT   TIME COMMAND-csh[user] (csh)
           15229 p2   S      0:04 find / -name myfile -print > find.out
           15781 p2   R      0:02 grep "hello again" /usr/file1 > grep.out
           15792 p2   T      0:01 ps
           15804 p2   R      0:00
```

The first example, **find / -name myfile -print > find.out &** starts a background job. The system returns a job number, identified by square brackets, and a process number. In the second example, **grep "hello**

again" /usr/file1 > grep.out was already running when stopped with ⟨ ⟨CTRL⟩-Z. In this case, the system does not report the process number and the job number.

The **ps** command (see Section 7.1.3) issued at this point displays four processes: the parent process **csh**, and three child processes, two for the background jobs and one for the **ps** command itself. The state field (**STAT**) indicates that the **ps** and **find** processes are running (**R**), the shell process (**csh**) has been inactive for a few seconds (**S**), and the **grep** process is stopped (**T**).

Note the use of the > metacharacter to redirect the output of the background process to a file. Without this redirection, the system outputs the results of the background jobs to **stdout**, the terminal (compare the VMS logical name **SYS$OUTPUT**). The simultaneous display of output from foreground and background jobs can be confusing. By redirecting the output to a file, you can easily review it at a later time. Another method for preventing the simultaneous display of output from multiple jobs is to issue the shell command **stty tostop**. With this command set, background jobs about to display output will stop processing until brought to the foreground. Of course, this method is less efficient than the first, inasmuch as it interrupts the processing of background jobs. The default **stty -tostop** negates the effect of **stty tostop**.

If background processes are likely to generate error messages, you should also redirect them from **stderr**, the terminal (compare the VMS logical name **SYS$ERROR**), to the same file capturing **stdout**; >**&** directs both standard output and error messages to the same file.

The system notifies you when a background job is completed. By default, the system notifies you just before the shell prompt reappears, that is, at the completion of a foreground command. C shell users can receive immediate notification by setting **notify**. **notify** without arguments toggles notification on and off. You can set **notify** in the .cshrc file to have it be in effect for every process generated.

8.3.2   *Examining Background Jobs*

You can use the **jobs** shell command to examine the status of any background jobs started by the current parent shell.

The fields displayed by the **jobs** shell command are:

[1]	Job number
+/−	Job status: current/next-to-current
Running/Stopped	State of each job
find / -name. . . .	Command being executed

Note that "current" does not imply processing order but relates to the order in which jobs are affected by the foreground process. The current background job is the last one affected by the foreground process, and the next-to-current background job is the one prior to the current background job that was affected by the foreground process.

The following section explains how to manipulate background jobs using either the *job number* or the *job status*.

8.3.3 Manipulating Background Jobs

In the following example, we have added to the two background jobs described in the previous example, a C language compilation (**cc**), a file edit (**vi**), and the display of a file (**more**). We will use this so-called *job stack* to illustrate the manipulation of background and foreground jobs.

```
example:    % stop %3
            [3] + Stopped   cc /usr/progs/calc.c >& errlog
form:       % kill job_number
example:    % kill %4
            [4]   Terminated   vi users.lis
```

The **jobs** command displays the current job stack. Note the additional information displayed for job 5 (**[5]**): **tty output** indicates that the **more** command was sending output to the terminal at the time it was stopped.

In the first example, **%2 &** changes the status of a background job (**[2]**) from stopped to running. The command **bg 2** (background 2) has the same effect. In the second example, **%5** brings job 5 to the foreground; **fg 5** (foreground 5) has the same effect. The commands **bg** and **fg** issued without arguments place the current job (+) in background or bring it to foreground, respectively. In the third example, **stop %3** changes the status of the third background job from running to stopped.

Note that when you change the status of a background job as in each of the above examples, that background job becomes the current job (+). Note also that if you change directory after submitting a background job, when you bring that job to foreground, the shell returns to the directory from which you issued the command to submit the background job. Once that job is completed, the directory to which you moved will once again become the current directory.[11]

In the fourth example, **kill %4** removes the fourth background job completely. Note the analogy to **kill** (see Section 7.3.1) for removing a process according to its process identification number.

8.4   *Batch Processing*

The fact that you can simultaneously execute a number of interactive tasks in UNIX but cannot do so easily in VMS reflects a basic difference in the typical use of each operating system. The VMS user is usually content with one interactive process and a number of batch jobs running in queues configured to prevent the degradation of interactive response time. The majority of UNIX versions, ULTRIX included, do not have batch processing capability. Rather, the user can simultaneously run a

---

11. See the discussion of the **at** command in Section 7.3.2.

foreground process and a number of background processes. A large number of background processes should not adversely affect interactive response time, because in most versions of UNIX the shell automatically lowers the priority of processes running in background for a system defined period of time. The UNIX method disadvantages the system administrator, who cannot easily exert the same level of control over the jobs running on the system as is possible in VMS when defining the many characteristics of a batch queue.

8.5 Summary

The following scenario illustrates the practical use of some of the commands introduced in this chapter.

User Jack receives a tape written at 1600 bpi in ASCII format with no tape label, a record size of 80 characters, and a block size of 3120 characters. The magnetic tape contains two files that are versions of the same program, one written in C and one in FORTRAN.

example:
```
UNIX
% pwd
/usr/jack
% mkdir newprog ; cd newprog
% dd if=/dev/rmt0h of=prog.c ibs=3120 cbs=80 conv=unblock
40 + 5 records in
27 + 1 records out
% mt rewind
% mt fsf 1
% dd if=/dev/rmt0h of=prog.f ibs=3120 cbs=80 conv=unblock
40 + 5 records in
27 + 1 records out
% ls
prog.c prog.f
% mt offline
% lpr prog.c prog.f
% lpq
Rank      Owner     Job     Files                    Total Size
1st       root      70      .login                     913 bytes
2nd       george    71      /tmp/T1500_reset            22 bytes
3rd       joyce     72      /usr/joyce/bigjob      4598376 bytes
4th       jack      73      /usr/jack/myprog         94738 bytes
% lprm -
dfA73 cuhhca dequeued
cfA73 cuhhca dequeued
% lpr -P fastprint prog.c prog.f
% lpq -P fastprint
```

```
Rank      Owner      Job      Files                    Total Size
Printing  jack       831      /usr/jack/myprog         94738 bytes
% cc -o progc.exe prog.c >& c.err &
[1]  73682
% f77 -o progf.exe prog.f >& f.err &
[2]  73688
% jobs
[1] -  Running          cc -o progc.exe prog.c >& c.err
[2] +  Running          f77 -o progf.exe prog.f >& f.err
```

First, Jack makes a subdirectory to contain the programs. Then he makes the subdirectory the present working directory with the command sequence **mkdir newprog ; cd newprog**. Jack places the magnetic tape on the drive and on-line, and reads the first file from the tape into the file **prog.c** with the command **dd if=/dev/rmt0h of=prog.c ibs=3120 cbs=80 conv=unblock**, which includes the block and record size specification of 3120 and 80 bytes respectively. Since Jack is not sure whether the tape device file causes the magnetic tape to rewind after each command, he uses the **mt rewind** command to reposition the tape at the beginning, moves forward one file with the **mt fsf 1** command, and reads the second file from magnetic tape into the output file **prog.f** with the command **dd if=/dev/rmt0h of=prog.f ibs=3120 cbs=80 conv=unblock**. Jack uses the **ls** command to verify that the two files have been copied. He then rewinds the tape and places the drive off-line with the **mt offline** command.

Jack decides to make a printed listing of the two programs. He uses **lpr prog.c prog.f** to send the two files to the default printer. Using the **lpq** command to display the contents of the default printer queue, Jack discovers that a large job, **/usr/joyce/bigjob**, is queued in front of his job. While wishing that print queue ordering were based on job size rather than time of submission, Jack decides to delete his own job and send it to another print queue to achieve a faster turnaround. He removes the print job from the default queue with **lprm -**. Since Jack knows that this is the only job he has queued, he uses this shorthand form of print job deletion, which removes all of his print jobs from the queue. Jack queues the job to a queue called **fastprint** with the command **lpr -P fastprint prog.c prog.f**. The command **lpq -P fastprint** verifies that the job is now printing in that queue.

While his file is printing, Jack compiles each program in background with the commands **cc -o progc.exe prog.c >& c.err &** for a C compilation and **f77 -o progf.exe prog.f** >& **f.err &** for a FORTRAN compilation (see Section 10.1). For both background jobs, Jack redirects standard output and standard error to appropriate files. Finally, Jack verifies that the two program compilations are running in background with the **jobs** command.

Chapter 9

Advanced File Management

One never notices what has been done; one can only see what remains to be done.

Marie Curie

Chapter 4 introduced UNIX commands and options for file management which a novice user might need in the first few terminal sessions. Now we turn our attention to more complex and diverse commands and options. Although used less frequently, they are important for the efficient management of files and directories. Once you understand the commands and options presented here, you will be ready to consult the man pages to obtain further information. Table 4.1 and Table 4.2 summarize most of the UNIX commands used in file management and the subset discussed in this book, respectively. This chapter follows the organization of Table 4.2: it divides commands into those that relate to directories and those that relate to individual files, and further divides them into commands that display directory and file contents, and those that modify directories and files. Two of the features presented here are unique to the C shell: the C shell variable **cdpath** and the creation of a *directory stack,* both of which simplify movement between commonly used directories.

Once you have read this chapter and experimented with the commands discussed herein, you should be ready to perform any file management task required by the average UNIX user. The UNIX features discussed herein include:

- Displaying files in new ways (Section 9.2)
- Copying whole directory structures (Section 9.3.1)
- Simplifying access to files in different directories (Section 9.3.2)
- Changing a file's protection (Section 9.4.1)
- Changing the group ownership of files (Section 9.4.2)
- Comparing files (Section 9.4.3)
- Finding and managing files in new ways (Section 9.4.4)
- Searching the contents of files (Section 9.4.5)
- Sorting file contents (Section 9.4.6)
- Updating a file's modification date (Section 9.4.7)
- Translating characters in a file (Section 9.4.8)
- Counting file contents (Section 9.4.9)
- Linking files together (Section 9.4.10)

Chapter 4 covered most of the frequently used options of the **ls** command for displaying directory contents. Here we discuss some extended features of **ls**.

9.1.1   *ls Revisited*

The command **ls -F** displays the name of the file followed by a flag describing the file type. **ls -F** offers a condensed listing rather than the long listing generated by **ls -l**, when you only need information about file type.

> UNIX
>
> **example:** % ls -F
>   **myfile.txt program.f* tmp/**
>   **zfoo@**

An * indicates that the file is executable. This does not mean that the file is an executable image (an **.EXE** file in VMS terminology), but rather that the file has a file protection rendering it executable. For example, a file that contains a list of shell commands may be readable, but the shell program will not interpret the contents unless the file is also executable. The default protection on a file created with UNIX does not usually include execute access. You must explicitly make the file executable with **umask** (see Section 3.2.1) or **chmod** (see Section 9.4.1). In VMS, the default file protection usually renders the file executable by the owner and other members of the group. / following the file name indicates that the file is a pointer to a subdirectory. @ signifies a *symbolic link* (see Section 9.4.10), and = signifies a *socket* (see Section 13.1).

The final four **ls** options that we will discuss refer not to the features of a file to be displayed but rather to the display format, which the following options modify.

	VMS	UNIX
example:	$ DIR/COLUMN=1	% ls -1
example:	$ DIR/PRINTER	% ls -C	lpr
example:		% ls -t
example:		% ls -r

In the first example, **ls -1** lists files at the terminal one per line rather than in multiple columns. The default gives multiple columns for terminal display and one file per line for output sent to any non-terminal device, including the printer. In the second example, **ls -C | lpr** illustrates how to override the printer default. The **C** option forces multiple column output, which is piped to the default printer. In the third example, **ls -t** sorts the file listing by date last modified rather than alphabetically, displaying the most recently modified file first. In the last example, **ls -r** displays files in reverse alphabetical order.

9.2   *Advanced File Display Commands*

In Section 4.8, we introduced the commands **cat** (catenate and print) and **more**, also called **page** (display a file a page at a time), for the display of file contents. We will now discuss the extended features of the **more** command and introduce the additional file display commands **od**, **head**, **tail**, and **pr**. The command **od** displays file contents in various formats and is useful in searching for non-printable characters such as control characters and tabs. The VMS command **DUMP** offers the same functions. The commands **head** and **tail**, as their names suggest, display the beginning and end of a file, respectively. The command **pr** does some simple page formatting useful for files you wish to send to a printer.

9.2.1   *more Revisited*

In Section 4.8, we compared the UNIX **more** command to the VMS command **TYPE/PAGE**, which displays the contents of a file one screen (default 24 lines) at a time. Using **more**, you can advance the file one screen by pressing ⟨SPACEBAR⟩, or one line by pressing ⟨CR⟩. Additional responses include:

i	Scroll **i** lines
t	Return to top of file
if	Skip **i** screens and print a screen
is	Skip **i** lines and print a screen full of lines
q or **Q**	Terminate file display
i/expr	Search for the **i**th occurrence of the expression
:f	Display the current file name and line number
. (dot)	Repeat the previous command
h	Display the above information on **more** options

As you can see, **more** offers some of the functions of a line editor when you use it in read only mode.

9.2.2   *Dump a File: od*

The UNIX command **od** (octal, decimal, hexadecimal, ASCII dump) corresponds to the VMS **DUMP** command. You can use **od** to examine the contents of files in various formats and to locate control and other non-printable characters. The VMS **DUMP** command is most useful for determining the format of magnetic tapes, whereas **od** is usually used on disk files that may have been read from tape with the **dd** command (see Section 8.2.2).

	VMS	UNIX
form:	$ DUMP[QUALIFIER(S)] - file-spec[, . . .]	% od [option(s)] file % cat file1 line 1
example:	$ DUMP FILE.	% od -a file1 0000000 ht l i n e sp 1 nl nl
example:	$ DUMP/OCTAL FILE.	% od -o file1 0000000 066011 067151 020145 005061 000012
example:	$ DUMP/HEXADECIMAL - FILE.	% od -h file1 0000000 6c09 6e69 2065 0a31 000a

These examples, **od -a**, **od -o**, and **od -h**, display the contents of **file1**, in this case a single line consisting of a tab followed by the words "line 1," in character, octal, and hexadecimal, respectively. Note that **od -a** denotes spaces with **sp**, new lines with **nl**, and tabs with **ht**.

9.2.3   *head, tail, and pr*

The command **head** displays the beginning of a file, and **tail** displays the end. Neither **head** nor **tail** has a VMS equivalent. The command **pr** formats one or more files which, without redirection or piping, appear at the terminal with page headers and page breaks. VMS achieves some features of the **pr** command with the **PRINT/HEADER** command.

	VMS	UNIX
form:	$ PRINT[/QUALIFIER(S)] file-spec[, . . .]	% head [-count] file(s) % tail [option(s)] file(s) % pr [option(s)] file(s)
example:		% head -30 /usr/test
example:		% head *.txt >> index

example:		% tail -30 /usr/test
example:		% tail -r /usr/test | lpr
example:	$ PRINT/HEADER FILE.DAT	% pr file.dat
example:		% pr -m file1 file2
example:		% pr -2 file1

In the first example, **head -30 /usr/test** lists the first thirty lines of the file. In the second example, **head *.txt >> index** lists the first 10 lines (default) of all the files ending in **.txt** and redirects the output to the file **index**. Note the use of >> redirection (compare >), which appends the result of each **head** operation to the file **index** rather than overwriting it. The entry for each **.txt** file in **index** is delimited by a flag of the form ===>**filename**<===. In the third example, **tail -30 /usr/test** displays the last 30 lines of the file. **tail -r /usr/test | lpr** reverses the order of the last 10 lines (default); that is, it displays the last line first, the second to last line second, and so on. The command pipes the result to the default printer.

The first example of printer formatting is the command **pr file.dat** without options, which formats **file.dat** for printing using the default file formatting characteristics. The default sets each page to a length of 66 lines, and prints the file name, date, and page number on each page with a five-line header and a five-line trailer. The command **pr -m file1 file2** prints **file1** and **file2** side by side, which is useful for comparing file contents. As with all forms of **pr**, this command truncates long lines rather than wraps them, so files are more likely to remain synchronized when displayed together. Finally, **pr -2 file1** prints **file1** in two columns, useful for saving paper when printing narrow files.

9.3 Advanced Directory Management Commands

Sections 4.4, 4.5, and 4.6 introduced commands for creating, deleting, and moving between directories. We now take the last step in directory management: copying the contents of a whole directory structure. We will also introduce two extensions of the C shell with which you can simplify access to files located in a variety of different directories.

9.3.1 Copying Whole Directories: cp -r

Used with the **r** option, the **cp** (copy) command accepts directories as arguments. You can use **cp -r** to graft one directory structure onto another. This use of **cp -r** corresponds to using the VMS **BACKUP** command to copy directory structures from disk to disk, rather than from disk to a backup save-set on magnetic tape.

	VMS	UNIX
form:	$ BACKUP[/QUALIFIER(S)] input- - specifier output-specifier	% cp -r [option(s)] directory1 directory2
example:	$ BACKUP [USER1. . .] - [USER2.USER1. . .]	% cp -r /user1 /user2

The result of the command in this example is illustrated below. Both directory structures remain intact, and the command grafts the directory **user1** and associated subdirectories onto **/user2** so that **user1** becomes an additional subdirectory of the directory **user2**.

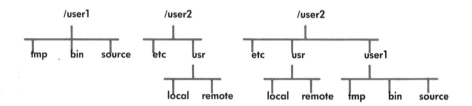

If you want to merge the contents of **/user1** and **/user2** while maintaining the lower-level directory structure—for example, changing **user1/bin**, **/user1/source**, and **/user1/tmp** to **/user2/bin**, **/user2/source**, and **/user2/ tmp** respectively—you would use the **tar** command (see Section 8.2.1).

9.3.2   C Shell Extensions

The C shell offers extensions to the shell-independent command **cd** for changing the current directory. These extensions are the shell variable **cdpath** and the *directory stack*. The variable **cdpath** lets you move easily to a commonly used directory irrespective of the current directory. In other words, you can move from the present working directory to a directory defined by **cdpath** without regard to the relative or absolute pathname required to get to that directory. The VMS **ASSIGN** command achieves a similar result, with one notable difference: **ASSIGN** establishes a pointer to a specific directory, whereas **cdpath** establishes a pointer to the parent directory of any subdirectory that is used frequently.

	VMS	UNIX
form:	$ ASSIGN equivalence-name[, . . .] - logical-name[:]	% set cdpath = directory-spec
example:	$ ASSIGN DUA2:[USER.TEST] TEST $ SHOW DEFAULT **DUA3:[PROGRAMS.NEW]** $ SET DEFAULT TEST $ SHOW DEFAULT **DUA2:[USER.TEST]**	% set cdpath = /user/test % pwd **/programs/new** % cd temp % pwd **/user/test/temp**
example:	$ ASSIGN DUA2:[USER.DOC] DOC $ ASSIGN DUA2:[USER.COM] COM	% set cdpath = (/user/doc /user/com)

In the first example, VMS **ASSIGN** establishes a synonym, **TEST**, for the directory specification **DUA2:[USER.TEST]**. The UNIX command **set cdpath = /user/test** establishes a pointer to all subdirectories of **/user/ test**. Hence, changing the directory to **temp** via a relative file definition makes **/user/test/temp** the present working directory irrespective of the current directory. The exception is the existence of **/programs/new/ temp** in which case that directory would have been preferentially made the present working directory. The last example, **set cdpath = (/user/ doc /user/com)**, illustrates giving multiple directory arguments to **cdpath** by enclosing them in parentheses and separating them with a blank.

A *directory stack* is a list of directory specifications retained by the C shell for the current terminal session only. Directory specifications can be made part of the stack and recalled as required. The present working directory is always at the top of the directory stack. The following scenario illustrates the use of a directory stack.

	UNIX	
example:	% pwd **/user2/programs/new**	
form:	% pushd dir	# Push /user2/programs/new onto the stack
example:	% pushd /usr	# and make /usr the current directory.
	/usr /user2/programs/new	
form:	% dirs	# Display the directory stack.
	dir	
example:	% dirs	
	/usr /user2/programs/new	
example:	% pushd /etc	# Push /usr onto the stack and move to /etc
	/etc /usr /user2/programs/new	
form:	% pushd +n	# Rotate the stack n times

```
example:   % pushd +1
           /usr /user2/programs/new /etc
form:      % popd          #Discard the present working directory and move
                               to the next entry on the stack
example:   % popd
           /user2/programs/new /etc
example:   % pwd
           /user2/programs/new
example:   % cd /tmp
example:   % dirs
           /tmp /etc
```

The examples begin in the directory **/user2/programs/new**. The command **pushd /usr** places (pushes) the directory **/usr** onto the directory stack, and makes it the present working directory. Note that the **pushd** command displays the directory stack; other commands that manipulate the stack also display it. Note also that **pushd** without arguments (not shown) switches the top two entries of the stack. The C shell command **dirs** interrogates the contents of the directory stack. Further use of the **pushd** command (**pushd /etc**) deepens the stack, and **/etc** becomes the present working directory. The command **pushd +1** makes the first directory stack entry the last, and the last the first: that is, it rotates the stack **+1** (one) time. The **popd** command discards the top of the directory stack (the present working directory), and makes the second entry in the stack the new present working directory. Note the use of **cd /tmp**, which changes the top entry in the stack to **/tmp** but does not change other entries in the stack.

9.4   *Advanced File Management Commands*

Section 4.2 described the various characteristics of UNIX files. This section discusses commands that change those characteristics, and introduces other advanced file management commands (see Table 4.2) that you may require from time to time.

9.4.1   *Change File Protection: chmod*

The UNIX command **chmod**, like the VMS **SET PROTECTION** command, changes the protection assigned to a file or directory. The command **chmod** provides two methods for specifying a change in file protection, as shown in the following examples.

	VMS	UNIX
form:	$ SET PROTECTION = - (CLASSIFICATION:LEVEL) file-spec[, . . .]	% chmod mode file(s)
example:	$ SET PROTECT = (O:RWED,G:RE,W:RE) A.DAT	% chmod 755 a.dat
example:		% chmod +x a.dat
example:		% chmod o-w,g-w \ a.dat
example:	$ SET PROTECT = (O:RWED,G,W) A.DAT	% chmod o = rwx a.dat

The first example illustrates the *absolute form* for specifying a file's protection. A level of protection is specified using an octal representation for each of the three types of user, owner, group, and world (in that order), where

owner	group	world
rwx	**rwx**	**rwx**
421	421	421

Hence,

7 = 4 + 2 + 1	Read, write, and execute
6 = 4 + 2	Read and write
5 = 4 + 1	Read and execute
4 = 4	Read only
3 = 2 + 1	Write and execute
2 = 2	Write only
1 = 1	Execute only

Note that specifying the levels of file protection with **chmod** is inverse to the **umask** command, where **7** implies no access, **1** implies read and write access but not execute access, and so on. The command **chmod 755 a.dat** changes the protection of the file **a.dat** to give the owner read, write, and execute access; group members read and execute access; and the world read and execute access.

The second and third examples use the *symbolic form* of the **chmod** command. The command **chmod +x a.dat** adds execute access to all types of users; that is, to the owner, group members, and the world. The command **chmod o-w,g-w a.dat** removes write access from the world and group members. Note that the symbolic forms of **chmod** use + (add) and − (minus) to add and subtract levels of protection, but do not change the protection for classes of users or protection levels not specifically addressed. That is, the second example gives execute access to the owner, group, and world, but does not change previously established read and write levels of protection. The equals sign (=) assigns protections absolutely. The last example, **chmod o = rwx a.dat**, illustrates absolute protection assignment by giving the owner read, write, and execute access to the file **a.dat** and removing all access from the group or the world.

For all uses of the **chmod** command, you must own the file for which you request a change in protection. Only the superuser may change the protection of files owned by other users.

9.4.2   *Change Group Ownership: chgrp*

The command **chgrp** changes the group ownership of a file. It corresponds to changing the Access Control Entry (ACE) for a VMS file, except that a VMS file can have multiple ACEs whereas a UNIX file can belong to only one group. To change group ownership, the UNIX user requesting the change must be the owner of the file and must be a member of the group being assigned to the file.

```
           VMS
form:      $ SHOW ACL/[OBJECT] object-spec
example:   $ SHOW ACL FILE1.
           Object type: file, Object name: DUA3:[SYSTEM]FILE1.:1, on 29-FEB-1988 -
             11:14:00.46
           (IDENTIFIER = PROJECTA,ACCESS = READ + WRITE + DELETE + CONTROL)
form:      $ SET ACL[/QUALIFIER(S)] object-name
example:   $ SET ACL FILE1./ACL = (IDENTIFIER = ADMIN.ACCESS = READ + WRITE -
             + DELETE + CONTROL)
           UNIX
form:      % groups [username]
form:      % chgrp [-f] group file(s)
example:   % groups ; ls- lg file1 ; chgrp admin file1 ; ls -lg file1
           admin projecta
           -rw-rw-r--   2 system   projecta 15 Feb 25 13:58 file1
           -rw-rw-r--   2 system   admin    15 Feb 25 13:58 file1
```

In the above example, the **groups** command indicates that the user (in this instance **system**) belongs to the groups **admin** and **projecta**. **ls -lg file1** indicates that user **system** owns **file1** and is therefore entitled to change the group from **projecta** to **admin**. **chgrp admin file1** changes the group ownership of the file **file1** from **projecta** to **admin**, which is verified by again issuing the command **ls -lg file1**.

9.4.3   *Compare File Contents: cmp and diff*

The UNIX commands **cmp** and **diff** serve the same function as the VMS command **DIFFERENCE** for reporting the differences between two files. The command **cmp** reports only the first difference found between two files; it is a useful quick-check to determine whether two files are identical. **cmp** is also useful for reporting the first difference found in two non-ASCII files. The command **diff** reports all the differences between two files or the contents of two directories. The VMS user familiar with the simple output of the **DIFFERENCE** command may find the output of the **diff** command difficult to interpret: **DIFFERENCE** displays the differences it finds, whereas **diff** displays the editing commands necessary to make the two files identical to one another.

```
             VMS                                    UNIX
             $ TYPE FILE1.,FILE2.                   % pr -m file1 file2
                                                    Maine          Texas
                                                    Montana        Montana
                                                    Nebraska       Illinois
                                                    Illinois       Alabama
                                                    Iowa           Maine
form:        $ DIFFERENCE[/QUALIFIER(S)] FILE1,FILE2    % cmp [option(s)] file1 file2
example:     $ DIFFERENCE/MATCH = 1 FILE1.,FILE2.       % cmp file1 file2
                                                    file1 file2 differ: char 1 line 1
************
File SYS$SYSROOT:[SYSMGR.SCRATCH]FILE1.:1
    1   Maine
    2   Montana
******
File SYS$SYSROOT:[SYSMGR.SCRATCH]FILE2.:1
    1   Texas
    2   Montana
************
************
etc.
             VMS
example:     $ DIFFERENCE/PARALLEL/MATCH = 1 FILE1.,FILE2.
             ------------------------------------      --------------------------------------
             File SYS$SYSROOT:[SYSMGR. -               | File SYS$SYSROOT:[SYSMGR. -
                SCRATCH]FILE1.;1                        SCRATCH]FILE2.;1
             ------------------- 1 ----------------    ------------------ 1 ------------------
             Maine                                     | Texas
             ------------------- 3 ----------------    ------------------ 3 ------------------
             Nebraska                                  |
             ------------------- 5 ----------------    ------------------ 4 ------------------
             Iowa                                      | Alabama
                                                       | Maine
             ------------------------------------      --------------------------------------
```

```
Number of difference sections found: 3
Number of difference records found: 4
DIFFERENCES /IGNORE = ()/MATCH = 1/PARALLEL-
    SYS$SYSROOT:[SYSMGR.SCRATCH]FILE1.;1-
    SYS$SYSROOT:[SYSMGR.SCRATCH]FILE2.;1
```

	UNIX
form:	% diff [option(s)] file1 file2
form:	% diff [option(s)] dir1 dir2
example:	% diff file1 file2
	1c1
	<Maine

	>Texas
	3d2
	Nebraska
	5c4.5
	<Iowa

	>Alabama
	>Maine

	VMS	UNIX
example:		% diff -e file1file2
example:	$ DIFFERENCE [DIR1...]*.*;* [DIR2...]*.*;*	% diff -r directory1 \
		directory2

In the first example, **cmp file1 file2** finds the first difference in the two files in the first character of the first line.

The command **diff file1 file2** reports each difference it finds, accompanied by up to four lines of information describing the changes required to make **file1** identical to **file2**.

Line 1   Consists of three fields:
1. The line number or range of line numbers in the first file prior to the change
2. A character to describe the type of change: **a** = append, **c** = change, **d** = delete.
3. The line or range of line numbers after the change

Line 2   The line(s) from the first file, if appropriate. The line(s) are identified by <.

Line 3   A delimiter (---) between the items of the first and second file, if appropriate.

Line 4   The line(s) from the second file, if appropriate. The line(s) are identified by >.

The output of the second UNIX example, **diff file1 file2**, indicates the following: Change Maine for Texas in **file1**, line 1 remains line 1. Delete line 3 (Nebraska) from **file1** so that line 3 becomes line 2. Change line 5 in **file1** from Iowa to two lines, Alabama and Maine, so that line 5 becomes lines 4 through 5.

The **e** option produces a slightly different form of output. For example, **diff -e file1 file2** displays (not shown) the commands that you must give to the **ed** editor to make **file1** identical to **file2**.

In the last example, **diff -r directory1 directory2** compares whole directories rather than individual files, and reports either the existence of a file in only one of the two directories (as determined by its name rather than its contents) or the differences found in files with the same name. The **r** (recursive) option compares all subdirectories of **directory1** and **directory2**.

9.4.4   *find Revisited*

Section 4.7 introduced the **find** command for locating files anywhere in the system, and illustrated its power to perform file management functions on any files it finds. We now continue our discussion of **find** by introducing more complex examples of finding files and executing commands on them. Note that the syntax of the **find** command is different from most other UNIX commands in that options consist of more than one character. Note also that options are position-sensitive.

	VMS	UNIX	
form:	$ DIRECTORY[/QUALIFIER(S)] - file_ spec	% find pathname_list criterion action	
example:	$ DIR/FULL[*. . .]MYFILE.	% find / -name myfile -exec file{} \;	
		/user1/bin/myfile:	executable
		/usr/local/myfile:	directory
		/etc/myfile:	empty
		/user3/myfile:	ascii text
		/user4/data/myfile:	data
		/user5/scripts/myfile:	commands
example:	$ DIR/MODIFIED/SINCE = -45-00 - [USER1. . .]	% find /user1 -mtime + 45 -print	
example:		% find /user1 -name '*.f' -atime -45 -print	
	UNIX		
example:	% find /usr/fred -name '*.f' -o (-mtime -3 -atime -6) -exec rm {} \;		

In the first example, **find / -name myfile -exec file {} \;** not only locates all occurrences of files named **myfile**, but also displays information about the file type. The construct **-exec file {} \;** executes the command **file** on each file **myfile** found. In contrast to **find**, **file** is a simple command that accepts a filename as an argument (in this example passed from **find**), examines the contents of that file, and returns the file type. The example shows some typical file types returned by the **file** command.

In the second example, **find /user1 -mtime +45 -print** displays all files down the directory hierarchy from **/user1** that were last modified (**mtime**) more than (+) 45 days ago. In the third example, **find /user1 -name '*.f' -atime -45 -print** displays all files that end in **.f** (FORTRAN source files) and have been accessed (**atime**) in the last (-) 45 days. Note that *modified* implies *written to,* whereas *accessed* implies *read from.* VMS has mechanisms to determine whether a file was modified (written) or created, but not when it was read.

The final example, **find /usr/fred -name '*.f' -o (-mtime -3 -atime -6) -exec rm {} \;**, introduces **o**, which functions as an OR Boolean operator: it deletes each file found from **/usr/fred** down the directory hierarchy that ends in **.f** and that was modified in the last three days or was accessed in the last six.

9.4.5   *Search File Contents: grep*

The UNIX command **grep** (compare the VMS command **SEARCH**) searches one or more files for a string of characters. Although **grep** has some useful features including the use of regular expressions (illustrated in the following examples), it lacks two features commonly used with the VMS **SEARCH** command: the **/WINDOW** qualifier for displaying records before and after the search string, and Boolean operators, available with the **/MATCH** qualifier.

As with every other UNIX command, the search string when using **grep** is case sensitive by default. This is not true of the VMS **SEARCH** command unless you use the **/EXACT** qualifier. A further inconvenience to a VMS user familiar with **SEARCH** is the syntax of the UNIX **grep** command, in which the search string precedes the file specification, which is the reverse of the syntax used by VMS **SEARCH**.

	VMS	UNIX
form:	$ SEARCH[/QUALIFIER(S)] file_ - spec string	% grep [option(s)] string file_spec
example:	$ SEARCH/EXACT FILE1. "HELLO - THERE"	% grep 'hello there' file1
	hello there, what a nice day	hello there, what a nice day
example:	$ SEARCH FILE*.TEXT "HELLO - THERE"	% grep -i 'hello there' file*.txt

```
*****************************        file1.txt:Hello there, what a nice day
SYS$SYSROOT:[SYSMGR.SCRATCH]FILE1.TXT;1  file2.txt:Hello there, what a horrible day
Hello there, what a nice day
*****************************
SYS$SYSROOT:[SYSMGR.SCRATCH]FILE2.TXT;1
Hello there, what a horrible day
```

example:	$ SEARCH/NUMBERS FILE3. - GOODBYE	% grep -n Goodbye file3
	12 Goodbye and have a nice day	12:Goodbye and have a nice day
example:	$ SEARCH/STATISTICS FILE3. - GOODBYE	% grep -c Goodbye file3 1

Files searched:	1	Buffered I/O count:	5
Records searched:	2	Direct I/O count:	5
Characters searched:	28	Page faults:	104
Records matched:	1	Elapsed CPU time:	0 00:00:00.16
Lines printed:	1	Elapsed time:	0 00:00:00.73

example:		% grep -v goodbye file3
example:		% vi `grep -l "include" *.f`
example:		% grep mode$ file4
example:		% grep "^ the" file5
example:		% ls -l	grep "^d"

In the first example, **grep 'hello there' file1** searches **file1** for all records that contain the string **hello there** and lists them. The single quotes, although not always necessary, delimit the string and ensure that meta-characters are taken literally rather than used to signify a special function when using the C shell.

In the second example, **grep -i 'hello there' file*.txt** uses the **i** option to make the command case insensitive. VMS users may feel more comfortable defining an alias such that **grep -i** becomes the default. This command lists records that match the search string, preceded by the name of the file containing the string.

In the third example, **grep -n Goodbye file3** searches for all records in **file3** that contain the string **Goodbye**. The **n** option displays the line numbers of records containing this string. In this example, the command found a single occurrence of the string on line 12.

In the fourth example, **grep -c Goodbye file3** once again searches for all records in **file3** that contain the string **Goodbye**. In this case, the **c** option displays the number of times the string was found. As you can see, this command supplies less statistical information resulting from a search than does the VMS command **SEARCH/STATISTICS**.

In the fifth example, **grep -v goodbye file3** displays all lines in **file3** except those that contain the string **goodbye** (not shown). The sixth example, **vi `grep -l "include" *.f`**, uses **grep** to extract filenames for further processing. The **l** option returns only the filename of any file ***.f** that contains the word **include**. The **vi** editor then edits any files found. The final three examples illustrate simple regular expressions: **grep mode$ file4** displays those lines of **file4** that end with the string **mode**; **grep "^the" file5** displays records of **file5** containing **the** at the beginning of the line and **ls -l|grep "^d"** lists those entries in a directory that are directory pointer files.

9.4.6   *Sort and Merge Files: sort*

The **sort** command sorts the contents of individual files or merges the contents of two or more sorted files. There are two major differences in the way VMS and UNIX sort files. First, VMS accepts more data types as sort keys. Second, you can define UNIX sort keys using any predefined delimiter, whereas in VMS you must define fields by fixed positions within the record.

	VMS	UNIX
form:	$ SORT[/QUALIFIER(S)] - INPUT_ FILE - OUTPUT_FILE	% sort [option(s)] [+ pos1] [-pos2] file(s)
example:	$ SORT FILE1. SYS$OUTPUT	% sort file1
example:	$ MERGE FILE1. FILE2. - SYS$OUTPUT	% sort file1 file2
example:	$ SORT FILE1. FILE.OUT	% sort -o file.out -n file1
example:	$ SORT/COLLATING_ - SEQUENCE= - MULTINATIONAL FILE1. 1.TMP $ SORT/COLLATING_ - SEQUENCE= - MULTINATIONAL FILE 2. 2.TMP	

The first example, **sort file1**, illustrates the simplest sort possible, using default settings for all characteristics: the sort key is the whole record for characters and the first digit for numbers, the ordering priority is the same as for listing files with the **ls** command (numbers first, uppercase before lowercase), and the sorted list is displayed at the terminal. In the second example, **sort file1 file2** functions the same way but merges the sorted lists for each file into a single display. In the third example, **sort -o file.out -n file1** uses the **o** option to direct output to the file **file.out**.[1] The **n** option sorts in strict ascending numeric order, using the whole number and not just the first digit. In the fourth example, **sort -f file1 file2** sorts, then merges, the contents of **file1** and **file2** disregarding the case of the alphabetic characters (**f** option). The fifth example, **sort +2 -4 file1**, illustrates the use of an alternative sort key to the default. In this instance, the sort key begins after (+) the second field (**2**) and ends (−) before the fourth field (**4**), that is, it uses the third field. By default, blanks delimit sort fields, that is, each word in a sentence constitutes a field. You can use other field separators, as in the sixth example, where **sort -t: +3n -5 +2n -4 /etc/passwd** sorts records in the password file. As we saw in Section 4.2, fields in the password file are separated by a colon. The **t** option indicates that the separator is a colon rather than a blank. The sixth example specifies two sort fields: **+3n -5**, the numeric field (**n**) beginning after the third field and ending before the fifth, namely the fourth or group field; and **+2n -4**, the numeric field (**n**) beginning after the second field and ending before the fourth, namely the third field, which represents the numeric identifier unique to each user.

9.4.7   *Create or Update a File: touch*

The command **touch** updates the modification date of a file by reading a character from the file and writing it back. In other words, **touch** edits the file without actually changing it. If the file you specify does not exist, touch will create it unless you have used the **c** option. **touch** has special

---

1. The **o** option for defining an output file is common to a number of commands.

significance when used with the **make** utility, as we will show in Section 10.2.

Creating empty files with **touch** can be very useful when experimenting with UNIX commands like those described in this chapter. **touch** always creates files with the same attributes because, as we saw in Section 2.3, having only one type of file structure is indigenous to the operating system. All UNIX files have the same attributes: a string of bytes with the block size defined by a given partition. Therefore, UNIX has no use for a File Definition Language (FDL) like that found in VMS.

	VMS	UNIX
form:	$ CREATE[/QUALIFIER(S)] - file- spec[, . . .]	% touch [option(s)] file(s)
example:	$ CREATE TEMP. (CTRL)-Z	% touch temp
example:		% touch -c temp

9.4.8 *Translate Characters: tr*

The **tr** command provides a simple mechanism for translating specified characters in a file into different characters without using an editor to perform a global edit. In the examples below, **tr** translates uppercase characters into lowercase or vice versa.

	UNIX
form:	% tr [option(s)] string1 [string2]
example:	% tr A-Z a-z < file1 > file2
example:	% tr -c A-Za-z '\012' < file1 > file2

In the first example, **tr A-Z a-z < file1 > file2** translates the alphabetic characters A through Z from **file1** to their lowercase counterparts and writes output to **file2**. Characters already lowercase in **file1** are copied unchanged to **file2**. In the second, more complex, example (taken from the **tr** man page), **tr -c A-Za-z '\012' < file1 > file2** performs the same translation, but outputs each word in **file1** on a separate line in **file2**. The **c** option indicates that each string of characters in **file1** will be followed with the delimited string **012**, the octal notation for new line. As we have seen, the \, acting as a metacharacter, prevents immediate interpretation by the C shell; instead, the command itself performs the interpretation. In sum, the command takes each word (anything containing characters from A through Z or a through z) from **file1**, follows each word with a new line, and outputs each word to **file2**.

9.4.9   *Word Count: wc*

We introduced **wc** in Section 2.5 to illustrate how different UNIX commands interpret wildcards. By default, **wc** lists the number of lines, words, and characters in a file.

	UNIX
form:	% wc [option(s)] file(s)
example:	% wc chapter3
	1723 7281 56388 chapter3

In this example, **wc chapter3** indicates that the file **chapter3** (an early draft of Chapter 3 in this book) consists of 1723 lines, 7281 words, and 56388 characters.

9.4.10   *Linking Files: ln*

A *link* provides a mechanism for assigning different names to the same file. The link does not create a separate copy of the file but a directory entry, providing different pathways to the same information. Since the same file can have multiple links, different users could for example read from a single file, each using a different file name but accessing the same information.

This use of links raises issues concerning maintenance of a file's integrity, for example, when two processes from the same or different users write to the file simultaneously. This issue relates to the broad subject of *file locking,* which VMS and UNIX handle differently. In VMS, a file by default is open to only one process at a time. This safeguard is usually not a limitation to an authorized user, since VMS users usually do not generate many processes at any one time. In UNIX, on the other hand, many different processes are likely to be running simultaneously, and files therefore must be accessible to a variety of processes. This situation increases the likelihood that a file could be corrupted inadvertently, and makes recovery of a corrupted file more difficult.

There are two types of links: a *hard link* (default) and a *soft* or *symbolic link*. A hard link maintains a directory entry which renders the link file indistinguishable from the original file but with a different name. If the original file were deleted, the link file would still exist and could be accessed in the same way as the original file. When a user makes a hard link to a file, the link count (see Section 2.3) for that file increases by one. A symbolic link simply provides a path to the original file. If the original file were deleted, the link would still exist but there would be no way of accessing the original file. A symbolic link does not increase the link count. Links are most often used to associate data files to be read or written by programs, as we shall see in Section 10.6. Hard links may not span file systems nor may they refer to directories, whereas symbolic links may do both.

A symbolic link in UNIX assumes the same role as the VMS **ASSIGN** command, with two notable exceptions. First, the **ASSIGN** command without qualifiers places an entry in the process name table, and removes it when the process terminates. Symbolic links, on the other hand, remain in effect until the link file is actually removed, that is, longer than a single terminal session. Second, VMS **ASSIGN** is often used with the qualifier **/USER_MODE**, which maintains the assignment, not for the duration of the terminal session but only as long as it takes to run a single executable image. UNIX links have no equivalent feature. VMS does not have the equivalent of a hard link.

	VMS	UNIX
form:	$ ASSIGN - [/QUALIFIER(S)] - equivalence-name - [, . . .] - logical-name[:]	% ln [-s] name1 [name2]
example:		% ls -l -rw-rw-r-- 1 system 15 Feb 25 13:58 file1.dat % ln file1.dat foo % ls -l total 1 -rw-rw-r-- 2 system 15 Feb 25 13:58 file1.dat -rw-rw-r-- 2 system 15 Feb 25 13:58 foo
example:	$ ASSIGN FILE2.DAT - FOO	% ln -s file2.dat foo
	$ SHOW LOGICAL - FOO	% ls -l total 1 -rw-rw-r-- 1 system 15 Feb 25 13:58 file2.dat

```
"FOO" = "FILE2.DAT"   lrwxrwxrwx   1 system   25 Feb 25 14:27 foo-> \
   (LNM$PROCESS_ -          file2.dat
   TABLE)
```

In the first example, **ln file1.dat foo** establishes a hard link between **file1.dat** and **foo**, so that writing to or reading from **foo** is identical to writing to or reading from **file1.dat**. As both files reside in the same directory, a simple long listing of the directory contents reveals two identical files. Compare the link count of two with the count of one for the non-linked file. The first link is always to the directory in which the file resides.

In the second example, **ln -s file2.dat foo** establishes a symbolic link between **file2.dat** and **foo**. Note the different format of the display provided by **ls -l** when the link is symbolic; the first column under **foo** contains **l** to indicate a symbolic link, and displays the actual link at the end of the record as **foo1 -> file1**.

9.5   *Summary*

The following series of examples summarizes the commands introduced in this chapter.

```
           UNIX
example:   % grep '/bin/csh' /etc/passwd | sort | awk -F: '{print $1}' > Cusers
example:   % cp -r /george/applic1 /usr/public/applic1
           % chmod 775 /usr/public/applic1/*
           % chgrp admin /usr/public/applic1/*
example:   % find /usr/public -name "*.f" -exec head -1 {} \; | sort > index
           % grep -i fft index
```

The first example comes from a UNIX user who has grasped the concept of complex command constructs built from relatively simple components. It pipes together three commands and then redirects the output to produce a file, **Cusers**, which lists all users who invoke the C shell by default at login time. This file could, for example, serve as a mailing list to relate information of importance only to C shell users. The construct **grep '/bin/csh' /etc/passwd** searches the password file for all records that define the C shell as the default. Recall that the file **passwd** contains one record for each user on the system, and that **/bin/csh** defines the default shell as the C shell. The command passes these records to **sort**, which sorts on the whole record since it has no arguments. Since the login name is the first entry of the record, **sort** sorts the records alphabetically by login name. The command then passes the sorted list to **awk -F: '{print $1}'**, which uses a colon as the field separator, as does the **/etc/passwd** file. The **awk** utility prints the first field of each record, which is redirected to the file **Cusers**.

In the second example, user George copies a set of files residing in the directory **/george/applic1** to a public area where all users can access them. George can do this since he is the owner of the directory **/usr/ public**. If any subdirectories of **/george/applic1** existed, they would become subdirectories of **/usr/public/applic1**. George then changes the protection of all files so the owner and the group have full access and all users can read and execute the files. Lastly, George changes the group ownership of the files so that members of the group **admin** can read, write, and execute the files.

In the last example, the **find** command locates all files in the public directories **/usr/public** that end in *.f*, that is, FORTRAN source files. The command pipes the first line of each file it finds through **sort** and redirects the sorted output to the file **index**. If all programs use the first record to declare the program name, then **index** contains a sorted list of all the programs on the system regardless of their file names. The command **grep -i fft index** searches this file **index** for all occurrences of the string **fft**, irrespective of the case of the string (**i** option).

Chapter 10

Programming

The wave of the future is coming and there is no stopping it.

Anne Morrow Lindbergh

This chapter introduces UNIX commands and utilities for compiling, debugging, profiling, and managing programs written in high-level languages. All the examples presented in this chapter use either the C or FORTRAN languages, although most features discussed here apply to any language for which a UNIX compiler is available. Readers who do not intend to use programming languages in the UNIX environment may skip this chapter.

Most versions of UNIX come with compilers for high-level languages. With VMS, you must purchase compilers as separate products. BSD is distributed with FORTRAN, C, and PASCAL; other compilers are available in the public domain. The advantages of both the BSD and public domain compilers are their low price—BSD itself is inexpensive to license—and their ability to run on any computer supporting BSD UNIX. Unfortunately, they do not use features of the hardware specific to each vendor. Consequently, they run compiled code slowly compared with native compilers that support such features as floating point accelerators, multiple processors, and vector processing units. The VAX FORTRAN and C compilers, available for both the VMS and ULTRIX operating systems, are examples of compilers taking advantage of specific hardware, in this case the VAX architecture. Readers who wish to determine what compilers are available on their systems should consult their system administrator or refer to on-line help using the command **man -k compile**.

In addition to specialized compilers, vendors may also offer proprietary software tools to assist in program development, such as language-sensitive editors, debuggers, and profilers. Irrespective of any additional proprietary software development tools all versions of UNIX possess programming tools, tools for which UNIX is well known. Table 10.1 summarizes these tools, a few of which we discuss in this chapter.[1]

First we describe the steps involved in producing executable code using both the FORTRAN and C compilers. Next, we introduce the **make** utility (compare the VMS layered product VAX DEC/MMS), a powerful UNIX tool for managing large programs that you need to compile repet-

---

1. Some of these tools are available to the VMS user as the layered product VNXset.

Table 10.1 Summary of UNIX Programming Tools

UNIX Tool[1]	VMS Equivalent	Function
adb	/DEBUG	General purpose debugging program
ar	LIBRARIAN	Archive and library maintainer
as	MACRO	Assembler language compiler
awk		Pattern matching and action program
bc		Arbitrary precision mathematical language
cb		C program beautifier
cc	CC[2]	C language compiler
ctags		Locates functions within a C or FORTRAN program
dbx	/DEBUG	Source level debugger
dc	DECalc[2]	Arbitrary precision desk calculator
error	/LIST	Analyzes and disperses in source compiler error messages
f77	FORTRAN[2]	FORTRAN-77 language compiler
fpr	PRINT	Prints files with FORTRAN carriage control
fsplit		Splits a multiroutine FORTRAN program into individual files
gcore	ANALYZE/PROCESS	Gets core image
gprof	PCA[2]	Profiles program execution
indent		Indents and formats C programs
ld	LINK	Loader (linker)
lex		Generates programs used in lexical analysis of text
lint		C program verifier
liszt		Franz LISP compiler
ln	ASSIGN	Links two files for reading or writing
lorder		Finds ordering relationship for an object library
make	VAX DEC/MMS[2]	Maintains groups of programs
mkstr		Creates a C error message file
nm	LINK/SYMBOL __TABLE	Prints the name list (symbol table) of an object file
pc	PASCAL[2]	PASCAL compiler
pdx	/DEBUG	PASCAL debugger
pmerge		PASCAL file merger
prof	PCA[2]	Profiles program execution
px		PASCAL interpreter
pxp		PASCAL execution profiler
pxref		PASCAL cross-reference program

Table 10.1   Summary of UNIX Programming Tools *(continued)*

UNIX Tool[1]	VMS Equivalent	Function
ranlib	**LIBRARIAN**	Randomizes libraries
sccs	VAX DEC/CMS[2]	Source code control system
size		Displays size of an object file
strings		Displays ASCII strings in a binary file
strip		Removes symbols and relocation bits
symorder		Rearranges name list
time	**SHOW PROCESS - /ACCOUNTING**	Determines system, user, and elapsed times
xstr		Extracts strings from C programs
yacc		Compiler writing assistant

1. These tools are taken from the ULTRIX version of UNIX. The available tools will vary slightly for different versions.
2. Available to the VMS user as a layered product.

itively. We do not discuss **sccs** (source code control system; compare the VMS layered product VAX DEC/CMS), a utility that extends the capabilities of **make**. **sccs** maintains the revision history and other features of a large program, typically coded by more than one programmer. To find more information about this utility, refer to the reading list in Appendix D.

Next, we discuss the debugging of programs. You can find errors in syntax using the **error** command (compare the **/LIST** qualifier of any VMS compiler), and errors in program logic using the interactive debugger **dbx** (compare the VMS qualifier **/DEBUG**). We then turn to improving program efficiency with the profiling commands **prof** and **gprof**, which indicate where and how the code uses CPU time (compare the VMS layered product VAX Performance and Coverage Analyzer).

Finally, we discuss the command **ar** (archive), the UNIX analogy to the VMS LIBRARIAN for maintaining groups of files. Of particular interest here is the use of **ar** for the creation and maintenance of *object libraries* to be included when linking.

10.1   Compiling and Linking

You invoke the BSD FORTRAN and C compilers with the commands **f77** and **cc**, respectively. Used without options (and assuming that no errors are found), these commands perform all the steps shown in Figure

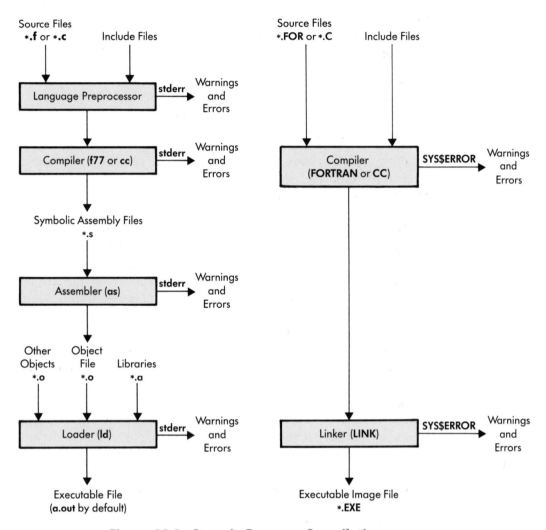

Figure 10.1 Steps in Program Compilation

10.1 to produce an executable image. Unlike VMS, you do not have to explicitly link the object code.

The filenames used in UNIX compilations traditionally carry file extensions. However, unlike VMS, UNIX uses such names only for file recognition purposes (the extensions are not assumed when used with commands). For example, in VMS, you can use the command **CC MYPROG** or **CC MYPROG.C** to compile the program contained in the file **MYPROG.C**; in UNIX, you must use the command **cc myprog.c**, for **cc myprog** will produce a "file not found" error.

The first step in producing an executable image invokes a *preprocessor,* which ignores all lines except those beginning with **#**. Refer to documentation on the compiler (for example, **man f77** or **man cc**) for a discussion of preprocessor instructions. Preprocessor instructions include:

- **#include "filename"**, useful for including additional user-written code shared by a number of programs, or for including a system routine (usually kept in subdirectories of **/usr/sys**)
- **#define** for replacing one string of characters with another

The second step in creating an executable image invokes the compiler proper to produce a *symbolic assembly file* with the file extension **.s**. The third step passes the symbolic assembly file to the assembler to produce an object file with an extension of **.o** (compare the VMS extension **.OBJ**). Note that BSD symbolic assembly code is independent of the language compiler that produced it; that is, the BSD assembler can interpret assembly code no matter what language compiler generated it. This feature has a number of benefits, including simplifying the writing of a new compiler and making applications more portable. If the system successfully produces an object file by default it deletes the symbolic assembly file (**.s**). The system then passes the object code and any other objects, either files or library entries, to the *loader* (*linker* in VMS), which produces an executable image retaining the object code (**.o**). Unless you call for an alternative file specification, the file containing the executable image is always named **a.out** (compare the VMS file extension **.EXE**). This last step is arcane and unimaginative. It may also be counterproductive if the novice UNIX user inadvertently overwrites an **a.out** file created during an earlier compilation of a different program.

The following examples illustrate the steps involved in producing an executable image and introduce options that you can use to retain intermediate files or produce executable files with more imaginative names. All the options presented in these examples apply to both the FORTRAN and C compilers.

	VMS	UNIX
form:	$ FORTRAN[/QUALIFIER(S)] source-file(s)	% f77 [option(s)] source-file(s)
form:	$ CC[/QUALIFIER(S)] source-file(s)	% cc [option(s)] source-file(s)
example:	$ FORTRAN MYPROG.FOR	% f77 myprog.f
	$ LINK MYPROG.OBJ	% chmod 755 a.out
	$ RUN MYPROG.EXE	% a.out
example:	$ FORTRAN MYPROG.C	
	$ LINK/EXECUTABLE=NEWNAME.EXE -	% cc -o newname.exe myproc.c

```
                  MYPROG.OBJ
example:  $ FORTRAN MYPROG.FOR               % f77 -c myprog.f
example:                                     % cc -S myprog.c
example:  $ FORTRAN MYPROG.FOR,[PUBLIC]*.FOR  % f77 -I/usr/public myprog.f
          $ LINK MYPROG,[PUBLIC]*.OBJ
example:  $ CC MYPROG.C                       % cc myprog.c -lplotlib
          $ LINK MYPROG, -
          SYS$LIBRARY:PLOTLIB.OLB/LIB
```

In the first example, **f77 myprog.f** without options produces an executable file **a.out**, to which the command **chmod 755 a.out** (see Section 9.4.1) gives an executable file protection. The file is executed simply by giving the name of the file. In the second example, **cc -o newname.exe myprog.c** also produces an executable file, but with the name **newname.exe** (**o** option). You should use this option and a unique filename in all compilations to prevent inadvertently overwriting executable files from prior program compilations.

In the third example, **f77 -c myprog.f** suppresses the loading stage (**c** option), producing an object file **myprog.o**. In the fourth example, **cc -S myprog.c** generates symbolic language code in the file **myprog.s** but stops there (**S** option). In the fifth example, **f77 -I/usr/public myprog.f** uses the **I** option to include an additional directory in the search path that the preprocessor uses to resolve references to **#include** files; usually, the preprocessor searches only **/usr/sys**. In the last example, **cc myprog -lplotlib** resolves references to calls to subroutines contained in the object code library **plotlib.a** (see Section 10.5). Note that this is a rare example where the file type (**.a**) is assumed. By default, the preprocessor searches the directories **/lib**, **/usr/lib**, and **usr/local/lib** in sequence to resolve references (compare the VMS logical name **SYS$LIBRARY**).

Subsequent sections introduce additional options to the **f77** and **cc** commands.

10.2 *Simplifying Compilation: make*

The UNIX utility **make** manages a group of files in some way dependent on each other. We will discuss the most common use of **make**: to maintain large programs. You can also, for example, use **make** to maintain a large document set, where changes in one document require corresponding changes in related documents.

In simple terms, **make** "remembers" which part of a program must be recompiled after you make a change. VMS users usually maintain a single large source file which they must recompile after making even a small change to a single routine or function. This programming practice is wasteful of both user time and system time. UNIX users, on the other hand, can maintain a number of smaller files, use **make** to "remember" which files they changed since the creation of the last executable image, and recompile only those parts of the program that they changed.[2]

Instructions to **make** are stored in a *makefile*. **make** searches for makefiles with the names **makefile** or **Makefile**. Before looking at the rules that govern a makefile, let us consider the sequence of events that take place when porting a VMS high-level language program to the UNIX environment. (Section 10.6 gives a specific example of porting a FORTRAN program from VMS to UNIX.)

1. Split the source code into smaller interdependent parts using the UNIX command **fsplit**, which splits FORTRAN source files into subroutines and functions
2. Write a makefile to manage the programs
3. Run **make** to create an up-to-date executable file
4. Run the program

You would repeat the last two steps each time you make a change to the program, recompiling only those subroutines and functions containing the code that you changed. If you wish to recompile all files, use the **touch** command (see Section 9.4.7) to update each file's modification date so that **make** includes it.

Some terms used in describing a makefile appear below. Note that we will not use all of these terms in the examples that follow.

commands	Tell **make** what action to take on a target file, for example, compilation
dependencies	Relationships between files, for example, the executable image is dependent on a number of object files, which in turn are dependent on a number of source code files
targets	Files produced as a result of commands and dependencies, for example, an executable image

---

2. The VMS layered product VAX DEC/MMS, part of the VNXset product, provides a VAX/VMS system with the capabilities of **make**.

flags	Strings of command options, for example, options to the **f77** or **cc** commands
macros	Shorthand means of specifying dependencies or commands; the macro name is made equal to a string once, and then used in subsequent references to the string
suffixes	Filename extensions that infer certain actions to be performed
prefixes	List of directories to be searched
comments	Any information preceded by **#** and ending with a new line.

These terms follow syntax rules, namely:

⟨TAB⟩	Designates the beginning of a command line following a dependency line
⟨TAB⟩-	Designates the beginning of a command line following a dependency line. If an error is found in this line **make** will not stop.
=	Assigns a name to a macro
@	At the beginning of a command line, causes the command to execute silently, that is, without displaying output on the screen
:	Separates a list of targets from a list of dependent files
a(b)	Indicates that filename **b** is stored in the archive (library) **a**
a((b))	Designates **b** as an entry point in a file stored in the archive **a**
s1.s2	Designates a second-level dependency, that is, files whose names end in **s2** depend on files whose names end in **s1**. An example is **.c.o**: files that have the file type **o** depend on files that have the file type **c**
\	Continues a command line or variable assignment onto the next line

The following example illustrates a simple makefile to print a long directory listing (**ls -l**) of the files residing in the directory **/usr/fred**. The listing resides in the file **list.out**, which is recreated only if the contents of the directory have changed since the last invocation of **make**.

```
            UNIX
example:   % cat makefile
           # Macro definitions:
           FILES = /usr/fred
           # Target definitions:
           Print: list.out
                   lpr list.out
           # Second level dependency:
           list.out: $(FILES)
                   ls -l $(FILES) > list.out
           % make -n
           ls -l /usr/fred > list.out
           lpr list.out
           % make
           ls -l /usr/fred > list.out
           lpr list.out
           % make
           lpr list.out
```

FILES = /usr/fred defines a macro for a *second-level dependency*. Dependencies are nested; that is, a first-level dependency is first dependent of a second-level dependency. The command line **ls -l $(FILES) > list.out** substitutes the value for the macro. The parentheses are obligatory. Compare this substitution to a C shell substitution (see Section 11.2), where **$FILES** would be valid. Since it follows a dependency, the **ls** command line is indented by a tab, indicating that the listing depends on the value associated with the macro. Similarly, the target **Print** depends on **list.out**. The **lpr** command, indented by a tab, follows the first-level dependency, **lpr** prints the directory listing on the default printer. **make -n** displays the commands that will be executed without actually executing them (**n** option), verifying that the makefile will function correctly. The first invocation of **make** creates the file **list.out**, a long listing of the files that reside in the directory **/usr/fred**, and sends it to the default printer. The second invocation illustrates the power of **make**: **make** determines that the contents of the directory **/usr/fred** have not changed since the listing file was made, and therefore prints the listing without recreating the file **list.out**.

Let us complete our discussion of **make** by introducing a *predefined symbol*. Predefined symbols, which begin with a period, appear in uppercase, and end with a colon, are names which signify a special function, as the following examples illustrate:

.DEFAULT:	Designates that a target depends on a file for which there are no specific commands or built-in rules to describe the dependency
.IGNORE:	Prevents **make** from halting when a command returns a non-zero status (see Section 11.8.7 for a discussion of error handling)
.PRECIOUS:	Prevents the target from being deleted if **make** is interrupted
.PREFIXES:	List of directories to be searched to resolve a reference to a file
.SILENT:	Executes commands without printing them to the screen
.SUFFIXES:	List of filename suffixes that have defined prerequisites in **make**, for example, **.c, .f, .s, .o,** and **.out**

The following example illustrates a makefile for compiling a group of C programs. This example and the makefile described in Section 10.6 may be used as templates for your own applications.

```
           UNIX
example:   % cat Makefile
           # macro definitions
           CSOURCE = a.c b.c c.c d.c
           OBJECTS = a.o b.o c.o d.o
           CFLAGS = -c -w -a
           # target definitions:
           prog.out: $(OBJECTS)
                   cc -o $@ $(OBJECTS)
           clean: $(OBJECTS)
                   rm -f $(OBJECTS)
           touch: $(CSOURCE)
                   touch $(CSOURCE)
           # second level dependencies
           .c.o: $(CSOURCE)
                   cc $(CFLAGS) $?
           # definitions
           .SUFFIXES: .out .o .c
           .PRECIOUS: prog.out
example:   % make
           cc -c -w -a a.c
           cc -c -w -a b.c
           cc -c -w -a c.c
           cc -c -w -a d.c
           cc -o prog.out a.o b.o c.o d.o
```

```
example:    % ex b.c
            : . . . .
            : wq
            % make
            cc -c -w -a b.c
            cc -o prog.out a.o b.o c.o d.o
example:    % make clean
            rm -f a.o b.o c.o d.o
example:    % make touch
            touch a.c b.c c.c d.c
```

The makefile maintains four files containing C source code which it compiles and loads into the executable image file **prog.out**. In the first example, **make** compiles each of the four files and creates an executable image. The second example invokes **make** after modifying one of the source code files using the **ex** editor. **make** recompiles only the source code file **b.c**, which has been modified, and uses the loader to create a new executable image file. The third example, **make clean**, illustrates the concept of *alternative entry points*: if the executable image file is current, it removes all object (**.o**) files; if the executable image is not current, it generates a current executable image and then removes all object files.

The last example, **make touch**, illustrates an important use of **make**: to force compilation even if a source file is up-to-date. The command **touch** updates the modification date of the file, thus causing **make** to recompile the source. Here, **touch** is invoked from the makefile using an alternative entry point. The source files could just have easily been touched with the UNIX command **touch *.c**, for example.

10.3   *Debugging Programs: error and dbx*

Table 10.1 lists several UNIX tools for debugging programs. Here, we consider two source-level debugging tools, the **error** command and the utility **dbx**. If you require an in-depth discussion of debugging tools, refer to the reading list in Appendix D.

The command **error** inserts error messages generated by incorrect syntax into the source code file. Compare the **/LIST** qualifier used by the VMS compilers, which provide a separate file (**.LIS**) locating syntax errors and displaying other useful information. The **error** lines appear in the source code file as comments, and therefore do not affect subsequent compilations. Since numerous messages make the source code difficult to read, you should make a copy of the source code before invoking **error** or perform a global edit and delete when the source code is completely debugged. For example, the **sed** command **sed /^C###/d myprog.f** removes all comments generated by **error** from the FORTRAN source code file **myprog.f** (see Section 5.3).

	VMS	UNIX
form:	$ FORTRAN/LIST source-file	% f77 source-file |&\ error
form:	$ CC/LIST source-file	% cc source-file |& error
example:	$ TYPE MYPROG.FOR	% cat myprog.f
	READ(5,*)A	read(5,*)a
	WRITE(6,*]A	write(6,*]a
	END	end
	$ FORTRAN/LIST MYPROG.FOR	% f77 myprog.f |& error
	%FORT-F-MISSDEL Missing operator or delimiter	1 file contains errors \ "myprog.f" (1)
	[write(6,*]] in module MYPROG$MAIN at line 3	File "myprog.f" has 1 \ error.
	. . . .	1 of these errors can be \ inserted into the file.
		You touched file(s): \ "myprog.f"
	$ TYPE MYPROG.LIS	% cat myprog.f
	. . . .	read(5,*)a
	0001 READ(5,*)A	C###2 [f77] Error on \ line 2 of myprog.f \ Syntax Error at \ "]"%%%
	0002 WRITE(6,*]A	write(6,*]a
	%FORT-F-MISSDEL. Missing operator or - delimiter	. . . .
	. . . .	

The command **f77 myprog.f |& error** performs a FORTRAN compilation of **myprog.f**, piping error messages to the **error** command, which inserts them at the appropriate places in the source code. Each error begins with **C###** followed by the line number, interpreted as a comment in later compilations (compare **/*###. . .*/** for C programs).

dbx is a BSD source-level interactive debugger for the C, FORTRAN, and PASCAL languages (compare the VMS utility **DEBUG**). Table 10.2 compares VMS and UNIX interactive debugger commands. Users of the VMS debugger may be disappointed with **dbx**. Although the VMS and

Table 10.2 Subset of dbx Commands

UNIX dbx	VMS DEBUG	Function
Execution and Tracing		
run [args]	GO [address-expression]	Begins executing
rerun [args]	GO [address-expression]	Restarts execution
trace [trace] [if]	SET TRACE/QUALIFIER(S) - [WHEN.. DO]	Traces execution of a line, a procedure, change to a variable, or print expression when line is reached
stop [if. at. in]	SET BREAK/QUALIFIER(S) - [WHEN.. DO]	Stops execution at some point
status	SHOW BREAK/QUALIFIER(S) SHOW TRACE/QUALIFIER(S)	Displays active trace and stop points
delete	CANCEL BREAK/QUALIFIER(S) CANCEL TRACE/QUALIFIER(S)	Removes active trace and stop points
cont	GO	Continues execution
step	STEP	Executes one source line
next		Steps to next line, executing calls
call [proc]		Executes object code associated with procedure
Printing Variables and Expressions		
dump [proc]	SHOW SYMBOL	Displays names and values of variables in procedure
print	EXAMINE/QUALIFIER(S)	Displays variables
whatis	SHOW TYPE	Displays declaration of variable, for example, real
where	SHOW MODULE	Prints active procedure and function
Source File Access		
/pattern/	SEARCH/QUALIFIER(S)	Searches forward or backward for pattern
edit [file]	EDIT [MODULE __NAME\LINE]	Invokes editor
file [file]	SET SOURCE	Changes current source file (or returns name if no argument is given)
func [function]	SET MODULE	Changes current function (or returns current function if no arguments are given)

Table 10.2 Subset of dbx Commands *(continued)*

UNIX **dbx**	VMS **DEBUG**	Function
list [line1,line2]	**TYPE line1:line 2**	Displays lines of text (default 10)
use [dirs]		Searches directory for source files
Aliases and Variables		
alias [chars string]	**DEFINE/QUALIFIER(S)**	Defines chars to be an alias for string
set var [=expr]	**DEPOSIT/QUALIFIER(S)**	Defines value for a variable
unalias [chars]	**UNDEFINE/QUALIFIER**	Removes an alias
unset var		Removes a variable
Miscellaneous		
help	**HELP**	On-line help
quit	**EXIT**	Quits the debugger
sh [command]	**SPAWN**	Passes command to shell for execution
source [file]	**@file-spec**	Reads commands from a file

UNIX debuggers offer similar functionality, albeit using a different syntax, the UNIX debugger is not as sophisticated. For example, in UNIX, without a windowing interface, you cannot use a split screen to simultaneously display the values of variables and the section of code that generated them.

The following example illustrates a simple use of the debugger: the user invokes the debugger, lists source code, sets a break point, examines a variable, changes the variable at the break point, and runs the program.

	VMS	UNIX
form:	**$ FORTRAN/DEBUG/NOOPT -** [source-file]	**% f77 -g [source-file]**
	$ LINK/DEBUG [object-file]	
	$ RUN [executable-file]	**% dbx**
	VAX DEBUG Version V4.7-1	**dbx version 2.0 of 4/2/87 22:10.**
	%DEBUG-I-INITIAL, language is - FORTRAN.	**Type 'help' for help.**
	module set to - FCONVERT$MAIN	enter object file name (default is \ 'a.out'):

```
                  DBG>                              reading symbolic information . . .
example:          $ ASSIGN HKL.IN FOR005            (dbx)
                  $ R FCONVERT.EXE
                  DBG> TYPE 1:7                      % dbx fconvert.exe
                                                     (dbx) list 1,7
                  1       integer h                  1       integer h
                  2       dimension fii(10)          2       dimension fii(10)
                  3       nref = 0                   3       nref = 0
                  4       read (5,2) nsf             4       read (5,2) nsf
                  5       write (6,2) nsf            5       write (6,2) nsf
                  6 10    read (5,2,end=100)h,k,l,fo,sigf, -   6 10    read (5,2,end=100)h,k,l,fo,sigf,stol, \
                          stol, (fii(i),i=1,nsf)                      (fii(i),i=1,nsf)
                  7       write (6,2) h,k,l,fo,sigf,stol, -   7       write (6,2) h,k,l,fo,sigf,(fii(i),i=1.nsf)
                          (fii(i),i=1.nsf)
                  DBG> SET BREAK %LINE 4             (dbx) stop at 4
                                                     [1] stop at 4
                  DBG> SHOW BREAK                    (dbx) status
                  breakpoint at -                    [1] stop at 4
                    FCONVERT$MAIN\%LINE 4
                  DBG> GO                            (dbx) run < hkl.in
                  break at FCONVERT$MAIN\%LINE 4     [1] stopped in MAIN at line 4
                  4:      read (5,2) nsf             4       read (5,2) nsf
                  DBG> EXAMINE NREF                  (dbx) print nref
                  FCONVERT$MAIN\NREF        0        0
                  DBG> DEPOSIT NREF = 4              (dbx) assign nref = 4
                  DBG> EXAMINE NREF                  (dbx) print nref
                  FCONVERT$MAIN\NREF        4        4
                  DBG> GO                            (dbx) cont
                  . . . .                            . . . .
```

dbx invokes the debugger (compare the VMS command **RUN/DEBUG**)
provided you previously compiled and loaded the source code with the
g option, which produces additional symbol table information needed
by the debugger. The debugger uses the file **a.out** if you specify no other
executable image. The debugger issues the **(dbx)** prompt (compare the
VMS prompt **DBG>**) when ready to receive commands. **list 1,7** (compare the VMS **DEBUG** command **TYPE 1:7**) lists the first seven lines of
the source file. **stop at 4** (compare the VMS **DEBUG** command **SET
BREAK %LINE 4**) sets a break point at line 4. **run < hkl.in** (compare the
VMS **DEBUG** command **GO**) executes the program. Rather than accept
input from the keyboard (stdin), the debugger reads input from the file
hkl.in. When execution stops at the breakpoint, **print nref** displays the
value of the variable **nref** (compare the VMS **DEBUG** command **EXAM-
INE NREF**). **assign nref = 4** changes this value (compare the VMS
DEBUG command **DEPOSIT NREF = 4**), and the **cont** command continues program execution (compare the VMS **DEBUG** command **GO**).

Profiling: prof and gprof

Profiling enables a programmer to determine how a program is spending its execution time. Profiling is useful if the programmer wishes to improve the efficiency of program code. Different versions of UNIX provide different utilities that work in different ways. The optional layered product VAX Performance and Coverage Analyzer (PCA) provides profiles for VMS users.

We will discuss two utilities available to BSD users, **prof** and **gprof**. **prof** provides a subset of the information available with **gprof**. Use the following steps to obtain profile data with **prof** or **gprof**:

1. Compile the program with either the **p** (**prof**) or **pg** (**gprof**) options.
2. Run the program to create the file used in profiling: by default, **mon.out** (**prof**) or **gmon.out** (**gprof**).
3. Invoke **prof** or **gprof**.

We will use the same program with which we illustrated **dbx** in the previous section to illustrate the use of **gprof** with default options. You should consult the **man** page on **gprof** for producing alternative profiles. Each time you invoke **gprof**, the output includes a description of each file displayed, as shown in the example.

	UNIX			
form:	% cc [-p or -pg] myprog.c			
	% f77[-p or -pg] myprog.f			
	% a.out			
	% prof (or gprof)			
example:	% f77 -pg fconvert.f			
	% a.out < hkl.in > /dev/null			
	% gprof			
	%time	**cumsecs**	**seconds**	**calls**	**name**
	42.7	2.71	2.71		mcount
	9.6	3.32	0.61	9172	_s_wsfe
	7.3	3.78	0.46	1091	_rd_ned
	6.9	4.22	0.44	8969	_ _flsbuf
	. . . . .				
	[continued below]				

The command **f77 -pg fconvert.f** produces an executable image file, **a.out**, which contains the information necessary to produce profile data. The command **a.out < hkl.in > /dev/null** runs the program, reading input from the file **hkl.in** and sending output to **/dev/null**. Recall that **/dev/null** (compare the VMS logical name **NL:**) is called the *bit bucket* and discards unwanted output. The command **gprof** displays profile data by reading the default files **a.out** and **gmon.out**. The first part of the **gprof** display is the so-called *flat profile,* also produced by **prof**. This section of the display does not describe the interrelationships between functions—for example, how often function **a** calls function **b**—but reports in descending order the percentage of total run time spent in each routine. The fields indicate the following:

%time The percentage of the total running time of the program that this function uses

cumsecs A running sum of the number of seconds used by this function and those listed above it

seconds The number of seconds used by this function alone: the major sort for this listing

calls The number of times this function was invoked, if profiled; otherwise blank

name The name of the function: the minor sort for this listing

The second part of the display is unique to **gprof** and describes the interrelationships among the various program functional units. There are three types of records in this display:

1. A single record for each function (listed second)
2. One or more parent records for each function (listed first)
3. Multiple child records for each function called by the parent (listed last)

The definition for each field in each of the three types of record is given, reading from left to right.

[gprof display continued...]

index	%time	self	descendents	called/total called+self called/total	parents name index children
					<spontaneous>
[1]	100.0	0.00	3.63		start [1]
		0.00	3.63	1/1	_main [2]
		0.00	3.63	1/1	start [1]
[2]	100.0	0.00	3.63	1	_main [2]
		0.03	3.58	1/1	_MAIN_ [3]
		0.00	0.01	17/17	_signal [28]

		0.00	0.01	1/1	_f_init [33]
		0.03	3.58	1/1	_main [2]
[3]	99.5	0.03	3.58	1	_MAIN_ [3]
		0.20	3.03	2183/2384	_do_fio [4]
		0.01	0.15	101/101	_e_wsfe [19]
		0.01	0.15	100/100	_e_rsfe [20]
		0.01	0.01	101/9070	_s_wsfe [7]
		0.00	0.00	101/9120	_s_rsfe <cycle 1> [14]
		0.00	0.00	1/1	_exit_ [50]

The function entries indicate the following:

index   The index of the function in the call graph listing as an aid to locating it (shown in square brackets)

%time   The percentage of the total time of the program accounted for by this function and its descendents

self   The number of seconds used by this function itself

descendents   The number of seconds used by the descendents of this function on behalf of this function

called   The number of times this function is called (other than recursive calls)

self   The number of times this function calls itself recursively

name   The name of the function, including its membership in a cycle, if any

index   As **index** above

The parent listings indicate the following:

self[3]   The number of seconds of this function's self-time due to calls from this parent

descendents[3]   The number of seconds of this function's descendent time due to calls from this parent

called[4]   The number of times this function is called by this parent; acts as the numerator of the fraction that

---

3. These fields are omitted for parents (or children) in the same cycle as the function. If the function (or child) is a member of a cycle, the propagated times and propagation denominator represent the self-time and descendent time of the cycle as a whole.

4. Static: only parents and children are indicated by a call count of 0.

divides the function's time among its
parents

total[3]
The number of times this function was called by all
of its parents; acts as the denominator of the
propagation fraction

parents
The name of this parent, including the parent's
membership in a cycle, if any

index
The index of this parent in the call graph listing as
an aid in locating it

The children listings indicate the following:

self[3]
The number of seconds of this child's self-time due
to being called by this function

descendent[3]
The number of seconds of this child's descendent's
time due to being called by this function

called[4]
The number of times this child is called by this
function; acts as the numerator of the propagation
fraction for this child

total[3]
The number of times this child is called by all
functions; acts as the denominator of the
propagation fraction

children
The name of this child, including its membership in
a cycle, if any

index
The index of this child in the call graph listing as an
aid to locating it

The cycle as a whole is listed with the same fields as a function entry.
Below it are listed the members of the cycle and their contributions to
the time and call counts of the cycle.

10.5   *Maintaining Libraries: ar and ranlib*

UNIX offers features similar to the VMS **LIBRARIAN** utility for maintaining files in an organized manner for easy access. As we shall see,
the UNIX user has to do a little more work and become familiar with
more than one command. The command **ar** (archive and library main-
tainer) creates libraries, adds files, replaces files, deletes files, and so
on. Once you create or modify the library, you usually randomize it with
the command **ranlib**. Randomization creates a table of contents to assist
in the location of files. The table of contents is available to the loader to

speed up the loading of files. This performance gain is useful in the main function of libraries: the storage of object files used by a variety of different programs at load time.

The following example illustrates the creation, manipulation, and subsequent use of an object library using the commands **ar** and **ranlib**.

	VMS	UNIX
form:	$ LIBRARIAN[/QUALIFIER(S)] LIBRARY - FILE(S)	% ar [option(s)] [position] \ archive file(s)
example:	$ LIB/CREATE PLOT.OLB START.OBJ, - STOP.OBJ, MOVE.OBJ, DRAW.OBJ	% ar cr plot.a start.o stop.o \ move.o draw.o
example:	$ LIB/LIST PLOT.OLB	

Directory of OBJECT library SYS$SYSROOT:[SYSMGR.SCRATCH]PLOT.OLB;1 on 19-SEP-1988 18:49:34

Creation date:	19-SEP-1988 18:48:20	Creator:	VAX-11 Librarian V04-00
Revision date:	19-SEP-1988 18:48:21	Library format:	3.0
Number of modules:	1	Max, key length:	31
Other entries:	1	Preallocated index blocks:	49
Recoverable deleted blocks:	0	Total index blocks used:	2
Max. Number history records:	20	Library history records:	0

DRAW
MOVE
START
STOP

UNIX
% ar t plot.a
start.o
stop.o
move.o
draw.o

example:	$ LIB/INSERT PLOT.OLB SYMBOL.OBJ	% ar q plot.a symbol.o
example:		% ar mb start.o plot.a move.o
example:	$ LIB/REPLACE PLOT.OLB SYMBOL.OBJ	% ar r plot.a move.o
example:	$ LIB/EXTRACT=MOVE/OUTPUT - =MOVE.OBJ PLOT.OLB	% ar x plot.a move.o

In the first example, **ar cr plot.a start.o stop.o move.o draw.o** creates a library **plot.a**, containing four object files (**c** option means create; **r** option means replace). Unlike the majority of UNIX command options, **ar** options are not preceded by a minus sign. Note that **.a** is the default file extension for libraries (compare the VMS extensions **.OLB** for object libraries and **.HLB** for help libraries). Unlike all other UNIX file extensions, compilers assume **.a**. For example, **cc myprog.c -lplot** is valid; **cc myprog.c -lplot.a** is not.

In the second example, **ar t plot.a** lists the contents of the library (**t** option). Unlike the VMS **LIBRARIAN**, **ar** does not store files alphabetically, but in the order received. Files added at a later date, therefore, will appear at the bottom of the library listing.

In the third example, **ar q plot.a symbol.o** adds the file **symbol.o** to the library (**q** option). **ar** does not perform a check to see if the file already exists in the library; it simply appends the file. If you inadvertently add a second file with the same name to the library, how do you delete the unwanted version? The answer to this question lies in the use of the positional parameter, as shown in the form of the command and illustrated in the next example.

ar mb start.o plot.a move.o uses a positional parameter to move (**m** option) **move.o** before (**b** option) **start.o**. The library entry to be moved is placed at the end of the command string; the library entry marking the move point immediately follows the command option. The order now becomes: **move.o**, **start.o**, **stop.o**, **draw.o**. The positional parameter can also pinpoint the file to be deleted, for example by indicating a file after (positional parameter **a** option) another file in the library.

In the fifth example, **ar r plot.a move.o** replaces the existing file **move.o** with a new version of the same file (**r** option), and places the new version at the end of the library.

In the final example, **ar x plot.a move.o** extracts a copy of the file **move.o** (**x** option): that is, the file remains in the library but a copy is extracted and placed in the current directory.

Once you are satisfied with the contents of an object library, you should randomize it with the **ranlib** command to improve the loader's access time when it loads the library with other source code files.

	VMS	UNIX
form:		% ranlib library
example:		% ranlib plot.a
example:	$ LINK MYPROG.OBJ,PLOT.OLB/LIBRARY	% cc myprog.c -lplot

The command **ranlib plot.a** randomizes the library created above for use by the loader. You should perform a randomization whenever you make a change to the library. **cc myprog.c -lplot.a** compiles and links the C program **myprog.c**, using object code from the library **plot.a** to resolve any external references. The compiler searches the directory paths specified by the shell variable path for the object library file. The directories **/lib** and **/usr/lib. .** contain system libraries (compare the VMS directory defined by the logical name **SYS$LIBRARY**). Site-dependent libraries usually reside in the directory **/usr/local/lib/. ..**

10.6   *Summary*

This summary once again uses examples from everyday use. The first example takes a FORTRAN program **prolsq.f**, copied from a VAX/VMS system and compiles and runs it.

```
                UNIX
example:   % fsplit prolsq.f
           prolsq.f already exists, put in zzz000.f
           symmin.f
           recip.f
           . . . .
           rtest.f
           % ls
           bcnvrt.f    disref.f    plnref.f    symmin.f    typescript
           bref.f      ellips.f    polar.f     symref.f    vdwref.f
           calc.f      expv.f      prolsq.f    teref.f     zzz000.f
           cgsolv.f    freeze.f    recip.f     torref.f
           chiref.f    matinv.f    rtest.f     torshn.f
           cross.f     matmul.f    scale.f     toss.f
           det3.f      plane.f     sfref.f     trig.f
           % mv prolsq.f prolsq.orig
           % mv zzz000.f prolsq.f
           % cat Makefile
           #
           OBJ =       prolsq.o symmin.o recip.o sfref.9 calc.o \
                       trig.o expv.o disref.o plnref.o plane.o \
                       chiref.o det3.o vdwref.o bref.o teref.o \
                       ellips.o bcnvrt.o torref.o torshn.o cross.o \
                       symref.o toss.o polar.o matinv.o cgsolv.o \
                       matmul.o scale.o freeze.o rtest.o
           f77 =       f77 -v
           .f.o:
                       $(f77) -c $*.f
           MAIN:       $(OBJ)
                       $(f77) -o MAIN $(OBJ)
           % make -n
           f77 -v -c prolsq.f
           f77 -v -c symmin.f
           . . . .
           f77 -v -c rtest.f
           f77 -v -o MAIN prolsq.o symmin.o . . . . rtest.o
```

The command **fsplit prolsq.f** breaks the large FORTRAN source code file into routines and functions to be managed by **make**. Because **prolsq.f** already exists, the main program cannot be called **prolsq.f**, so the command renames it **zzz000.f**. The user then renames **prolsq.f** as **prolsq.orig**, and **zzz000.f** as **prolsq.f**. The command **cat Makefile** displays the makefile written to maintain this group of routines. **OBJ = . . .** defines a macro **OBJ** for the object files; note that the backslash denotes the continuation of the macro definition. **f77 = f77 -v** defines a macro for the compilation that includes the **v** option to display the version number of the compiler. **.f.o:** defines the dependency, that is, the existence of an **.o** file depends on the existence of an **.f** file. The dependency is followed by the command **$(f77) -c $*.f**, beginning after a tab; the **c** option suppresses the loading phase. A further dependency, **MAIN**, appears, which depends on the **OBJ** macro. The command **$(f77) -o MAIN $(OBJ)** (after a tab) loads the object files into an executable image file **MAIN**. The command **make -n** then displays the commands that **make** will execute without actually executing them.

example:
```
                 UNIX
        % make
        f77 -v -c prolsq.f
        Berkeley F77, version 1.0
        prolsq.f
        MAIN prolsq:
        Error on line 45 of prolsq.f Declaration error. .
        . . .
        % f77 prolsq.f |& error
                1 non-specific errors follow
        [unknown] MAIN prolsq:
        [unknown] Error. No assembly.
        1 file contains errors "prolsq.f" (1)
        File "prolsq.f" has 1 error
                1 of these can be inserted in the file
        You touched file(s): "prolsq.f"
        % more +45 prolsq.f
        DATA DMIN /5.0,3.0,2.5,2.0/
        C###45 [f77] Error on line 45 of prolsq.f Declaration \
            error. . .
```

Once **make** is functioning correctly, the program can be debugged. **make** without options invokes the makefile called **Makefile** and compiles each routine. **make** finds only one error, in the parent program **prolsq.f**. This parent program is compiled again, external to **make**, with the command **f77 prolsq.f |& error**. The error message generated by the compilation is piped to the **error** command, which embeds the error message at the appropriate place in the source file. The command **more +45 prolsq.f** displays the file beginning at line 45, since the compilation indicated that the error was at line 45. Assuming the error was fixed, a further invocation of **make** would compile just the **prolsq.f** file and create an executable image file called **MAIN** from all the object files.

Once the program is compiled and running, the user decides to profile a typical execution to determine where the program uses most of its CPU time. The user plans to recode the most CPU-intensive parts of the program, thus improving its efficiency.

```
            UNIX
example:    % ex Makefile
            :/-c/
                        $(f77) -c $*.f
            :s/-c/-c -pg/
                        $(f77) -c -pg $*.f
            : wq
            % touch *.f ; make
            % cat run
            #
            ln IDISK fort.3
            ln JDISK fort.4
            ln ../protin/ATMDST.8 fort.10
            ln SHIFT.IN fort.15
            ln SHIFT.OUT fort.16
            ln ../fconvert/prolsq.hkl fort.20
            ln FOFC.OUT fort.31
            ln XYZBG.OUT fort.32
            date
            time MAIN < data
            date
            rm -f fort.*
            % run
            % gprof MAIN gmon.out
```

First, the user modifies the makefile with the **ex** editor to include the option **pg** for each compilation. The command **touch *.f ; make** updates the modification dates of all the FORTRAN source files (***.f**) so that the subsequent **make** will recompile each file with the profile options (**pg**). The user runs the program with the script file named **run**, which assigns data files to the various FORTRAN unit numbers and runs the program. Notice that a hard link assigns files to FORTRAN unit numbers. In the example, writing to FORTRAN unit number 3 would, by default, write to the file **fort.3**, but the link causes data to be written to the file **IDISK**. After the program runs, the user removes the hard links with the command **rm -f fort.***. Recall that if the user had set soft links, the **IDISK** file would have also been deleted.[5] The user then invokes **gprof** with the executable file defined as **MAIN** in the makefile, and **gmon.out**, the default profile produced at run time. The example does not show the output of **gprof**, but it would look similar to the output shown in Section 10.4.

---

5. Different UNIX FORTRAN compilers use different methods for assigning data files.

Chapter 11

Shell Programming

Civilization advances by extending the number of important operations that can be performed without thinking of them.

Alfred North Whitehead

Shell programming involves grouping together a number of shell commands and constructs into a file (called a *shell script*) to perform a routine task. The analogy in VMS is the creation of a Digital Command Language (DCL) command procedure. The syntax of a shell script varies according to the shell in use; in this chapter, we restrict our discussion to C shell syntax. Since the man page for **csh** is terse, this chapter explains the features of C shell programming in greater detail. If you are versed in DCL command procedures, you should be aware that achieving equivalent functionality in UNIX requires becoming adept at writing shell scripts. This chapter will get you started. The following comparisons and contrasts will help to orient the VMS user to shell programming in UNIX.

- Both shell scripts and DCL command procedures use only commands and constructs that the standard operating system can interpret. Use of a high-level language compiler is not necessary.
- As a general rule, scripts execute faster than DCL command procedures.
- The debugging of scripts and DCL command procedures relies on the error-reporting features of the shell and command language interpreter, respectively. Error reporting by the shell is uninformative.
- DCL command procedures may utilize comprehensive string-handling capabilities. The shell has poor string-handling capabilities, but you may supplement them with the extensive string-handling capabilities of **awk** and **sed**.
- Compared to a high-level language, both the shell and DCL are slow in performing integer arithmetic.
- Neither the shell nor DCL is capable of non-integer arithmetic.
- UNIX has an extensive set of commands and utilities that you can incorporate in scripts.
- Shell scripts are like C; if you can program in C, then you will find shell programming easy.

Figure 11.1 illustrates the various components of shell programming and indicates the organization of this chapter. The guts of a shell script are

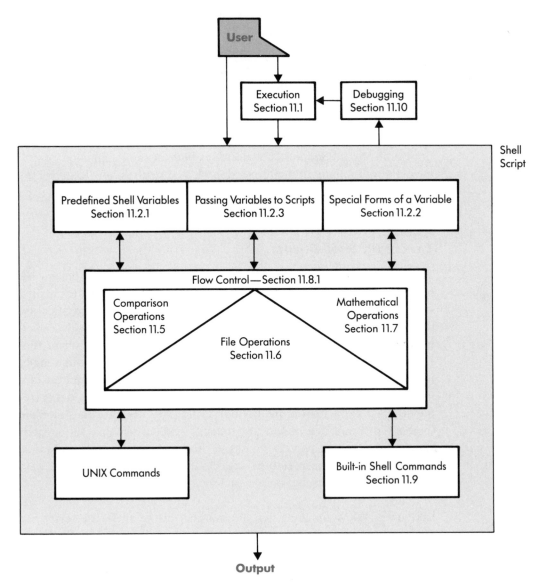

Figure 11.1 Shell Programming Overview

the UNIX commands and utilities, many of which we have discussed already. Script programming adds flow control, argument handling, error handling, and the like to help you use UNIX commands more effectively. The features of script programming are built in to the shell.

Section 11.1 presents the execution of shell scripts. Beginning with execution may seem premature, but remember that a shell script does not have to be complex. A shell script can be no more than a shorthand notation for a single command string, many of which we have discussed already. We are therefore more than ready to execute our first shell script. Section 11.2 describes how shell scripts handle variables. Section 11.3 describes how they handle filename modification, and Section 11.4 describes how they handle variable expansion. Sections 11.5 to 11.7 describe the various types of operators available. Section 11.8 discusses flow control, and Section 11.9 discusses built-in shell commands useful in shell programming. Finally, Section 11.10 discusses how to debug the mess we have created.

11.1   *Executing Shell Scripts*

The VMS user executes a DCL command procedure by placing @ before the name of the command file; the UNIX user executes a shell script using only the name of the script file. If no directory specification precedes the script file name, the C shell will search the paths described by the shell variable **path** to resolve the reference to the script file. Entries such as **/etc** and **/usr/bin** (see Section 2.3), which contain many of the programs and scripts that make up the UNIX command set, are followed by a period, signifying the current directory. UNIX users frequently add paths (before the period) of the type ˜**user/bin** and ˜**user/etc** to the file **.cshrc** (see below) to indicate directories that the system should search to resolve references to their own shell scripts and other programs. To be interpreted by the shell, the shell script must have a file protection that renders it executable by the user.

Like all UNIX commands that are not part of the shell, the script file executes in a child shell forked by the parent shell. Normally this child shell takes on all the predefined variables assigned to the parent shell as well as those defined by the user in the file **.cshrc** (another shell script). However, **#!/bin/csh -f** appearing as the first line of the script file invokes a fast start of the C shell and does not execute the commands in **.cshrc**. This line could represent significant time savings if the **.cshrc** file is long and complex. The following example illustrates a simple shell script.

	VMS	UNIX
example:	**$ TYPE TEST.COM**	**% cat test_script**
		#!/bin/csh -f

```
$!Test command procedure    # test script
$ SHOW USERS                who
$ EXIT                      exit
$ @TEST.COM                 % chmod +x test
                            % test
        VAX/VMS Interactive Users    system ttyp0 Aug 6 09:00
  Total number of interactive users = 1
SYSTEM      _RTA1:      000004AE  RTA1:
```

Note the following:

- Commands in scripts are not preceded by the shell prompt (compare $ for DCL command procedures).

- The script file is first made executable with the **chmod** command. This is necessary if the script file has not been given a file protection rendering it executable by the owner, as is usually the case (see the discussion of **umask** in Section 4.2).

- The procedure is terminated with the **exit** command (compare the VMS command **EXIT**), which returns control to the parent shell. Since the **exit** command is assumed by default if an EOF is reached, it is not essential in this example.

- The example shows a fast start of the shell.

- Anything following **#** in a command line is interpreted as a comment (compare **!** in VMS), with the exception of **#!/bin/csh -f**.

11.2   *Variables*

You can assign variables in shell scripts using the **set** command. Note the following differences in assigning values to variables and returning variable values between shell scripts and DCL command procedures:

- UNIX does not make the same distinction as VMS between defining variables for the duration of the command procedure and defining variables for the duration of the terminal session (that is, globally). The **set** command always assigns variables for the current process. Including the variable assignment in the **.cshrc** file gives the equivalent of global definitions, because this file is usually executed each time a shell (process) is started (that is, for each command or script file executed). The exception, as noted above, is a fast start of the C shell.

- No distinction is made in defining a shell variable as an integer or a text string (compare the VMS = and := , for example).

- UNIX always treats uppercase and lowercase strings differently. VMS translates lowercase to uppercase unless the text string is surrounded by double quotes.
- To return the value of a variable, you should precede the variable name with the **$** metacharacter (compare VMS, where the variable name is surrounded by single quotes).

Once you have assigned a name to a variable, you can use the shell command **echo** (compare the VMS command **WRITE SYS$OUTPUT**) to write to **stdout** (standard output), returning either the numeric or text string value of a variable.

	VMS	UNIX[1]
form:	**$** VARIABLE_NAME = local_integer/text	**%** set variable_name = \
	$ VARIABLE_NAME = = global_integer/-text	value
	$ VARIABLE_NAME := local_text	
	$ VARIABLE_NAME := = global_text	
example:	**$** SAMPLE = 1	**%** set sample = 1
	**$** WRITE SYS$OUTPUT "Number ''SAMPLE'''"	**%** echo "Number $sample"
	Number 1	**Number 1**
	**$** WRITE SYS$OUTPUT "Number sample"	**%** echo "Number sample"
	Number sample	**Number sample**
example:	**$** STRING = = "hello there"	**%** set string = "hello there"

1. These examples follow the C shell prompt, indicating that they were issued as commands and not executed as part of a script.

In the first example, **set sample = 1** assigns a value of 1 to the variable **sample**. Note that the **$** metacharacter forces the value of the variable to be returned. In the second example, **set string = "hello there"** equates the variable named **string** to a text string. Unlike VMS, UNIX makes no distinction between equating a variable name to an integer or a text string.

11.2.1 *Predefined Shell Variables*

Section 3.3.2 introduced *predefined shell variables,* the most common of which appear in Table 11.1. You can display a complete list on-line using the **set** command without arguments. The VMS analogy to predefined shell variables are the symbol definitions found in the system logical name table. You should avoid using predefined shell variable

Table 11.1   Predefined C Shell Variables

	Variable	
UNIX	VMS[1]	UNIX Meaning
user	**F$USER( )**	Username
path		Current path specification
home	**SYS$LOGIN**	Home, or parent directory, of user
shell		Current shell
term	**F$GETDVI("DEVICE","DEVTYPE")**[2]	Terminal type
status	**$STATUS**	Status returned by last command: 0 = no error, 1 = error[3]

1. The predefined C shell variables either have no analogy in VMS, or loosely correspond to either a system defined logical name or a result obtainable from a lexical function.

2. **term** returns an alphanumeric string: **F$GETDVI** returns an integer value.

3. **status** and **$STATUS** are redetermined each time a command is executed. Compare the UNIX definition to VMS, where **0001** implies no error and any other hexadecimal value implies an error.

names when defining your own variables. The following examples illustrate typical values returned for common predefined shell variables.

	VMS	UNIX
example:	$ WRITE SYS$OUTPUT "''F$USER()'''" [FRED]	% echo $user # username fred
example:		% echo $path # command reference /usr/fred/bin /usr /bin /usr/bin

example:	$ SHOW LOGICAL SYS$LOGIN
	 "SYS$LOGIN" = -
	    "SYS$SYSROOT:[SYSMGR]"
	       (LNM$JOB_802B0A50)
		% echo $home # parent directory
		 /usr/fred

example:	$ SHOW TERMINAL Terminal: TTA4: Device_type VT100 - Owner: FRED	% echo $term # terminal type vt100
example:	. . . . $ SHOW SYMBOL $STATUS $STATUS = = "%X00000001	% echo $status # error condition 0

The discussion of error handling in Section 11.8.7 will illustrate the importance of **status**.

Table 11.2 Special Forms of C Shell Variable

Form		UNIX Meaning
UNIX	**VMS**	
$?name	1	Returns **0** if variable name is not defined, **1** if defined
$#name	2	Returns integer specifying the number of elements of variable **name**
$name[m-n]	2	Returns elements **m** through **n** of variable **name**, where **m** and **n** are integers
$name[m-]	2	Returns elements **m** through the last element of variable **name**, where **m** is an integer
$name[*]	2	Returns all elements of variable **name**
$name[$]	2	Returns last element of variable **name**
${0}		Returns name of script being executed
$?0		Returns **0** if name of script being executed is known, **1** if not
$a ($argv[a])	**Pa**	Returns **a**th variable passed to script
$*		Returns all variables passed to script
$$	**F$PID( )**	Returns process number of current shell
$<	**INQUIRE**	Takes input from terminal keyboard

1. Not directly obtainable, but achieved with an error handler.
2. Not directly obtainable, but achieved by decomposing a variable into elements with the **F$ELEMENT** lexical function.

11.2.2   *Special Forms of a Variable*

Table 11.2 illustrates the special forms of a variable. You can break the value of a variable into separate elements, where each element is separated by a blank. The C shell can then conveniently address these elements. What if you wish to define elements of a variable other than those delimited by blanks? You cannot do this easily with shell commands, for the C shell does not offer the convenience of the VMS lexical functions to manipulate strings—for example, **F$EXTRACT** to decompose a variable according to the position of each character in a string, and

F$CVS and F$FAO for integer/character string conversions. However, as we saw in Section 5.4, this shortcoming is remedied with **awk**, the pattern-matching and action utility, which can decompose a string in the same way as the VMS lexical functions. Table 11.2 also lists the $< construct (compare the VMS command **INQUIRE**) for entering the value of a variable to a shell script from **stdin**. The following shell script illustrates some of these features.

	VMS	UNIX
example:	$ TYPE TEST.COM	% cat test_script
	$! Special forms of a variable	# Special forms of a variable
	$!	#
	$ INQUIRE NAME "Enter Text String: "	echo -n "Enter Text String: "
	$!	set name = $<
	$!	echo "This script is called ${0}"
	$ WRITE SYS$OUTPUT "Processed by -	echo "This script is being \
	"F$PID(A)'"	processed by PID $$"
		#
	$ NUM = 0	echo "The string entered has \
		$#name elements"
	$ LOOP:	echo "The first word is \
		$name[1]"
	$ LABEL = F$ELEMENT(NUM," ",NAME)	echo "The last word is $name[$]"
	$ IF (LABEL .EQS. " ") THEN GOTO END	exit
	$ COUNT = NUM + 1	
	$ WRITE SYS$OUTPUT "Word "COUNT'="LABEL'"	
	$ NUM = NUM + 1	
	$ GOTO LOOP	
	$ END: WRITE SYS$OUTPUT "The string entered has -	
	"COUNT' elements"	
	$ EXIT	
	$ @TEST COM	% chmod 744 test_script ; test_ \
		script
	Enter text string: test of string -	Enter text string: test of string \
	manipulation	manipulation
		This script is called test_script
	Processed by 00000043	This script is being processed by \
		PID 27183
	Word 1 = test	The string entered has 4 elements
	Word 2 = of	The first word is test
	Word 3 = string	The last word is manipulation
	Word 4 = manipulation	
	The string entered has 4 elements	

Note the variation in the use of **echo**. The **n** option prevents skipping to the next line, and so you may enter a response after the string echoed (the default condition for the VMS command **INQUIRE**). You can equate the string entered to the variable **name** with **set name = $<**, and then manipulate it using the definitions outlined in Table 11.2. That is, the variable **name** consists of four elements, the words "test of string manipulation." Recall from Section 5.4.8 that the **awk** construct **substr($name,1,6)** could have been used to return, for example, an element of "test o"; a substring of **name** starting at character 1, and 6 characters long. Thus we have an element that includes blanks but is not delimited by blanks.

11.2.3 *Passing Variables to Scripts*

Table 11.2 illustrates how variables are passed to scripts from the command line. The variable name **argv** is reserved for arguments entered on the command line. Thus **argv[1]** is the first argument (also called **$1**; compare in VMS **P1**), and **argv[$]** is the last (also called **$$**; compare in VMS **Pn**). You must enclose any argument passed to a script that contains a blank or a shell metacharacter in double quotes. VMS limits the number of variables (parameters) that you may pass to a command procedure to eight. UNIX has no such restriction; that is to say, the number of variables that you may pass to a script file is so large that the average user will never reach it. If you wish to know about this and other restrictions, refer to the **man** page for **csh**.

	VMS	UNIX
example:	$TYPE TEST.COM	%cat test_script
	$! return parameters passed to procedure	# return variables passed to \
		script
	$ WRITE SYS$OUTPUT " "P1" "	echo "argv[1]"
	$ WRITE SYS$OUTPUT " "P2" "	echo "$2"
	$ WRITE SYS$OUTPUT " "P3" "	echo "$$"
	$ EXIT	exit
	$@ TEST [DIRECTORY] TEST "HELLO -	%chmod 744 test_script
	THERE"	test_ script "[directory]" test \
		"hello there"
	[DIRECTORY]	[directory]
	TEST	test
	HELLO THERE	hello there

The above example illustrates the passing of variables to shell scripts. The double quotes around **[directory]** prevent the normal interpretation of the open and close square brackets as metacharacters. Similarly, the double quotes cause **"hello there"** to be interpreted as a single variable.

Table 11.3 Filename Modifiers

	Modifier		
UNIX	VMS		UNIX Meaning
:r	F$PARSE(file-spec..."NAME")		Returns portion of filename preceding a period; if filename does not contain a period, returns complete filename
:e	F$PARSE(file-spec..."TYPE")		Returns portion of filename following a period; if filename does not contain a period, returns null
:h	F$PARSE(file-spec..."DEVICE") + F$PARSE(file-spec..."DIRECT")		Returns head (path) of file specification
:t	F$PARSE(file-spec..."NAME") + F$PARSE(file-spec..."TYPE")		Returns tail of file specification, excluding path

11.3 *Filename Modifiers*

Filename modifiers cause the system to return portions of an absolute or relative filename, as defined in Table 11.3. VMS users familiar with the **F$PARSE** lexical function, which calls the **$PARSE** RMS service for extracting portions of a file specification, can achieve similar results using a shell script with filename modifiers. UNIX has no direct way of modifying filenames on a remote UNIX computer. Compare the VMS command **F$PARSE(file-spec. . ."NODE")**. However, as we shall see in Section 13.3.1, you can pipe a remote file lookup to a filename modifier to return portions of the filename, but not the remote host name. The following example illustrates the use of the filename modifiers outlined in Table 11.3.

VMS	UNIX
example: $TYPE TEST.COM	%cat test_script
$! Return portions of a filename	# Return portions of a \ filename
$ INQUIRE FILENAME "Enter filename: "	echo -n "Enter filename: "
$!	set filename = $<

```
$ WRITE SYS$OUTPUT """F$PARSE(FILENAME-        echo "$filename:r"
...  "NAME")'"                                 #
$ WRITE SYS$OUTPUT """F$PARSE(FILENAME-        echo "$filename:e"
...  "TYPE")'"                                 #
$ WRITE SYS$OUTPUT """F$PARSE(FILENAME-        echo "$filename:h"
...  "DIRECTORY")'"                            #
$ A := 'F$PARSE(FILENAME..."NAME")'            echo "$filename:t"
$ B := 'F$PARSE(FILENAME..."TYPE")'            #
$ C = A + B                                    #
$ WRITE SYS$OUTPUT """C'"                      #
$ EXIT                                         exit
$ @TEST.COM                                    % test_script
Enter filename: [FRED]PROGRAM.C               Enter filename /usr/fred/ \
                                                   program.c
PROGRAM                                        program
C                                              c
[FRED]                                         /usr/fred
PROGRAM.C                                      program.c
```

The variable **filename** is set using input from **stdin**, and then modified
by following the variable with a colon and the appropriate modifier.

11.4   *Variable Expansion*

The result of variable expansion depends on whether the variable is surrounded by single forward quotes, double quotes, or single backward
quotes. A single forward quote prevents any kind of variable expansion
(compare VMS variable name only). The variable name is returned literally, and alias or wildcard expansion does not take place. A double
quote groups characters or numbers into a single argument (as shown
above), allows variable expansion, and prevents wildcard expansion
(compare VMS double quotes). A single backward quote causes the
immediate execution of a command argument (compare VMS single forward quote). The following example illustrates these three kinds of variable expansion.

```
             VMS                              UNIX
example:     $ NAME = "DIR *.FOR"            % set name = "ls *.f"
                                             % echo $name
                                             ls program.f
             $ WRITE SYS$OUTPUT "NAME"       % echo '$name'
             NAME                            name
             $ WRITE SYS$OUTPUT """NAME'"    % echo "$name"
             DIR *.FOR                       ls *.f
```

echo **$name** returns the variable substitution with the metacharacter expanded. **echo '$name'** prevents any variable substitution and returns the variable name. **echo "$name"** returns the substitution for the variable name, which includes the non-expanded metacharacter *. Finally, **echo `$name`** causes immediate command execution: the result of executing the command between backward quotes becomes part of the command line. **ls *.f** indicates that one file of the file type **.f**, **program.f**, resides in the present working directory.

11.5 Comparison Operators

Table 11.4 illustrates the comparison operators supported by the C shell. We will encounter numerous uses of comparison operators in subsequent examples. We now introduce the **if** statement, discussed in greater detail under flow control in Section 11.8, to show how comparison operators function. The major distinction between UNIX and VMS comparison operators, as we have already seen, is that UNIX uses the same operator for both text and integer variables, and VMS uses a different comparison operator for each.[2]

	VMS	UNIX
example:	$! EQUAL TO	# equal to
	$ IF (I .EQ. 10) THEN	if ($i = = 10) then
	$ IF (STRING .EQS. "FALSE") THEN	if ($string = = "false") then
example:	$! NOT EQUAL TO	# not equal to
	$ IF (I .NE. 10) THEN	if ($i != 10) then
	$ IF (STRING .NES. "FALSE") THEN	if ($string != "false") then
example:	$! GREATER THAN 1 AND LESS THAN 10	# greater than 1 and less than \
	$ IF (I .GT. 1 .AND. I .LT 10) THEN	10
		if ($i>1 && $i<10) then
example:	$! EQUAL TO 0 or 1	# equal to 0 or 1
	$ IF (I .EQ. 0 .OR. I .EQ. 1) THEN	if ($i = =0 ||$i = =1) then
example:	$! EQUAL TO TRUE OR FALSE	# equal to true or false
	$ IF (STRING .EQS. "TRUE" .OR. STRING -	if ($string = = "true" || $string \
	.EQS. "FALSE") THEN	= = "false") then
example:	$! NOT LESS THAN OR EQUAL TO 10	# not less than or equal to 10
	$ IF (I .GT. 10) THEN	if (!($i< =10)) then

---

2. Unlike most functions in VMS, the string comparison operators are case-sensitive when enclosed in double quotes, for example **"false"** is not equal to **"FALSE"**.

Table 11.4 Comparison Operators

UNIX Operator	VMS Operator	UNIX Meaning
=	= == := :==	Assign value to variable
==	.EQ. .EQS.	Equal to
!	.NE. .NES.	Boolean not, for example, not equal to
&&	.AND.	Boolean and
||	.OR.	Boolean or
>	.GT. .GTS.	Greater than
<	.LT. .LTS.	Less than
>=	.GE. .GES.	Greater than or equal to
<=	.LE. .LES.	Less than or equal to

Each example compares either the variable **i** to some integer value or the variable string to some text string, as described in the comment that precedes the command. The last example, **if(!($i<=10)) then**, is noteworthy because it illustrates the nesting of comparison operators: variable **i** is neither less than nor equal to 10, that is, it is greater than 10 (identical to **if ($i>10) then**).

11.6   *File Operators*

Table 11.5 lists a type of C shell operator that tests the characteristics of a file. There is no analogy to these UNIX C shell *file operators* in VMS, although you can use values returned by the **F$FILE_ATTRIBUTES** lexical function to determine the attributes of a VMS file. The features returned by **F$FILE_ATTRIBUTES** do not translate into UNIX file operators because of the different ways in which VMS and UNIX treat files. A VMS file is highly structured, and **F$FILE_ATTRIBUTES** returns information about that structure. A UNIX file is nothing more than a string of bytes. Since a UNIX file has no file structure information, file operators only return features like file ownership and protection.

	VMS	UNIX
form:	FFILE_ATTRIBUTES (file-spec,- condition)	if (file_operator file) then
example:		# true if /usr/fred is a directory if (-d /usr/fred) then
example:		# true if /tmp/file1 exists if (-e /tmp/file1) then

```
example:        # true if /usr/fred/text contains text
                if (-f /usr/fred/text) then
example:        % whoami
                fred
                # true if fred owns /usr/fred/file
                if (-o /usr/fred/file) then
example:        # true if /usr/fred/file is readable
                if (-r /usr/fred/file) then
example:        # true if /usr/fred/file is writeable
                if (-w /usr/fred/file) then
example:        # true if /usr/fred/file is executable
                if (-x /usr/fred/file) then
example:        # true if /usr/fred/file is empty
                if (-z /usr/fred/file) then
```

Table 11.5   File Comparison Operators

UNIX	VMS	UNIX Meaning
-d		True if file is a directory
-e	1	True if file exists
-f		True if file contains text
-o	2	True if executor of file is owner
-r	2	True if file is readable by executor
-w	2	True if file is writable by executor
-x	2	True if file is executable by executor
-z	2	True if file is empty

1. Same results could be achieved with an error handler.
2. There is no VMS equivalent to return the Boolean value
described. However, the **F$FILE_ ATTRIBUTES** lexical func-
tion returns results that may be manipulated as a string variable to produce the desired effect.

File comparison operators check whether a file is readable, writable, or
executable by looking at the *protection mask,* that is, the protection
assigned to the file. In the above examples, **/usr/fred/file** will be
reported executable if its protection level renders it such, irrespective of
whether the file is an executable image, shell script, or plain text.

11.7   *Mathematical Operators*

We have seen that the UNIX **set** command associates a value to a variable, and that such values may be integers or text: for example, **set a =
1** or **set a = "test"**. VMS uses = to equate a variable to an integer value

Table 11.6 Mathematical Operators

UNIX	VMS	UNIX Meaning
Integers		
+	+	Add
−	−	Subtract
*	*	Multiply
/	/	Divide
+ +		Increment by 1
− −		Decrement by 1
%		Modulo
Bits		
>>		Right bit shift
<<		Left bit shift
~	.NOT	1's complement
!		Logical negation
|	.OR.	Inclusive or
^		Exclusive or
&	.AND.	And

and = = to equate a variable to a text value. The VMS user can perform mathematical operations on either text or integer values. The UNIX C shell permits only mathematical operations on integer variables. The C shell @ metacharacter equates a variable name to the result of a mathematical operation using integer variables. Table 11.6 lists mathematical operators used by the C shell.

example:

```
              VMS                                      UNIX
          $ TYPE TEST.COM                          % cat test_script
          $ I = 15                                 set i = 15
          $ J = 3                                  set j = 3
          $!                                       #
          $! ADDITION                              # addition
          $ K = (I + J)                            @ k = ($i + $j)
          $ WRITE SYS$OUTPUT "addition: "K'"       echo "addition: $k
          $!                                       #
          $! SUBTRACTION                           # subtraction
          $ K = (I - J)                            @ k = ($i - $j)
          $ WRITE SYS$OUTPUT "subtraction: "K"     echo "subtraction: $k
          $!                                       #
```

```
$! DIVISION
$ K = (I / J)
$ WRITE SYS$OUTPUT "division: "K'"
$!
$! MULTIPLICATION
$ K = (I * J)
$ WRITE SYS$OUTPUT "multiplication: "K'"
$!
$!
$!
$!
$!
$!
$!
$!
$!
$!
$!
$!
$!
$!
$! INVERT BITS
$ K = .NOT. I
$ WRITE SYS$OUTPUT "Invert bits: "K'"
$!
$!
$!
$!
$!
$! BITWISE INCLUSIVE OR
$ K = (I .OR. J)
$ WRITE SYS$OUTPUT "Logical or: "K'"
$!
$!
$!
$!
$!
$! BITWISE AND
$ K = (I .AND. J)
$ WRITE SYS$OUTPUT "Bitwise and: "K'"
$ EXIT
$ @TEST.COM
addition: 18
subtraction: 12
division: 5
multiply: 45
-
-
-
invert bits: -16
-
logical or: 15
```

```
# division
@ k = ($i / $j)
echo "division: $k"
#
# multiplication
@ k = ($i * $j)
echo "multiplication: $k"
#
# modulo
@ k = ($i % $j)
echo "modulo: $k
#
# right bit shift
@ k = ($i >> 2)
echo "right bit shift by 2: $k"
#
# left bit shift
@ k = ($i << 2)
echo "left bit shift by 2: $k"
#
# invert bits
@ k = (~ $i)
echo "invert bits: $k"
#
# logical negation
@ k = (! $i)
echo "logical negation: $k"
#
# bitwise inclusive or
@ k = ($i | $j)
echo "bitwise inclusive or: $k"
#
# bitwise exclusive or
@ k = ($i ^ $j)
echo "bitwise exclusive or: $k"
#
# bitwise and
@ k = ($i & $j)
echo "bitwise and: $k"
exit
% test_script
addition: 18
subtraction: 12
division: 5
multiplication: 45
modulo: 0
right bit shift by 2: 3
left bit shift by 2: 60
invert bits: -16
logical negation: 0
bitwise inclusive or: 15
```

The above examples illustrate the use of the major mathematical operators. You should take care with the syntax used in these expressions: for example, **@k** is not the same as **@ k**, nor is **~$i** the same as **~ $i**. Blanks are not necessarily ignored.

For readers unfamiliar with the characteristics of mathematical operators, we explain the above examples further. The definitions hold for VMS as well as UNIX. Note that subscripts indicate the counting base: hence 3_{10} is 3 to the Base 10, and 1111_2 is 1111 to the Base 2 (binary).

- division **(i / j)** returns an integer value rounded down. For example, **15 / 3** returns 5, and **15 / 4** returns 3.
- modulo **(i % j)** returns the remainder after division. For example, **15 % 3** returns 0, and **15 % 4** returns 3.
- bitwise right shift **(i >> j)** shifts **i** **j** bits to the right, discarding the first **j** bits. For example, **15 >> 2)** shifts **15** two bits to the right so that 1111_2 becomes 11_2, which is 3_{10}.
- bitwise left shift **(i << j)** shifts **i** **j** bits to the left and pads with zeros. For example, **(15 << 2)** shifts **15** two bits to the left and pads with zeros, so that 1111_2 becomes 111100_2, which is 60_{10}.
- **~** or 1's complement changes 0's to 1's and vice-versa including the sign bit, thus it has the effect of making the integer value n become $-(n + 1)$. For example **~ 15** becomes -16.
- **!**, logical negation, returns 0 for any result not equal to 0 and 1 for any result equal to 0.
- **|** signifies a bitwise inclusive or: a bit that is 1 in either variable returns 1.
  For example, **(15 | 3)** $15_{10} = 1111_2$
  $$3_{10} = 0011_2$$
  (15 | 3) $= 1111_2 = 15_{10}$
- **^** signifies a bitwise exclusive or: a bit that is 1 in both variables returns 0, and a bit that is 1 in only one of the variables returns 1.
  For example, **(15 ^ 3)** $15_{10} = 1111_2$
  $$3_{10} = 0011_2$$
  (15 ^ 3) $= 1100_2 = 12_{10}$
- **&** signifies a bitwise and: a bit that is 1 in both variables returns 1, and other bits return 0.
  For example, **(15 & 3)** $15_{10} = 1111_2$

$$3_{10} = 0011_2$$
$$(15 \And 3) \qquad = 0011_2 = 3_{10}$$

11.8   *Flow Control*

The statements **IF** and **GOTO** provide flow control in VMS command procedures. The UNIX C shell also offers **if** and **goto** and the additional statements **while**, **foreach**, **switch**, and **shift** to control the logical flow of a shell script. As with DCL command procedures, you can exert flow control in response to error conditions (see Section 11.8.8).

11.8.1   *if*

The **if** statement provides a one- or two-way conditional branch. You can nest **if** statements, as the more complex examples in Section 11.9 show.

	VMS[3]	UNIX
form:	$ IF (expression) THEN [$] command	if (condition) then
		. . . .
		else
		. . . .
		endif
example:	$ TYPE TEST.COM	% cat test_script
	$! report a files executable status	# report a files executable status
	$ INQUIRE A "Enter filename: "	echo -n "Enter filename: "
	$ IF (F$PARSE(A. . . "TYPE") .NES. -	set a = $<
	".EXE") THEN GOTO NO	if (-x $a) then
	$ WRITE SYS$OUTPUT ""'A' is -	echo "$a is executable"
	executable"	
	$ EXIT	else
	$ NO:	echo "$a is not executable"
	$ WRITE SYS$OUTPUT ""'A' is not -	endif
	executable"	
	$ EXIT	exit
example:	$ TYPE TEST.COM	% cat test_script
	$! display a non-empty file	# display a non-empty file
	$ IF (F$FILE_ATTRIBUTES('P1',"EOF") -	if (-z $1) then
	.EQ. 0) THEN GOTO EMPTY	echo "File is empty"
	$ TYPE 'P1'	endif
	$ EXIT	more $1
	$ EMPTY: "WRITE SYS$OUTPUT "File is -	exit
	empty"	
	$ EXIT	

3. The **IF. . THEN. . ELSE. .** construct has been added to VMS 5.0.

In the first example, **if (-x $a) then** defines a two-way branch that reports whether or not the file is executable (compare the VMS lexical function **F$PARSE**, which determines whether a file extension is **.EXE**, that is, if the file is likely to be executable). In the second example, **if (-z $1) then** defines a one-way conditional branch. If the file is empty, the fact is reported. Then, in both the empty and the non-empty case, the example displays the file with the **more** command; there is no **else** condition.

11.8.2 *while*

Taken literally, the **while** statement means, "while a condition is in effect, perform a specific task."

	VMS	UNIX
form:		while (expression)
		. . . .
		end
example:	$ TYPE TEST.COM	% cat test_script
	$! time waster	# display calendar by month
	$ I = 1	set i = 1
	$ LOOP:	while ($i != 13)
	$ IF (I .GE. 13) THEN EXIT	cal $i 1988
	$ WRITE SYS$OUTPUT "No calendar - available"	@ i = ($i + 1)
	$ I = I + 1	end
	$ GOTO LOOP	echo "Calendar complete"
	$ EXIT	exit

This example introduces the **cal** command, which displays a calendar for any given year. If you give only the year argument, **cal** displays the year with four months across the screen. The shell script **test_script** displays the months one after the other. By using the month option to **cal** (variable **i**), the script repeats the loop, increasing **i** by one each time. As long as **i** is less than 13, the script continues. When **i** reaches 13, the script terminates.

11.8.3 *foreach*

foreach performs some function on a file in a list of files that meet the specified criterion. **foreach** sequentially defines each file that meets the specified criterion as a variable and performs some operation on it. In VMS, you first create a list of files in a temporary file, then read back the temporary file, performing the appropriate operation on each file in the list.

	VMS	UNIX
form:		**foreach variable (filelist)**
		. . . .
		end
example:	$ TYPE TEST.COM	% **cat test_script**
	$! Type all .TXT files	# **Display all .txt files**
	$ DIR/COL = 1/OUTPUT = A.OUT *.TXT	**foreach i (*.txt)**
	$ OPEN/READ INFILE A.OUT	**cat $i**
	$ READ INFILE SCRATCH	**end**
	$ READ INFILE SCRATCH	
	$ READ INFILE SCRATCH	
	$ LOOP:	
	$ READ INFILE PROG	
	$ IF (PROG .EQS. "") THEN GOTO END	
	$ TYPE 'PROG'	
	$ GOTO LOOP	
	$ END: CLOSE INFILE	
	$ EXIT	

foreach i (*.txt) sequentially displays each **.txt** file in the current directory with the command **cat $i**. Obviously, **cat *.txt** has the same effect as this script.

11.8.4   *switch*

switch directs the flow of a script to a particular *case label,* a point in the script which matches the possible conditions defined by the **switch** statement. You may define a default condition **default:** in case none of the **switch** statements matches a case label. The **breaksw** statement directs flow to the statement following the **endsw** statement. If no condition is met and no default condition is defined, execution continues after the **endsw** statement. Sound confusing? The following simple example helps to clarify the use of **switch**.

	VMS	UNIX
form:		**switch (string)**
		case string:
		. . . .
		breaksw
		case string:
		. . . .
		breaksw
		default:
		. . . .
		endsw

example:

```
$ TYPE TEST.COM                                    % cat test_script
$! Select a printer                                # Select a printer
$ ON WARNING THEN GOTO WRONG                        #
$ WRITE SYS$OUTPUT "Select a printer"              echo "Select a printer"
$ INQUIRE PR "Enter 1 or <CR> for laser -          echo "Enter 1 or <CR> for
                                                      laser; \
  2 for plotter; 3 for character printer"             2 for plotter; 3 for character"
$ IF (PR .EQS. "") THEN GOTO 1                      set p = $<
$ GOTO 'P1'                                         switch $p
$ 1:                                                case 1:
$ PRINT/QUEUE=LASER 'P1'                               lpr -Plaser $1
$ GOTO DONE                                         breaksw
$ 2:                                                case 2:
$ PRINT/QUEUE=PLOTTER 'P1'                             lpr -Pplotter $1
$ GOTO DONE                                         breaksw
$ 3:                                                case 3:
$ PRINT/QUEUE=CHARACTER 'P1'                           lpr -Pcharacter $1
$ DONE:                                             breaksw
$ EXIT                                              default:
$ WRONG:                                               lpr -Plaser $1
$ WRITE SYS$OUTPUT "Invalid Entry"                  endsw
$ EXIT                                              exit
```

In this example, the **switch** statement directs the printing of a file to a specific printer queue. The user issues a response of **1**, **2**, **3**, or ⟨CR⟩ to choose a printer. The script directs flow to the appropriate case label corresponding to the user's response. The **lpr** command queues the file and passes control to the **endsw** statement label. If the user enters the default condition ⟨CR⟩ or any character other than **1**, **2**, or **3**, control passes to the **default** statement label, which prints the file of the default print queue **laser**. Compare this to VMS, where you must introduce an **ON WARNING** condition to handle an erroneous character. Shell scripts also have error handling capabilities, as we shall see in Section 11.8.7.

Note that nested **if. .then. .else** constructs could have exerted the same flow control. Where case labels are constants, however, **switch** is more convenient.

11.8.5   *goto*

You can use the UNIX C shell **goto** statement the same way as the VMS **GOTO** statement to achieve flow control, by directing flow to a statement label ending with a colon. Shell script statement labels must appear on a line by themselves, unlike their VMS counterparts which may precede any valid DCL command line.

	VMS	UNIX
form:	$ GOTO LABEL	goto label
	. . . .	. . . .
	$ LABEL: [command]	label:
example:	$ TYPE TEST.COM	% cat test_script
	$ IF (P1 .EQS. "") THEN -	if ($1 = = "") then
	GOTO UNDEFINED	goto undefined
	$ WRITE SYS$OUTPUT "THE VALUE -	endif
	OF PARAMETER 1 is: "P1'"	echo "The value of variable 1 is: $1"
	$ EXIT	exit
	$ UNDEFINED: WRITE SYS$OUTPUT -	undefined:
	"PARAMETER 1 IS UNDEFINED"	echo "Variable 1 is undefined"
	$ EXIT	exit

In this example, if the value of the first variable passed to a script is undefined (null), the **goto** statement directs flow to the label **undefined:**.

11.8.6 *shift*

shift does not direct the flow to a specific line in the script, but to a different element of the same variable. **shift** downgrades each element number by one, discarding element one. For example, using **shift** on variable **test** reassigns element **n** of **test** (**test[n]**) to element **n-1** (**test[n-1]**). The element **test[2]** becomes **test[1]**, and the original **test[1]** is discarded. In VMS, you assign variable names to the elements of the original variable using the **F$ELEMENT** lexical function to decompose the variable into separate elements with blanks as delimiters, and then reassign the value of **element** to **element-1** via a conditional loop. **shift** is particularly useful for performing the same operation on each of the arguments passed to the script file by shifting **argv**. In this example, **shift** progressively decrements the elements of the variable **z** and echoes the result.

	VMS	UNIX
form:		shift variable
example:	$ TYPE TEST.COM	% cat test_script
	$! VMS analogy to UNIX C-	# Using shift
	shell shift	
	$ Z := " ONE TWO THREE"	set z = "one two three"
	$ NUM = 1	echo "Before using shift there are $#z elements"
	$ LOOP1:	while ($#z > 0)
	$ EL'NUM' = -	echo "$z[1]"
	F$ELEMENT('NUM'," ",Z)	

```
$ IF (EL'NUM' .EQS. "") -        shift z
    THEN GOTO NEXT
$ NUM = NUM + 1                  end
$ GOTO LOOP1                     echo "After using shift there are $#z elements"
$ NEXT:                          exit
$ TOTAL = NUM - 1
$ WRITE SYS$OUTPUT -
    "Start with "TOTAL'"
$ NEW_NUM = NUM - 1
$ LOOP2:
$ IF (NEW_NUM .EQ. 0) -
    THEN GOTO END
$ EL'NUM' = EL'NEW_ -
    NUM'
$ TEST = = EL'NUM'
$ WRITE SYS$OUTPUT -
    ""TEST'"
$ NEW_NUM = NEW_ -
    NUM - 1
$ NUM = NUM - 1
$ GOTO LOOP2
$ END:
$ WRITE SYS$OUTPUT -
    "No elements left"
$ EXIT
$ @TEST.COM                      % test_script
Start with 3 elements            Before using shift there are 3 elements
THREE                            one
TWO                              two
ONE                              three
No elements left                 After using shift there are 0 elements
```

11.8.7   *Error Handling and Flow Control*

VMS uses the constructs **ON ERROR THEN**, **ON WARNING THEN**, and **ON SEVERE_ERROR THEN** to direct the flow of a DCL command procedure when it finds an error or warning condition. The error or warning condition applies to all command lines following the statement until you introduce a new condition or turn error handling off with **SET NOON**. UNIX handles errors on a command-by-command basis, using the built-in shell variable **status**.

You can also invoke error handling for piped commands using the comparison operators || and **&&**. The conditions that apply to these operators are as follows:

command1 succeeds	operator	command2 executes
yes	||	no
no	||	yes
yes	&&	yes
no	&&	no

We will illustrate each form of the operator with an example.

UNIX

form: % command1 || command2
example: % cc test.c >& err1 || mail fred < err1
form: % command1 && command2
example: % grep csh /etc/passwd > cusers && lpr cusers

The construct **cc test.c >& err1 || mail fred < err1** compiles a C program. If the compilation reports no errors, command execution stops. If an error occurs, the file containing the error messages is mailed to user **fred**.

The construct **grep csh /etc/passwd > cusers && lpr cusers** searches the **/etc/passwd** file for **csh**, records that contain the names of users who use the C shell by default. If any such records are found, they are output to the file **cusers** and then printed on the default line printer. If **grep** fails to find any entries, the **&&** condition fails and the null file is not sent to the printer.

Now we discuss the use of the predefined shell variable **status**.[4] The variable **status** is redetermined after the execution of any command or shell script. You can display it with the command **echo $status**. Unfortunately, the value it returns is not consistent from command to command. For example, **find /dir -name test -print**, which finds all files named **test** down the directory hierarchy from **/dir**, returns a status of **0** if **/dir** does not exist. **lpr file1**, on the other hand, returns a status of **1** if the file **file1** does not exist. Both commands return a non-zero status if command syntax is incorrect. You should experiment with status values returned by commands before using the values as conditional branches

---

4. The name of the UNIX variable is **status**; preceding it with the **$** metacharacter indicates variable substitution. In VMS, on the other hand, the logical name is **$STATUS**; **$** is part of the symbol name.

in script files. You may find the following rule of thumb useful: **0** indicates that execution was successful, **1** indicates that there was nothing wrong with the command but that it did not achieve what it set out to do, and any other value indicates that there is a problem with the command syntax.

	VMS	UNIX

example:	`$ SEARCH MYFILE.DAT FRED`
	fred
	`$ SHOW SYMBOL $STATUS`
	$STATUS = = "%X00000001"
		`% grep fred myfile.dat`
		fred
		`%. echo $status`
		0

example:	`$ SEARCH MYFILE.DAT JILL`
	%SEARCH _I_ NOMATCHES, no strings -
	  matched
	`$ SHOW SYMBOL $STATUS`
	$STATUS = = "%X08D78053"
		`% grep jill myfile.dat`
		%
		
		`% echo $status`
		1

example:	`$ SEARCH MYFIL.DAT FRED`
	-RMS-E-FNF, file not found
	`$ SHOW SYMBOL $STATUS`
	$STATUS = = "%X08D7804A"
		`%. grep fred myfil.dat`
		myfil.dat: no such file or directory
		`% ιecho $status`
		2

These three examples illustrate the above statement using the **grep** command. If the command executes correctly and finds the search string, it returns a value of **0**. If the command executes correctly but does not find the search string, it returns a value of **1**. If the file itself is not found, the condition is more severe and a value of **2** is returned. Compare VMS, where **$STATUS** returns an odd value if the command execution is successful.

We will now put this all together in a shell script. This example reports on the type of error found when using **grep**, based on the value of **status**.

	VMS	UNIX

example:	`$ TYPE TEST.COM`
	`$! error handling`
	`$ SET NOON`
	`$ SEARCH 'P2' 'P1'`
	`$ IF ($SEVERITY .EQ. 1) THEN GOTO 1`
	`$ IF ($SEVERITY .EQ. 2) .OR. -`
	
	`      $SEVERITY .EQ. 4) THEN GOTO 2`
	`$ IF ($SEVERITY .EQ. 3) THEN GOTO 3`
	`$ EXIT`
		`% cat test_script`
		`# error handling`
		`grep $1 $2`
		`set error = $status`
		`if ($error = = 0) then`
		`echo "execution \`
		`    successful"`
		`goto end`
		`endif`
		`if ($error = = 1) then`

```
$ 1: WRITE SYS$OUTPUT "Execution successful"      echo "nothing found"
$ EXIT                                            goto end
$ 2: WRITE SYS$OUTPUT "Error"                     endif
$ EXIT                                            echo "severe error found"
$ 3: WRITE SYS$OUTPUT "Nothing found"             end:
$ EXIT                                            exit
```

11.9   *Built-in C Shell Commands*

C shell users do not have to worry about the distinction between built-in C shell commands and separate programs called by the C shell. However, users who invoke the Bourne or Korn shells, either on the same computer or on different computers, will discover that the built-in C shell commands are not available. Some built-in shell commands that we have already discussed are **dirs**, **pushd**, and **popd** for manipulating the directory stack; **fg**, **bg**, and **jobs** for background processing; **at**, **kill**, and **nice** for affecting processes; and **history** for reviewing the history list.

We now introduce several new built-in C shell commands particularly useful in shell programming: **onintr** (on interrupt; compare the VMS command **ON CONTROL_Y**), which redirects the control of a script when an interrupt is issued; **eval**, which executes a command built from variables, that is, it forces the current process to interpret any shell metacharacters before performing the variable substitution; **time** (compare the VMS command **SHOW STATUS**), which determines the execution time and elapsed (wall clock) time of a command or shell script; and **source**, which forces the execution of commands or shell scripts by the parent shell.

11.9.1   *onintr*

The shell command **onintr** redirects the flow of a script following a ⟨CTRL⟩-C interrupt (compare the VMS command **ON CONTROL_Y**). Interrupt redirection is particularly useful to the VMS user writing captive command procedures, that is, procedures which do not let the user escape to the command language interpreter. UNIX captive shell scripts cannot be created so easily, since the user always has the option to stop the current process with ⟨CTRL⟩-Z and fork another copy of the shell.

	VMS	UNIX
form:	$ ON CONTROL_Y THEN GOTO LABEL	onintr label
	. . . .	. . . .
	$ LABEL:	label:
example:	$ TYPE TEST.COM	% cat test_script
	$! Partial example of interrupt handling	# Partial example of interrupt \ handling
	$ ON CONTROL_Y THEN GOTO END	onintr end
	. . .	. . .
	$ EXIT	exit
	$ END:	end:
	$ TYPE SYS$OUTPUT -	echo "Script abnormally \ terminated"
	"Procedure abnormally terminated"	exit
	$ EXIT	

The example illustrates a construct that exits a script: if you issue a ⟨CTRL⟩-C interrupt, flow control passes to the statement label **end** and a message reporting abnormal termination is displayed.

11.9.2 *eval*

The built-in C shell command **eval** has no analogy in VMS. If the VMS user issues a command, the same process that invoked it executes it, assuming it is not spawned. UNIX, on the other hand, often forks a child process to execute the command. Since this child process, forked to execute a command string defined as a variable by the parent process, takes each element of the variable literally and not as a command string, **eval** forces execution by the parent process, which interprets the command string correctly.

	VMS	UNIX
example:	$ TEST = = "DIR/ - OWNER"	% set test = "ls -l | grep root"
	$ 'TEST'	% $test
	[files listed here]	/ not found
		grep not found
		root not found
		% eval $test
		-rwxr-xr-x 2 root 2560 Jun 13 11:17 rootfile

In this example, the problem is that the child shell forked to process the command takes variable substitutions literally; that is, it interprets metacharacters not as such but as elements of the variable. Thus, the shell searches for files with the names |, **grep**, and **root**, and not for files in the user's directory owned by **root** as intended. **eval** forces execution by the current (parent) shell, which takes the elements of the variable as arguments to the command. You can think of **eval** as taking a string, converting it into an argument list using spaces as delimiters, and causing that string to be interpreted by the curent (parent) shell.

11.9.3　　**time**

The built-in C shell command **time** (compare the VMS command **SHOW STATUS**) reports the time it takes commands and shell scripts to execute. If no argument is given, **time** reports the time used by the parent process and all the child processes it has generated since the beginning of the terminal session.

	VMS	UNIX
form:		% time [command]
example:	$ SHOW STATUS	
	$ @TEST.COM	
	$ SHOW STATUS	% time myscript
		0.2u 0.1s 0.22 33% 1+2k 1+1io 1pf+0w

	VMS
example:	$ SHOW STATUS
	Status on 2-AUG-1988 15:30:37.97 Elapsed CPU : 0 00:41:56.73
	Buff. I/O : 5216 Cur. ws. : 350 Open files : 0
	Dir. I/O : 423 Phys. Mem. 177 Page Faults : 7688

UNIX

% time
2.8u 3.3s 20:46 1% 38+40k 38+25io \
55pf+0w

The example **time myscript** returns the time it takes to execute the script file myscript, as follows:

0.2u	0 minutes and 2 seconds of user CPU time
0.1s	0 minutes and 1 second of system CPU time
0.22	0 minutes and 22 seconds of wall clock time
33%	33% of the available CPU resources
1+2k	1k of physical memory + 2k of the memory stack
1+1io	1 page input + 1 page output to disk (a page equals 512 bytes)
1pf+0w	1 page faulted in, + 0 pages faulted out

The second example shows the output of **time** without arguments.

11.9.4   *source*

You can nest scripts by including the name of a script file as a command line in the current script file. Compare VMS, where **@COMMAND_ PROCEDURE** is a command line in the current procedure. The shell running the current script file usually forks a child process with its own set of characteristics for the nested script to execute in. At the end of the nested script, control returns to the current script. Any definitions made by the child process are not passed back to the parent (compare VMS global definitions, which become part of the parent command procedure). Preceding the nested script with the built-in C shell command **source** prevents the forking of a child process and forces the current process to perform the execution, so that any definitions that the nested script makes become active for the current script.

The following two examples illustrate other important uses of the **source** command.

	VMS	UNIX
form:	$ @ command_procedure	% source [-h] script_file
example:	$ @LOGIN.COM	% source .cshrc
example:		% source -h history_list

In the first example, **source .cshrc** invokes definitions for the parent shell if they have just been made through modification to the **.cshrc** file. If **source** had not been invoked, the user would have had to log out of the C shell and log back in again for the new definitions to take effect in the parent process. If **.cshrc** was excecuted without the **source** command, the child process forked to execute the command would make the definitions, which would immediately be lost when control returned to the parent process. In the second example, **source -h history_list** adds a predefined set of commands, contained in the file **history_list**, to the history list. You could have created the file **history list** with the command **history -h 15 > history_list**, for example. Note that you may save a specified number of commands from the history list with the shell command **set savehist n**, which retains the last **n** commands. The history list is saved in the hidden file **.history** and automatically made part of the history list at the beginning of the next terminal session with the command **source -h ˜/.history**, invoked by the shell at startup time.

11.10　　*Debugging Shell Scripts*

You can debug shell scripts by explicitly invoking the C shell program
with the command **csh**, using one or more options to execute the script.
The result is similar to using the VMS command **SET VERIFY**, either prior
to or as part of a command procedure.

	VMS	UNIX
form:	$ SET VERIFY	% csh [option(s)] script_file
	$ @ command_procedure	
	$ TYPE TEST.COM	% cat test_script
	$ DIR/FULL 'P1'	ls -l $1
	$ EXIT	exit
	$ SET VERIFY	
example:	$ @TEST_SCRIPT A	% csh -x test_script a
	$ DIR/FULL A	ls -l a
	[directory listing here]	-rwxr-xr-x 1 fred 32 Aug 8 19:19 a
	$ EXIT	exit
example:		% csh -v test_script a
		ls -l $1
		-rwxr-xr-x 1 fred 32 Aug 8 19:19 a
		exit

The construct **csh -x test_script a** echoes the command lines after variable substitution (**x** option), and **csh -v test_script a** echoes the command
lines prior to variable substitution (**v** option). Hence, the **x** option is useful for locating problems in variable substitution, and the **v** option is
useful for locating the line on which a script file is failing. The **X** and **V**
options (not shown) extend the features of **x** and **v** to include the **.cshrc**
file when you have not used a fast start of the C shell.

11.11　　*Summary*

A discussion of three annotated script files summarizes the features presented in this chapter.

The first script file, **run_program**, on the basis of the user's response to
a number of questions, creates a script file containing the commands
necessary to run a program called **prolsq**. The flow of the script depends
on whether the user includes arguments as part of the command line. If
the user specifies no arguments, the system prompts for the appropriate
input.

example:

```
% cat run_program
#!/bin/csh -f
# run_program: Use symbolic links to associate data files to the program
#              PROLSQ and then execute the program.
#
# Display banner message
echo "= = = = = = = = = = = = = = = = = = = = = = = = = = = = = ="
echo "                    Prolsq Submission Procedure"
echo "= = = = = = = = = = = = = = = = = = = = = = = = = = = = = ="
echo " "
if ($1 = = "help") then            # redirect flow if help required
goto info
endif
if ($1 = = " ") then
   echo "Interactive input\        # determine if 1st argument defined
        mode..."                   # yes: assume all arguments defined
   echo " "                        # no: interactively prompt for arguments
else
   echo "Predefined input \
        mode..."
   echo " "
     if ($7 = = "") then           # exit if all 7 arguments not defined
     echo "Incorrect number of \
          arguments"
     exit
     endif
   set card1 = $1                  # assign variables to input arguments
   set card2 = $2
   set card3 = $3
   set card4 = $4
   set card5 = $5
   set card6 = $6
   set card7 = $7
   goto start_execution            # move to execution phase
endif                              # begin interactive input phase
echo -n "CONTROL DATA FILE (<cr> = prolsq.dat):"
set card1 = $<                     # prompt for each input variable
if ($card 1 = = "") then           # and assign it offering a default
   set card1 = "prolsq.dat"
endif
echo -n "INPUT RESTRAINTS FILE (<cr> = atmdst.dat):"
set card2 = $<                     # repeat for remaining 6 arguments
if ($card2 = = "") then
   set card2 = "atmdst.dat"
endif
echo -n "INPUT SHIFTS FILE (<cr> = shift.in):"
set card3 = $<
if ($card3 = = "") then
   set card3 = "shift.in"
```

```
endif
echo -n "OUTPUT SHIFTS FILE (<cr> = shift.out):"
  set card4 = $<
if ($card4 = = "") then
  set card4 = "shift.out"
endif
echo -n "REFLECTION INPUT FILE (⟨cr⟩ = prolsq.hkl)
set card5 = $<
if ($card5 = = "") then
  set card5 = "prolsq.hkl"
endif
echo -n "STRUCTURE FACTOR OUTPUT FILE (⟨cr⟩ = prolsq.fofc)"
  set card6 = $<
if ($card6 = = "") then
  set card6 = "prolsq.fofc"
endif
echo -n "COORDINATE OUTPUT FILE (⟨cr⟩ = prolsq.outxyz):"
  set card7 = $<
if ($card7 = = "") then
  set card7 = "prolsq.outxyz"
endif
#
start_execution:
# write all program parameters to a script file run_prolsq.scr
echo "#" > run_prolsq.scr                          # open run_prolsq.scr
echo "cd $cwd" >> run_prolsq.scr                   # append to run_prolsq.scr
echo "ln -s $card2 fort.10" >>run_prolsq.scr
echo "ln -s $card3 fort.15" >> run_prolsq.scr
echo "ln -s $card4 fort.16" >> run_prolsq.scr
echo "ln -s $card5 fort.20" > run_prolsq.scr
echo "ln -s $card6 fort.31" >> run_prolsq.scr
echo "ln -s $card7 fort.32" >> run_prolsq.scr
echo "ln -s /stripe/idisk fort.3" >> run_prolsq.scr
echo "ln -s /stripe/jdisk fort.4" >> run_prolsq.scr
echo "time prolsq.exe < $card1" >> run_prolsq.scr # stdin defined by
$card1
run_prolsq.scr                                     # run program giving the
                                                   # execution time

exit                                               # output is written to
                                                   # stdout

#   helpful information
info:
echo " "
echo      "Prolsq arguments:"
echo   "argv(1)    control data file        (unit 5)     default prolsq.dat"
echo   "argv(2)    input coordinates        (unit10)     default atmdst.dat"
echo   "argv(3)    input shifts             (unit15)     default shifts.in"
echo   "argv(4)    output shifts            (unit16)     default shifts.out"
echo   "argv(5)    reflection list          (unit20)     default newrefs.dat"
echo   "argv(6)    structure factor output  (unit31)     default fofc.out"
```

```
echo  "argv(7)    coordinate output        (unit32)    default xyz.out"
echo " "
echo  "NB idisk (unit3) and jdisk (unit4) are scratch files written and"
echo  "   read in a stripe partition i.e. simultaneously writes to 2"
echo  "   file systems"
exit
```

First, **run_program** tests for input arguments. If the first argument is **"help"**, control passes to the statement label **info**, which displays information on running the script, and then exits. If the first argument is not defined as **"help"**, the script assumes that all arguments have been defined on the command line and that interactive prompting is not required. Flow passes to a statement that checks whether all seven required arguments have been specified. If they have, control passes to the statement label **start_execution**. If all seven arguments have not been defined, the script terminates with an error message. If no arguments have been specified, the script prompts the user for the appropriate input, offering default responses.

Once the variables **card1** through **card7** have been defined in a script file, **run_prolsq.scr** is generated, containing the appropriate symbolic links to associate data files with FORTRAN unit numbers.[5] The program **prolsq.exe** then executes with the **time** command providing timing information; any program output is sent to **stdout**, the terminal.

The second example, **menu_script**, illustrates the use of a menu interface to access a simple database consisting of a number of files. Each file in the database contains a field called a recognition code at the end of each record, which is part of the name of the file. Each menu option that accepts a recognition code uses that code to point to one or more files.

example:
```
UNIX
%cat menu_script
#!/bin/csh -f
# ====================================
#            menu_script: simple menu driven database lookup
# ====================================
#
#
```

---

5. How data files are associated with FORTRAN unit numbers depends on the version of UNIX and the version of the FORTRAN compiler (see Section 10.1).

```
# retain original directory pointer and move to database directory
pushd /data1/pdb
# present banner
echo "  cuhhca Brookhaven Database Utility Program 'date   "
# ' (back quote) causes immediate execution of the date command
# to return the time the script was invoked
#
onintr menu                              # on interrupt return to menu
menu:
echo " "                                 # present menu of options
echo "  The following options are available:"
echo " "
echo "      I   list identity of the database"
echo "      D   list a directory of the database contents"
echo "      SD   search the directory listing for keywords"
echo "      SF   search full database for keywords"
echo "      T   list a database entry at the terminal"
echo "      C   copy database entry with possible format conversion"
echo "      Q   quit the database"
echo " "
echo -n "Option> "                       # user enters option here
set command = $<
goto $command                            # branch to option
#
# identity option - describes latest database update
#
I:                                       # account for upper and
i:                                       # and lowercase user response
echo "  This database is the April 1986 release"
#
goto menu                                # return to menu
#
# directory option - display a file summarizing all database entries
#
D:
d:
echo " Type ⟨CTRL⟩-C to return to menu"
echo " "
echo " Use the 4 character recognition code at the end of each entry"
echo " to address entries with subsequent menu options"
# The file directory contains header information for each file in the
# directory and was created with the command head -4 *.dat >> directory
#
cat directory
goto menu
#
# search directory for keywords using grep - records returned contain
# filename from where they were originally extracted with the head command
#
SD:
```

```
sd:
echo " "
echo -n "keyword(s).- "
set string = $<
grep -i "$string" directory              # disregard case or string (i)
goto menu
#
# search all files for string N.B. this is much slower than
# searching the file directory and should be used only after
# the search directory option has failed to return useful
# information
#
sf:
SF:
echo -n "Keyword(s):- "
set string = $<
grep -i $string *.dat                     # search all data files
goto menu
#
# list a database entry
#
T:
t:
echo -n "Enter recognition code:-"        # code obtained from a search option
set entry = $<
cat 'entry'
goto menu
#
# Copy entry - calls a program format.exe which will format a
# database entry suitable for editing. The user is
# prompted for the output file and appropriate symbolic links
# established for the input file (database entry) and output file
# (user file)
#
C:
c:
echo -n "Enter recognition code:- "
set temp_filein = $<
set filein = '/data1/pdb/pdb'$temp_filein
echo -n "Filename for output coordinates [/group/user/file]: "
set fileout = $<
ln -s $filein fort.1
ln -s $fileout fort.2
format.exe
rm fort.*                                 # remove symbolic links
goto menu
#
# FINITO - gracefully exit the script from the menu
#
Q:
```

```
q:
echo "   Exit Brookhaven database utility program      `date`"
popd                                                # return user to original directory
exit
```

The script file **menu_script** presents a menu of options to the user. The user's response to the option list directs flow control. The script retains the present working directory for later recovery using **pushd** and **popd**. Files are searched with **grep** for strings specified by the user, entries are typed with **cat**, or the program **program.exe** is executed, performing a format conversion specified by the user.

In the last example, **which** locates the path to any commands given as arguments provided the path is in the user's path list. **which** is useful for finding the directory where a system program or user program resides. This example comes directly from the BSD version of UNIX, with additional comments for clarity.

```
                  UNIX
example:   % cat /etc/ucb/which
           #! /bin/csh -f
           # fast start of the C shell
           #
           # @(#)which.csh 4.2 (Berkeley)          83/02/14
           #
           # which : locate the path to a command i.e. what directory it is in
           #
           set prompt                              # pretend this shell is interactive \
                                                      -strike
           set path2 = $PATH                       # save PATH in case it gets changed in \
                                                      .cshrc
           # if .cshrc exists, execute it in the current shell to establish
           # any aliases
           if ( -e ~/.cshrc ) source ~/.cshrc
           setenv PATH $path2                      # restore PATH
           # prevent variable name expansion
           set noglob
           #
           # loop for each argument (i.e. command) given
           #
           foreach arg ( $argv )
           set alius = `alias $arg`                # determine if the argument is an alias
           switch ( $#alius )                      # 0 = no ; 1 = yes
           case 0 :                                # if so use the first real command \
                                                      name
```

```
            breaksw
      case 1 :
         set arg = $alius[1]
         breaksw
      default :
         echo ${arg}: "       " aliased to $alius
         continue
      endsw
      unset found
      if ( $arg:h != $arg:t ) then              # if a path is specified
            if ( -e $arg ) then                 # if file exists in current directory
                  echo $arg
            else
                  echo $arg not found
            endif
            continue
      else                                      # only command name given
            foreach i ( $path )                 # check for existence in each element \
            if ( -x $i/$arg && ! -d $i/$arg \     of path
      ) then
                        echo $i/$arg
                  set found                     # found exists
                  break
                  endif
            end
      endif
      if ( ! $?found ) then                     # if found does not exist
            echo no $arg in $path
      endif
      end
```

The **which** BSD command script accepts multiple arguments (in this case commands). For each argument, **which** determines whether that command is an alias. If so, it uses the standard command name to determine the path. **which** then determines whether a path has been included as part of the argument. If so, the script determines whether the file exists in the directory specified (that is, it functions like the **ls** command) and then exits. If a path is not specified, **foreach** is used to check each directory in the path list. If the command is found, is not a directory, and is executable, the path is reported and the script exits or checks the next argument supplied. If, on the other hand, after exhausting the path list, the command is not found, that fact is reported and the script exits or checks the next argument.

Chapter 12

Text Processing

It is always good
When a man [or woman] has two irons in the fire.

Francis Beaumont and John Fletcher

This chapter discusses the standard UNIX text processing tools available to users familiar with VMS DSR (Digital Standard Runoff).[1] UNIX has a number of powerful text processing tools which require programming skills to fully utilize, and which therefore may appear bewildering to the novice (see Table 12.1). We will restrict our discussion to UNIX features that perform simple text processing approximately equivalent to VMS DSR. Users who are already familiar with VMS DSR and who need to create a formatted document on a UNIX system will find this chapter useful.

VMS DSR and UNIX text processing tools both require embedded flags in the text to specify the formatting features. Today, many users regard this requirement as arcane, for two reasons.[2] First, text processing on personal computers has introduced many easy-to-use software products. Second, these products are "interactive": changes to the format of the document occur as you add or delete text. You do not have to make changes to the text with an editor, modify the text processing flags, process the document with the text processor, and then review the results. Although true WYSIWYG (What You See Is What You Get) software—the exact representation on the terminal screen of what you get on paper—is rare (some say nonexistent), many hardware and software combinations come close. The Apple Macintosh running any one of a number of software packages (for example, PageMaker) is of course a good example. True WYSIWYG requires a bit-map terminal capable of displaying a whole page using exactly the same fonts available to the printer. These features are available on some of today's workstations.

Many third-party software vendors, along with Digital Equipment Corporation, have addressed the needs of VMS users for interactive text

---

1. We define text processing as the manipulation of text to produce a document in a desired format. We make no attempt to distinguish among the features that characterize word processing, desktop publishing, and typesetting.

2. Text processing is another example of a religious war that rages over which is the best piece of software: users of Tex and SCRIBE are likely to disagree with this statement.

Table 12.1 UNIX Text Processing Tools

Tool	Function
Basic Tools	
nroff	Basic text formatting tool
troff	Extension of **nroff** to support typesetting and laser printers
ditroff	Device-independent **troff**
Macros	
ms	Distributed with UNIX Version 7 and BSD
mm	Distributed with System V
me	Newer version available mainly with BSD
Preprocessors	
eqn	Formats mathematical equations
pic	Simple line drawing
refer	Bibliography generation
tbl	Table processing

processing tools; this book was written with one of them. These tools are usually a compromise between VMS DSR and true WYSIWYG. The compromise is necessary to accommodate the disparity between the limited features of most terminals and the high-resolution, multiple-font laser printers attached to many VAX/VMS computers. For example, you can perform interactive text filling and centering, but you must still indicate font changes with embedded flags. There are fewer interactive text processing products available for UNIX, but this situation is changing as UNIX gains acceptance in the commercial sector.

Given the availability of easy-to-use, interactive text processing tools, why bother with UNIX text processing tools at all? The answer is twofold. First, like VMS DSR, since the tools are part of the operating system you can use them at no additional cost. Second, because UNIX can function on a variety of hardware types, you can produce the same formatted document on any hardware that supports UNIX. The **man** pages exemplify this fact. They are distributed as unformatted files: when you invoke the **man** command, it formats the **man** page for display using the standard UNIX text processing tools. Hence, you can easily write or modify a **man** page and display it in the same format on any computer that supports UNIX (see Section 12.4).

What tools does UNIX offer for text processing? The first tool was **roff** (*runoff,* abbreviated in the customary UNIX manner). This tool was extended and became **nroff** (*new runoff*). One version of **nroff** was further extended to support a typesetter. This new tool is known as **troff** (*typesetter runoff*), and supports proportional spacing, multiple fonts, and the like. Today, versions of **troff** have been extended to support laser and other printers possessing many of the features of a typesetting system. These versions often go by different names; for example, **iroff** designates **troff** support for the Imagen laser printer series, and **ditroff** (device-independent typesetter runoff), available on some systems, consolidates the different versions of **troff** intended for use on different output devices. Finally, **psroff** supports PostScript-compatible printers.

The major difference between **troff** and VMS DSR is its use of macros and preprocessors. A macro is called by a single flag yet imposes a number of formatting features. Calls to macros are denoted by flags in uppercase, in contrast to the lowercase flags used for single formatting features. You may customize the **troff** macros to suit your own needs or write your own macros. Of course, there may be more than one macro package available on a given UNIX system: **ms** was the first; **mm** extends the features of **ms** and is distributed with UNIX System V; and **me** comes with BSD and offers some of the capabilities of **ms** and **mm** plus some of its own, for example a simple index generator.

Preprocessors simplify specialized tasks by generating the appropriate **troff** commands for parts of a document: **refer** assists in producing bibliographies; **pic** produces line drawings; **tbl** produces tables; and **eqn** simplifies the processing of mathematical equations. Preprocessors use pipes: the preprocessor pipes output to **troff** for subsequent processing.

This chapter is not intended as an in-depth discussion of UNIX text processing tools; for example, we do not discuss the preprocessors. Refer to Appendix D for citations of several good texts. Rather, this chapter provides a cross-reference table between VMS DSR and **troff** flags to help the VMS user either porting VMS DSR documents to UNIX or writing new documents get started. Users familiar with DSR should read this chapter first and then turn to the UNIX text processing documentation as they write their first **troff/nroff** documents. The cross-reference table should continue to be a useful reference.

Table 12.2 cross-references the VMS DSR flags and embedded commands with the commonly used **troff/nroff** commands and macro. Important similarities and differences between them include the following:

- Both **troff** and DSR use global and embedded commands. Global commands in both utilities begin with a period appearing as the first character of a line which contains only the command. Embedded commands can be located anywhere in the text; embedded **troff** commands begin with \.

- **troff** provides more built-in formatting features than DSR. That is, without specifying global or embedded commands, **troff** sets default values for many options. These values depend on which macro package you are using, if any.

- **troff** uses both uppercase and lowercase commands. Lowercase means a **troff** command; uppercase means a macro command. Commands contained in the **ms** macro package do not necessarily follow these rules.

- **troff** macros are a powerful feature not available with DSR, although you can achieve some of their functionality with the DSR **.REQUIRE** command. For example, you can keep a letterhead you wish to use in a variety of correspondence in the file **HEAD.RNO**, and then include it in a variety of DSR documents with **.REQUIRE HEAD.RNO**. The **troff** user would define a macro, perhaps contained in a file with many other macros, as follows:

```
.de HE
[letterhead here]
. .
```

The command **.HE** would include the letterhead in a new document.

- An important difference between a **troff** macro and the DSR **.REQUIRE** command is that you can pass variables to a macro but not to a file included with the **.REQUIRE** command. For example, if the **HE** macro were used by all personnel in a company, their individual names could be used as follows:

```
.de HE
\\$1
[letterhead here]
. .
```

Table 12.2 Comparison of VMS DSR and UNIX Text Processing

VMS DSR	UNIX	Function
Page Formatting Commands		
.[NO]AUTOSUBTITLE		Disable/enable automatic subtitling
.[NO]DATE		Disable/enable date in running headings
.DISPLAY NUMBER		Format for page numbering
.DISPLAY SUBPAGE		Format for subpage numbering
.[END]SUBPAGE		End/begin new page format
.FIRST TITLE		Include title on first page
.[NO]HEADERS	.OH 'L'C'R'	Disable/enable page headings
	.EH 'L'C'R'	**O** = odd page; **E** = even page
	.OF 'L'C'R'	**H** = header; **F** = footer
	.EF 'L'C'R	**L** = left title; **C** = center; **R** = right
	.LH .CH .RH	
	.LF .CF .RF	
.HEADERS UPPER		The heading word **page** appears as **PAGE**
.HEADERS LOWER		The heading word **page** appears as **page**
.HEADERS MIXED		The heading word **page** appears as **Page**
.LAYOUT	.nf	Define layout for headers and footers
.[NO]NUMBER PAGE		Disable/enable page numbering
.NUMBER SUBPAGE		New sequence of subpage numbers
.NUMBER RUNNING	.pn	New sequence of page numbers
.PAGE SIZE	.FM	Set the page size
	.HM	**FM** = footer margin; **HM** = header margin
	.PO	**PO** = page offset; **LL** = line length
	.LL	
	.pl	Page length
.[NO]PAGING		Disable/enable paging
.[NO]SUBTITLE		Disable/enable subtitle for page headings
.TITLE		Specify title for running headings

Table 12.2 Comparison of VMS DSR and UNIX Text Processing *(continued)*

VMS DSR	UNIX	Function
	.2C/.1C	Two/one column format: **CW** = column width; **GW** = gutter width
	.vs	Vertical spacing
	.ll	Line length
Text Formatting Commands		
.[NO]AUTOJUSTIFY		Automatic right margin justification
.[NO]AUTOPARAGRAPH		Automatic paragraphing
.[NO]AUTOTABLE		Opposite effect of **AUTOPARAGRAPH**
.[BEGIN/END] BAR		Begin/end vertical bar as first character
.[EN/DIS]ABLE BAR		Enable/disable vertical bars
.BLANK	.sp	Insert blank lines
.[EN/DIS]ABLE BOLDING	.bd	Enable/disable bolding
.BREAK	.br	Temporarily disable filling and justification
.CENTER	.ce	Center line of text
.DISPLAY ELEMENTS		Format of list items
.FIGURE	.ne/.sp	Leave space for a figure
.[NO]FILL	.nf/.fi	No fill/fill lines with text
	.DS/.DE	No fill and **.KS**
	.DS L/.DE	As above, but start flush left
	.DS C/.DE	As above, but line-by-line center
	.DS B/.DE	As above, but centered until turned off
	.CD/.DE	No fill, each line centered, no **.KS**
	.LD/.DE	No fill, flush left, no **.KS**
	.ID/.DE	No fill, indented, no **.KS**
.[END] FOOTNOTE	.FS/.FE	Start/end footnote
.[EN/DIS]ABLE HYPHEN	.ny/.nh	Enable/disable hyphenation
	\\%**word**	Disable hyphenation of word
.INDENT	.ti	First line following indented
.[NO]JUSTIFY	.na/.ad	Disable/enable right justification
.[NO]KEEP		Disable/enable keeping of blank lines

Table 12.2 Comparison of VMS DSR and UNIX Text Processing *(continued)*

VMS DSR	UNIX	Function
.LEFT MARGIN	**.RS/.RE**	Set/unset left margin
.[END] LIST		Delimit a list
.LIST ELEMENT		Denote first item in a list
.[END] LITERAL	**\e**	End/start literal presentation of text
.NUMBER LIST		Start numbering list elements
.[END] NOTE		Delimit text as a note
.[EN/DIS]ABLE OVERSTRIKING	**.bd**	Enable/disable overstriking of text
.PAGE	**.bp**	Force a new page
.PARAGRAPH	**.PP**	Invoke paragraph parameters
	.LP	**PP** = normal indent; **LP** = no indent;
	.IP	**IP** = all lines indent
	.QP	**QP** = indent left and right
	.XP	**XP** = exdent (bibliography)
.[NO]PERIOD		Control spaces after certain punctuation
.RIGHT		Position text relative to right margin
.RIGHT MARGIN	**.ll**	Set right margin
.SET PARAGRAPH	**.PI/.PD**	Set paragraph parameters
		PI = set paragraph indent.
		PD = set space between paragraphs
.SKIP	**.ls**	Skip number of lines according to spacing
.SPACING	**.vs**	Space between lines of text
.TAB STOPS	**.ta**	Change position of tab stops
.TEST PAGE	**.ne**	Test to see if block of text will fit page
	.KS/.KE	Start/end keep (block of test on one page), leave partial page blank
	.KF/.KE	As above but fill to end of page, placing block at start of new page
.[EN/DIS]ABLE UNDERLINING		Enable/disable underlining
	.EQ/.EN	Begin/end equation

Table 12.2 Comparison of VMS DSR and UNIX Text Processing *(continued)*

VMS DSR	UNIX	Function
Section Formatting		
.APPENDIX		Denotes start of an appendix
.CHAPTER		Denotes start of a chapter
.DISPLAY APPENDIX		Specify form of appendix numbering
.DISPLAY CHAPTER		Specify form of chapter numbering
.DISPLAY LEVELS		Specify form of sequential numbering
.ENTRY		Create index entry without page number
.[NO]FLAGS INDEX		Disable/enable index recognition character
.[NO]FLAGS SUBINDEX		Disable/enable subindex recognition character
.HEADER LEVEL	**.NH n**	Specify header level
	.SH	**NH** = next header; **SH** = subheader
.INDEX		Create index entry with page number
.[EN/DIS]ABLE INDEXING		Enable/disable indexing
.NUMBER APPENDIX		Beginning letter of appendix
.NUMBER CHAPTER		Beginning number of chapter
.NUMBER LEVEL		Beginning number of sequence of headers
.SEND TOC		Send DSR commands to table of contents
.SET LEVEL		Preset section headers
.STYLE HEADERS		Set format of headers
.[EN/DIS]ABLE TOC		Enable/disable table of contents
.X[LOWER/UPPER]		Control case of index entries
	.XS/.XE	Delimit table of contents entry
	.PX	Display table of contents
	.AB/AE	Begin/end abstract
	.AI	Specify author's institution
	.AE	Specify author

Table 12.2   Comparison of VMS DSR and UNIX Text Processing *(continued)*

VMS DSR	UNIX	Function
Font Specifications		
	.ft	Change font
	.fp	Mount font
	.ps n	Set point size: **n** = absolute; −**n** = decrease by **n**; +**n** = increase by **n**
	\sn	In-line point size change: **n** as above; **\s0** = restore previous point size
	\fn	In-line font change: **n** = 1 plain; **n** = 2 italics; **n** = 3 bold
	.SM	Decrease point size by 2
	.LG	Increase point size by 2
	.NL	Reset point size
	.R	Roman font
	.I	Italic
	.B	Bold
Accent Marks		
	*e	Acute
	*^o	Circumflex
	*Cc	Hacek
	*:u	Umlaut
	*'e	Grave
	*~n	Tilde
	*.c	Cedilla
Flag Recognition Commands		
.[NO]FLAGS ACCEPT		Disable/enable accept flag recognition
.[NO]FLAGS ALL		Disable/enable all flags
.[NO]FLAGS BOLD		Disable/enable bold flag recognition
.[NO]FLAGS BREAK		Disable/enable break flag recognition
.[NO]FLAGS CAPITALIZE		Disable/enable capitalize flag recognition
.[NO]FLAGS COMMENT		Disable/enable comment flag recognition
.[NO]FLAGS HYPHENATE		Disable/enable hyphenation flag recognition

Table 12.2 Comparison of VMS DSR and UNIX Text Processing *(continued)*

VMS DSR	UNIX	Function
.[NO]FLAGS LOWERCASE		Disable/enable lowercase flag recognition
.[NO]FLAGS OVERSTRIKE		Disable/enable overstrike flag recognition
.[NO]FLAGS PERIOD		Disable/enable period flag recognition
.[NO]FLAGS SPACE		Disable/enable space flag recognition
.[NO]FLAGS SUBSTITUTE		Disable/enable substitute flag recognition
.[NO]FLAGS UNDERLINE		Disable/enable underline flag recognition
.[NO]FLAGS UPPERCASE		Disable/enable uppercase flag recognition

Miscellaneous

VMS DSR	UNIX	Function
.[NO]CONTROL CHARACTERS		Accept control characters as normal characters
.IF, .IFNOT, .ELSE, .ENDIF.		Conditional commands to control processing
.NOSPACE		Prevent the end of line space
.REPEAT		Repeat character specified number of times
.REQUIRE		Include another DSR file in output
.SET DATE		Permit date substitution
.SET TIME		Permit time substitution
.VARIABLE		Used with the **IF[NOT]** block

Flags

VMS DSR	UNIX	Function
—	\e	Treat next character literally
*	.B	Make next character bold
|	.hw	Break word here if at end of line
<		Capitalize all characters in next word
!	\"	Begin comment
.	.	Start command
=	\%	Allow hyphenation of word here
>		Index or subindex next word
\		Make next character lowercase

Table 12.2 Comparison of VMS DSR and UNIX Text Processing *(continued)*

VMS DSR	UNIX	Function
%	\o	Overstrike previous character with next character
+		Insert extra interword space after character
#		Insert unexpandable space
$	.DA [date]	Insert date or time
	.ND	**DA** = date at bottom of page; **ND** = disable **DA**
&	.ul	Underline next character
	.cu	Continuous underline
^		Make next character uppercase
	%	Substitute page number
Macro Commands		
	.de xx yy	Define or redefine macro **xx**; end at **yy** (default **..**)
	.am xx yy	Append to a macro
	.ds xx string	Define **xx** containing string
	.as xx string	Append string to **xx**
	.rm xx	Remove request, macro, or string **xx**
	.rn xx yy	Rename request, macro, or string **xx** to **yy**
	.em xx	End macro is **xx**

The command **.HE "Phil Bourne"** includes my name as the first line of the letterhead, for my name is equated to the first argument (**$1**) to the macro. Note that if the argument to be passed to the macro is more than one word long, you must enclose it in quotes. Note also that you could pass further arguments to the macro as **$2**, **$3**, and so on. The \\ is required: the first backslash defines an embedded command, and the second backslash insures that the argument is interpreted when the line is interpreted by **troff**, and not when you define it.

- You can modify the effects of commands by flags in DSR and by number and string registers in **troff**. To modify the value of a number register, use the **.nr** command. For example,

```
.nr HM 4.5i
.nr FM 2i
.nr PO 3.25i
.nr LL 4i
```

adjusts the default page size, which is approximately a 1-inch bor-
der all around on an 8½ by 11-inch page, to the following: a header
margin (**HM**) of 4.5 inches; footer margin (**FM**) of 2 inches; page off-
set (**PO**) or left margin of 3.25 inches; and line length (**LL**) of 4
inches. To modify the value of a string register, use the **.ds** command:

```
.ds CH
.ds CF Page %
```

First, the center header (**CH**) string is cleared by setting it to a null
string, and then the center footer (**CF**) is set to the string **Page** followed by the page number (**%**).

- Both **troff** and DSR allow you to follow some commands with an
  optional argument. For example, in DSR, **.sp2** indicates that two
  lines should be left blank. The corresponding **troff** command is **.sp
  2**. Note that you must leave a space between the command and the
  argument.

- Some **troff** commands are in effect only for the current line. Refer
  to the discussion of bolding (**.B**) in Section 12.4 for an example.

- DSR supports only Digital Equipment Corporation printers,
  whereas **troff** supports printers from various manufacturers.

- You declare the printer you are using with **troff** on the **troff** command line; nothing within the document relates it to a specific
  printer. Hence, you can easily print the same document on a variety of printers. Of course, the appearance of the document may
  vary depending on the characteristics of each printer. Commands
  not recognized by a specific printer are ignored.

- **troff** permits explicit indications of character size, line spacing, and
  related characteristics in a variety of units, as you would expect of
  a typesetting program.

12.3 *troff/nroff Arguments and Options*

The arguments and options used with **troff** or **nroff** may depend on the
printer you are using. In these examples, the output is sent to **stdout**,
the terminal screen.

	VMS	UNIX
form:	$ RUNOFF[/OPTION(S)] DSR _file	% nroff [-option(s)] [file(s)]
		% troff [-option(s)] [file(s)]
example:	$ RUNOFF/PAGE="1,3,11:19" MYDOC.RNO	% troff -o1,3,11-19 mydoc
example:		% nroff -man /usr/man/\
		man1/cat.1 \
		| ul | more -s -f

In the first example, **troff -o1,3,11-19 mydoc** formats pages 1, 3, and 11 through 19 (**o** option). In the second example, **nroff -man /usr/man/ man1/cat.1 | ul | more -s -f** has the same effect as the command **man cat**. **man** (the **m** option followed by **an**) invokes the macro package **an**, written specifically for the **man** pages. Like all macro packages, it resides in the directory **/usr/lib/tmac**. You can produce your own **man** pages, as the example of UNIX text processing below shows. The file **/usr/man/ man1/cat.1** contains the unformatted **man** page for the **cat** command, as discussed in Section 3.5. The output from **nroff** is piped to the **ul** (underline) command; **ul** decides whether to underline the output by looking at the environment variable **TERM** and matching it to the **/etc/termcap** entry to see if the terminal supports underlining (see Section 3.1). The output of **ul** is piped to **more -s -f** (compare the VMS command **TYPE/ PAGE**), which displays the formatted (possibly underlined) text, pausing after each screen. The **s** option compresses multiple blank lines. The **f** option filters out escape sequences that **nroff** generates and that are not part of the document, but that control specific printers.

12.4   *Summary*

The following simple example summarizes this overview of UNIX text-processing tools. This example shows the unformatted **man** page for the **cat** command, and then the output after formatting by the **man** command. Using this example as a template, you should be able to create your own formatted **man** pages.

	UNIX
example:	% cat /usr/man/man1/cat.1
	.TH cat 1
	.SH name
	cat \- concatenate and print
	.SH SYNTAX
	.B cat
	[

```
.B \-b
] [
.B \-e
] [
.B \-n
] [
.B \-s
] [
.B \-t
] [
.B \-u
] [
.B \-v
]
file. . .
.br
.SH DESCRIPTION
The
.PN cat
command reads each
.I file
in sequence and displays it on the standard output. Thus
.PP
.ti + 15n
cat file
.PP
displays the file on the standard output, and
.PP
.ti + 15n
cat file1 file2 >file3
.PP
concatenates the first two files and places the result on the third.
.PP
If no input file is given, or if the argument '\-' is encountered.
.PN cat
reads from the standard input file.
Output is buffered in 1024-byte blocks unless the standard
output is a terminal, in which case it is line buffered.
.PP
The
.B \-b
option ignores blank lines and precedes all other output with
line numbers.
.PP
The
.B \-e
option displays a dollar sign ($) at the end of each output
line.
.PP
The
.B \-n
```

option precedes all output lines (including blank lines) with
line numbers.
.PP
The
.B \-s
option squeezes adjacent empty lines so that the
output is displayed single spaced.
.PP
The
.B \-t
option displays all non-printing characters including tabs
in the output.
In addition to those representations used with the
.B \-v
option, all tab characters are displayed as ^I.
.PP
The
.B \-u
option makes the output completely unbuffered
.PP
The
.B \-v
option displays non-printing characters (except tabs)
.CT x
(control character x) prints as ^X
The delete character
(octal 0177) prints as ^?.
Non-ascii characters (with the high bit set) are printed as M-
(for meta) followed by the character of the low 7 bits.
.PP
.SH RESTRICTIONS
Beware of 'cat a b >a' and 'cat a b >b', which destroy
the input files before reading them.
.SH "SEE ALSO"
cp(1), ex(1), more(1), pr(1), tail(1)

example: % man cat   cat(1)

NAME
    cat - concatenate and print
SYNTAX
    cat [-b] [-e] [-n] [-s] [-t] [-u] [-v] file. . .
DESCRIPTION
    The <u>cat</u> command reads each <u>file</u> in sequence and displays it
    on the standard output. Thus
            cat file
    displays the file on the standard output, and
            cat file1 file2 >file3
    concatenates the first two files and places the result on
    the third.
    If no input file is given, or if the argument '-' is encoun-
    tered, <u>cat</u> reads from the standard input file. Output is

buffered in 1024-byte blocks unless the standard output is a terminal, in which case it is line-buffered.

The **-b** option ignores blank lines and precedes all other output with line numbers.

The **-e** option displays a dollar sign ($) at the end of each output line

The **-n** option precedes all output lines (including blank lines) with line numbers

The **-s** option squeezes adjacent empty lines so that the output is displayed single spaced.

The **-t** option displays all non-printing characters including tabs in the output. In addition to those representations used with the **-v** option, all tab characters are displayed as ˆI.

The **-u** option makes the output completely unbuffered.

The **-v** option displays non-printing characters (except tabs). ⟨CTRL/x⟩ (control character x) prints as ˆX. The delete character (octal 0177) prints as ˆ?. Non-ascii characters (with the high bit set) are printed as M- (for meta) followed by the character of the low 7 bits.

RESTRICTIONS
Beware of 'cat a b >a' and 'cat a b >b', which destroy the input files before reading them.

SEE ALSO
cp(1), ex(1), more(1), pr(1), tail(1)

In the first example, **cat /usr/man/man1/cat.1** displays the unformatted **man** page. In the second example, **mat cat** displays the familiar format of the **man** page. Let us reconcile some of the flags and embedded commands with the results they produce:

.TH	Title formatted according to a macro.
\	Treat next character literally, not as a formatting command
.B	Bold till end of line reached
.br	Break
.SH	Subheading
.PN	Alternate font, ignored by most terminals
.I	Italics, ignored by most terminals
.PP	Invoke paragraph parameters
.ti+15n	Temporary indent, standard indent + 15 spaces

These few commands should be enough to show you how to produce your own simple **man** pages.

Chapter 13

Processor-to-Processor Communications

The new electronic independence recreates the world in the image of a global village.

Marshall McLuhan

The days of a single central mainframe computer accessible only to the anointed behind glass walls are over. The 1980s have seen a movement towards distributed processing, brought about by the availability of less expensive yet powerful minicomputer systems, personal computers, and, more recently, single-user workstations. This trend is expected to continue, resulting in the further expansion of computer networks to connect processors of different types offered by many vendors.

In the environment shaped by this trend, the UNIX user will have occasion to perform tasks on two or more processors simultaneously. This chapter identifies those tasks and describes the command required to perform them. Unfortunately, the procedure is not a comparatively simple matter of defining a single command for each task: the commands vary according to the type of connection existing between the UNIX computers and the type of access permitted by the system administrator of each computer. For the purposes of this discussion, we consider two types of connections:

1. *Network,* a fast connection using dedicated wiring that permits interactive communication, called Internet.[1]
2. *Modem,* a slow connection using telephone lines, in which tasks are often queued for transmission by means of the UNIX UUCP utility.

To further complicate the situation, the commands used in network communications are subdivided according to whether the connection is to a UNIX *trusted* or *non-trusted host.* The VMS analogue to a UNIX trusted host is a proxy login. To perform a task on another VAX/VMS computer, VMS users issue a given command whether they have a proxy login or not. The VMS user provides username and password information for the other computer only if a proxy login is not available. For example, to copy a VMS file to another VAX/VMS computer, the user invokes the **COPY** command and provides username and password information in the instance of a non-proxy login but no username and password information in the case of a proxy login. UNIX users issue

---

1. The terms *network connection* and *Internet* are used interchangeably throughout this chapter.

completely different commands depending on whether file copying occurs between trusted or non-trusted hosts: **rcp** between trusted hosts, and **ftp** between non-trusted hosts. The syntax used by these two commands is different. **rcp** resembles the **cp** command for local file copying (see Sections 4.9 and 9.3.1), whereas **ftp** uses a syntax different from anything we have encountered before. Hence, copying to a trusted host simplifies file transfer because there is no new syntax to remember. The disadvantage of communicating with trusted hosts is that the security of a user's files may be more easily compromised than when communicating with non-trusted hosts. As we shall see, if an intruder gains access to a user's files on one computer, it is a simple matter to gain access to that same user's files on any trusted host computer.

This chapter is organized into two major divisions based on the type of connection between the host computers: Section 13.2 covers network connections and Section 13.3 covers modem connections. Each of these two divisions is further subdivided based on task. Table 13.1 summarizes these tasks and indicates the section of the chapter where you can find additional information.

The tasks of remote login, file transfer, and sending mail require no further clarification. Remote command execution involves issuing a command on one computer for execution on another computer. Remote file access involves transparently accessing files located on a remote computer as if those files were located on the local computer. Experienced DECnet users should note that task-to-task communications, whereby a program on one node interacts directly with a program on another node, is beyond the scope of this book. Refer to the reading list in Appendix D for further information on task-to-task communications.

Several features of processor-to-processor communication, not necessarily obvious from Table 13.1, need to be understood from the outset:

- The commands **uucp**, **uusend**, and **uux** are part of the UUCP (UNIX to UNIX CoPy) utility for performing tasks between local and remote hosts. **tip** and **cu** are separate programs that may use the same modems as UUCP to dial remote hosts on which they can conduct terminal sessions.
- Tasks based on network connections use **r**, or *remote*, commands— **rcp**, **rlogin**, and **rsh**—for trusted hosts, and **telnet** and **ftp** for non-trusted hosts.

Table 13.1 Commands Used for Communication Between UNIX Hosts

Task	Network		Modem
	Trusted Host	Non-Trusted Host	
Remote login	**rlogin** (13.2.4.1)[1]	**telnet** (13.2.4.2)	**tip/cu** (13.3.3)
File transfer	**rcp** (13.2.6.1)[1]	**ftp** (13.2.6.2)	**uucp/uusend** (13.3.5)
Sending mail	**mail** (13.2.5)	**mail** (13.2.5)	**mail** (13.2.5)
Remote command execution	**rsh** (13.2.7)		**uux** (13.3.6)
Remote file access	NFS (13.2.8)[2]	NFS (13.2.8)[2]	

1. **telnet** and **ftp** can also be used on trusted hosts, but **rlogin** and **rcp** simplify usage.
2. NFS is not a command but a protocol that permits access to remote file systems with standard UNIX commands.

- Sending mail to users on other computers employs the **mail** utility (see Chapter 6) regardless of the type of connection between the computers. The format of the mail address, however, differs from computer to computer.
- Remote file access via Network File System (NFS) is available only using network connections.

The use of NFS requires further discussion.

NFS is not a standard part of the UNIX operating system, but you can obtain it under license from Sun Microsystems, Inc. Many vendors of computers that use UNIX also offer NFS. NFS is not a command; you can think of it as a set of programs with which a file system mounted on one computer may also be mounted on a remote computer. This means that you can access a file with the file management commands discussed in Chapters 4 and 9, whether the file resides on a local or remote computer. The VMS analogy to UNIX NFS is the Local Area VAXcluster (LAVC).

This chapter concludes with a brief discussion of two topics which, although not concerned with commands, can be important to the UNIX user faced with a distributed computing environment. The first introduces Usenet, a UNIX bulletin board for the dissemination of electronic information. The second explains network communications between UNIX and VMS computers.

Before examining how you may perform tasks on a number of computers, you should have a basic understanding of how communication occurs between computers: between both UNIX processors and UNIX and non-UNIX processors. We start with a simple discussion of how computers communicate, introducing nomenclature used throughout the remainder of the chapter. Included in this discussion are examples of several UNIX commands with which you can inquire into the characteristics and status of UNIX computers communicating via network or modem.

13.1　Communication Overview

Once two UNIX computers are connected by a physical link, the potential exists for communication between them. Each computer is called a host (compare the VMS node). Hosts are characterized by a host name (in VMS, a node name). The computer to which a user's terminal is connected is called the local host (in VMS, local node), and all other computers are called remote hosts (in VMS, remote nodes).

The speed with which communication takes place varies greatly, and is a function of the physical link. Modem connections are generally slow, typically transferring data using regular telephone lines at 300, 1200, or 2400 baud (bits per second), whereas network connections are much faster, in the range of 56,000 to 10 million baud, and use dedicated wiring.

Modem connections are simple. The host receiving data via a modem treats it no differently from input from any terminal. If a UNIX host has a modem that can both originate and answer calls, the UUCP software (part of nearly all versions of the UNIX operating system) enables the host to join a large conglomeration of UNIX processors for file, mail, and news exchange. To reduce telephone costs, exchange usually occurs via a number of intermediate hosts on a *store-and-forward* network. Each intermediate host receives a complete copy of the file being transferred before it passes it along to the next host. The system administrator maintains data for remote hosts (for example, telephone numbers) and the types of connection they afford in the files **/usr/lib/uucp/L.***. Typically, at some predetermined time each day, one UNIX host will automatically dial another and exchange files, mail, or news. The time delay from queuing the information precludes any interactive access.

To establish a network-based connection between hosts is not as simple as establishing a modem-based connection using an RS-232 (terminal) interface. High-speed data transmission and the ability to perform task-to-task communication require specialized hardware and software. If computers from different manufacturers running different operating systems wish to communicate, they must adopt a standard interface. One such interface, Ethernet, is used by VMS and most UNIX-based processors. Ethernet defines not only the wiring and type of plugs that connect computers but also the format of the data sent. Data is broken into discrete entities called *packets*. Each packet contains a part of the data being sent, the local host name, the remote host name, and a sequence number. The receiving host uses the sequence number to reassemble packets in the correct order, particularly important if packets must be resent because an error occurred during transmission.[2]

VMS and UNIX format data differently in that part of the packet devoted to user data. VMS uses a format called DECnet, and UNIX uses Transmission Control Protocol/Internet Protocol (TCP/IP). You can use DECnet and TCP/IP on the same Ethernet network, but only a host that understands the format you use can interpret it; a format that the host cannot interpret is ignored. Different versions of UNIX use the TCP/IP definition in different ways. BSD uses a *socket* and System V uses a *stream*. Discussion of sockets and streams is beyond the scope of this book; they do not affect how the average user performs networking tasks. In BSD, however, you may encounter a file type that indicates a socket (see Section 2.3.2).

Modem-based communications first require that you establish a physical connection, accomplished by one host dialing another on the telephone exchange in the same way voice connections are established. Hosts on a network are always connected; during transmissions over the network each host looks at each packet to determine whether it is destined to receive it. If so, it responds immediately, thus making interactive communications possible. Computers on a network supporting the TCP/IP protocol are said to be part of the Internet network. Appendix D includes references to more detailed discussions of TCP/IP.

---

2. Modem-based data transfers may be simply a stream of data, started and stopped in the same way data from a terminal is started and stopped. However, some software supporting modem-based data transfers, like Kermit, also transfer data in packets.

Table 13.2   VMS and UNIX Mail Address Formats

Address Type			Format
VMS			
	DECnet	Form:	**NODE::USER**
		Example:	**BOSTON::FRED**
UNIX			
	Network	Form:	**user@host**
		Example:	**fred@boston.chem.mit.edu**
	Modem	Form:	**site1\!site2\!user**
		Example:	**newyork\!boston\!fred**

13.1.1   Addressing Communications

Network and modem communications to a user on a remote host require an address akin to a postal address. Each user's address is defined uniquely using a combination of the login name and the name of the local host. The format of the address differs for network and modem communications, and both of these differs from the VMS DECnet network address. Table 13.2 summarizes each format.

The UUCP (modem-based) host name does not have to be the same as the network host name if the host supports both types of communication. However, to avoid confusion, the system administrator usually makes them identical. Network and UUCP addresses are discussed further below.

13.2   Network Communications

This section is devoted to a discussion of communications among UNIX processors connected via a network. Readers who do not intend to access remote hosts via a network should proceed to Section 13.3.

13.2.1   Network Addresses

A user may determine the name of the local host in a network environment with the command **hostname** (compare the VMS command **SHOW LOGICAL SYS$NODE**). Usually this is unnecessary, as the host name is displayed as part of the banner message prior to the login prompt.

	VMS	UNIX
example:	$ SHOW LOGICAL - SYS$NODE CUHHCA::	% hostname cuhhca
example:		% grep cuhhca /etc/hosts 128.59.98.1 cuhhca.hhmi.columbia.edu cuhhca babbage.columbia.edu babbage.hhmi babbage.hhmi.columbia.edu babbage cuhhca.columbia.edu cuhhca.hhmi

The file **/etc/hosts** stores definitions of the local and remote hosts potentially reachable on Internet. In the above example, **grep cuhhca /etc/hosts** searches this file for the host **cuhhca**. Associated with the host name is an Internet address (**128.59.98.1**) and one or more other names. The first name (**cuhhca.hhmi.columbia.edu**) is the official Internet host name; any others (for example, **cuhhca**) are aliases. A user wishing to access a remote host can use the Internet address, the official name, or any of the aliases. Obviously, it is easiest to use an alias.

A user wishing to communicate with a remote host on the network can confirm its existence by searching **/etc/hosts**. It is just as simple, however, to attempt to communicate. If the system returns the message host unknown, it does not necessarily mean that the host is unreachable; the host simply may not be defined in the **/etc/hosts** file. You should consult the system administrator in such cases, unless you know the Internet address, which you should then use.

13.2.2   *Network Status*

Section 7.2.2 introduced the command **netstat** for monitoring the utilization of a network. Network utilization statistics are of little concern to many users. What is of concern is the status of a remote host. Just because a network host exists does not necessarily mean it is available; it may be down for preventive maintenance or because of hardware failure. The command **ruptime** (compare the VMS command **SHOW NETWORK** for non-end nodes) displays which network hosts are available in the immediate vicinity.[3]

---

3. Information will not be given for remote hosts beyond the network gateway.

		1	0	0	(Local)	->	1.9	CUMBG
		5	3	3	UNA-0	->	1.130	CURTRA
		6	8	4	UNA-0	->	1.130	CURTRA
		. . . .						
1.1	CMCFRF	0	6	3	UNA-0	->	1.130	CURTRA
1.2	CMCFRD	0	6	3	UNA-0	->	1.130	CURTRA
1.9	CUMBG	0	0	0	(Local)	->	1.9	CUMBG
. . . .								

UNIX

example: % ruptime

apne292b	up	48+03:00	1 user.	load	0.01,	0.00,	0.00
columbia	down	??:??					
cucca	up	18+04:00	4 users.	load	0.09,	0.11,	0.14
cuhhca	up	6+21:15	8 users.	load	6.72,	6.38,	5.93
cuhhmd	up	18+05:04	5 users.	load	0.77,	0.46,	0.27

The fields displayed by **ruptime** (taking cuhhca as an example) are as follows:

cuhhca	Remote host name
up 6+21:15	System has been up for 6 days, 21 hours, and 15 minutes
8 users	8 users are currently logged into the system
load 6.72 6.38 5.93	5 minutes ago the system load was 6.72, 10 minutes ago it was 6.38, and 15 minutes ago it was 5.93

13.2.3   *What Is a Trusted Host?*

Before we examine specific commands used in network communication, we must elaborate on the concept of a *trusted host*. As stated in Section 13.1, the commands used to communicate with a trusted host may differ from those used to communicate with a non-trusted host. As we shall see, trusted host commands simplify access by bypassing the password security check otherwise required. The system administrator of each host defines which remote hosts and which users on those hosts are trusted. Let us follow the sequence of events when user, login name

fred, on local host **a**, attempts to communicate with remote host **b** using a trusted host **r** command. To simplify the initial discussion, we assume that Fred has identical login names on both hosts **a** and **b**, although, as we shall see, this is not a requirement.

To communicate, **fred** on host **a** must have access to an account on host **b**. When **fred** makes a communication request from host **a** to host **b**, for example for a remote login or a file copy, host **b** first checks the file **/etc/hosts.equiv** to see if host **a** is defined. **/etc/hosts.equiv** contains official Internet host names for trusted hosts. If it finds an entry for host **a**, host **b** checks its **/etc/passwd** file for the login name **fred**. If it is found, access is given to account **fred** on host **b** without checking password information. That is, if an entry for host **a** exists in host **b**'s **/etc/hosts.equiv** file, any user who has the same login name on host **a** and **b** has trusted host access.

If an entry for host **a** is not found in host **b**'s **/etc/hosts.equiv** file, then the hidden file **˜user/.rhosts** (˜**fred/.rhosts** in this example) is searched for personalized trusted host access. This file, if it exists, contains a list of Internet hosts, one per line. Each host name listed may be followed by one or more login names separated by spaces, defining which users from that host may make **r** command requests. If an entry for host **a** is found in this file, assuming that no login name(s) follow the entry for host **a**, then the **/etc/passwd** file is checked for the login name **fred** (that is, the login names on the local and remote hosts are assumed to be the same). If login name **fred** is found, access is given to the system. Once again, the password is not checked.

What if the user's login names are not the same on host **a** and **b**? By default, **˜user/.rhosts** on host **b** is the file **.rhosts** in the directory **˜user**, where **user** is the name of the user making the request from host **a**. The user's communication request from host **a** can specify the search of an alternative **˜user/.rhosts** file. If this alternative file is searched, access is given to host **b** only if the **˜user/.rhosts** file specified contains an entry for host **a** followed by the login name of the person on host **a** making the request.

For example, let us again consider login name **fred** on host **a**, this time making a communication request to login name **george** on host **b**. First, the login name **george** must exist on host **b**. Second, **˜george/.rhosts** must contain an entry for host **a** followed by the login name **fred**. As you can see, access of this type is useful if a user has different login names on two hosts and wants the convenience of trusted host access.[4]

The following example emphasizes the concept of trusted host access.

	VMS	UNIX
example:	$ SHOW LOGICAL SYS$NODE	% hostname ; whoami
	CUHHCA::	cuhhca
		fred
	$ SHOW NETWORK	% cat /etc/hosts.equiv
	[not shown]	cuhhmd.hhmi.columbia.edu
		cubsun.biol.columbia.edu
		% cat ~fred/.rhosts
		cuchmc.hhmi.columbia.edu george

User **fred** on network host **cuhhca** displays the file **/etc/hosts.equiv**. It indicates definitions of two trusted hosts. Any remote user on **cuhhmd. hhmi.columbia.edu** or **cubsun.biol.columbia.edu** who has an identical login name on **cuhhca** can access **cuhhca** with trusted host **r** commands.

Further, **~fred/.rhosts** indicates that user **george** from host **cuchmc.hhmi. columbia.edu** can access account **fred** on **cuchca**. Note that this does not imply that **fred** on **cuhhca** can access account **george** on **cuchmc. hhmi.columbia.edu**.

With these concepts in mind, we now turn to the specific commands that perform tasks on remote UNIX hosts both trusted and non-trusted.

13.2.4   *Remote Login*

Two UNIX commands perform remote network logins: **rlogin** for trusted hosts and **telnet** for all other Internet hosts (compare the VMS command **SET HOST**).

13.2.4.1   *Trusted Host: rlogin*

rlogin is an example of an **r** command for trusted host access.

---

4. Some system administrators may regard the creation of a ~**user/.rhosts** by the user as too great a security risk. One alternative, available on some BSD UNIX systems, is to have the user **root** own the ~**user/.rhosts** file.

	VMS	UNIX
form:	$ SET HOST [/QUALIFIER(S)] NODE_ - NAME	% rlogin host_name -[option(s)]
example:	$ SHOW LOGICAL SYS$NODE: CUHHMC:: $ SHOW PROCESS Pid: 00000A31 Proc. name: FRED - UIC: [FRED.GRP] Priority: 4 Default file spec: - DUA1:[FRED]	% hostname; whoami cuchmc fred
	$ SET HOST CUHHMD Welcome to CUHHMD	% rlogin cuhhmd Last login: Fri May 27 15:44:01 \ from 1.81
	Last interactive login on Friday, 27- - MAY-1988 15:34 Last non-interactive login on - Friday, 27-MAY-1988 01:10 $	ULTRIX V2.0-1 System #2: Mon \ May 2 17:04:56 EDT 1988 %
example:		% rlogin cuhhca -lgeorge . . . .
example:		% hostname cuhhca % ˜(CTRL)-Z % hostname cuhhmc % fg rlogin cuhhca -lgeorge % hostname cuhhca

In the first example, **rlogin cuhhmd** logs **fred** on the local host **cuchmc** into the account **fred** on remote host **cuhhmd**. In the second example, **rlogin cuhhca -lgeorge** requests a remote login to the trusted host **cuhhca**. Note that rather than requesting a login to the default account **fred**, this command requests a login to the account **george** with the **l** option. If the directory **˜george** on the trusted host **cuhhca** contains an **.rhosts** entry that permits access from **fred** on host **cuchmc**, then the connection is successful. If the user's **rlogin** attempt is invalid, the remote host requests password information rather than rejecting the request (compare **telnet** below).

A useful feature of **rlogin**, also offered by **telnet** but not available from VMS **SET HOST**, is the ability to toggle between the local and the remote host, as illustrated in the third example. ⟨CTRL⟩-Z stops the process on the remote host and returns control to the shell on the local host. **fg** (foreground) restarts the stopped process and reconnects the user to the remote host. Hence, once you make a connection to a remote host, you can use both the local and the remote host without having to reestablish the connection with **rlogin**.

13.2.4.2   *Non-Trusted Host: telnet*

The command **telnet** establishes a login session on a remote host, trusted or non-trusted. In either instance, the remote host requests login name and password information.

```
              VMS                    UNIX
form:         $ SET HOST             % telnet host
example:      $ SET HOST CUHHIA      % telnet cuhhia
              CUHHIA:: VMS NODE      Trying...
                                     Connected to cuhhia.hhmi.columbia.edu.
              Username:              Escape character is '⟨CTRL⟩]'
              Password
              Welcome to VMS 4.7     IRIS UNIX (cuhhia)
                                     login: system
                                     Password.
                                     IRIS Workstation
                                     % ⟨CTRL⟩-]
                                     telnet>z
                                     Stopped
                                     % hostname
                                     cuhhca
                                     % fg
                                     telnet cuhhia
                                     % hostname
                                     cuhhia
```

In this example, **telnet cuhhia** makes a connection to the Internet remote host **cuhhia**, which then prompts for a login name and password (compare **rlogin**). Like **rlogin**, a useful feature of **telnet** is the ability to toggle between the local and the remote host, issuing commands in either environment. ⟨CTRL⟩-] (close square bracket) escapes to the **telnet>** prompt; the **telnet** command **z** generates a new copy of the shell on the local host which can accept commands (C shell only), in this example **hostname**, **fg** returns the **telnet** shell to foreground as described in Section 8.3, and the terminal session resumes on the remote host as shown by the display of the remote host's name in response to the **hostname** command. Additional commands that you may issue at the **telnet** prompt appear in Table 13.3.

Table 13.3   telnet Commands

Command	Function
open host	Open a connection to the named host
close	Terminate a session and return to **telnet** prompt
quit	Terminate a session and return to local shell
z	Suspend **telnet** and invoke copy of local shell
escape (char)	Set the escape character (default ⟨**CTRL**]⟩)
status	Report current **telnet** status
options	Toggle options indicated by **status**
crmod	Toggle carriage return mode
?	Get help on the above

13.2.5   *Sending Mail*

Chapter 6 discussed the **mail** utility extensively. We now discuss the elements unique to sending mail to remote network hosts. Users need only an understanding of the format of the mail address. Recapping from Table 13.2, VMS supports a DECnet mail address of the form **NODE::USERNAME**. UNIX, on the other hand, supports two forms of mail address; for Internet mail there is **user@host**, and for UUCP mail there is **host!user**. Since each is discussed on-line in the **man** page **mail-addr**, only a synopsis is given here.

The Internet host name is a hierarchical arrangement. For example, the address **cuhhca.hhmi.columbia.edu**, which we have seen on several occasions, implies that the address will be interpreted by the **edu** routing tables, which sends the message to the **columbia** gateway, then to the subdomain **hhmi**, and lastly to the host **cuhhca**. For the average user, the terms *routing table, gateway,* and *subdomain* are not important. You only need to know that **edu** is the name of all computers in educational institutions, **columbia** is a gateway to all Internet hosts at Columbia University, **hhmi** covers all computers in the Howard Hughes Medical Institute at Columbia University, and **cuhhca** is the specific computer. You do not need to remember such routing if the system administrator defines a simple alias in the **/etc/hosts** file.

	VMS	UNIX
form:	To: NODE::USER	% mail user@host
example:		% mail fred@cuhhmc.chem.columbia.edu

File Transfer

How you perform file transfer between a local and a remote UNIX host depends on whether trusted host access is available. If trusted host access is available, you can use the command **rcp** (remote copy). **rcp** uses the same syntax as **cp** (copy, Section 4.9), along with a host name followed by a colon. Compare **rcp** to VMS proxy login access, which extends the features of the **COPY** command to include a node name followed by **::** (double colon). **COPY** is similar to **rcp** in that username and password information are not required.

If trusted host access is not available, you can use the utility **ftp**. **ftp** first requires that you establish a connection to the remote host, and then use a command syntax different from both **cp** and **rcp** to transfer files.

UNIX differs from VMS in both types of file transfer in that the user must have an account on the remote machine to enable file transfer even when the remote file is readable by all users. VMS users may copy a world-readable file from a remote node whether they have a username on that node or not. The inability of UNIX to let remote hosts read world-readable files becomes a problem when you have files you wish to make available for export. A method commonly used to circumvent this problem is to establish a guest account (often called **anonymous** or **guest**), which permits **ftp** connections to the directory where these files reside.

13.2.6.1   ***Trusted Host: rcp***

The following examples show various uses of **rcp** and compares them to their VMS proxy login counterparts.

	VMS	UNIX
form:	$ COPY[/QUALIFIER(S)] NODE:: - source_file target_file	% rcp hostname:source_file target_\ file
example:	$ COPY CUHHMD::DUA0:[USER1] - JUNK.DAT MYFILE.DAT	% rcp cuhhmd:/usr/user1/junk \ myfile
form:	$ COPY/QUALIFER(S) source_file - NODE::target_file	% rcp source_file hostname:target_\ file
example:	$ COPY MYFILE.DAT - CUHHMD::DUA0: - [USER1]JUNK.DAT	% rcp myfile cuhhmd:/usr/user1/\ junk
form:		% rcp -r source_directory hostname:target_directory

example:		% rcp -r ˜fred/programs cuhhmd:/\
		usr/fred/programs
example:	$ COPY MYFILE.CUHHMD::DUA2: -	% rcp myfile cuhhmd:programs/junk
	[.PROGRAMS]JUNK.	
example:	$ COPY MYFILE.CUHHMD::DUA2: -	% rcp myfile cuhhmd:programs
	[.PROGRAMS]	

In the first example, **rcp cuhhmd:/usr/user1/junk myfile** copies the file **/usr/user1/junk** from the trusted remote host **cuhhmd** to **myfile** in the present working directory on the local host. In the second example, **rcp myfile cuhhmd:/usr/user1/junk** copies **myfile** in the present working directory on the local host to **junk** in the directory **/usr/user1** on the remote trusted host **cuhhmd**. For file transfer to occur, the same login name must own the remote directory **/usr/user1** on **cuhhmd** as well as the files on the local host, unless modified by a **cuhhmd:˜user/.rhosts** entry. Moreover, the directory **/usr/user1** must already exist on **cuhhmd**; the command will not create it.

The third example, **rcp -r ˜fred/programs cuhhmd:/usr/fred/programs**, illustrates copying a directory structure (**r** option for recursive copying) across the network. You cannot do this in VMS with the **COPY** or **BACKUP** commands, since neither copies directory structures between local and remote nodes. The VMS user must create a **BACKUP** save-set on the local node, copy it to a remote node as a single file, and then recreate the directory structure using the **BACKUP** command again on the remote node. In the UNIX example given here, the local directory **programs**, any subdirectories of **programs**, and all files therein are recreated on the remote host **cuhhmd** in the directory **/usr/fred/programs** in the same way as the **cp** command copies directory structures on a single host (see Section 9.3.1).

In the fourth example, **rcp myfile cuhhmd:programs/junk** illustrates the use of a relative pathname to specify a file on the remote host. The command copies **myfile** to **˜user/programs/junk** on the remote host. Relative pathnames on a local host start from the present working directory; relative pathnames on a remote host start from the parent directory of the user. Note that if the directory **˜user/programs** on the remote host did not exist, it would not have been created. Rather, an error would have occurred.

The last example extends the concept of using a relative pathname. **rcp myfile cuhhmd:programs** does not include an output filename (**programs** is a directory), hence the file is copied with the same name to **˜user/programs/myfile**.

13.2.6.2 ### *Non-Trusted Host: ftp*

Section 13.2.6.1 showed that file transfer between trusted hosts is no more cumbersome than transfers between VMS nodes using DECnet, and offers the additional feature of simple directory structure copying. Copying between non-trusted hosts is not so straightforward.

ftp (file transfer program), a UNIX utility for file transfer between non-trusted network hosts, establishes a connection to a remote host for which a login name and password are required. Once an **ftp** connection is established, you can issue a variety of commands on either the local or the remote host, including **?**, which provides help on available **ftp** commands. A subset of commonly used **ftp** commands appears in Table 13.4. As a pleasing departure from standard UNIX practice, you may abbreviate these commands.

You can avoid entering your login name and password each time you make a connection with **ftp** by using the hidden file **˜user/.netrc**, which resides in the parent directory of the local host (compare **˜user/.rhosts**, which resides on the remote host).

UNIX

form:	machine host login username password password
example:	% cat ˜fred/.netrc
	machine cuhhmd.hhmi.columbia.edu login fred password mypassword

In this example, the user can make an **ftp** connection to the remote host **cuhhmd.hhmi.columbia.edu** using the login name **fred** and the password **mypassword**. The host name must be the official Internet host name, that is, the first entry for the host in the **/etc/hosts** file and not an alias. As the **˜user/.netrc** file contains a user's password on a remote host, the file should not be readable by anyone except the user (and **root**). In fact, **˜user/.netrc** will not function if the world or group has access to the file.[5] The following examples show **ftp** connections to a remote host, both with and without a **˜user/.netrc** file.

---

5. This may not be true of all versions of UNIX. In those implementations that do function despite world or group access to **˜user/.netrc**, the security risk is significant.

Table 13.4   A Subset of ftp Commands

Command	Function
!	Issue shell command on local host
ascii	Set file transfer type to ASCII (default)
binary	Set file transfer type to binary
bye (or quit)	Terminate connection to remote host and exit **ftp**
cd	Change present working directory on remote host
close	Terminate connection to remote host do not exit **ftp**
delete	Delete a file on remote host
get (or recv)	Copy file from remote to local host
help (or ?)	Get help on available commands
lcd	Change directory on the local host
ls	Directory listing on remote host
mdelete	Delete multiple files on remote host
mget	Retrieve multiple files from remote host
mkdir	Create a directory on remote host
mput	Copy multiple files from the local to remote host
open	Establish a connection to a remote host
prompt	Toggle interactive prompting
put (or send)	Copy single file from local to remote host
pwd	Display current working directory on remote host
rename	Rename a file on the remote host
rmdir	Remove a directory on remote host
status	Display the status of **ftp**

UNIX

form: % ftp [option(s)] [host]
example: % ftp cuhhmd
Connected to cuhhmd.hhmi.columbia.edu.
220 cuhhmd FTP server (Version 4.1 Tue Mar 31 21:45:47 EST 1987) ready.
Name (cuhhmd.hhmi.columbia.edu:): fred
Password (cuhhmd.hhmi.columbia.edu:fred): [password entered here - not \
  echoed]
331 Password required for fred.
230 User fred logged in.
ftp> pwd
251 " /usr/users/fred" is current directory.
ftp> bye
221 Goodbye.
%

```
example:    % cat .netrc
            machine cuhhmd.hhmi.columbia.edu username fred password mypassword
            % ftp cuhhmd
            Connected to cuhhmd.hhmi.columbia.edu.
            220 cuhhmd FTP server (Version 4.1 Tue Mar 31 21:45:47 EST 1987) ready.
            331 Password required for fred.
            230 User fred logged in.
            ftp> pwd
            251 " /usr/users/fred" is current directory.
            ftp> bye
            221 Goodbye
            %
```

Only the second example uses a ˜**user/.netrc** file. In both examples, the
ftp command **pwd** is issued on the remote host to determine the current
working directory on that host. In both examples, **ftp** is terminated with
the command **bye**, which logs the user off the remote host and returns
the local shell prompt.

We now turn to **ftp** commands that may be used once a connection has
been made.

```
            UNIX
example:    ftp> !ls bob.txt
            bob.txt
example:    ftp> put
            (local-file) bob.txt
            (remote-file) old.txt
example:    ftp> put bob.txt
example:    ftp> ls bob.txt
            200 PORT command okay.
            150 Opening data connection for /bin/ls (128.59.93.1,1651) (0 bytes).
            bob.txt
            226 Transfer complete.
            211 bytes received in 0.39 seconds (0.54 Kbytes/s)
example:    ftp> mget
            (remote-files) batch.out.*
            mget batch.out.223? y
            mget batch.out.234? y
            mget batch.out.235? y
example:    ftp> status
            Mode: stream; Type: ascii; form: non-print; Structure: file
            Verbose: on; Bell: off; Prompting: on; Globbing: on
            Hash mark printing: off; Use of PORT cmds: on
example:    ftp> prompt
            Interactive mode off
example:    ftp> mput batch.out.*
            ftp>
```

In the first example, **!ls bob.txt** determines that the file **bob.txt** exists in the current directory of the local host. Any command that begins with **!** instructs **ftp** to pass the command to the shell on the local host for execution; that is, **ftp** forks a new shell to execute the local command. In the second example, **put** without arguments prompts **ftp** to request first the name of the existing file to be copied from the local host, and second the name it is to receive on the remote host. Then **bob.txt** on the local host is copied (**put**) to **old.txt** on the remote host. The third example, **put bob.txt**, illustrates a situation in which the local but not the remote file name is given: the file is copied (**put**) to the remote host with the same name that it had on the local host. In the fourth example, **ls bob.txt** verifies that the copy was successful by checking for the existence of **bob.txt** on the remote host.

In the fifth example, **mget** copies (gets) multiple files from the remote host. By default, the user is prompted to copy each file (compare the VMS command **COPY/CONFIRM**). You may turn off interactive prompting in one of two ways. First, the **ftp** command **prompt** will toggle the value of interactive prompting; you can determine the current value (on or off) with the **ftp status** command. The last example, **mput batch.out.***, illustrates multiple copying from the local to the remote host with interactive mode off: all files are copied without comment. Second, you can invoke **ftp** with the **i** option (not shown), which suppresses interactive prompting.

In the fourth example, **ftp** displays diagnostic messages indicating the total number of bytes transferred and the rate of transfer. These diagnostics are displayed during all **ftp** transfers, but have been omitted from all but the fourth example for the sake of brevity.

13.2.7   *Remote Command Execution: rsh*

You may not issue commands on a remote host from a local host unless the local host is trusted by the remote host. For non-trusted hosts, the local user must first login to the remote host and then issue commands either through **telnet** or **ftp**.

rsh (remote shell) executes a command or a shell script on a remote trusted host by invoking a shell on the remote host, which then executes the command. Any command that can be interpreted by the shell on a remote host is valid. VMS commands are always interpreted by the local node. This fact does not present a problem when accessing files, as VMS file specifications may include a remote node. For example, the VMS user wishing to display the contents of a directory on node **BOSTON** might enter the command **DIRECTORY BOSTON::DUA2:[FRED]**. The UNIX user accomplishes the same task with the command **rsh boston "ls ˜fred"**. Both the VMS and the UNIX commands are straightforward. However, what if the local user wishes to review the list of interactive users on node **BOSTON**?

	VMS	UNIX
example:	$ TYPE BOSTON::DUA2:[FRED]CMD.COM $ DEFINE/USER SYS$OUTPUT SYS$NET $ 'P1'	% rsh boston "who"
example:	$ TYPE BOSTON::DUA2:[FRED]- "TASK = CMD SHOW USERS"	

UNIX accomplishes the task by invoking a remote shell to execute the **who** command. VMS requires invoking a command procedure created on the remote node.

The following examples illustrate the functionality of **rsh** when combined with piping and input/output redirection.

	VMS	UNIX
form:	$ COMMAND[/QUALIFIER(S)] - NODE::DEVICE:[DIRECTORY]FILE	% rsh host [option(s)] command(s)
example:	$ PRINT/REMOTE - CUHHMD::DUA1:[FRED]- MYFILE.DAT	% rsh cuhhmd "cat /usr/fred/\ myfile" | lpr
example:	$ COPY - CUHHMD::DUA1:[FRED]A.DAT - CUHHMD"FRED - MYPASS"::DUA1[FRED]B.DAT	% rsh cuhhmd "cat /usr/fred/a > \ /usr/fred/b"
example:	$ COPY MYFILE.DAT - CUHHMD::SYS$PRINT	% cat myfile | rsh cuhhmd "lpr -"
example:	$ TYPE - CUHHMD::DUA2:[GEORGE]- MYFILE.	% rsh cuhhmd -lgeorge "cat myfile"

The first example, **rsh cuhhmd "cat /usr/fred/myfile"** | **lpr**, illustrates local printing of a file resident on the remote host **cuhhmd**. Rather than displaying the remote file **/usr/fred/myfile**, the output is piped to the default line printer (see Section 8.1.1). Note that the pipe is interpreted by the local shell because it is not contained in double quotes. In the second example, **rsh cuhhmd "cat /usr/fred/a > /usr/fred/b"** redirects the output of the **cat** command to the file **/usr/fred/b**; since double quotes surround the output redirection, the remote host performs the operation. Note that the result would be the same using the command **rsh cuhhmd "cp /usr/fred/a /usr/fred/b"**. In the third example, **cat myfile | rsh cuhhmd "lpr -"**, rather than displaying the contents of **myfile**, pipes the output to the **rsh** command, which prints it on the default line printer attached to the remote host **cuhhmd**. The last example, **rsh cuhhmd -lgeorge "cat myfile"**, illustrates further the use of the **l** option (compare **rlogin**). The local user invokes the remote shell through the account **george** on the remote host **cuhhmd**, assuming the file ˜**george/.rhosts** is present to permit remote access by the local user initiating the request. The file **myfile** in the parent directory of user **george** will be displayed.

13.2.8   *Transparent File Access: NFS*

The Network File System (NFS) software permits a UNIX user to access files physically located on devices attached to remote hosts as if they were attached to the local host. The NFS software must reside on both the local and the remote host. VMS users familiar with the Local Area VAXcluster (LAVC) should note that the features of NFS and LAVC are similar. A LAVC user requests access to a file using the logical device name **SYS$COMMON**; the NFS user specifies a file system. In both cases, the physical location of the file is irrelevant. For example, the user who lacks access to NFS and wishes to display a file on a remote trusted host would use the **rsh** (remote shell) command, which includes the remote host name. If the file system on which the file resides is available via NFS, however, the user can issue the **cat** command.

NFS is licensed by Sun Microsystems, Inc., and runs on a variety of computers that support a version of the UNIX operating system.[6] Therefore, you can directly access files on a variety of hardware types. You can determine whether NFS is running on your system by looking for the NFS daemon. A daemon is a process owned by the superuser (**root**); it is usually started at boot time and performs some background function. In this example, **ps -aux | grep nfsd** searches the list of all processes running on the system for **nfsd**, the NFS daemon.

---

6. NFS is now available for the VMS operating system, permitting files to be shared between UNIX and VMS computers (see Section 13.5).

```
              VMS                        UNIX
example:      $ SHOW CLUSTER             % ps -aux | grep nfsd
              SYSTEMS    MEMBERS         system 12384  0.4  0.2  72  36  p3  S  0:00  grep nfsd
              NODE  SOFTWARE  STATUS     root    3989  0.0  0.1  68   0   ?  I  1:19  nfsd 4
              CUMBG   VMS 4.7            root    3990  0.0  0.1  68   0   ?  I  1:13  nfsd 4
                                         root    3988  0.0  0.1  68   0   ?  I  1:16  nfsd 4
                                         root    3987  0.0  0.1  68   0   ?  I  1:06  nfsd 4
```

If one or more NFS daemons are running, you can list remote file systems available locally with the **df** command.

```
              UNIX
example:      % df
              Filesystem          kbytes     used    avail  capacity  Mounted on
              /dev/da0a           18067     13708     2552    84%      /
              /dev/da0h          108645     96273     1507    98%      /usr
              cuhhia:/usr1        56144     26315    26318    50%      /cuhhiausr1
```

Remote file systems accessible via NFS are displayed in the form **hostname:filesystem**, where **hostname** is the first part of the Internet host name and **filesystem** is the name of the file system on the remote host. The above example displays three file systems, two local and one remote. The remote file system **cuhhia:/usr1** is accessed as **/cuhhiausr1** on the local host.

```
              UNIX
example:      % ls /cuhhiausr1
              aronson   horton     mms      purnick    weiss
              % rlogin cuhhia
              IRIS Workstation
              % ls /usr1
              aronson   horton    mms      purnick     weiss
```

ls /cuhhiausr1 provides a directory listing of the remotely mounted file system **cuhhia:/usr1**. This directory listing is verified by an **rlogin** to the remote host **cuhhia**, which has the identical file system known locally as **/usr1**.

You can list the local file systems available for mounting on remote hosts by displaying the file **/etc/exports**.

```
               UNIX
   example:    % hostname ; cat /etc/exports
               cuhhca
               # nfs exports file      4/5/88
               #
               /data1
               /usr
```

hostname ; cat /etc/exports indicates that the local host **cuhhca** has two file systems, **/data1** and **/usr**, available for remote mounting.

13.3   *Modem Communications*

We now turn to communications via standard telephone lines using modems attached to the local and the remote computer. Users who do not intend to use modem connections may proceed to Section 13.4.

13.3.1   *UUCP Addresses*

The format of a UUCP address (see Table 13.2) requires further explanation. First, \ prevents the interpretation of the ! C shell metacharacter as a history substitution (see Section 3.4). The address is therefore interpreted correctly by the local or remote host as **site!user**. Second, the address may also be a path indicating that the message must pass through an intermediate **site1** to reach the final destination **site2**.

The UUCP user may determine the UUCP host names of the local and reachable remote hosts using the commands **uuname -l** and **uuname**, respectively.

```
               UNIX
   form:       % uuname [-l]
   example:    % uuname
               c1apple
               cucard
   example:    % uuname -l
               cuhhca
```

These examples show two systems, **c1apple** and **cucard**, that can be reached directly by UUCP, and that the UUCP name of the local host is **cuhhca**.

13.3.2   *UUCP Status*

UUCP offers no mechanism to determine whether a remote host is currently reachable. If a remote host is not available when UUCP attempts to make a connection, UUCP will continue making attempts at regular intervals defined by the system administrator until a connection is made.

13.3.3   *Remote Login: tip and cu*

UUCP provides only batch processing (spools requests), and therefore precludes any type of interactive communication including remote login. However, if dial-out and dial-in modems are available, you can use the commands **tip** and **cu** (compare the VMS command **SET HOST/DTE**) to conduct a terminal session on a remote host. Both **tip** and **cu** require that you physically initiate a session; UUCP automatically establishes a connection at some predefined time. The commands **tip**, **cu**, and those of UUCP may share the same modems.

BSD UNIX systems include **tip** but not **cu**, so **tip** is the command discussed here. The system administrator of the local host maintains a file **/etc/remote**, which contains characteristics of the remote hosts reachable via **tip**. This simplifies access to remote hosts, since you do not need to explicitly specify the characteristics required to make a connection each time you attempt communication.

```
             UNIX
example:     % cat /etc/remote
             # sample entry from a /etc/remote file
             #
             cuccfa/1200 Baud Able Quadracall attributes:\
             :dv = /dev/cua0:br#1200:cu = /dev/cua0:at = vadic:du
form:        % tip [-v] [-speed] system name or phone #
example:     % tip -2400 cuccfa
```

The first example, **cat /etc/remote**, illustrates the format of the file for defining the characteristics of remote hosts. Since this file is established by the system administrator, we will not discuss it further. The command **tip -2400 cuccfa** establishes a connection to the remote host defined in the **/etc/remote** file. Rather than the default baud rate of 1200 (**br#1200**), 2400 is specified. Alternative phone numbers can be maintained in a file which defaults to **/etc/phones**, but may be a user's private telephone directory, which is pointed to by the environment variable defined by the command **setenv PHONES path**.

Table 13.5 Subset of tip Commands

Command	Function
˜⟨CTRL⟩D˜.	Logout of remote machine and exit **tip**
˜c [name]	Change directory on the local host to **name**
˜!	Exit to shell on local host (C shell only)
˜>	Copy file prompted for from local to remote host
˜<	Copy file prompted for from remote to local host
˜p from [to]	Like ˜>
˜t from [to]	Like ˜<
˜|	Pipe output from a remote command to local process
˜s	Set a variable
˜?	Help with these commands

Once a connection has been made, you can issue a variety of commands to the **tip** program to initiate some action on the local or remote host. Table 13.5 summarizes these commands, including commands to transfer files, issue commands on the local or remote host, and set a variable.

13.3.4 ### *Sending Mail*

Sending UUCP mail uses the **mail** utility discussed in Chapter 6. The only variation to note here is the format of the mail address. In a UUCP mail message address, as we have previously discussed, **!** is a C shell metacharacter, and you therefore must precede it with \ to prevent immediate interpretation. Thus, although an address might be displayed as **c1apple!bobs**, you would give it as **c1apple\!bobs** to use it as an actual mail address.

UUCP mail messages which need explicit routing to reach a distant site by passing through other sites take the form **site1\!site2\!site3\!user**. That is, the message passes first to **site1**, then to **site2**, and then to **user** at **site3**. Users should consult the system administrator for information on the explicit routing required to reach remote hosts.

	VMS	UNIX
form:		% mail host\!user
example:	$ MAIL	% mail c1apple\!bobs
	MAIL> SEND	
	To: CUHHMD::FRED	

File Transfer: uucp and uusend

The commands **uucp** and **uusend** are part of the UUCP group of programs. **uucp** copies only to an immediate neighbor, that is, a remote host
dialed directly, whereas **uusend** can pass files to remote hosts through a
number of intermediate host connections. You should use these commands only when no network connection is available, since they are
spooled for processing via slow modem connections rather than processed interactively using a fast network.

Note the distinction between **uucp** (lowercase) and UUCP (uppercase).
UUCP refers to a collection of programs used for modem communications that includes **uucp** and **uusend**. These commands, like their UUCP
counterpart **uux**, use a similar syntax. You can use **uucp** to copy in both
directions, both from and to a remote host, whereas **uusend** will copy
only from a local to a remote host.

For **uucp** and **uusend** to function local, remote, and (in the case of
uusend) intermediate hosts must be running UUCP. An account **uucp**
handles the request spooled by the local host. Like any user account,
uucp has a parent directory **˜uucp** (C shell syntax), usually designated /
usr/spool/uucp. Unlike a normal user account, the parent directory has
world read, write, and execute access, for it must be able to receive
UUCP files from remote hosts. Alternatively, you may have a subdirectory with world read, write, and execute access to receive UUCP files
from a user on a remote host. If so, the user sending a file to this directory via UUCP must know of its existence.

We will look at some examples of using **uucp** before turning to **uusend**.

	UNIX
form:	% uucp [option(s)] local_file remote_file
example:	% uucp myfile cuhhmd\!˜uucp
example:	% uucp -m myfile1 myfile2 myfile3 cuhhmd\!˜fred/scratch
form:	% uucp [option(s)] remote_file local_file
example:	% uucp cuhhmd\!˜fred/book/chap\[0-9\] ˜george/book
example:	% uucp myfile cuhhmd\!˜uucp/fred/yourfile

In the first example, **uucp myfile cuhhmd\!˜uucp** spools the local file
myfile for copying to the public directory **uucp** on the remote host
cuhhmd; by default the remote file will be given the name **myfile**. (Recall
the **host\!user** address syntax of UUCP from Section 13.3.1). The local

user may inform the remote user destined to receive the file of its impending arrival by mail. You notify the recipient with the option **nuser**: for example, **nfred** will cause UUCP on the remote host to automatically send a mail message to remote user **fred** informing him of the arrival of the file.

The second example, **uucp -m myfile1 myfile2 myfile3 cuhhmd\!˜fred/scratch**, illustrates the copying of multiple files to the subdirectory, **scratch** of user **fred** on the remote host **cuhhmd**. The **m** option directs UUCP to send mail to the local sender when successful file transfer has occurred. Without this option, the local user sending the file has no way of knowing when the file transfer occurred.

The third example, **uucp cuhhmd\!˜fred/book/chap\[0-9\] ˜george/book**, illustrates copying from a remote to a local host, and further use of \. Any file from **chap0** through **chap9** in the subdirectory **book** of remote user **fred** is copied to local user **george**'s subdirectory **book**. Note that the remote directory ˜**fred/book** and the files **chap0** through **chap9** must be world readable, and that the local directory ˜**george/book** must be world writable. The characters **[** (open square bracket) and **]** (close square bracket) are C shell metacharacters, and therefore must be preceded by \ to prevent immediate interpretation by the shell on the local host.

The last example, **uucp myfile cuhhmd\!˜uucp/fred/yourfile**, illustrates directory creation with **uucp**. **myfile** on the local host is copied to a subdirectory, **fred** of ˜**uucp**. If that subdirectory did not exist on the remote host, it would have been created.

We now turn to **uusend**. As noted above, **uusend** sends but does not receive files through intermediate hosts to a final destination. Each host must have **uusend**. UUCP does not necessarily imply **uusend**, as some versions of UNIX UUCP support **uucp** but not **uusend**. One disadvantage of **uusend** as compared to **uucp** is its lack of a mechanism to determine whether a file has arrived at a remote host. One advantage of **uusend** over **uucp** is that you may set file protections when the file reaches a remote host; with **uucp** the remote file is always world readable, and therefore not secure.

UNIX
form: % uusend local_file site1\!site2\. . .\!sitex\!remote_file
example: % uusend myfile cuhhca\!cuchmc\!c1apple\!˜uucp

In the first example, **uusend myfile cuhhca\!cuchmc\!clapple\!⌐uucp** copies the local file **myfile** to the final destination **⌐uucp/myfile** on remote host **clapple**. Note that the name of the remote file defaults to **myfile**. To get to the final destination, the file passed through the intermediate hosts **cuhhca** and **cuchmc**. In the second example, **uusend - cuhhca\ !cuhhmc\!clapple\!⌐uucp/outfile** follows the same route as the first example. However, the - (dash) metacharacter indicates that input is **stdin** and not a file. All text entered at the terminal will be sent to the remote file **⌐uucp/outfile** on **clapple** until you issue a ⟨CTRL⟩-D. The third example, **myprog | uusend - cuhhca\!cuhhmc\!clapple\!⌐uucp/outfile**, expands on this concept. Rather than send the output of the program **myprog** to the terminal, it is piped to the **uusend** command which copies it to **⌐uucp/ outfile** on the remote node **clapple**.

The last example, **uusend -m 700 myfile cuhhca\!cuchmc\!clapple\!/usr/ fred/scratch/outfile**, illustrates the use of the **m** option to set the protection of the file copied to the remote host. **myfile** is copied to the final destination of **/usr/fred/scratch/outfile**. Although the directory **/usr/ fred/scratch** must allow world write access in order to accept the file, the protection of the file is set to **700**, which indicates full access by the owner and no access by other classes of user.

13.3.6   *Remote Command Execution: uux*

uux is a UUCP program for executing a small subset of commands on a remote host. Like other UUCP modem-based requests, requests generated by **uux** are spooled for processing. Its response, therefore, is not fast enough to be interactive. The system administrator of the remote host defines the commands that you can run on that host. The commands reside in the file **/usr/lib/uucp/L.cmds**.

UNIX
example: % cat /usr/lib/uucp/L.cmds
PATH=/bin:/usr/bin:/usr/ucb
rmail
rnews

```
lpr
uusend
bnproc
unbatchnews
uux
```

In the **L.cmds** file shown above, **PATH = /bin:/usr/bin:/usr/ucb** indicates the directories that will be searched to locate the allowable commands. The allowable commands follow, one per line. Some versions of UNIX extend the functionality of this file, for example, by stating explicitly which commands can be executed by which remote hosts. The features described here are common to all versions.

If a remote command request is unsuccessful, the local user is notified by mail on the local machine. The following examples illustrate various uses of **uux**, using either local or remote files for both input and output.

	UNIX
form:	% uux host\!command "input-output control"
example:	% uux cuhhmd\!who "> ˜fred/scratch/who.out"
example:	% uux cuhhmd\!who "> cuhhmd\!˜uucp/scratch/who.out"
example:	% uux \!lpr "< cuhhmd\!˜uucp/scratch/who.out"
example:	% uux \!diff cuhhmd\!/tmp/file1 cuhhca\!/tmp/file2 "> \!diff.out"
example:	% uux -m cuhhmd\!lpr < printfile.txt

In the first example, **uux cuhhmd\!who "> ˜fred/scratch/who.out"** executes the **who** command on the remote host **cuhhmd**. The result of the **uux** command is output to the file **who.out** on the local host. **uux** output must always be output to a local file, since **stdout** has no meaning to the **who** command executed remotely. Note also the use of double quotes: without them, the shell directs the output of the local **uux** command to the file **who.out**. With them output from the remote execution of **who** is placed in the local file **who.out**. As **who.out** is to be written by the UUCP utility and not the user issuing the **uux** command, the directory to which it writes the output must be world writable, and an absolute pathname must be given unless the file is to be written to a directory owned by the **uucp** account.

In the second example, **uux cuhhmd\!who "> cuhhmd\!˜uucp/scratch/who.out"** copies the result of the remote **who** command to the file ˜uucp/scratch/who.out on the remote host **cuhhmd**, rather than to the local host. The third example, **uux \!lpr "< cuhhmd\!˜uucp/scratch/who.out"**, illustrates the execution of a command on the local host using a file from the remote host **cuhhmd**. **!lpr** without a preceding host name indicates a file to be printed on the default line printer on the local host. The fourth example also illustrates local command execution, but introduces the use of files from two remote hosts as input to the command. **uux \!diff cuhhmd\!/tmp/file1 cuhhca\!/tmp/file2 "> \! diff.out"** executes the **diff** command locally using two remote files located on hosts **cuhhmd** and **cuhhca**. The output is placed in the local file **diff.out**.

The fifth example, **uux -m cuhhmd\!lpr < printfile.txt**, illustrates how to print a local file on a remote line printer connected to **cuhhmd**. The **m** option notifies the user on the local host by mail when the command has been executed, in this instance, when the file is spooled for printing.

13.4   *Usenet: Electronic Bulletin Board*

Usenet grew out of the expanding UUCP network to disseminate information of interest to UNIX users. Usenet is like a newsstand where each magazine on that newsstand is a *newsgroup* covering a particular topic. Examples of newsgroups are:

- Public domain software
- Hardware/software technological reviews
- Employment opportunities
- Games
- Bug fixes
- Field topics such as biology, medicine, and chemistry

Usenet differs from a newsstand in that users can reply to news (like a letter to the editor, perhaps?) and can post news. The programs that permit these activities and that the system administrator uses to manage news are known as Netnews. Netnews was developed at Duke University in the late 1970s. The programs that the UNIX user will encounter are:

readnews	Basic read and reply
rn	Advanced read and reply
vnews	Full-screen read and reply
postnews	Post news articles

You should consult your system administrator to find out whether any news is received at his or her site. If news is received by the local host, you can review the file **/usr/lib/news/newsgroups** to determine the current newsgroups. If a useful newsgroup is available but is not received by the local host, ask your system administrator to receive the one you want. For the details of how to use Usenet, see the excellent discussion of the topic by Anderson, Costales, and Henderson in *UNIX Communications* (Appendix D).

<table>
<tr><td>13.5</td><td>

Communications Between VMS and UNIX

</td></tr>
</table>

A number of vendor-dependent solutions permit communications between VMS nodes and UNIX hosts. It is beyond the scope of this book to discuss each of these. Rather, we give an overview based on the simple discussion of computer communications in Section 13.1.

As indicated, modem communications between UNIX and VMS processors are accomplished simply by taking into consideration the requirements for each computer as if the user were connecting a terminal directly to each computer. File transfer is then easily accomplished with either **tip** or a variety of third-party software packages, most notably Kermit. The use of UUCP is not possible unless the VMS node supports a UNIX emulator or a native version of UUCP for VMS can be found.[7]

Communications between a VMS node and a UNIX host attached to a network require software and sometimes hardware to convert DECnet to TCP/IP packets and vice versa. Obviously, if one VMS machine must communicate with a number of UNIX machines, the most efficient solution is to provide TCP/IP emulation for the single VMS node. Similarly, in the case of one UNIX host that must communicate with a number of VMS nodes, DECnet emulation for the UNIX host represents the most efficient solution.

In a truly heterogeneous environment of processors, with a number of VMS and UNIX hosts, the best solution is to dedicate a processor for performing conversions from TCP/IP to DECnet and vice versa. The ULTRIX version of UNIX supports both TCP/IP and DECnet, and can be used to fulfill this function as a DECnet-Internet gateway. The VMS user can then access a remote UNIX host with familiar VMS commands such as **COPY** and **DELETE**. Correspondingly, the UNIX user can access the VMS nodes with commands like **ftp** and **telnet**.

---

7. The VAX Systems Special Interest Group of the Digital Equipment Corporation Users Society (DECUS) offers a native implementation. The software is available on the DECUS Software Library magnetic tapes.

Once again, a scenario from daily use will summarize the networking features described in this chapter. UNIX user Janet Smith has just relocated and must develop applications on two UNIX hosts. On the host **apple**, to which her terminal is connected, her login name is **smithj**. On the other host, **orange**, her login name is **janet**.

```
                UNIX
example:    % whoami ; hostname
            smithj
            apple
example:    % grep orange /etc/hosts
            126.21.36.1    orange.dept.company.edu    orange
            % telnet orange
            Trying...
            Connected to orange.dept.company.edu
            Escape character is '(CTRL)]'.
            UNIX. RELEASE BSD 4.3 (orange)
            login: janet
            Password
            Never logged in
example:    % set prompt = "orange>"
example:    orange> cat /etc/hosts.equiv
            grape.dept.company.edu
            pear.dept.company.edu
            peach.dept.company.edu
example:    orange> ls -l .rhosts
            -rw-rw-r--  1 root      30 Jun 11 09:25 .rhosts
example:    orange> cat .rhosts
            apple.dept.company.edu    smithj
            orange> logout
            Connection closed
example:    % rlogin orange -ljanet
            Last login: Thu Jun 16 10:58 from apple
            orange> logout
            Connection closed
example:    % uuname
            amsterdam
            london
            purdue
example:    % uucp -m purdue\!~janet\*.\* ~uucp/smithj
            [some time later]
example:    % cp ~uucp/smithj/*.* ~smithj
example:    % rsh orange -ljanet "rcp apple:~smithj/*.* ~janet/*.*"
example:    % mail purdue\!root
            Subject: Thanks
            Thank you for your help over the years
            .
            Cc:
```

Janet Smith logs in and issues the command **whoami ; hostname**, which displays her login name and the name of the local host. Knowing that the remote UNIX host she is going to use is on the same network, she searches the **/etc/hosts** file to see if it is defined. **grep orange /etc/hosts** reveals that the host she seeks is defined, with the official name **orange.dept.company.edu** and the alias **orange**. She uses the command **telnet orange** to login to this remote host using the login name **janet**. To avoid any confusion that may arise by not knowing what host she is using at any given time, Janet changes the prompt of the remote host, from the default **%** for the C shell to the name of the remote host, with the command **set prompt = "orange>"**. Note that the prompt is contained in quotes to prevent the C shell from misinterpreting **>** as a shell redirection metacharacter. Janet also includes this **set** command in the file **.login** so that the prompt is set to **orange>** the next time she logs in (not shown).

The command **cat /etc/hosts.equiv** establishes that the system administrator of the remote host **orange** does not consider **apple** a trusted host. However, the commands **ls -l .rhosts** and **cat .rhosts** reveal that the system administrator has established a user-specific trusted host definition indicating that **smithj** from host **apple.dept.company.edu** may access this account without supplying password information. She tests her access by logging out of the remote host and issuing the command **rlogin orange -ljanet**, which indeed gives her trusted host access to the remote host.

Next, Janet checks the remote hosts available from host **apple** using UUCP with the command **uuname**. Since she can reach **purdue**, the computer she used at her previous location, Janet issues the command **uucp -m purdue\!˜janet*.* ˜uucp/smithj** to copy files from her home directory at the old location to the subdirectory **smithj** of **uucp**. The **m** option informs her by **mail** when the copy operation has taken place. Some time later, Janet issues the command **cp ˜uucp/smithj/*.* ˜smithj** to copy the files to her parent directory on the local host **apple**. **rsh orange -ljanet "rcp apple:˜smithj/*.* ˜janet/*.*"** copies these files to the remote host **orange**. Note that Janet must use **rsh** even though **rcp** is simpler, because **rcp** does not support the **l** option which Janet needs as her local and remote login names differ. **ljanet** indicates that the remote login is to the account **janet** rather than the default **smithj**.

Finally, Janet sends UUCP mail to the address **purdue\!root** to thank the system administrator of host **purdue** for her help over the years (system administrators need this kind of encouragement!)

Epilogue

No passion in the world is equal to the passion to alter someone else's draft.
                                                              H. G. Wells

Welcome, UNIX user! If you have read Chapters 1 through 5 and other chapters pertinent to your own needs, you have made a good start. If you have also sat at the terminal and experimented with commands like the ones presented in this book, then you are well on the way to joining the growing number of competent UNIX users.

Early UNIX terminal sessions are likely to incite an entire spectrum of emotion in any reader who regards VMS as an old friend. For example:

- Awe at the endless number of complex command constructs that can be built from simple UNIX commands.
- Disdain for whoever chose the names for some of these commands, like **cat**, **biff**, **awk**, and **grep**.
- Anger at the limited error-reporting features of the UNIX shell.
- Frustration at the clumsiness of UNIX command line recall and editing.
- Anxiety while reading about the concept of a UNIX file system, followed by relief when you realize it is elegant and simple to use.
- Laughter followed by bewilderment as you explore the UNIX documentation, either on-line or in printed form.

The list goes on, but the best emotion is yet to come: satisfaction, the satisfaction that comes from developing complex applications using this powerful medium.

I hope that this book will continue to be a useful reference after you have reached the top of the learning curve and the sense of satisfaction is upon you. To this end, Appendix A provides a quick cross-reference to help you locate a command or an option to a command, and points to the section of this book containing a detailed discussion. Appendix B is a quick cross-reference guide to both the **ex** line editor and the **vi** screen editor. Appendix C indicates where information on important UNIX files is to be found. Appendix D provides an extensive reading list. The UNIX documentation is poor, but many good supplementary texts are available if you know where to look.

Future UNIX users will have the opportunity to hide the operating system behind a windowing interface common to both UNIX and VMS. This certainly is a powerful feature for occasional UNIX users, but for the serious user looking through the window is not enough. You need to step through and experience the inner world first-hand. I encourage you to do so, and wish you well in this endeavor.

P.B.

Appendix A

Command Summaries

Table A.1   VMS Commands with UNIX Equivalents

VMS Command	UNIX Equivalent	Section	UNIX Function
:= =	alias	3.2.2	Define alias for C shell
	set	3.2.2, 11.2	Set shell variable
:= = = =	setenv	3.2	Define an environment variable
@	source	11.9.4	Have parent process invoke a script
ASSIGN	ln	9.4.10	Assign one file to another
	ln -s		Assign one file to another across file systems
BACKUP	tar	8.2.1	Backup files into a tar file
BACKUP/INIT	tar -c		Initialize output device
BACKUP/LIST	tar -t		List contents
BACKUP/LOG	tar -v		Report progress
	tar -x		Restore files
	tar -r		Write at end of existing tar files
	tar -u		Write only files not already on tape
	tar -f		Use alternative special device file

VMS Command	UNIX Equivalent	Section	UNIX Function
	tar -m		Update files modification date upon restore
CC	cc	10.1	(See **FORTRAN**)
COPY	cp	4.9, 9.3.1	Copy a file
COPY/CONFIRM	cp -i		Confirm before copying
	ftp	13.2.6.2	Copy to/from non-trusted remote host
	rcp	13.2.6.1	Copy to/from trusted remote host
	rcp -r		Recursively copy subdirectories
CREATE	touch	9.4.7	Create or update a file
	touch -c		Existing files only
CREATE/DIRECTORY	mkdir	4.5	Create a subdirectory
DEBUG	dbx	10.3	Debug a program
DELETE	rm	4.11	Delete a file
DELETE/CONFIRM	rm -i		Confirm deletion
	rm -r	4.6	Delete a directory and all subdirectories
	rmdir	4.6	Delete an empty subdirectory
DELETE/ENTRY	lprm	8.1.3	Remove queued line printer job
	lprm -		Remove all jobs owned by user
DELETE/QUEUE	lprm -Pqueue		Remove all jobs from **queue**
DIFFERENCE	cmp	9.4.3	Display first difference in two files
	diff	9.4.3	Display all differences in files or directories
	diff -i		Ignore case differences
	diff -e		Generate editing changes for **ed**
	diff -r		Compare directories
DIRECTORY	ls	4.1, 9.1.1	List files
DIRECTORY [. . .]	ls -R		Recursively list subdirectories subdirectories

VMS Command	UNIX Equivalent	Section	UNIX Function
DIRECTORY/ COLUMN = 1	**ls -1**		List one file per line
	ls -a		Include hidden files
DIRECTORY/DATE	**ls -c**		List by creation/ modification time
	ls -d		List directory name only
	ls -F		Append character to designate file type
DIRECTORY/FULL	**ls -l**		Long listing
	ls -r		List in reverse order
DIRECTORY/OWNER	**ls -g**		Include group (used with l)
DIRECTORY/SIZE	**ls -s**		Include size
	ls -u		List according to access time
	ls -C		Override one file per line
	ls -t		Sort by date last modified
DIRECTORY/SIZE/TOTAL	**du**	7.1.4	Summarize disk usage
	du -a		All files
	du -s		Total size only
DIRECTORY [. . .]	**find**	4.7, 9.4.4	Find a file
	find -atime[+ /-]n		Modified in more (+) or less (-) than **n** days
	find -exec cmd {} \;		Issue command on files found
	find -group		In specified group
	find -name		By name
	find -newer file		Modified more recently than **file**
	find -ok cmd {} \;		As **-exec** but requests confirmation of action
	find -perm		By file protection
	find -print		Print path to each file found
	find -type		By file type
	find -user		By ownership
DUMP	**od**	9.2.2	Dump a file in various formats
	od -a		ASCII

Table A.1   VMS Commands with UNIX Equivalents *(continued)*

VMS Command	UNIX Equivalent	Section	UNIX Function
DUMP/OCTAL	**od -o**		Octal
DUMP/HEXADECIMAL	**od -h**		Hexadecimal
EDIT/EDT	**vi**	5.2	Screen editor
EDIT/RECOVER	**vi -r**		Recover screen editing session
	ex	5.1	Line editor
EDIT/RECOVER	**ex -r**		Recover line editing session
	ed	5.1	Line editor
EXCHANGE	**dd**	8.2.2	Backup/restore non-standard files
	ltf	8.2.4	VMS to ULTRIX tape exchange
EXIT	**exit**	11.1	Terminate a script
FORTRAN	**f77**	10.1	Compile and link FORTRAN program
	f77 -c		Suppress linking
	f77 -g		Create symbol table for profiling
	f77 -gp		Create object file for profiling
	f77 -S		Save assembler code
/OUTPUT=**file**	**f77 -ofile**		Place executable in **file**
	f77 -llib		Include library in load step
/LIST	**error**	10.3	Place syntax errors in code
HELP	**man**	3.6	On-line help
HINTS	**man -k topic**		Summarize help by topic
	man -f command		Summarize help by command
LIBRARY	**ar**	10.5	Library maintainer
LIBRARY/CREATE	**ar -cr**		Create library
LIBRARY/EXTRACT	**ar -x**		Extract module(s)
LIBRARY/INSERT	**ar -q**		Insert module(s)
LIBRARY/LIST	**ar -t**		List module(s)
LIBRARY/REPLACE	**ar -r**		Replace module(s)
	ar -m		Move module(s)
	ranlib	10.5	Randomize library
LINK		10.1	(See **FORTRAN**)
LOGOUT	**logout**	3.3	Terminate a terminal session

VMS Command	UNIX Equivalent	Section	UNIX Function
MAIL	**mail**	6.1	Send or receive electronic mail
MAIL DELETE	**mail d**		Delete message(s)
MAIL DIR	**mail f [user] or h**		Display header lines [from user]
MAIL DIR/FOLDER	**folders**		Display existing folders
MAIL EDIT	**mail e**		Edit message(s)
MAIL EXIT	**mail q**		End, saving unread message(s)
MAIL EXTRACT	**mail s file**		Store message(s) in **file**
MAIL HELP	**mail ?**		Get help on **mail** commands
MAIL MOVE	**mail s +folder**		Move message(s) to **folder**
MAIL NEXT	**mail n**		Go to next message
MAIL QUIT	**mail exit**		End, leaving **mail** environment unchanged
MAIL READ	**mail t**		Read message(s)
MAIL REPLY	**mail r**		Reply to all receivers
	mail R		Reply to sender only
MAIL SEND	**mail m**		Send a mail message
MAIL/EDIT	**mail ~e**		Invoke the editor defined by **EDITOR** in **.mailrc**
MAIL SET	**mail .mailrc**		Define **mail** environment
MAIL SET FOLDER	**mail -f folder**		Use specified folder
	mail !		Issue a shell command
	mail ch dir		Change directory to **dir** (default **$home**)
	mail ~d		Include the **dead.letter** file
	mail ~h		Optionally change all characteristics
	mail ~m #		Include message number # in current message
	mail ~p		Display entire message
	mail ~r file		Include **file** in message
	mail ~t users		Add **users** to those receiving message
	mail u		Undelete messages
	mail ~v		Invoke the **vi** editor
ON CONTROL _ Y	**onintr**	11.9.1	On interrupt

VMS Command	UNIX Equivalent	Section	UNIX Function
PHONE	**talk [ttyname]**	6.2	Communicate interactively with another user
PRINT	**lpr**	8.1.1	Print a file on the default line printer
PRINT/QUEUE	**lpr -Pqueue**		On specified queue
PRINT/COPIES=n	**lpr -#n**		**n** copies
	lpr -f		Format using FORTRAN carriage control
PRINT/NOHEADER	**lpr -h**		No header page
PRINT/FLAG	**lpr -Jjobn**		Include **jobn** on first page
	lpr -m		Send mail upon completion
PRINT/PAGE	**lpr -p**		Preformat with **pr**
PRINT/DELETE	**lpr -r**		Remove file after printing
	lpr -s		From user directory, not spool directory
	pr	9.2.3	Preformat file before printing
	pr -f		Use form feeds, not blank lines
	pr -h string		Replace header with **string**
	pr -l n		Make page **n** lines (default=66)
	pr -m		Merge files and print side by side
	pr +n		Begin at page **n**
	pr -n		**n** column output
	pr -t		Omit default page header and trailer
	pr -w n		Set line width to **n** (default=72)
RECALL/ALL	**history**	3.5	Recall command lines
RENAME	**mv**	4.10	Rename a file
RENAME/CONFIRM	**mv -i**		Confirm
	mv -f		Override conformation
RUNOFF	**nroff/troff**	12.3	Format text
RUNOFF/PAGE	**-o**		Selected pages only
	-mmacro		Use definitions in macro
SEARCH	**grep**	9.4.5	Search file(s) for strings

VMS Command	UNIX Equivalent	Section	UNIX Function
SEARCH/STAT	**grep -c**		List only count of lines that match
	grep -i		Ignore case distinctions
SEARCH/NUMBERS	**grep -n**		Precede each match with line number
	grep -v		List only lines that do not match
	grep -l		Return only filename that contains match
SET BROADCAST	**mesg y**	6.2	Permit broadcast interruptions
=NOMAIL	**biff n**	3.2.1	No incoming mail notification
SET DEFAULT	**cd**	4.4	Change directory
SET FILE/OWNER	**chgrp**	9.4.2	Change group ownership of a file
SET HOST	**rlogin**	13.2.4.1	Network login to trusted host
	rlogin -luser		With different login name
	telnet	13.2.4.2	Network login to non-trusted host
SET HOST/DTE	**tip**	13.3.3	Dial remote host
SET PASSWORD	**passwd**	3.2.3	Change the password
SET PROCESS			
/PRIORITY	**nice, renice**	7.3.3	Change the priority of a process
	limit	7.3.4	Limit the values of a process's resources
SET PROTECTION	**chmod**		Change file protection
[. . .]	**chmod -R**		Recursively descend directories
/DEFAULT	**umask**	3.2.4.2	Change the default protection
SET TERMINAL	**tset, stty**	3.1	Set the terminal characteristics
SET VERIFY	**csh**	11.10	Verify command/script execution
	csh -x		Echo after variable substitution
	csh -v		Echo command line prior to execution
	csh -X		As **-x**, but include **.cshrc**
	csh -V		As **-v**, but include **.cshrc**

Table A.1   VMS Commands with UNIX Equivalents *(continued)*

VMS Command	UNIX Equivalent	Section	UNIX Function
SHOW DEFAULT	pwd	4.3	Display current directory
SHOW DEVICE			
/ALLOCATED	tty	3.1	Display device to which a terminal is connected
/FULL	df [filesystem]	7.2.3	Display information on a file system
	df -i		Give block and fragment size
SHOW LOGICAL	printenv	3.2	Display environment characteristics
SYS$NODE	hostname	13.2.1	Display local host name
SHOW MEMORY	vmstat	7.2.1	Display memory utilization
SHOW NETWORK	netstat	7.2.2	Display network utilization
	ruptime	13.2.2	Display uptime of remote hosts
SHOW PROCESS	whoami	7.1.1	Display login name
	ps	7.1.3	Display information on processes
/ALL	ps -l		Long listing
	limit	7.1.5	Display resource limits
SHOW QUEUE	lpq	8.1.2	Display default print queue status
	lpq -Pqueue		For **queue**
	jobs	8.3.2	Display background job queue
SHOW STATUS	time	11.9.3	Display resources used by a process
SHOW SYSTEM	ps -aux	7.1.3	Show features of all processes
SHOW TIME	date	5.4.8	Display date and time
SHOW UIC	groups	3.1	Display group membership
SHOW USERS	who	7.1.2	Who is using the system
	w		Who is using the system (long)
	rwho		Who is using remote hosts (in last 30 minutes)
	rwho -a		All users
	rwho -h		Order alphabetically by host
	users		Who is using the system (short)

VMS Command	UNIX Equivalent	Section	UNIX Function
SORT	sort	9.4.6	Sort and merge
SORT/KEY	sort -n/ +n		Before/after field **n**
SORT/OUTPUT	sort -o file		Direct output to **file**
	sort -tn		Alternative field separator **n**
	sort -n		Strict ascending numeric order
	sort -f		Disregard case of alphanumerics
STOP/ID	kill -9	7.3.1	Remove a process
SUBMIT	at	7.3.2	Start a process at a later time
	bg	8.3.1	Move a process to background
TYPE	cat	4.8	Display a file
	cat -n		With line numbers
	cat -s		Suppress multiple blank lines
TYPE/PAGE	more (page)	4.8	Pause after each page
	more -c		Refresh screen
	more -f		Truncate rather than wrap long lines
	more -n		Display **n** lines (default = 24)
	more +n		Begin at line **n**
	more /string		Display 2 lines before next string
	head	9.2.3	Display the beginning of a file
	head -n		First **n** lines
	tail	9.2.3	Display the end of a file
	tail -n		Last **n** lines
	tail -r		In reverse order
WRITE	echo	11.2	Write to standard output
	echo -n		Leave cursor at end of line

Table A.2 UNIX Commands with No VMS Equivalents

Command	Section	Function
awk	5.4	Stream (batch) editor
-Fsep		Define field separator as **sep**
-ffile		Use commands contained in **file**
bc/dc	1.2	Calculator
cal [month] year	11.8.2	Display calendar
clear	3.3	Clear the terminal screen
dirs	9.3.2	Display the directory stack
eval	11.9.2	Force evaluation by parent process
fg	8.3.3	Bring job to foreground
fsplit	10.2	Split FORTRAN source code file into functional units
gprof	10.4	Extended profile of program execution
kill	8.3.3	Remove a background job
make	10.2	Maintain dependent files
-n		Echo but do not perform commands
mt	8.2.3	Magnetic tape manipulation
bsf [count]		Move back **count** files
bsr [count]		Move back **count** records
eof		Write EOF
fsf [count]		Move forward **count** files
fsr [count]		Move forward **count** records
rewind		Rewind tape
popd	9.3.2	Make top of directory stack the current directory
prof	10.4	Simple profile of program execution (see **gprof**)
pushd	9.3.2	Place a directory on the directory stack
+n		Rotate the stack **n** times
rsh	13.2.7	Remote command execution
script [file]	Preface	Make a transcript of a terminal session (default file transcript)
sed	5.3	Stream (batch) editor
-n		Display only modified lines
-e		Combine editing commands
set noclobber	2.1.3	Prevent redirection from overwriting existing file
spell	1.2	Check file for spelling errors
stop	8.3.3	Stop a background job
tr	9.4.8	Translate characters in a file
-c string		Include **string** in each translation
uucp	13.3.5	Send/receive file(s) via UUCP
uuname	13.3.1	Display remote host names reachable via UUCP
-l		Display local UUCP host name

Table A.2   UNIX Commands with No VMS Equivalents *(continued)*

Command	Section	Function
uusend	13.3.5	Send file(s) via UUCP
uux	13.3.6	Remote command execution via UUCP
wc	9.4.9	Count the number of lines, words and characters in a file
-l		Lines only
-w		Words only
-c		Characters only

Appendix B

Editor Summaries

Table B.1   VMS EDT Line Mode versus UNIX ex

EDT	ex	ex Function
Display Commands		
Tx	**x**	Display line **x**
Tx:y	**x,y**	Display lines **x** through **y**
T.:END(TREST)	**.,$**	Display current line to end of file
T1..	**1,.**	Display line 1 to current line
TWHOLE	**1,$**	Display whole line
Tstring	**/string/**	Display first line containing **string** below current line
T-string	**?string?**	Display first line containing **string** above current line
Ta:b,x:y	**a,b x,y**	Display lines **a** through **b** followed by lines **x** through **y**
	x,ynu	Display lines **x** through **y** with line numbers
Manipulation Commands		
I	**a**	Append after current line
D	**d**	Delete current line
Dx:y	**x,yd**	Delete lines **x** through **y**
S/S1/S2/	**s/s1/s2/**	Substitute String 1 for String 2
S/S1/S2/1:END	**s/s1/s2/g**	Substitute String 1 for String 2 throughout the file
R.	**c**	Delete current line and insert
Mx:y TO z	**x,ym z**	Move lines **x** through **y** and paste after **z**
WRITE FILE x:y	**x,ya [name]**	Copy lines **x** through **y** to buffer **name**
	y [name]	Put lines from buffer **name** after current line

Table B.1 VMS EDT Line Mode versus UNIX ex *(continued)*

EDT	**ex**	**ex** Function
INCLUDE FILE	**r file**	Include file after current line

Miscellaneous Commands

HELP		Get help
	undo	Reverse last command
QUIT	**q!**	Quit without saving changes
EXIT	**wq**	Exit saving changes

Form:	EDT	* command linea:lineb
	ex	: linea,lineb command options

Table B.2 VMS EDT Screen Mode Versus UNIX vi

EDT	**vi**	**vi** Function
Entering Text		
(default)	**a**	Append text after the cursor
	i	Insert text after the cursor while overwriting
[PF1][0] [1]	**o**	Open a new line below the cursor
	O	Open a new line above the cursor
	R	Replace characters
	⟨**ESC**⟩	Terminate input mode
Cursor Movement		
arrow keys	arrow keys	Move the cursor right or left, up or down
[2]	**$**	Move to the end of the line
backspace (**F12**)	**^**	Move to the beginning of the line
	H	Move cursor to the top of the screen
	L	Move cursor to the bottom of the screen
	M	Move cursor to the middle of the screen
[4][8]	⟨**CTRL**⟩**-F**	Scroll file forward one screen
[4][8]....	**#**⟨**CTRL**⟩**-F**	Scroll file forward # screens
[5][8]	⟨**CTRL**⟩**-B**	Scroll file backward one screen
[5][8]....	**#**⟨**CTRL**⟩**-B**	Scroll file backward # screens
	⟨**CTRL**⟩**-D**	Scoll file forward one-half screen
	⟨**CTRL**⟩**-U**	Scroll file backward one-half screen
[4][1]	**w**	Move forward one word
[4][1]....	**#w**	Move forward # words
[5][1]	**b**	Move backward one word
[5][1]....	**#b**	Move backward # words
	e	Move to last character of current word

EDT	vi	vi Function
[4][PF1][PF3]x	**fx**	Move forward to next character **x**
[5][PF1][PF3]x	**Fx**	Move backward to next character **x**
	)	Move forward one sentence
	(	Move backward one sentence
	}	Move forward to end of paragraph
	{	Move backward to beginning of paragraph
[4][PF1][PF3]string	**/string**	Move forward to **string**
[PF3]	**n**	Move forward to next occurrence of **string**
[5][PF1][PF3]string	**?string**	Move backward to **string**
[PF1][7]T#	**#G**	Move to line number **#**

Changing Text[2]

[.]	**r**	Replace a single character
	R	Replace until terminated by ⟨ESC⟩
[.]	**x**	Delete a single character
⟨**DEL**⟩, ⟨**CTRL**⟩**-H**	⟨**DEL**⟩, ⟨**CTRL**⟩**-H, X**	Delete character before the cursor
[-]	**dw**	Delete from cursor to beginning of next word
[PF1][2]	**d$**	Delete from the cursor to the end of the line
[-]	**cw**	Delete from cursor to beginning of next word and insert
[PF1][2]	**c$**	Delete from the cursor to the end of the line and insert
	dd	Delete the whole line containing the cursor
	cc	As **dd** and insert at the beginning of the line

Cut and Paste

[.]...[6]	**y**	Yank (copy) text into an alternative buffer
[.][2][6]	**yy**	Yank (copy) current line into alternative buffer
[PF1][6]	**p**	Paste deleted or yanked text after the cursor
	P	Paste deleted or yanked text before the cursor
[PF1][7] INCLUDE FILE	**r file**	Include an external file
[PF1][7] WRITE FILE	**w file**	Write to an external file

Miscellaneous Commands

[PF1][7].	⟨**CTRL**⟩**-G**	Identifies line number containing cursor
[PF1]command	**u**	Undo last command
	U	Undo all changes on the current line

Table B.2 VMS EDT Screen Mode Versus UNIX vi *(continued)*

EDT	vi	vi Function
	!	Enter a shell command
[PF1][7]	:	Enter an **ex** command
Leaving the Editor		
⟨**CTRL**⟩-**Z EXIT**	:w	Write and save the current file
⟨**CTRL**⟩-**Z QUIT**	:q	Quit the editor without saving
	:wq (or **ZZ**)	Write and quit
	:q!	Quit without saving changes
Using Editors in **vi**		
[PF1][7]	:	Prompt at bottom of screen for an **ex** command
⟨**CTRL**⟩-**Z**	Q	Quit **vi** without saving and begin an **ex** session

1. EDT keypad keys appear in square brackets.
2. Commands that move the cursor can be combined with commands that change text to provide wide-ranging functionality. For example, **d)** deletes from the cursor to the beginning of the next sentence.

Appendix C

Important UNIX Files

File	Section	Purpose
/lib	10.1	System libraries
/vmunix	2.2	The UNIX system kernel
/lost + found	2.2	Directory containing a file system's lost files
~user/.cshrc	3.2.2	Define environment for the C shell
~user/.exrc		Define environment for the **ex** editor
~user/.forward	6.1.4	Define a forwarding mail address
~user/.history	11.9	Maintain history list for following terminal session
~user/.hushlogin	3.1	Silences login messages
~user/.login	3.2.1	Define environment for the whole terminal session
~user/.logout	3.3	Commands to be executed upon logout
~user/.mailrc	6.1.8	Define environment for the **mail** utility
~user/.netrc	13.2.6.2	Define information for **ftp** access
~user/.profile	3.2.2	Define environment for the Bourne shell
~user/.rhosts	13.2.3	Define private remote hosts
~user/dead.letter	6.1	Contains interrupted mail message
~user/mbox	6.1	User's read mail file (compare the VMS MAIL folder)
/bin/login	3.1	Login program
/dev/null	2.2	Null device (bit bucket), used to discard output or input an immediate EOF (end-of-file)

File	Section	Purpose
/dev/tty. . .	3.1	Special file associated with a terminal connection
/dev/ptty. . .	3.1	Special file associated with a pseudo-terminal; a network connection
/dev/Stty. . .	3.1	Special file associated with a terminal server connection
/etc/cron	7.1.3	Program to perform tasks at preset intervals
/etc/disktab	2.2	Description of the characteristics of each physical disk type, for example, partition size and location
/etc/dumpdates	8.2.1	Maintained by **dump** to record last full and incremental file system backups
/etc/environ	3.1	Program to establish environment variables
/etc/exports	13.2.8	File systems that may be exported, that is, mounted by other hosts supporting NFS
/etc/fstab	3.2	File system location and characteristics
/etc/getty	3.1	Program to determine terminal characteristics
/etc/gettytab	3.1	Terminal line description
/etc/group	3.1	Name of group and login names of the members
/etc/hosts	13.2.1	All hosts reachable via network
/etc/hosts.equiv	13.2.3	Trusted hosts reachable via network
/etc/init	3.1	Program to initiate a terminal session
/etc/motd		Message-of-the-day file maintained by the system administrator
/etc/passwd	3.1	Information defining each user of the system
/etc/phones	13.3.3	System-wide remote phone number database of systems commonly accessed via the **tip** command
/etc/printcap	8.1	Description of available lineprinters
/etc/rc.local		Site-specific startup information
/etc/remote	13.3.3	Remote systems available to the **tip** command
/etc/tapecap	8.2	Description of available tape drives
/etc/ttys	3.1	Terminal initialization data read by **/etc/init**
/etc/ttytype	3.1	Maps the terminal type (defined in **/etc/termcap**) to each computer port available on the system
/etc/update	7.1.3	Maintains file system integrity
/etc/utmp	7.1.2	Who is currently logged on the system
/usr/adm/wtmp	7.1.2	Records all logins and logouts
/usr/lib	10.1	Directory containing infrequently used system libraries

File	Section	Purpose
/usr/lib/crontab	7.3.2	Schedule of programs to be run by **/etc/cron** at preset intervals
/usr/lib/Mail.rc	6.1.8	System-wide **mail** environment
/usr/lib/news/newsgroups	13.4	News groups maintained by Usenet
/usr/lib/tmac	12.3	Location of **nroff/troff** macro packages
/usr/lib/uucp/L.commands	13.3.5	**uusend** commands accepted from remote hosts
/usr/lib/uucp/L-devices	13.3.1	Characteristics of dialout modems used by UUCP
/usr/lib/uucp/L-dialcodes	13.3.1	Common dial codes used by the UUCP dialers
/usr/lib/uucp/L.sys	13.3.1	Dialing characteristics used by UUCP in reaching remote hosts
/usr/local/lib	10.1	Local system-wide libraries
/usr/skel	3.8	Default user environment files
/usr/spool/mail/user	6.1	Incoming mail postbox for **user** (compare the VMS NEWMAIL folder)
/usr/spool/uucp	13.3.5	Parent directory of **uucp** account
/usr/spool/uucp/ERRLOG	13.3.1	Error log maintained by the UUCP utility
/usr/spool/uucp/LOGFILE	13.3.1	Log of UUCP activity
/usr/spool/uucp/SYSLOG	13.3.1	Log of UUCP file transfer activity
/usr/sys/. . .	10.1	System routines used by the preprocessor

Appendix D

Additional Reading

The books in this list were selected using the BRS Colleague Bibliographic Search Service, which contains a database of all books in print in the United States. Not all the books have been reviewed by the author. The articles cited as "Unix Document Set" are usually part of the UNIX documentation distributed with the operating system software. Consult your system administrator for details. The dates for these articles come from Digital Equipment Corporation's ULTRIX-32m Version 2.0 document set, and may differ from the documentation distributed with other UNIX versions.

General: Beginners

Brown, P., and P. Birns. *UNIX for People*. Englewood Cliffs, NJ: Prentice-Hall, 1984.

Christian, K. *The UNIX Command Reference Guide: The Top 50 UNIX Commands, What They Are and How to Use Them*. New York: Wiley, 1987.

Lomuto, A. N., and N. Limuto. *A UNIX Primer*. Englewood Cliffs, NJ: Prentice-Hall, 1983.

McGilton, H., and R. Morgan. *Introducing the UNIX System*. New York: McGraw-Hill, 1983.

Pasternack, I. *Exploring the UNIX Environment*. New York: Bantam Books, 1985.

Silvester, P.P. *UNIX: An Introduction for Computer Users*. New York: Wiley, 1984.

Silvester, P.P. *The UNIX System Guidebook*. New York: Springer-Verlag, 1988.

Strong, B., and J. Hosler. *UNIX for Beginners: A Step-By-Step Introduction*. New York: Wiley, 1987.

Todino, G., and D. Dougherty. *Learning the UNIX Operating System*. Newton, MA: O'Reilly and Associates, Inc., 1987.

The Waite Group. *UNIX Primer Plus*. Indianapolis, IN: Howard W. Sams & Co., 1983.

Whiddett, R.J., and R.E. Berry. *UNIX: A Practical Introduction for Users*. New York: Halsted Press, 1985.

General: Intermediate

AT&T Staff and M.I. Bolsky. *The UNIX System User's Handbook*. Englewood Cliffs, NJ: Prentice-Hall, 1986.

Budgen, D. *Making Use of the UNIX Operating System*. Englewood Cliffs, NJ: Prentice-Hall, 1986.

Christian, K. *The UNIX Operating System. 2nd Edition*. New York: Wiley, 1988.

Farkas, D. *UNIX for Programmers*. New York: Wiley, 1987.

Kernighan, B.W., and R. Pike. *The UNIX Programming Environment*. Englewood Cliffs, NJ: Prentice-Hall, 1984.

Kochan, S.G., and P.H. Wood. *Exploring the UNIX System*. Indianapolis, IN: Hayden Books, 1985.

Martin, D. *UNIX System Bible*. Indianapolis, IN: Howard W. Sams & Co., 1987.

McNully Development, Inc. *UNIX Reference Guide*. Englewood Cliffs, NJ: Prentice-Hall, 1986.

Sobell, M.G., *A Practical Guide to the UNIX System*. Menlo Park, CA: Benjamin-Cummings, 1984.

Thomas, R., and J. Yates. *The Programmer's Guide to the UNIX System*. Reading, MA: Addison-Wesley, 1983.

Thomas, R., and J. Yates. *User Guide to the UNIX System*. Berkeley, CA: Osborne–McGraw-Hill, 1985.

The Waite Group. *UNIX Papers for Developers and Power Users*. Indianapolis, IN: Howard W. Sams & Company, 1987.

Walker, A. *The UNIX Environment*. New York: Wiley, 1984.

Weinberg, P.N., and J.R. Groff. *Understanding UNIX: A Conceptual Guide*. Carmel, IN: Que Corporation, 1988.

General: Advanced

AT&T Staff. *UNIX Programmer's Manual, Volumes 1 Through 5*. New York: Holt, Rinehart and Winston, 1986.

Bach, M.J. *The Design of the UNIX Operating System*. Englewood Cliffs, NJ: Prentice-Hall, 1986.

Bell Laboratories Staff. *UNIX*. New York: Holt, Rinehart and Winston, 1983.

Franzosa, B. (Ed.). *The UNIX System Encyclopedia*. Palo Alto, CA: Yates Vent, 1985.

Mikes, S. *UNIX: Power User's Guide*. Berkeley, CA: Osborne–McGraw-Hill, 1988.

Prata, S. *Advanced UNIX: A Programmer's Guide*. Indianapolis, IN: Howard W. Sams & Company, 1985.

Sage, R. *Tricks of the UNIX Masters*. Indianapolis, IN: Howard W. Sams & Company, 1987.

UNIX System Administration

AT&T Staff. *UNIX System Administrator's Reference Manual*. Englewood Cliffs, NJ: Prentice-Hall, 1988.

Backhurst, N., and P. Davies. *System Management Under UNIX*. Larchmont, NY: Book Clearing House, 1987.

Burke, F. *UNIX System Administration*. San Diego: Harcourt Brace Jovanovich, 1987.

Fiedler, D., and B.H. Hunter. *UNIX System Administration*. Indianapolis, IN: Hayden Books, 1986.

Foxley, E. *UNIX for Super-Users*. Reading, MA: Addison-Wesley, 1985.

Seyer, M.D., and W.J. Mills. *DOS UNIX: Becoming a Super User*. Englewood Cliffs, NJ: Prentice-Hall, 1986.

Shaw, M.C., and S.S. Shaw. *UNIX Internals: A Systems Operations Handbook*. Blue Ridge Summit, PA: Tab Books, 1987.

Wood, P.H., and S.G. Kochan. *UNIX System Security*. Indianapolis, IN: Hayden Books, 1987.

UNIX for Microcomputers

Chirlian, P.M. *UNIX for the IBM PC*. Columbus, OH: Merrill Publishing Company, 1987.

Clukey, L.P. *UNIX and XENIX Demystified*. Blue Ridge Summit, PA: Tab Books, 1985.

Deikman, A. *UNIX Programming on the 80286-80386*. Redwood City, CA: M&T Publishing, 1988.

Nutshell Handbooks. *DOS Meets UNIX*. Newton, MA: O'Reilly and Associates, 1987.

Shaw, M.C., and S.S. Shaw. *UNIX V and XENIX System V: Programmer's Toolkit*. Blue Ridge Summit, PA: Tab Books, 1986.

Specialized System Consultants. *UNIX-XENIX Text Processing Reference*. Seattle, WA: Specialized Systems, 1987.

Topham, D.W., and H. Trong. *UNIX and XENIX. A Step-by-Step Approach for Micros*. New York: Brady Computer Books, 1985.

Topham, D.W., and H. Van Truong. *The System V Guide: A UNIX and XENIX Tutorial*. New York: Brady Computer Books, 1986.

Miscellaneous

Chorafas, D.N. *Fourth- and Fifth-Generation Programming Languages, Volume 2: Which UNIX? AT&T, IBM, and Other Operating System Environments*. New York: McGraw-Hill, 1986.

Christian, K. *UNIX Dictionary*. New York: Wiley, 1988.

Egan, J.I., and T.J. Teixeira. *Writing a UNIX Device Driver*. New York: Wiley, 1988.

Manis, R., and R. Jorgenson. *Relational Database Management in the UNIX Environment*. Englewood Cliffs, NJ: Prentice-Hall, 1988.

Poole, P.C., and N. Poole. *Using UNIX by Example*. Reading, MA: Addison-Wesley, 1986.

Schreiner, A.T., and H.G. Friedman. *Introduction to Compiler Construction with UNIX*. Englewood Cliffs, NJ: Prentice-Hall, 1985.

Shirota, Y., and T.L. Kunit. *First Book on UNIX for Executives*. New York: Springer-Verlag, 1984.

Yates, Y.L., and R. Thomas. *The Business Guide to the UNIX System*. Reading, MA: Addison-Wesley, 1984.

System III

Specialized Systems Consultants. *UNIX Command Summary System III*. Seattle, WA: Specialized Systems, 1983.

System V

AT&T Staff. *UNIX System Software Readings*. Englewood Cliffs, NJ: Prentice-Hall, 1988.

AT&T Staff. *UNIX System V Programmer's Guide*. Englewood Cliffs, NJ: Prentice-Hall, 1987.

AT&T Staff. *UNIX System V Reference Manual*. Englewood Cliffs, NJ: Prentice-Hall, 1987.

AT&T Staff. *UNIX System Readings and Applications*. Englewood Cliffs, NJ: Prentice-Hall, 1987.

AT&T Staff. *UNIX System V Utilities Handbook*. Englewood Cliffs, NJ: Prentice-Hall, 1985.

AT&T Staff. *Computer Software Catalog: UNIX System V Software*. Englewood Cliffs, NJ: Prentice-Hall, 1987.

Balay, R.H. *User's Introduction to UNIX V*. Dubuque, IA: Kendall-Hunt, 1988.

Bourne, S.R. *The UNIX V Environment*. Reading, MA: Addison-Wesley, 1986.

Byers, R.A. *Introduction to UNIX System V*. New York: McGraw-Hill, 1985.

Coffin, S. *UNIX: The Complete Reference, System V, Release 3*. Berkeley, CA: Osborne–McGraw-Hill, 1988.

Morgan, R., and H. McGilton. *Introducing the UNIX System V*. New York: McGraw-Hill, 1987.

Nutshell Handbooks. *UNIX in a Nutshell, System V Edition*. Newton, MA: O'Reilly and Associates, 1987.

Prata, S. *UNIX System V Primer*. Indianapolis, IN: Howard W. Sams & Company, 1987.

Sobell, M.G. *A Practical Guide to the UNIX System V*. Menlo Park, CA: Benjamin-Cummings, 1985.

Specialized System Consultants. *UNIX Command Summary (System V)*. Seattle, WA: Specialized Systems, 1987.

Thomas, R., and J.L. Yates. *Advanced Programmer's Guide to UNIX System V*. Berkeley, CA: Osborne–McGraw-Hill, 1985.

BSD

Nutshell Handbooks. *UNIX in a Nutshell, Berkeley Edition*. Newton, MA: O'Reilly and Associates, 1987.

Olczak, A. *The UNIX Reference Guide for BSD*. Hasslet, MI: Systems Publications, 1987.

Quaterman, J.S., and A.P. Stettner. *The Design and Implementation of the 4.3BSD UNIX Operating System*. Reading, MA: Addison-Wesley, 1988.

Specialized System Consultants. *UNIX Command Summary (BSD 4.2)*. Seattle: Specialized Systems, 1984.

Specialized System Consultants. *UNIX Command Summary for Berkeley 4.2 & 4.3 BSD*. Seattle: Specialized Systems, 1984.

Wang, P.S. *An Introduction to Berkeley UNIX*. Belmont, CA: Wadsworth, 1988.

Chapter 1: Introduction

UNIX World. Mountain View, CA: Tech Valley Publishing. Published monthly.

UNIX Review. San Francisco: Miller, Freeman Publications. Published monthly.

Chapter 2: Fundamentals

Bach, M.J. *The Design of the UNIX Operating System*. Englewood Cliffs, NJ: Prentice-Hall, 1986.

Ritchie, D.M., and K. Thompson. *The UNIX Time-Sharing System*. Comm. ACM *17*, 365 (1974).

Silvester, P.P. *The UNIX System Guidebook*. New York: Springer-Verlag, 1988.

Chapter 3: Getting Started

Kernighan, B.W. *UNIX for Beginners*. UNIX Documentation Set (1984).

Chapter 4: Introductory File Management

Nutshell Handbooks. *UNIX in a Nutshell, Berkeley Edition*. Newton, MA: O'Reilly and Associates, 1987.
Nutshell Handbooks. *UNIX in a Nutshell, System V Edition*. Newton, MA: O'Reilly and Associates, 1987.

Chapter 5: Editing

Aho, A.V., Kernigan, B.W., and P.J. Weinberger. *Awk—A Pattern Scanning and Processing Language, Second Edition*. UNIX Documentation Set, 1978.
El, L.M. *Editing in a UNIX Environment: The Vi-ex Editor*. Englewood Cliffs, NJ: Prentice-Hall, 1985.
Hansen, A. *Vi: The UNIX Screen Editor*. Haverford, PA: Bradly Communications, 1985.
Joy, W. *Ex Reference Manual*. UNIX Documentation Set, 1980.
Joy, W. An Introduction to Display Editing with Vi. UNIX Documentation Set, 1984.
Lamb, L. *Learning the vi Editor*. Newton, MA: O'Reilly and Associates, 1987.
McMahon, L.E. *SED: A Non-interactive Text Editor*. UNIX Documentation Set, 1978.
Sonnenscheim, D. *A Guide to Vi: Visual Editing on the UNIX System*. Englewood Cliffs, NJ: Prentice-Hall, 1986.
Strong, B. *UNIX Word Processing Book. Step by Step Guide for the Vi Editor*. New York: Wiley, 1987.
Strong, B., and J. Hosler. *UNIX for Beginners: Basic Word Processing Skills with Ed*. New York: Wiley, 1988.

Chapter 6: Communicating with Other Users

Shoens, K. *Mail Reference Manual*. UNIX Documentation Set, 1984.
The Waite Group. *UNIX Communications*. Indianapolis, IN: Howard W. Sams & Company, 1987.

Chapter 9: Advanced File Management

Nutshell Handbooks. *UNIX in a Nutshell, Berkeley Edition*. Newton, MA: O'Reilly and Associates, 1987.

Nutshell Handbooks. *UNIX in a Nutshell, System V Edition*. Newton, MA: O'Reilly and Associates, 1987.

Chapter 10: Programming

Digital Equipment Corporation. *Guide to the Source Code Control System.* ULTRIX-32 Documentation Set, Order Number AA-ME84A-TE. Maynard, MA: 1989.

Dunsmuir, M.R., and G.J. Davies. *Programming the UNIX System*. New York: Halsted Press, 1985.

Farkas, D. *UNIX for Programmers: An Introduction*. New York: Wiley, 1988.

Feldman, S.I. *Make—A Program for Maintaining Computer Programs.* UNIX Documentation Set, 1978.

Gehani, N. *UNIX ADA*. Englewood Cliffs, NJ: Prentice-Hall, 1987.

Horspool, N.R. *C Programming in the Berkeley UNIX Environment*. Englewood Cliffs, NJ: Prentice-Hall, 1987.

Hume, J.N., and R.C. Holt. *PASCAL Under UNIX*. Englewood Cliffs, NJ: Prentice-Hall, 1983.

Lapin, J.E. *Portable C and UNIX Systems Programming*. Englewood Cliffs, NJ: Prentice-Hall, 1986.

Moore, R.F. *Programming in C with a Bit of UNIX*. Englewood Cliffs, NJ: Prentice-Hall, 1985.

Peters, J.F. *UNIX Programming: Methods and Tools*. San Diego: Harcourt Brace Jovanovich, 1988.

Rochkind, M.J. *Advanced UNIX Programming*. Englewood Cliffs, NJ: Prentice-Hall, 1985.

Rochkind, M.J. *Advanced C Programming for Displays: Character Displays, Windows and Keyboards for UNIX and MS-DOS*. Englewood Cliffs, NJ: Prentice-Hall, 1988.

Salama, B., and K. Haviland. *UNIX System Programming: A Programmer's Guide to Software Development*. Reading, MA: Addison-Wesley, 1987.

Schirmer, C. *Programming in C for UNIX*. New York: Halsted Press, 1987.

Schreiner, A.T., and G.H. Friedman Jr. *Introduction to Compiler Construction with UNIX*. Englewood Cliffs, NJ: Prentice-Hall, 1985.

Chapter 11: Shell Programming

Anderson, G., and P. Anderson. *The UNIX C Shell Field Guide*. Englewood Cliffs, NJ: Prentice-Hall, 1986.

Arthur, L.J. *UNIX Shell Programming*. New York: Wiley, 1986.

Bourne, S.R. *An Introduction to the UNIX Shell*. UNIX Documentation Set, 1984.

Joy, W. *An Introduction to the C Shell*. UNIX Documentation Set, 1984.

Manis, R., and M.H. Meyer. *The UNIX Shell Programming Language*. Indianapolis, IN: Howard W. Sams & Company, 1986.

Chapter 12: Text Processing

Barron, D.W., and M.J. Rees. *Text Processing with UNIX*. Reading, MA: Addison-Wesley, 1987.

Brown, C.C., and R.D. Sperline. *Preparing Documents with UNIX*. Englewood Cliffs, NJ: Prentice-Hall, 1986.

Emerson, S.L., and K. Paulsell. *Troff Typesetting for UNIX Systems*. Englewood Cliffs, NJ: Prentice-Hall, 1986.

Kernighan, B.W. *A Troff Tutorial*. UNIX Documentation Set, 1984.

Krieger, M. *Word Processing on the UNIX System*. New York: McGraw-Hill, 1985.

Lesk, M.E. *Tbl—A Program to Format Tables*. UNIX Documentation Set, 1984.

O'Reilly, T., and D. Dougherty. *UNIX Text Processing*. Indianapolis, IN: Howard W. Sams & Company, 1987.

Ossanna, J.F. *Nroff/Troff User's Manual*. UNIX Documentation Set, 1984.

Roddy, K.P. *UNIX nroff-troff: A User's Guide*. New York: Holt, Rinehart and Winston, 1985.

Chapter 13: Processor-to-Processor Communications

AT&T Staff. *UNIX System V Network Programmer's Guide*. Englewood Cliffs, NJ: Prentice-Hall, 1989.

AT&T Staff. *UNIX System V Streams Primer*. Englewood Cliffs, NJ: Prentice-Hall, 1987.

AT&T Staff. *UNIX System V Streams Programmer's Guide*. Englewood Cliffs, NJ: Prentice-Hall, 1989.

O'Reilly, T., and D. Dougherty. *Managing UUCP and USENET*. Newton, MA: O'Reilly and Associates, 1987.

Todino, G. *Using UUCP and USENET*. Newton, MA: O'Reilly and Associates, 1987.

The Waite Group. *UNIX Communications*. Indianapolis, IN: Howard W. Sams & Company, 1987.

Glossary

. (dot)   The current directory.

.. (dot-dot)   The parent directory of the current directory.

Absolute pathname   A pathname that starts at the root directory, that is, with /.

Alias   The C shell mechanism for abbreviating a command line (compare the VMS construct :=).

Argument list   The list of words from the command line that the C shell passes to a command.

ASCII   American Standard Code for Information Exchange: a standard character encoding scheme.

Background job   A job that is not receiving input from the terminal.

Baud   Bits per second; a unit used to describe the transmission speed of data.

Bit bucket   Name for the file **/dev/null**. Characters written here are "thrown away"; characters read from here cause an immediate EOF.

Bit map   Mapping of the screen such that each pixel is represented in physical memory.

Break point   A point set in a source code program which stops the debugger during execution.

BSD   Berkeley Software Distribution, the version of UNIX originating at the University of California at Berkeley.

Built-in command   A command whose code is internal to the C shell; the C shell does not fork a process to execute the command.

Card image   A terminal display representation of a punched card, 80 characters per record.

Child process The process created when the parent process executes the **fork** system routine.

csh Shorthand for **/bin/csh**, the C shell program.

Current directory The directory to which commands refer by default.

Daemon A system-generated process that performs some system management function in a manner transparent to the user.

Debugging Correcting errors in a program or procedure.

Detached job A job that continues processing after the user has logged out.

Device See *Physical device*.

Directory A UNIX file that contains names of other files or directories.

Directory hierarchy The arrangement of directories in a UNIX file system. The root directory is at the top of the directory hierarchy and contains pointers to all file systems, and hence to all directories on the system.

Directory stack A data structure that stores directories for later recall.

Disk partition Part of a disk onto which a file system is mounted.

Environment The set of characteristics describing a UNIX user's terminal session. The characteristics include the open files, the user and group identification, the process identification, and environment variables.

Environment variable A variable exported automatically to subsequent programs. Environment variables are defined with the **setenv** command.

EOF End-of-file character(s) that denote the end of a file, usually ⟨CTRL⟩-D.

Ethernet Local area network standard providing the two lower levels of the ISO/OSI (International Standards Organization/Open System Interconnect) seven-layer reference model.

Event Past command stored in the history list.

Executable image An executable file located in physical memory.

Extension The part after the . (period) in a pathname. Also called file extension.

Field separator One or more characters used to separate fields in a record; defaults to one or more blanks.

File A stream of bytes stored under a unique pathname.

File and device independence Using filenames and device names in commands equivalently; for example, **who > out** and **who > /dev/lp**.

File descriptor The number UNIX assigns to an open file.

Filename A set of characters used to reference a file. Any character is legal, but it is best to choose from the alphanumeric character set, period, and underscore. BSD filenames may contain up to 255 characters.

Filename expansion Matching filenames in the specified directory according to the following rules: * matches any character sequence including null; ? matches any single character; [ ] delimits a set of characters; [n-m] matches the range of characters **n** through **m** inclusive; ˜ matches the home directory; and {} delimits different parts in a common pathname (see also *globbing*).

File system   A hierarchical arrangement of files beginning at the root and mounted in a disk partition.

Filter   A program that reads from the standard input, processes it, and writes it to the standard output. Filters are typically used in pipes.

Floating point accelerator   Hardware designed specifically to enhance the speed with which mathematical operations are performed on floating point data types.

Foreground job   A job that must be completed or interrupted before the shell will accept more commands; a job receiving input from the terminal.

Fork   The system routine that creates a new process by duplicating the calling (parent) process.

Globbing   Filename expansion using metacharacters.

Group ID   A numeric identification designating the group to which a user belongs. The number corresponds to an entry in the **/etc/group** file.

Hard link   Associates the same file contents with two or more file names within the same file system.

Header   The directory containing the filename.

History list   List of previously issued commands.

Home directory   The user's default working directory, specified in the **/etc/passwd** file.

Host   A computer on a network (compare the VMS node).

Host name   The name given to a host (compare the VMS node name).

Inode   Pointers used in locating data on a physical device.

Input   Data read by a command or user program.

Interrupt   A signal, typically generated at the keyboard, which causes the currently executing process to terminate unless special action is taken by the process to handle the signal.

Interrupt handler   A set of statements executed upon receipt of an interrupt.

Job   A task consisting of one or more processes assigned a job number by the C shell and executing in either foreground or background.

Job control   Ability of the C shell to control multiple jobs.

Job number   The number that uniquely identifies a job within a C shell session.

Job stack   Queue of jobs maintained by the C shell.

Job states   The current state of a job. (see also *Suspended, Terminated,* and *Detached.*)

ksh   Shorthand for **/bin/ksh**, the Korn shell program.

Link   An entry in a directory (that is, a filename) that points to an existing file. Hard links may not span file systems. Symbolic links, also called soft links, may.

Link loader   Software that combines all the separate modules of a program to create an executable file.

Lock file   A file whose existence prevents some function (for example, access to a common database, printing device, or other shared facility).

Login name   The name assigned to a user (compare the VMS username).

Metacharater   A character with a special meaning (for example, > denotes redirection of output).

Modifier   See *Variable modifier.*

Multiprocessor   Two or more processors sharing common physical memory.

Network contention   Two or more packets demanding simultaneous access to the network.

NFS   Network File System, a network protocol developed by Sun Microsystems, Inc., to permit access to files on remote computers as if they were located on the local computer (compare the VMS Local Area VAX-cluster).

Object files   Files containing object code produced as the result of a compilation.

Object library   A library containing object files.

Option   Modifies command execution.

Output   Data produced by a command or user program.

Packet   A unit of data and other information, for example, local host address, remote host address, sent on a network.

Page   The unit of interchange between physical memory and a swapping device; 512 bytes for VAX computers.

Parent directory   The directory above the current directory; the directory one level closer to the root.

Parent process   The originator of the fork call that creates a child process.

Partition   Segment of a physical disk onto which a file system is mounted.

Parsing order   The order in which the C shell evaluates a command line and instigates any special mechanisms (**history, alias**, and so on).

Password   A special code word known only by the user to permit access to the system. A user's password is stored in encrypted form in the file **/etc/passwd**.

Pathname   The names of all the directories that must be traversed to reach a given destination (file or directory).

Pathname qualifier   See *Variable modifer*

Physical device   A piece of hardware attached to the computer, for example, a disk drive, tape drive, printer, or terminal.

Physical device name   The name given to a physical device. For example, **/dev/tty01** (compare the VMS name **TTA1:**), **/dev/da0a** (compare the VMS name **DUA0:**), and **/dev/rmt0h** (compare the VMS name **MUA0:**).

Pipe   A connection that allows one program to get its input directly from the output of another program.

Pipelining   A hardware architecture that permits different components of an instruction to simultaneously process different data elements.

Pixel A picture element: a point on the screen that is directly addressable by the computer.

Predefined variable A shell variable defined and maintained by the C shell.

Prepend To append to the front.

Preprocessor Software that performs modifications to data so that the data conforms to the input requirements of some other standard software.

Present working directory See *Current directory*

Priority A number assigned to a process which determines the system resources that the process may receive.

Process A program that is being executed or is waiting to be executed.

Process identification or process id An integer that uniquely identifies a process within the system.

Profiling Monitoring how system resources are utilized in a given program.

Protection mask The protection assigned to a file.

Recursion Defined relative to itself; calling a procedure from within a procedure.

Redirection Designating the source or destination of input or output to be a named file or device.

Relative pathname The names of all directories either above or below the current directory that must be traversed to reach a given destination (file or directory).

Regular expression Incorporation of metacharacters to define the characteristics of a string.

RISC Reduced Instruction Set Computer: a hardware architecture that concentrates on performing the most frequently used instructions at an accelerated rate. The less often used instructions are performed by the operating system software.

Root Another name for the superuser.

Root directory Top level of the UNIX directory hierarchy; all directories derive from it.

RS-232 A standard interface used to connect a terminal to a host computer.

Script A shell procedure or program (compare the VMS DCL command procedure).

Search path The ordered list of directories that the C shell searches to find commands.

sh Shorthand for the file **/bin/sh**, the Bourne shell program.

Shell The UNIX command interpreter (compare the VMS DCL command language interpreter).

Shell variable An identifier that can hold one or more strings of characters.

Socket Defines an endpoint for a network communication (BSD only).

Soft link Associating the same file contents with two or more file names either within the same file system or across file systems; also called a symbolic link.

Standard error (stderr) Where error messages are written; the terminal by default (compare the VMS logical name **SYS$ERROR**).

Standard input (stdin) Where input is taken from; the terminal by default (compare the VMS logical name **SYS$INPUT**).

Standard output (stdout)   Where output is written to; the terminal by default (compare the VMS logical name **SYS$OUTPUT**).

Status   The state in which a program exists. By convention, 0 indicates a successful exit, non-zero an error.

Store-and-forward   A type of network connection in which a complete transmission is passed to one intermediate host before transmission to the next intermediate host begins.

Stream   Same function as a socket, used by System V.

Subdirectory   A directory that exists within another directory; any directory other than the root directory.

Superuser   The login name that has total access to the system; also called **root**.

Suspended   Temporarily stopped foreground or background job.

Symbolic link   See *Soft link*

System load   The demand that all processes are placing on the computer. Usually expressed as a number: 1.0 represents 100% utilization; 0.1 represents 10% utilization of system resources.

System routines   The set of resident procedures callable by the user.

Tail   The last part of a file; or a filename without a directory specification.

Task   A defined activity.

TCP/IP   Transmission Control Protocol/Internet Protocol: the network protocol used by UNIX-based computers.

Terminal session   The interaction that occurs between the user and the computer between login and logout.

Terminated job   Permanently stopped job.

Tool   A command or utility designed to help get a job done, for example, **make** or **dbx**.

Trusted host   A host that permits access without the need to supply password information (compare the VMS proxy login).

Uptime   Wall clock time since the system was last booted.

User identification or user id   The number associated with each login name. This number is stored in the **/etc/passwd** file.

Usenet   Network of UNIX-based computers for the exchange of every imaginable type of information.

Utility   A command with many options, for example, **mail** or **awk**.

Variable expansion   Replacing the variable identifier with its associated string or strings in a shell command line.

Variable modifier   Symbol referring to part of a variable, usually under the assumption that its value is a pathname.

Vectorization   Hardware that permits a single instruction to act upon multiple data elements.

Word   A string separated by blanks, tabs, or the C shell special characters >, <, |, **&**, ;,), and (.

Wordlist   A C shell variable consisting of more than one word.

Index